Mancuso's
SMALL BUSINESS
RESOURCE GUIDE

Mancuso's
SMALL BUSINESS
RESOURCE GUIDE

Joseph R. Mancuso

PRENTICE HALL PRESS
New York London Toronto Sydney Tokyo

Prentice Hall Press
Gulf + Western Building
One Gulf + Western Plaza
New York, New York   10023

Portions of this work were originally published by Prentice-Hall, Inc., in the
The Small Business Survival Guide, 1980.

PRENTICE HALL PRESS and colophon are registered trademarks of
Simon & Schuster, Inc.

Library of Congress Cataloging in Publication Data
Mancuso, Joseph.
    [Small business resource guide.]
    Mancuso's small business resource guide/Joseph R. Mancuso.
        p.   cm.
    "Sections of this book were originally published in 1980 in Small business survival
guide by Prentice-Hall, Inc."—T.p. verso.
    Includes index.
    ISBN 0-13-813080-9 ISBN 0-13-551888-1 (pbk.)
    1. Small business—Management—Information services—United States—Direc-
tories. 2. Small business—Management—Bibliography.
I. Mancuso, Joseph. Small business survival guide. II. Title.
HD62.7.M367 1988
658'.022'072—dc19   87-27015
                                                                         CIP

Designed by C. Linda Dingler

Manufactured in the United States of America

10 9 8 7 6 5 4 3 2 1

First Edition

It's not the critic who counts or the observer who watches from a safe distance. Wealth is created only by doers in the arena who are marred with dirt, blood, and sweat. These producers strike out on their own, come up short time and again, know high highs, low lows, and great devotions, and overextend themselves for worthwhile causes. Without exception, they fail more than they succeed, and they appreciate this reality even before venturing out on their own. When these producers of wealth fail, they do so with style and grace, recognizing that failure is only a resting place, not a place in which to spend a lifetime. Their place will never be with those nameless souls—the takers—who know neither victory nor defeat, who receive weekly paychecks regardless of their week's performance, who are hired hands laboring in someone else's garden. These doers are producers: No matter what their lot may be at any given moment, their place is alone, in the sun.

Contents

120525

Introduction

My secret desire has always been to have available to all small business owners an 800 (toll-free) telephone number which would be an entrepreneur's lifeline to sources of help.* While I still fantasize about this, I have come to realize that it would soon become a security blanket. It's often so lonely in an entrepreneurial venture that the need to talk to someone who can understand, empathize, or share the burden might cause people to use this number in the same way that they "dial a prayer."

The best idea is to dial a friend who can give help and understanding. The cost of just *one* 800 number line would be about $5,000 per month—without including the salary of the person who answers the telephone, and so on.

In fact, I envisioned this 800 number to be so wonderful that we'd need more than one telephone line. Although I hadn't calculated how many lines would be needed, I realized that one line would not be enough, and in my daydreams, this issue of the number of telephone lines kept nagging at me.

So, I did what any sensible entrepreneur would do: I made a rough estimate. First, I knew there were 12 million small businesses in the United States because I had read such a statistic published by the Small Business Administration (SBA). Second, I concluded that not every small business owner would use the toll-free number, so I guessed that one-third would use it and two-thirds would ignore it. But then I realized that people other than small business owners would use the service. In fact, its greatest users were likely to be would-be entrepreneurs. I didn't really know of any published statistics on how many would-be entrepreneurs existed, so I checked again with the SBA and discovered that they only knew "it is a lot." I asked the friends in my universe and concluded that more would-be entrepreneurs existed than practicing entrepreneurs—at a ratio of at least 3 to 1. The number of potential users was back to my original estimate of about 12 million people.

But of course they wouldn't all use the toll-free number every day. Even so, the 800 number could be receiving a million calls a day, if it were a quality service. Do you know how much it would cost to staff an 800 number that handled a million calls each day? The cost would be staggering, well beyond the financial reach of any individual and surely infinitely beyond my resources.

But it still seemed like a sound concept. Then it occurred to me that the only entity able to deal in such large numbers would be the U.S. government. Maybe this was the solution! The government could foot the bill for the toll-free number to offer help and advice to entrepreneurs.

This "solution" could have fearful consequences: The cure could turn out to

---

*The Small Business Administration has installed a toll-free number in order to provide quick delivery of free SBA pamphlets, but it's really not the same thing: (800) 328-5855.

be worse than the disease! Not only would entrepreneurs discover that the telephone lines were always busy, they'd probably get bad advice, which is worse than no advice at all. How could the people who brought us social security and the swine flu vaccine help my little business?

At that point in my daydreams, an old joke that put the government's effectiveness into a revealing perspective flashed through my mind:

> The Lord's Prayer is composed of 50 words. The Gettysburg Address is composed of 266 words. The Ten Commandments have 297 words. And a recent government proclamation setting the price of cabbage had 26,911.

That settled it—my dreams wouldn't work. That's when I decided to compile this book. I hope you like it!

This book is *not* a general reference book. It is *not* a comprehensive sourcebook of help for small businesses. It does *not* necessarily include all of the best sources of aid for entrepreneurs in each category, and the dozen or so sources listed in each category are neither complete nor ideal.

That's what makes *Mancuso's Small Business Resource Guide* a great book!

Designed as a starting point for the small business owner who wants to receive information on a topic, the book is limited in size by intent. My objective was to include no more than 600 sources—about a dozen sources for 50 categories. I have exceeded this goal.

I judged that this size was manageable; the book would lose its operational value if more chapters were added. I typically turn to these sources for an answer, a reference, a book, a person, or another information source to receive more information. Compiled from my Rolodex card file and those of members of the Center for Entrepreneurial Management, Inc. and the Chief Executive Officers Clubs, these sources will steer you toward the answer to your question, even if they do not solve your immediate problem.

I believe you'll find *Mancuso's Small Business Resource Guide* useful as a starting place for an information search.

—Joseph R. Mancuso
The Center for Entrepreneurial Management

Mancuso's
SMALL BUSINESS
RESOURCE GUIDE

Accounting

Accounting is the science of organizing the financial information essential to the operation of a business. A certified public accountant (CPA) can analyze your costs and assist in making financial projections under various scenarios. The individuals listed below are highly recommended.

Edward B. Beanland, Partner
Arthur Young & Co.
2121 San Jaquinto St., Ste. 700
Dallas, TX 75201
(214) 969-8702
CPAs

Douglas L. Blensly, Partner
Martin Werbelow & Co.
100 S. Los Robles Ave., Ste. 600
Pasadena, CA 91101
(815) 577-1440
CPAs

John F. Curtis, Partner and Director of
    Entrepreneurial Services Group
Arthur Young & Co.
One Boston Pl., Ste. 2700
Boston, MA 02102
(617) 723-7570
CPAs

Irwin S. Friedman, Managing Partner
FER & S
401 N. Michigan Ave.
Chicago, IL 60611
(312) 644-6000
CPAs

Harvey Goldstein, Managing Partner
Singer, Lewak, Greenbaum & Goldstein
10960 Wilshire Blvd., Ste. 826
Los Angeles, CA 90024
(213) 477-3924
CPAs

Philip H. Graff, Managing Partner
M. J. Berger & Co.

778 Frontage Rd.
Northfield, IL 60093
(312) 441-7800
CPAs

Mark Lancaster, Partner
Deloitte, Haskins & Sells
1400 Lincoln Plaza, Lock Box 4
Dallas, TX 73201
(214) 954-4628
CPAs

Joseph C. Murphy, Partner
Price Waterhouse
16479 Dallas Pkwy., Ste. 810
Dallas, TX 75248
(214) 733-1212
CPAs

Martin Nachbar, Managing Partner
Seidman & Seidman
100 Merrick Rd.
Rockville Center, NY 11570
(516) 536-5760
CPAs and management consultants

Francis Percuoco, Managing Partner
Gerald T. Reilly & Co.
424 Adams St.
Milton, MA 02186
(617) 696-8900
CPAs

Grant E. Rollin, Partner
Deloitte, Haskins & Sells
1676 N. California Blvd., Ste. 600
Walnut Creek, CA 94596
(415) 935-1001
CPAs

Stanley P. Snyder, Managing Partner
Snyder, Newrath & Co., P.C.
4520 East-West Hwy., Ste. 400
Bethesda, MD 20814
(301) 652-6700
CPAs

Jay William Trien, Managing Partner
Weiner & Co.
177 Madison Ave.

Morristown, NJ 07969
(201) 267-4200
CPAs

Alan S. Zelbow, Partner
Mann Judd Landau
441 Stuart St.
Boston, MA 02116
(617) 536-0020
CPAs for closely held businesses

ACCOUNTING FIRMS

Reference is often made to the "Big Eight" American accounting firms. They are listed below.

Arthur Andersen & Co.
1345 Avenue of the Americas
New York, NY 10105
(212) 708-4000

Arthur Young & Co.
277 Park Ave.
New York, NY 10172
(212) 407-1500

Coopers & Lybrand
1251 Avenue of the Americas
New York, NY 10020
(212) 536-2000

Deloitte, Haskins & Sells
One World Trade Center
New York, NY 10048
(212) 669-5000

Ernst & Whinney
787 Seventh Ave.
New York, NY 10019
(212) 830-6000

Peat, Marwick, Mitchell & Co.
345 Park Ave.
New York, NY 10154
(212) 758-9700

Price Waterhouse
153 E. 53d St.
New York, NY 10022
(212) 371-2000

Touche Ross & Co.
1633 Broadway
New York, NY 10019
(212) 489-1600

Two Musts for Small Businesses

It's surprising how many things small businesses have in common, even if their products and customers are different. Bookkeeping and payroll are two of those things. Since everybody has to deal with them, why not make the processes easier and more efficient?

Bookkeeping. The one-write check system is a "must" for small businesses. One-write systems, which can be ordered from a number of stationery firms but not from most banks, simplify bookkeeping; a carbon strip on the back of each check automatically posts the check in the ledger as it is written. Any business that writes more than 25 checks a month can benefit; posting errors are eliminated and the bookkeeping process is streamlined.

Payroll. An outside service to handle both payroll and tax reporting is another "must" for efficient operations. It saves time and keeps the payroll confidential, helping to avoid potential hard feelings among employees. The cost may be as little as $30 per pay period.

Many firms supply one-write check systems and payroll services. The Center for Entrepreneurial Management (CEM) vouches for those listed below.

For checks:
Safeguard Business Systems
470 Maryland Ave.
Fort Washington, PA 19034
(215) 643-4811

For payroll services:
Automatic Data Processing (ADP)
One ADP Blvd.

Roseland, NJ 07068
(800) CALL-ADP
(201) 994-5000 (in NJ)

Russell S. Holdstein, CEO
Pay Day
One Decision St.
San Francisco, CA 94103
(415) 621-2121

Acquisitions

Often the wisest course for an entrepreneur is to purchase an existing business with its preexisting name recognition, market share, and experienced personnel. Exciting new financial techniques, notably leveraged buyouts (LBOs), will frequently make it possible to do this at a surprisingly low cost to the purchaser. The businessperson thinking about selling a company should be well informed about these new techniques and about the possibilities open to the seller.

ASSOCIATIONS

The Institute of Certified Business Counselors is an association of business brokers.
W. R. Stabbert, CEO
Institute of Certified Business Counselors
3206 Peachwillow La.
Walnut Creek, CA 94598
(415) 945-8440

The 35 members of the International Association of Merger and Acquisition Consultants (IMAC) are experienced merger/acquisition specialists with particular expertise in transactions involving medium-size businesses with sales in the range of $1 million to $15 million. IMAC distributes business information on available merger or acquisition prospects, maintains a database on all buyer/seller listings in its network, and publishes a monthly newsletter.
International Association of Merger and Acquisition Consultants
903 N.W. Commerce Bank Bldg.
9575 W. Higgins Rd.
Rosemont, IL 60018
(312) 696-4330

The Association for Corporate Growth is an organization of 2,800 members organized in 22 chapters across the United States. Its members are mostly corporate officers concerned with mergers and acquisitions.
Association for Corporate Growth
104 Wilmot Rd.
Deerfield, IL 60015
(312) 940-8800

MISCELLANEOUS SERVICES

One of the best merger and acquisition businesses in the country.
John York, Pres.
Robert E. Lend Co., Inc.
One N. LaSalle St.
Chicago, IL 60602
(312) 346-2111
(mergers and acquisitions)

DAW Tech III Corporation specializes in mergers and acquisitions.
Isaac I. Daniel
DAW Tech III Corp.
215 N. Marengo Ave.
Pasadena, CA 91101
(818) 793-4266

Geneva Business Services has offices around the United States and conducts seminars and provides information on buying and selling a business.
Gary Roelke
Geneva Business Services
Glenpointe Centre West
Teaneck, NJ 07666
(201) 692-1600

David Hoods
Geneva Marketing Services
575 Anton Blvd.
Costa Mesa, CA 92626
(714) 966-2700

The central office of SBA provides a national list of businesses whose SBA loans have "gone bad"; almost all of the businesses are for sale. Also see the SBA Liquidation Officer in your area for a local list.
Liquidation Officer
Small Business Administration
1441 L St., N.W.
Washington, DC 20416
(800) 424-5201

The International Business Network offers very detailed material on "Buying a Business with No Money Down." Their 15-hour audiotape program costs $250; an excellent workbook is included. They also offer a one-day seminar on the same subject; the cost is about $595. Contact the following source for more information.

Gordon Bizar
International Business Network
12400 Wilshire Blvd., Ste. 340
Los Angeles, CA 90025
(213) 826-3442

PUBLICATIONS

The *Business and Acquisition Newsletter* advises readers of companies, product lines, and patents available for sale. International in scope, it provides information on how to find and make good acquisitions and mergers. The cost is $250 per year.
Len Fox
Business and Acquisition Newsletter
Newsletters International
2600 S. Gessner Rd.
Houston, TX 77063
(713) 783-0100

The *First List* is an excellent quarterly listing of about 900 businesses.
First List
First National Bank of Maryland
25 S. Charles St., 15th Floor
Baltimore, MD 21201
(301) 244-7943

How to Do a Leveraged Buyout for Yourself, Your Corporation, or Your Client, 2d edition, by Nicholas Wallner and J. Terrance Greve, is an excellently detailed (and expensive at $90) 250-page guide (plus appendix) that offers many source materials on LBOs. Business Publications also offers a 44-page catalog of material on LBOs. The catalog and book are available from the following source.
Business Publications, Inc.
8505 Commerce Ave.
San Diego, CA 92121
(800) 523-7543
(800) 453-2646 (in CA)

The *Handbook of Small Business Valuation Formulas* ($40; 140 pages) and the *Business Valuation Handbook* ($43; 450 pages) contain statistics on valuation prices that can be useful for buyout valuation clauses for different types of businesses.
Glenn Desmond
Valuation Press
13160 Mindanao Way, Ste. 247
Marina Del Rey, CA 90292
(213) 822-3691

BUY YOUR OWN BUSINESS

High-ticket LBOs are very much in the news. Pantry Pride acquires Revlon: $1.6 billion. Kohlberg Kravis Roberts & Company purchases Storer Broadcasting: $2.5 billion. But big, well-known companies are not the only targets for LBOs. Businessmen seeking a quick route to entrepreneurship buy small- and medium-size businesses every day.

In LBOs, the buyer borrows against the assets of the company he intends to purchase. These buyouts require very little, if any, of the buyer's own money. That's what prompted John and Carri Hammett to give up their careers to become business owners. (He was an executive in a small manufacturing company, and she was an executive in a large corporation.) The process they went through is typical of low-ticket LBOs.

The Hammetts screened more than 150 firms, looking for one that was undervalued. There are several ways to locate such companies. Tap into key small business sources like business brokers, accountants, lawyers, and insurance agents. Review "Chapter 11" listings; bankrupt companies are often good buys. Check into companies in your field of interest, even those not up for sale; although some of them may not be on the block, many owners *will* sell for the right price.

The Hammetts searched full time for ten months, investigating businesses that produced everything from rattan furniture to medical equipment. They finally selected Coes Knife Company in Worcester, Mass., which was founded in 1830 by Loring Coes, the inventor of the monkey wrench. The company was financially sound. It had a steady market for its industrial knives among nearby textile plants, and the Hammetts saw potential for a large increase in production. But more important, the owners of Coes Knife Company were willing to sell. Owners of other businesses had told the Hammetts that they were interested in selling their companies only to see what outsiders would pay, thereby wasting the couple's time. "The best deal," explains John Hammett, "is the deal that can be done."

Negotiating the Buyout

Knowing why the owners want to sell can often help the buyer strike a better deal at the negotiating table. For example, owners who have grown frustrated with the business may lower the price if the buyer agrees to expedite the deal. The Hammetts learned that Coes Knife Company was a fourth-generation family business. The current owners had lost interest in running the company, but they wanted to remain associated with it. Consequently, the Hammetts suggested that the owners help finance the deal. The Hammetts would pay back the loan over many years, giving the sellers a nice retirement income and some substantial tax breaks.

Although a company's owner is by far the best source for financing, buyers should also approach asset bankers located near the business targeted for the buyout. The bulk of the Hammetts' financing came from an asset bank near Worcester. These banks lend money based on a company's assets—a perfect situation for LBOs. In addition, they have a vested interest in keeping local businesses alive. If your search for asset-based lenders doesn't pan out, try other local banks. Seek financing from national institutions only after you've exhausted local prospects.

When seeking financing, the buyer needs a solid business plan, just as he does with a typical start-up. Unlike the plan for a start-up, which describes a theoretical business, a buyout plan must show how an existing business will be overhauled to produce enough additional revenue to warrant a loan. Plans for LBOs should include three important elements.

1. A description of the new management team: Potential lenders want to know if the new team has the background to turn the company around.

2. A description of the marketing strategy: Explain why the new strategy will be significantly more effective than the old one.

3. A description of the financial status: Trace the financial history of the company and project the estimated future income.

Although purchasing a company is easier in some ways than starting one, LBOs require hard work. Turning a company around takes a lot of time and effort. In 1986, John Hammett worked 100 hours during the week of Christmas. If it hadn't been for the holiday, he says, he would have worked more hours.

Advertising

Resources in this chapter concern promoting and advertising both products and services for an entrepreneurial venture. Many entrepreneurs avoid hiring advertising agencies because they consider the cost to be prohibitive. They refuse to pay for advertising help or advice until they reach an impasse in their marketing plans; at that point it is often too late to solve what may be a fundamental problem.

Find a good, small agency, where your account will get the attention of the top executives. Work with a firm of about a dozen people. You may come to consider the agency as a junior member of your team.

Select an agency early in your company's development. An integrated corporate communications concept for letterheads, business cards, envelopes, and logos will establish a valuable corporate identity. When all of the corporate communications are well coordinated from the beginning, your company can avoid the embarrassment of not being taken seriously because of unprofessional standards.

After you've found the right advertising agency, let it do its job. Be candid and honest, and give the agency all of the necessary information about your product and your markets, but don't try to impose your own artistic taste. If the agency has solid information, it can serve you effectively.

The standard 15-percent-of-the-media-costs method of agency compensation prevails. Most approved media will allow an accredited agency to deduct a 15-percent discount (just as airlines will allow travel agencies to deduct a 10-percent discount). For example, an advertising agency that annually places $100,000 of media advertising for a client can be directly compensated by paying the various media $85,000 while billing the client at the published rates totaling $100,000. It is impossible for an agency to work profitably on a straight commission basis unless the media expenditures are considerable. Remember, the agency is in business to make a profit, too. There could be a conflict of interest for the agency using this method, because putting your advertising dollars into "commissionable" media is to its advantage.

The best course for your company may be direct mail or another noncommissionable medium. Do you want the agency to work for your company or for the commissionable advertising media? Conflict between what is good for the media and what is good for the client is possible. An agency that is reimbursed only for print and electronic media may be unreceptive to designing brochures or trade literature. An estimate of the annual advertising budget should be the foundation for determining an agency's compensation. This process allows a fairer, more informed choice of the optimal allocations between commissionable and noncommissionable activities.

The most practical and fairest method of agency compensation is a monthly retainer fee that amounts to about 10 percent more than the commissions the agency would receive on an annual forecasted commissionable media expenditure. This method eliminates the conflict of interest: The agency is free to worry about what's best for you, not about what's best for itself.

My advice on advertising is to get help early and often. Businesspeople often believe that they are advertising experts; they try to do it themselves. Adopting this approach may be disastrous. The following resources are offered to supplement, not to supplant, your selection of an advertising agency.

PUBLICITY DIRECTORIES

The procedure for contacting trade journals varies from industry to industry. For example, some journals will accept color photos, some will accept only black-and-white photos, and some will not accept photos. You can obtain a list of newspapers, magazines, and trade journals relevant to your business, as well as their requirements for publicity releases, by consulting the following six directories.

The most comprehensive source of print media information is *The Gale Directory of Newspapers and Periodicals* (the former *Ayer Directory of Publications*).

Gale Research Co.
Book Tower
Detroit, MI 48226
(800) 223-GALE

Bacon's Publicity Checker is the finest comprehensive source of publicity information in the United States. This is the source used by most public relations firms. It is published annually; four seasonal supplements list magazines and daily and weekly newspapers in the United States and Canada. Listings include information on circulation, frequency, publication dates, and types of publicity used. The cost is $140.

Bacon's
332 S. Michigan Ave.
Chicago, IL 60604
(312) 922-2400
(800) 621-0561

Standard Periodicals Directory is an excellent comprehensive list of periodicals. This service offers 11 separate directories, and gives advertising rates, specifications, and circulation for publications, broadcast stations, and other media.

Patricia Hagood
Oxbridge Communications
150 Fifth Ave., Ste. 301
New York, NY 10011
(212) 741-0231

Ulrich's Directory of Periodicals, available in most libraries, is also an excellent source.

R. R. Bowker Co.
205 E. 42d St.
New York, NY 10017
(212) 916-1600

Standard Rate & Data is an extensive source of both print and electronic media; it is a classic source of detailed information.
Standard Rate & Data
3004 Glenview Rd.
Wilmette, IL 60091
(312) 256-6067

Internal Publications Directory is an all-in-one directory of house organs. It's a good and unusual method of obtaining publicity.
National Research Bureau
424 N. Third St.
Burlington, IA 52601
(319) 752-5415

PERIODICALS

Advertising Age, which is published weekly, is the leading newspaper serving the advertising industry. Presented in a tabloid format, issues exceed 100 pages. This widely read and often-quoted paper focuses on advertising in the broadest sense.
Advertising Age
Crain Communications
740 N. Rush St.
Chicago, IL 60611
(312) 649-5200

Adweek publishes five weekly regional editions that report on the advertising industry: *Adweek/East, Adweek/Midwest, Adweek/Southeast, Adweek/Southwest,* and *Adweek/West.* Look in your local Yellow Pages or contact the publisher at the address below.
Adweek
ASM Communications
49 E. 21st St.
New York, NY 10010
(212) 529-5500

AGENCIES

The JN Company is a very creative agency.
Jerome Naidus, CEO
The JN Co.
510 Broadhollow Rd.

Melville, NY 11747
(516) 752-8800

The Madelyn Miller Agency offers a flair for the colorful.
Madelyn Sue Miller, Pres.
The Madelyn Miller Agency
101000 N. Central, #430
Dallas, TX 75243
(214) 987-2553

The Blaine Group specializes in public relations.
Devon Blaine, Pres.
The Blaine Group
7465 Beverly Blvd.
Los Angeles, CA 94104
(213) 938-2577

Jamison & Associates specializes in retail advertising.
David McKay Jamison, Pres.
Jamison & Associates
130 Sutter St., Seventh Floor
San Francisco, CA 94104
(415) 398-2848

Stephen L. Geller Advertising excels at placing magazine advertising on a barter basis.
Stephen L. Geller Advertising
800 Second Ave., Ste. 1317
New York, NY 10017
(212) 986-6642

MISCELLANEOUS SERVICES

Established in 1953, the Harvey Research Organization provides market research services, including custom reports on market behavior, advertising effectiveness, and recognition profiles, to the business community.
Harvey Communication Measurement
Harvey Research Organization, Inc.
Temple Bldg., Rm. 1400
Rochester, NY 14604
(716) 232-4268

The *Small Business Adwriting Planner* explains how to develop advertisements for small business operations. The cost is $150.
National Retail Merchants Association
100 W. 31st St.

New York, NY 10001
(212) 244-8780

Gebbie Press Inc. is a good source of media information.
Gebbie Press Inc.
Box 1000
New Paltz, NY 12561
(914) 255-7560

Alternative Businesses

ASSOCIATION

The National Association for the Cottage Industry provides information for home-based businesses. It publishes a monthly newsletter, *Mind Your Own Business at Home,* and also publishes *Cottage Connection.*

National Association for the Cottage Industry
P.O. Box 14460
Chicago, IL 60614
(312) 472-8116

MISCELLANEOUS SERVICES

A growing small business in Maine, Millrock, Inc. manufactures store displays and has fabulous contacts for alternative businesses.

Rocco J. Zappia, Pres.
Millrock, Inc.
P.O. Box 974
Sanford, ME 04073
(207) 324-0041

PUBLICATIONS

In Business is written for owners of very small businesses (less than $1 million annual sales). The relations of the business with its community are strongly emphasized. Small successful alternative businesses are profiled. Contact JG Press for this highly recommended source.

Jerry Goldstein
JG Press, Inc.
P.O. Box 323
18 S. Seventh St.
Emmaus, PA 18049
(215) 967-4135

New Hope Communications is an especially good source for food specialty information.

Doug Greene
New Hope Communications
328 S. Main St.

New Hope, PA 18938
(215) 862-9414

The Craft Report provides good information on home-based crafts businesses.
The Craft Report
700 Orange St.
P.O. Box 1992
Wilmington, DE 19899
(302) 656-2209

A monthly publication like *Reader's Digest,* the *Utne Reader* excerpts material from the Alternative Business Press.
Eric Utne
Utne Reader
Lens Publishing Co.
2732 W. 43d St.
Minneapolis, MN 55410
(612) 929-2670

Associations of Small Businesses

These organizations can benefit small businesses in many ways: providing business advice, making contacts, lobbying local, state, and federal governments for favorable legislation, and so on. The *Encyclopedia of Associations* is a directory of *all* associations. The cost is $400. It is also available in lower-priced regional editions.

 Gale Research Co.
 Book Tower
 Detroit, MI 48226
 (313) 961-2242
 (800) 223-GALE

NONPOLITICAL

Within the American Management Association (AMA) there is an exclusive 2,000-member group called the President's Association (P/A), which runs an effective five-day management course for presidents. P/A also offers a Limited Company Membership; there are an additional 3,000 members in this group.

 President's Association
 American Management Association
 135 W. 50th St.
 New York, NY 10020
 (212) 586-8100

The Chief Executive Officers (CEO) Club is a group of about 300 CEOs who are dedicated to improving the quality and profitability of their enterprises through shared experience and personal growth. Eight meetings a year are held in each of seven regional locations (Boston, New York, Chicago, Dallas, Los Angeles, San Francisco, Washington, DC). This is an elite group of CEOs who run businesses with more than $2 million in annual sales.

 The three CEO Clubs also sponsor an intensive three-day Management Course for CEOs and a three-day Negotiating Course for CEOs, which are conducted several times annually in resort locations across the United States. Contact the following for more information.

 Joseph R. Mancuso, Pres.
 Chief Executive Officers Clubs
 180 Varick St., Penthouse
 New York, NY 10014-4606
 (212) 633-0060

Several hundred R&D-based small companies belong to the American Association of Small Research Companies.

American Association of Small Research Companies
1200 Lincoln Ave.
Prospect Park, PA 19706
(215) 522-1500

The Young Presidents Organization is an international group of 5,000 company presidents. This group has strong local chapters.

Young Presidents Organization
52 Vanderbilt Ave.
New York, NY 10017
(212) 867-1900

The Association of Venture Founders is a group of several hundred successful business founders. It is headed by Arthur Lipper III and his wife, Annie Lipper. Arthur is the chairman of *Venture* magazine.

Annie Lipper
Association of Venture Founders
521 Fifth Ave.
New York, NY 10175
(212) 682-7373

There are 22 groups of The Executive Committee in California alone; groups can also be found in New Mexico, Texas, Wisconsin, Michigan, Florida, Illinois, and Japan (total of 30). Groups of a dozen CEOs meet monthly. Annual fees are about $7,000.

Pat Hyndman, Dir.
The Executive Committee
3737 Camino Del Rio South, Ste. 206
San Diego, CA 92108
(619) 563-5875

The *Directory of Business, Trade & Public Policy Organizations* is published by the SBA.

Small Business Administration
Office of Advocacy
1725 I St., N.W.
Washington, DC 20416

The National Association of Entrepreneurs offers the opportunity for networking with other entrepreneurs, mostly in Colorado.

National Association of Entrepreneurs
8735 N. Sheridan
Westminster, CO 80003
(303) 426-1166

It is estimated that 80 percent to 95 percent of U.S. businesses are family operated. The Center for Family Business can offer aid.

Leon Danco
Center for Family Business
P.O. Box 24268
Cleveland, OH 44124
(216) 442-0800

The headquarters of the Chamber of Commerce has resources specifically geared for small enterprises.

Center for Small Business
U.S. Chamber of Commerce
1615 H St., N.W.
Washington, DC 20062
(202) 659-6180

POLITICAL

With more than 600,000 dues-paying members, the National Federation of Independent Business (NFIB) provides a strong voice for small business interests. NFIB publishes a newsletter, the *NFIB Mandate,* eight times a year through which it polls its membership to determine lobbying positions.

John Sloan, Pres.
National Federation of Independent Business
150 W. 20th Ave.
San Mateo, CA 94403
(415) 341-7441

National Federation of Independent Business
Capital Gallery East, Ste. 700
600 Maryland Ave., S.W.
Washington, DC 20024
(202) 554-9000

The National Small Business United serves manufacturers, service businesses, retailers, wholesalers, and "anybody who thinks they're small." About 50,000 members strong, it exerts powerful legislative influence.

John Galles, Pres.
National Small Business United
1155 15th St., N.W., Ste. 710
Washington, DC 20005
(202) 293-8830

The Small Business Legislative Council is a coalition of trade and professional associations and is an effective lobbying group.

John Satagaj
Small Business Legislative Council
1025 Vermont, Ste. 1201
Washington, DC 20005
(202) 639-8500

Founded by the legendary Texas oil man, entrepreneur T. Boone Pickens, Jr., the United Shareholder Association is a nonprofit group dedicated to representing shareholders' rights in Congress.

T. Boone Pickens, Jr.
United Shareholders Association
1667 K St., N.W., Ste. 770
Washington, DC 20006
(202) 393-4600

Bankruptcy

Bankruptcy filings continue to climb, despite the increasing strength of the U.S. economy. The Administrative Office for U.S. Courts reports that the number of bankruptcy petitions filed in U.S. bankruptcy courts for the period ended December 31, 1986, and for the four prior years were as follows:

	Chapter 7	Chapter 11	Chapter 12	Chapter 13	Nonbusiness	Total
1982	42,000	14,712	—	6,963	310,552	374,235
1983	40,973	17,819	—	7,265	296,261	362,328
1984	39,138	17,783	—	7,051	284,534	348,488
1985	43,400	20,401	—	7,464	341,233	412,510
1986	50,626	21,370	517	8,491	448,989	530,008

ASSOCIATION

The National Association of Credit Management provides valuable information on bankruptcy.

National Association of Credit Management
520 Eighth Ave.
New York, NY 10016
(212) 947-5070

MISCELLANEOUS SERVICES

Contact a crisis management consultant before filing a Chapter 11 petition. A consultant like The Pace Group might help to revitalize a troubled company.

Langdon G. Johnson, Pres.
The Pace Group
Crisis Management Consultants
30 Tower La.
Avon, CT 06001
(203) 677-5515

I recommend Joseph Braunstein as a bankruptcy specialist.

Joseph Braunstein, Attorney
Riemar & Braunstein, Inc.
3 Center Plaza
Boston, MA 02108
(617) 523-9000

PUBLICATIONS

Highlights of the Bankruptcy Reform Act of 1978 is a free brochure prepared by the commercial collection agency section of the Commercial Law League of America for Mid-Continent Adjustment Company. It presents some of the major provisions of the new bankruptcy code. A more detailed discussion is available in the *Bankruptcy Reform Act Manual* ($27.50). Write to the following source for copies of either publication.

Gordon Calvert, Exec. Dir.
Commercial Collection Agency Section
Commercial Law League of America
P.O. Box 34-531
Bethesda, MD 20817
(301) 365-2224

Les Kirschbaum, Pres.
Mid-Continent Agencies, Inc.
3703 W. Lake Ave.
Glenview, IL 60025
(312) 729-8300

It is always a good idea to review the experience and credentials of each firm, and attorneys tend to specialize even within the general sphere of bankruptcy—consumer or commercial, debtor or creditor representation. The most definitive source available is *The Directory of Bankruptcy Attorneys,* edited by Lynn M. LoPucki ($59).

The Directory of Bankruptcy Attorneys
Prentice-Hall Law and Business
855 Valley Rd.
Clifton, NJ 07013
(800) 831-7799

A wide variety of bankruptcy articles and reprints, as well as a newsletter, is available from Mid-Continent Adjustment Company. Offices are located in Chicago, Buffalo, New York, Atlanta, and Louisville, Kentucky.

Les Kirschbaum
Mid-Continent Agencies, Inc.
3703 W. Lake Ave.
Glenview, IL 60025
(312) 729-8300

How to Get Out of Debt, by Ted Nicholas, is a large workbook which contains practical advice on how to solve debt problems. Enterprise publishes a number of fine books about small business, especially on legal topics.

Enterprise Publishing
1725 Market St.
Wilmington, DE 19801
(302) 575-0440

The National Bankruptcy Reporter is an interesting but expensive (about $1,000
annually) newsletter which contains hard-to-find data on business bankruptcy filings
in New York and other states.
Andrews Publications, Inc.
P.O. Box 200
Edgemont, PA 19028
(215) 353-2565

Credit Executive is a bimonthly magazine published by the New York Credit &
Financial Management Association exclusively for its members. The subscription
charge is included in the membership fee.
Credit Executive
71 W. 23d St.
New York, NY 10010
(212) 741-2266

EXCELLENCE IN FAILURE

When we think of the greats of the automobile industry, the same names always
come to mind: Henry Ford, Ransom Olds, Walter Chrysler, and Louis Chevrolet.
It's only natural. Olds didn't dub his car the "Speed-Buggy" or the "Road-King."
His name was Olds, and he was building automobiles, so Oldsmobile was a logical
name for his product. For decades, each Olds on a highway or Ford in a driveway
has been a monument to the companies' founders.

But what about the less well-known entrepreneurs who keep their family crests
off their goods? Are these innovators less worthy of recognition? Hardly. In fact, one
of the greatest legends in automobile history is a person who's rarely spoken of
today.

From the beginning of his long career, William "Billy" Durant believed that
a good product would be a "self-seller." Such a self-seller came along in 1886, when
the 25-year-old Durant happened to ride in a road cart that featured a new kind of
spring—one that smoothed out travel on rough roads. He borrowed $2,000 to buy
the patent and formed a partnership with J. Dallas Dort. By 1901, the Durant-Dort
Carriage Company, 14 plants strong, was the nation's largest buggy maker.

A zealous promoter, Durant was always scouting out new products. In 1904,
he was invited to look at a failing company run by David Buick, a plumbing supplier
and tinkerer. Impressed by an experimental car which Buick had developed, Durant
purchased the company. He is said to have financed the firm in a single day by selling
$500,000 of Buick stock.

By 1908, Durant decided to form an auto combine. Incorporating under the
name General Motors (GM), he proceeded to buy, with Buick stock, the Oldsmobile,

Cadillac, and Oakland motor companies. With nearly 30 companies under the GM umbrella, the business was valued at $37 million in 1910.

A Remarkable Recovery

GM seemed prosperous, but the economy was fickle, the industry was young, and Durant was too busy building to think about planning and safeguards. During the Panic of 1910, GM found itself squeezed for cash, and a coalition of Eastern bankers squeezed Durant out. This scenario is not uncommon in the lore of entrepreneurship—but what happened afterward is.

When Durant left GM, he took several long-time associates with him. In two years they founded a half-dozen car companies, most notably the Chevrolet Motor Company (with race-car driver Louis Chevrolet). Durant consolidated the firms under the Chevrolet banner. By 1915, Chevrolet was valued at $80 million. Through the years Durant had continued to buy stock in GM; by 1915, he controlled enough stock to retake the company.

Under his renewed tutelage, GM continued to grow. Among his acquisitions were a small refrigeration firm (christened Frigidaire by Durant), the Delco Company (adding the brilliant engineer Charles Kettering to his GM team), and the Hyatt Roller Bearing Company (adding Alfred P. Sloan to his GM team). GM built a $20-million office building in Detroit which was dubbed the Durant Building.

The postwar economy declined in 1920. GM, which only a year before had $38 million in cash, was $200 million in debt. Durant lost more than $90 million—his entire fortune—trying to bolster GM stock. Shortly after leaving GM in 1920, Durant sent out letters to raise money for a new company, Durant Motors, which would strive to manufacture "a real good car." He had commitments for $7 million within 48 hours. His first car, the Durant Four, was designed and built in 47 days.

By 1927, Durant planned to compete head to head with GM by consolidating more than 28 percent of the U.S. auto manufacturers under the name "Consolidated Motors." But when the stock market crashed in 1929, Consolidated Motors became a forgotten dream: Durant Motors was on the ropes, and Durant himself was nearly broke. In 1936, one of America's greatest entrepreneurs filed for bankruptcy at the age of seventy-five.

Durant's accomplishments should not be diminished because he didn't leave a "Durantmobile" or a university endowment for posterity. He should not be overlooked, even if his spectacular Durant Building in Detroit has been redubbed the General Motors Building. Despite the fortunes won and lost, Durant lived and died as an entrepreneur: Being an innovator was the only thing he knew how to do.

Banks

A close and sympathetic relationship with a commercial bank can be very helpful to a small business, not only in facilitating loans but also in securing valuable business advice.

ASSOCIATIONS

Any information you might need on the status of the banking industry is available from the American Bankers Association, a trade organization which has about 14,000 members.

American Bankers Association
1120 Connecticut Ave., N.W.
Washington, DC 20036
(202) 663-5000

The Independent Bankers Association, another good trade organization, works with banks that help small businesses.

Independent Bankers Association
P.O. Box 267
1168 S. Main St.
Sauk Center, MN 56378
(612) 352-6546

MISCELLANEOUS SERVICES

Robert Morris Associates is the predominant training organization for commercial lenders. They also provide valuable industry statistics and financial ratios for industries.

Robert Morris Associates
1616 Philadelphia National Bank Bldg.
Broad & Chestnut Sts.
Philadelphia, PA 19107
(215) 665-2858

The Robert Morris "Projection of Financial Statements" form is widely used by entrepreneurs in preparing financial statements for business plans. It is available from the following source.

Bankers Systems, Inc.
P.O. Box 1457

St. Cloud, MN 56302
(612) 251-3060

In order to cut through some of the red tape involved in getting an SBA-guaranteed loan, SBA has instituted the Preferred Lenders Program (PLP), in which individual banks are granted the authority to make SBA loans. To locate a bank approved by SBA in the PLP, call this toll-free number: SBA answer desk (800) 368-5855. Contact Veribank if you're interested in checking up on the financial health of your bank.

Veribank
P.O. Box 2963
Woburn, MA 01888
(617) 245-8370

How to Get a Business Loan Without Signing Your Life Away is a three-hour videotape program, by Joseph R. Mancuso, which offers a wealth of information on small business banking, including "How to Get and Stay Off Personal Loan Guarantees." (A four-hour audiotape program is also available.) Contact the following source for more information.

The Center for Entrepreneurial Management
180 Varick St., Penthouse
New York, NY 10014-4606
(212) 633-0060

A former bank president who lectures on bank/entrepreneur issues, Somers White is an extremely effective speaker. He has produced excellent books and tapes on obtaining bank loans.

Somers White
4736 N. 44th St.
Phoenix, AZ 85018
(602) 952-9292

PUBLICATIONS

Bank Mergers and Acquisitions, an authoritative newsletter devoted exclusively to mergers and acquisitions, provides in-depth reportage, analysis, and interpretation. It also keeps you abreast of new regulatory developments.

Curran & Roemer, Inc.
3107 Kingsbridge Ave.
Bronx, NY 10463
(212) 769-4800

Polk's Bank Directory is the most complete source of bank information and bank listings we've found. The North American Edition costs $170.

R. L. Polk & Co.
2001 Elm Hill Pike

Nashville, TN 37210
(615) 889-3350

The *Encyclopedia of Banking and Financing,* an excellent directory, can be obtained
from Banker's Publishing Company. *Banker and Tradesman* and the *Commercial
Record* are also published by this group.
Bankers Publishing Co.
210 South St., 5th Floor
Boston, MA 02111
(617) 426-4495

Offshore Banking News is offering a free 12-page pamphlet on the benefits of offshore
banking titled *Offshore Banking Is Not Evil.* Topics covered include "What Offshore
Banking Really Is—and What It Isn't," "How to Investigate Offshore Banking and
Investment Opportunities," "How to Open a Swiss Bank Account," "How to Borrow Offshore," and "When It Is Necessary to Report Offshore Movement of Funds
and When It Isn't."
Offshore Banking News
301 Plymouth Dr., N.E.
Dalton, GA 30720
(404) 259-6035

ARE YOU ON GOOD TERMS WITH YOUR BANK?

To be your bank's best customer, score 175 points or more on this quiz.

1. Can you draw an organizational chart of the bank with your banker included? You need to know where the decision-making power is and where your
banker fits in. (25 points)
2. Did you give your banker a small Christmas present last year? A small gift
is something like a book. (For example, if you know he has a hobby give him a book
on the subject.) (20 points; add 10 points if your banker came to your Christmas
party)
3. Do you know where your banker went to school? One of the first things two
people do when they get to know one another is look for some common ground.
Knowing what school your banker went to not only tells you something about him
but also provides an opener for conversation. (10 points)
4. Do you know the first name of your banker's spouse? People tend to trust
those they are familiar with (up to a point, of course), so it helps if you know the
name of your banker's spouse and ask about him or her once in a while. (10 points)
5. Do you know the first and last names of your banker's boss? Bankers tend
to move up quickly in their jobs, either by changing banks or by bouncing from one
branch to another. If you know your banker's boss, then it's possible that when your
banker moves, your account will be passed up to the boss rather than down to the
new loan officer. And the higher the rank of the person you're dealing with, the
better off you are. (15 points)
6. Do you know the names and backgrounds of at least two members (exclud-

ing your banker) of the loan committee? Ninety percent of the time, your loan officer makes the decision on your loan, but he has to get the approval of the loan committee. Knowing who's on the committee (and that they know you) will smooth the process. (40 points)

7. Do you know your banker's home town? Friendly interest is one key to a good relationship. (10 points)

8. Do you know your banker's birthday? When I mention that it's a good idea to give your banker a quick phone call on his birthday, the average person laughs and tells me it's a corny idea. He laughs, but on *his* birthday he gets a kick out of the fact that someone remembers. (Also, calling your banker on his birthday tells him that you have a good memory for dates and will remember when your loan payments are due.) (15 points)

9. Have you taken your banker and/or his boss on a tour of your company in the past six months? It's amazing how impressed a banker is when he actually sees a product being produced, sold, and shipped. (25 points)

10. Have you been out socially (*not* as part of a loan request) with your banker in the past six months? Socially means no business. Don't make the mistake of asking a touchy question after a pleasant meal. And let your banker do 90 percent of the talking. The more you let him talk about his interests, the better impression you'll make. (30 points)

HOW TO TURN YOUR BANKER INTO A COMPANY SUPPORTER

There comes a time in the life of every entrepreneur, sometime between the beginning of his company and the time it achieves success, when a banker will have to be contacted. Maybe there won't be enough collateral, or the paperwork won't be completely in place, and the banker must decide whether or not to proceed with a loan that may make or break the company.

The entrepreneur obviously wants the banker to say, "Hey, this guy's okay. I know him and I know his company, and I think we ought to make the loan." But the very nature of commercial banking in the United States is conservatism. Banking is a low-profit, low-risk business, and if you haven't done your homework with your banker, chances are slim that he is going to "risk" a nickel of the bank's money on you.

The first thing that anyone starting a new business must understand is that raising capital isn't necessarily a function of the need to raise capital. In other words, just because you need to raise $50,000 by the end of the month doesn't mean you'll be able to get it. Therefore, it pays to be on good terms with your banker. And that means more than a good track record at paying back your loans.

In order to become your bank's best customer, you need to make your banker your best friend. What does this mean? It means that when you go to the bank for a loan, you shouldn't be interested only in what your banker can do for you but in what you can do for your banker. In fact, you'll find that asking his advice can be quite beneficial. "Money always follows advice" is my first law of raising capital. It pays to follow a few basic guidelines as you begin your search for a good commercial lender.

Never pick a bank, pick a banker. One thing you'll quickly discover about bankers is that they're ambitious. It's not uncommon to find out that six months after you've negotiated a loan, your loan officer has been promoted and no longer handles your account. When that happens, it usually means starting over—explaining your business, plans, and needs to a new loan officer. But it doesn't have to happen this way.

When a banker moves up the ladder, he can continue to handle your account. Commercial loan officers hang on to certain accounts all the way up the corporate ladder. But if you visit your banker only once or twice a year when you need money, and forget about him the rest of the time, you can bet that he'll forget about you after his promotion. In other words, if you want the banker to take a genuine interest in your business, take a genuine interest in his business.

Find a banker who understands the idiosyncracies of your business and industry. A common complaint is that the bank just isn't there when the company needs it the most. That's probably because the banker doesn't understand the particular business. Or, to put it bluntly, the banker doesn't even know when the company needs help. To avoid this problem, find a banker who speaks the language of your industry or is willing to learn. (It also helps if you learn to speak his language.) A banker who knows your industry will know what your needs are and when and why they occur.

Good preparation is the key to getting off on the right foot with your banker. Whenever you raise capital, it's essential to bring the element of risk down to an acceptable level (and for bankers, an acceptable level of risk is zero).

When you walk in the door of your bank, you should be prepared to answer the following five questions.

1. How much money do you need?
2. How long do you need it for?
3. What are you going to do with it?
4. When and how are you going to repay it?
5. What will you do if you don't get the loan?

Furthermore, arrange your financial data in a format that is readily understandable.

Let your banker know what you're doing. After you have established a relationship with a banker, keep him informed. Let him know if you're doing anything new, such as innovations in manufacturing or in collecting receivables, or if you've hired new managerial talent. The more he knows about your business, the better. This is especially true in a closely held company where the banker is actually lending to management. Let your banker know what management is doing and thinking.

Be enthusiastic about your business. This is seldom a problem for entrepreneurs. No one is more enthusiastic and gung ho about what they're doing than entrepreneurs. But even entrepreneurs may sometimes feel that they need to take a more conservative approach when dealing with bankers. This simply isn't the case. If you can get your enthusiasm across to your banker, you can bring him over to your side.

Never take your banker by surprise. Bankers hate surprises. Keep your banker posted on good *and* bad company events. Never surprise him with bad news. In fact, a banker often plays a vital role in a growing business so that he really is a part of your management team. As such, he should be someone you can talk to in good times or in times of crisis.

After your business is on its feet, there are a number of ways to keep your banker informed about what you're doing. Perhaps the best thing you can do is to have him visit your facility. Let him see the product being produced, sold, and shipped. Bring your banker along to trade shows. It's a great opportunity to let him get hands-on experience with the industry. And, more important, it provides an excellent opportunity for him to actually see you writing orders!

If you're in a service business, try to show your banker other results of your business's activities. For example, if you're in real estate, take your banker to see the houses and property you've sold in the past and the houses and property you currently have listed.

Nothing makes a banker happier than to see the bank's money making money and to know that he is a part of it. Even if you don't have any earthshaking news to report, it's a good idea to call your banker from time to time just to chat about business—both yours and his. Your banker will go out of his way to help your business grow if he feels that he's a part of your business.

You're not doing your job if you go into the bank only when you need to borrow. A bank's best customer is not necessarily its biggest customer. The best customer is the one the banker wants to keep. And it's the entrepreneur's job to become the best customer of the bank by making his company as indispensable to the bank as the bank is to his company. The advantages of good banking relations to a growing company cannot be underestimated. And the secret to good banking relations is to find the right banker and to stick with him.

PREFERRED LENDER PROGRAM

SBA Business Loan Guarantees

SBA has been guaranteeing bank loans to small businesses since its creation by Congress in 1953. Because these guarantees of up to 90 percent of the loan value are available only to small businesses that have already been turned down by private commercial lenders, the program enables entrepreneurs to obtain long-term credit that otherwise would not be available at reasonable terms and conditions.

The SBA has guaranteed more than 384,000 regular business loans, also known as 7(a) loans, because Section 7(a) of the Small Business Act authorizes this activity. These loans total almost $41 billion. The agency guaranteed 14,206 7(a) loans in fiscal year (FY) 1986. SBA's portfolio of outstanding guaranteed loans now stands at $9.9 billion.

What Lender Certification Does

SBA's "regular service" on 7(a) loan guarantees requires an SBA application review and decision that duplicates to some extent the work already done by the lender. Lender certification eliminates the duplicative paperwork.

The Certified Lenders Program (CLP) invites lenders who have been more heavily involved in SBA's "regular service" loan guarantees, if they meet certain criteria, to accept delegations of authority that will result in much faster service to the lender by the agency.

Lender certification offers two levels of participation. Certified lenders receive a partial delegation of authority, and their loan guarantee applications are given a three-day turnaround by the local SBA office, assuming everything is in proper order. Preferred lenders enjoy a full delegation of authority and can decide unilaterally on SBA participation in eligible business loans.

SBA's present authority for developing PLP, the ultimate step in the lender certification process, is based on Public Law 96-302, Section 114. This law authorizes SBA, with respect to guaranteed business loans, to delegate to certain lending institutions the authority to determine eligibility, creditworthiness, loan structuring, loan monitoring, loan collection/servicing, and loan liquidation actions, and to make necessary decisions at each stage of the procedure without, in most instances, SBA's prior review or consent. However, PLP loans currently have a maximum SBA guarantee of only 75 percent.

Lender certification benefits the loan applicant, the lender, and SBA. Loan applicants and lenders receive faster service, and the agency is able to leverage its resources to provide better assistance to more small businesses.

How the Program has Developed

CLP generated 29.6 percent of the $2.13 billion in 7(a) general business loan guarantees approved by SBA during FY1986. In many SBA offices, the average turnaround time for CLP loans was shorter than the three days promised. There were approximately 650 certified lenders by the end of FY1986.

PLP was made available throughout the United States during FY1986. Seventy-six preferred lenders generated 662 PLP loans, valued (gross) at $169.437 million in 7(a) regular business loan guarantees. SBA's guaranteed share of these loans was $125.2 million. Currently, there are approximately 140 lenders approved for the program.

SBA's "regular service" for business loan guarantees from lenders continues unchanged (except as amended by Public Law 99-272, which became effective on April 7, 1986) for those participant lenders that have executed with SBA only the *Loan Guaranty Agreement (Deferred Participation) (SBA Form 750 and/or 750B),* which has neither certified nor preferred status.

Lender certification is part of a total SBA effort to switch from retailing to wholesaling its services. Loan guarantee activity by certified and preferred lenders requires less staff time and paperwork by SBA than the "regular service" program. This improvement enables the agency to better use its limited staff resources to handle a greater volume of loan applications and to devote needed resources to portfolio management and other agency responsibilities.

Criteria for Lender Certification

Lenders interested in lender certification ordinarily must be active in the agency's "regular service" loan guarantee program. Only lenders with whom SBA has had good experience (measured by a set of criteria) will be able to graduate from "regular service" to certified lender status. Only lenders with at least one year of certified lender status will be considered for preferred lender status.

How Does the Program Work?

Early in 1983, SBA launched a pilot program in three regions of the United States: New York/New Jersey, the Midwest, and the West Coast. In those regions SBA designated its most active and best-performing lending partners as preferred lenders. Under the program, PLP lenders handle all loan paperwork, including the processing, closing, servicing, and, if necessary, liquidation of SBA loans. The program was designed to reduce paperwork and loan delays.

Approximately 140 lending institutions in 44 states are now participating in PLP. These lenders must first be successful participants (for at least one full year) in the agency's CLP. The areas without PLP participants are Delaware, Kentucky, New Hampshire, North Dakota, Oregon, Rhode Island, the District of Columbia, Puerto Rico, and the Virgin Islands.

For loan approvals, the PLP lender makes all decisions related to eligibility, creditworthiness, and loan closing with no prior review by SBA. After the closing, the PLP lender also makes most final decisions regarding the administration and, if necessary, the liquidation of the loan.

SBA examines the PLP lender's SBA portfolio periodically (usually each quarter) to ensure that it meets agency requirements. Every two years, PLP lenders must renew their authority, and if they do not perform up to SBA standards, their authority is not renewed.

Financial institutions interested in applying to the program should contact their local SBA office. The Office of Financial Institutions in the SBA Central Office can provide additional information; call (202) 653-2585.

SBA Guarantees of PLP Loans

Because of the special procedures of PLP, SBA guarantees PLP loans only to a maximum of 75 percent, versus 85 or 90 percent for general SBA loans (depending upon the size of the loans, etc.), as authorized by the Small Business Act (amended on April 7, 1986).

Although the 75-percent guarantee has eliminated some marginal loans from consideration, many top-notch lending institutions find PLP appealing for the following reasons.

1. Lenders can sell the SBA-guaranteed portion of the loan on the secondary market; this is the case with most SBA-guaranteed loans.

2. Lenders can offer expeditious service to their borrowers, thus improving their competitive position.

3. Lenders often get referral business from other lending institutions that are not as familiar with SBA's loan guarantee programs.

4. Lenders handle PLP loans with minimal SBA interaction (and consequent delays).

5. Lenders know that PLP will continue to improve and expand, benefiting all parties involved in the program.

PLP LENDERS

Region I

Connecticut
Hamden	American National Bank
Waterbury	Colonial Bank

Maine
Augusta	Key Bank of Central Maine

Massachusetts
Boston	First National Bank of Boston
Boston	Shawmut Bank, NA
Peabody	Essexbank
Springfield	Bank of New England–West
Worcester	Guaranty Bank & Trust Company

Vermont
Brattleboro	Vermont National Bank
Burlington	Chittenden Bank
Burlington	The Merchants Bank
Randolph	Randolph National Bank

Region II

New Jersey
Jackson	Garden State Bank
Lodi	National Community Bank of New Jersey
Newark	First Fidelity Bank, NA, New Jersey
North Plainfield	North Plainfield State Bank
Union	The Money Store Investment Corporation

New York
Albany	New York Business Development Corporation
Buffalo	Liberty National Bank and Trust Company
Buffalo	Manufacturers and Traders Trust Company
New York City	Chase Manhattan Bank, NA
New York City	Chemical Bank
New York City	Citibank, NA
Rochester	Security Norstar Bank, Rochester

Region III

Pennsylvania
Erie	Marine Bank
Perkasie	Bucks County Bank and Trust Company
Pittsburgh	Mellon Bank, NA
Pittsburgh	Pittsburgh National Bank
Reading	Meridian Bank

Virginia
Richmond	Sovran Bank
Richmond	United Virginia Bank

West Virginia
Huntington	The First Huntington National Bank

Region IV

Alabama
Birmingham	Central Bank of the South

Florida
North Miami Beach	First Western SBLC, Inc.
Orlando	Sun Bank, NA
Panama City	Bay Bank & Trust Company
Panama City	The First National Bank of Panama City

Georgia
Atlanta	First National Bank of Atlanta
Atlanta	Fulton Federal Savings
Atlanta	Southern Federal Savings & Loan
Atlanta	Southern National Bank
Atlanta	The Business Development Corporation of Georgia, Inc.
Atlanta	The Citizens and Southern National Bank
Augusta	Bankers First Savings & Loan Association

Mississippi
Jackson	Deposit Guaranty National Bank

North Carolina
Winston-Salem	Wachovia Bank & Trust Company, NA

South Carolina
Columbia	Bankers Trust of South Carolina

Tennessee
Elizabethton	Citizens Bank
Memphis	National Bank of Commerce
Memphis	Union Planters National Bank
Nashville	Commerce Union Bank
Nashville	First American National Bank
Nashville	Third National Bank

Region V

Illinois
Benton	United Illinois Bank of Benton
Chicago	South Shore Bank of Chicago
Joliet	First Midwest Bank/Joliet
Urbana	Busey First National Bank

Indiana
Fort Wayne	Lincoln National Bank of Fort Wayne

Michigan
Midland	Chemical Bank and Trust Company

Minnesota
Minneapolis	First National Bank of Minneapolis
St. Cloud	First American Bank of St. Cloud

Ohio
Bowling Green	Mid-American National Bank and Trust Company
Cincinnati	First National Bank of Cincinnati
Columbus	Bank One of Columbus
Columbus	Huntington National Bank
Dayton	First National Bank of Dayton

Wisconsin
Madison	First Wisconsin National Bank of Madison
Milwaukee	Associates Commerce Bank
Milwaukee	First Wisconsin National Bank of Milwaukee
Milwaukee	M&I Northern Bank
Milwaukee	Marine Bank, NA
Sheboygan	First Wisconsin National Bank of Sheboygan
Wausau	First American National Bank of Wausau

Region VI

Arkansas
Little Rock	Commercial National Bank of Texarkana

Louisiana
Baton Rouge	Capital Bank and Trust Company

New Mexico
Albuquerque	First National Bank in Albuquerque

Oklahoma
Stillwater	Stillwater National Bank and Trust Company

Texas
Brownsville	Texas Commerce Bank–Brownsville
Corpus Christi	First National Bank of Corpus Christi
El Paso	Texas Commerce Bank–El Paso, NA

Region VI

El Paso	First City Bank–West, NA
Houston	Texas American Bank–Spring Branch
Longview	Longview Bank and Trust Company
Lubbock	First National Bank at Lubbock
Seguin	Southwestern Commercial Capital, Inc.

Region VII

Iowa

Cedar Rapids	Merchants National Bank of Cedar Rapids
Davenport	Davenport Bank and Trust Company
Des Moines	Norwest Bank Des Moines
Sioux City	Toy National Bank
West Des Moines	West Des Moines State Bank

Kansas

Liberal	First National Bank of Liberal
Wichita	Fourth National Bank and Trust Company

Missouri

Columbia	First National Bank & Trust Company
Jefferson City	Central Trust Company
Kansas City	United Missouri Bank of Kansas City, NA
Springfield	The Boatmen's National Bank of Springfield
St. Louis	Mercantile Trust Company, NA

Nebraska

Lincoln	First National Bank & Trust Company
Lincoln	Union Bank and Trust Company

Region VIII

Colorado

Denver	Republic National Bank of Englewood

Montana

Whitefish	Mountain Bank

South Dakota

Sioux Falls	Western Bank of Sioux Falls

Utah

Salt Lake City	First Security Bank of Utah
Salt Lake City	Tracy Collins Bank & Trust Company
Salt Lake City	Valley Bank and Trust Company

Wyoming

Cheyenne	First Wyoming Bank, NA, Cheyenne

Region IX

Arizona
Phoenix	The Valley National Bank of Arizona
Phoenix	Thunderbird Bank

California
Bakersfield	San Joaquin Bank
Hollywood	American Pacific State Bank
San Francisco	Bank of America NT & SA
San Francisco	Wells Fargo, NA
San Luis Obispo	First Bank of San Luis Obispo

Hawaii
Honolulu	Bank of Hawaii

Nevada
Las Vegas	Valley Bank of Nevada

Region X

Alaska
Anchorage	Alaska Pacific Bank
Fairbanks	First National Bank of Fairbanks

Idaho
Boise	The Idaho First National Bank

Washington
Lynwood	City Bank
Seattle	Rainier National Bank
Spokane	Washington Trust Bank

Barter

Entrepreneurs often overlook the opportunity to barter for services with other entrepreneurial ventures. A growing interest has developed in bartering, and many publications and services have emerged. These services and publications are entrepreneurial in their own right; the claim is made that several billion dollars are exchanged annually through barter. Bartering has an obvious advantage: It avoids taxes. In other words, if a doctor gives you medical service worth $100 and you do labor for him in his home worth $100, neither of you has really declared $100 of income. You have swapped services, and this exchange is not a taxable transaction.

It's interesting to note that the government maintains accurate figures on its Gross National Product (GNP), which is the aggregate of U.S. output on the basis of products and services that are sold for cash. Barter does not enter into the GNP picture. Bartered goods that are not individually exchanged for cash are not recorded in government statistics.

Another aspect of barter that appeals to entrepreneurs involves the possibility of a good bargain. Unfortunately, a good bargain isn't always attainable because people who are bartering services for goods or goods for services often tend to inflate their prices. Be wary of unscrupulous buyers and sellers when examining barter alternatives.

The sources of information on barter provided in this chapter may be helpful in securing new products or services for your firm, or in offering your firm's services or products to others. Unfortunately, low quality is often associated with barter. You must not ignore this fact of small business life. Usually the sources of barter information are themselves poor businesses; therefore, they go out of business faster than their customers. A few of the better sources are listed below.

Barter News is issued quarterly as a magazine for the barter industry.
>   Robert B. Meyer
>   *Barter News*
>   P.O. Box 3024
>   24721 Tarazona
>   Mission Viejo, CA 92690
>   (714) 855-4618

The International Reciprocal Trade Association is a good source of information.
>   Paul Suplizio, Dir.
>   International Reciprocal Trade Association
>   4012 Moss Pl.
>   Alexandria, VA 22304
>   (703) 823-8707

The National Association of Trade Exchange is the industry's trade association.
Gary Monkman
National Association of Trade Exchange
2832 Belvedere, Ste. 114
Waukeegan, IL 60085
(312) 249-3080

The Welt International Corporation is a good international barter group.
Leo Welt
Welt International Corp.
1413 K St., N.W., Ste. 800
Washington, DC 20005
(202) 371-1343

Countertrade Outlook is one of the original publishers of barter information.
Judith Fischer, Publisher
Countertrade Outlook
P.O. Box 3141
Alexandria, VA 22302
(703) 370-3817

Uniclub is an organization which provides a credit card to barter and also allows the customer to charge on this card, paying 15 percent less than the amount that is charged.
Uniclub
40 W. 27th St.
New York, NY 10117
(212) 696-4949

Business Development Corporations and State Business Development Agencies

The purpose of business development corporations (BDCs) is to attract and retain businesses in their respective states, and thus to increase employment. Although they sound like government agencies, BDCs are *private* organizations that operate within a state. Their shareholders are usually other private financial institutions located within the state, mainly savings banks and insurance companies, although industrial companies are sometimes investors.

Interest rates on BDC loans are usually a function of the prime rate and range from 2 to 4 percent above the prevailing rate. In addition, some BDCs charge application fees and commitment fees. These fees generally do not total more than 1½ percent of the loan. A prime advantage of BDC loans is the longer maturities available. A bank will rarely offer more than five years for a term loan; however, BDC loans have averaged maturities of between four and ten years.

Although most BDCs require collateral, many will accept second liens. The owners should be prepared to assign key-man life insurance and personally to guarantee the loan if the business is closely held.

BDCs are lenders, not investors, and are usually not interested in equity positions in the business. However, a few, such as the New York Business Development Corporation, have formed small business investment company subsidiaries (SBICs). The SBIC will take equity positions, generally via subordinated debt with warrants (or a convertible feature), to round out a financing package.

BDCs are specifically designed to provide long-term capital to small businesses. It's tough to get capital today, so it's a good idea to become familiar with your state BDC.

For more information, you can contact your local chamber of commerce or the following source.

National Association of Business Development Associations
Industrial Development Corp. of Florida
801 N. Magnolia Ave., Ste. 218
Orlando, FL 32803
(305) 841-2640

The National Association of Business Development Corporations has members at the following locations.

Alaska State Development Corp.   Juneau, AK 99811
Pouch D   (907) 586-2775

George H. Eagen, Exec. V.P.
First Arkansas Capital Corp.
800 Pyramid Pl.
Little Rock, AR 72201
(501) 374-9247

First Arkansas Development Finance Corp.
910 Pyramid Life Bldg.
Little Rock, AR 72201
(501) 374-9247

David Johnson, Exec. V.P.
The Business Development Corp. of Georgia
4000 Cumberland Pkwy., Ste. 1200A
Atlanta, GA 30339
(404) 434-0273

Don Albertson, Exec. V.P.
Iowa Business Development Corp.
901 Insurance Exchange Bldg.
Fifth & Grand Aves.
Des Moines, IA 50309
(515) 282-2164

George L. Doak
Kansas Development Credit Corp.
Bank 4 Tower, Ste. 1030
1 Townsite Plaza
Topeka, KS 66603
(913) 235-3437

Jess C. Dixon, Jr., Exec. V.P.
Business Development Corp. of Kentucky
382 Starks Bldg.
Louisville, KY 40202
(502) 964-6498

Kenneth J. Smith
Massachusetts Business Development Corp.
One Liberty Sq.
Boston, MA 02109
(617) 350-8877

Richard Bourke, V.P.
Development Credit Corp. of Montana
P.O. Box 916
Helena, MT 59624
(406) 442-3850

James H. Childe, Exec. V.P.
Business Development Corp. of Nebraska
139 S. 52d St.
Lincoln, NE 68510
(402) 483-0382

Gino Del Carlo
Nevada Financial Development Corp.
350 S. Center St., Ste. 380
Reno, NV 89501
(702) 323-3033

Albert Hall III, Mgr.
New Hampshire Business Development
  Corp.
10 Center St.
Concord, NH 03301
(603) 224-1432

Kevin Dotson
New Mexico Business Development Corp.
6001 Marble N.E., Ste. 6
Albuquerque, NM 87110
(505) 268-1316

Robert W. Lazar, Exec. V.P.
New York Business Development Corp.
41 State St.
Albany, NY 12207
(518) 463-2268

Paul Mitchel, Pres.
Bryan Fischer
SE Pennsylvania Development Fund
1 Penn Center, Ste. 1360
Philadelphia, PA 19103
(215) 568-4677

Greg Rudman
Joseph Dougherty
Western Pennsylvania Development Credit
  Corp.
Frick Bldg., Ste. 1220
437 Grant St.
Pittsburgh, PA 15219
(412) 288-9206

James Stevenson, Pres.
Business Development Corp. of Rhode
  Island
30 Exchange Terr.
Providence, RI 02903
(401) 351-3036

Vern Amick, Exec. V.P.
Business Development Corp. of South
  Carolina
P.O. Box 21823
Columbia, SC 29221
(803) 798-4064

V. Gibson Sears, Exec. V.P.
Greater Spokane Business Development
 Association
Municipal Bldg., Rm. 250
W. 808 Spokane Falls Blvd.
Spokane, WA 99201-3333
(509) 456-4380

Larry McDonald
Wyoming Industrial Development
 Corp.
P.O. Box 3599
Casper, WY 82602
(307) 234-5351

STATE BUSINESS DEVELOPMENT AGENCIES

State business development agencies can provide guidance, programs, or services in the following areas:

Business development
Procurement assistance
Financial assistance
Opportunities for businesses run by minorities and women

ALABAMA
Alabama Development Office
135 S. Union St.
State Capitol
Montgomery, AL 36130
(205) 263-0048

ALASKA
Office of Enterprise
Department of Commerce
Pouch D
Juneau, AK 99811
(907) 465-2018

ARIZONA
Office of Business and Trade
Department of Commerce
1700 W. Washington St., 4th Floor
Phoenix, AZ 85007
(602) 255-5371

ARKANSAS
Small Business Development Center
University of Arkansas (Little Rock)
Library Bldg., Rm. 512
Little Rock, AR 72204
(501) 371-5381

CALIFORNIA
Office of Small Business Development
Department of Commerce
1121 L St., Ste. 600
Sacramento, CA 95814
(916) 445-6545

COLORADO
Business Information Center
Office of Regulatory Reform
1525 Sherman St., Rm. 110
Denver, CO 80203
(303) 866-3933

CONNECTICUT
Small Business Services
Department of Economic Development
210 Washington St.
Hartford, CT 06106
(203) 566-4051

DELAWARE
Economic Development Office
99 King's Hwy.
P.O. Box 1401
Dover, DE 19903
(302) 736-4271

DISTRICT OF COLUMBIA
Office of Business and Economic Development
1111 E St., N.W., Ste. 700
Washington, DC 20004
(202) 727-6600

FLORIDA
Small Business Development Center
University of West Florida, Bldg. 8
Pensacola, FL 32514
(904) 474-2908

GEORGIA
Small Business Development Center
1180 E. Broad St.
Chicopee Complex
Athens, GA 30602
(404) 542-1721

HAWAII
Small Business Information Service
250 S. King St., Rm. 724
Honolulu, HI 96813
(808) 548-7645

IDAHO
Division of Economic and Community
  Affairs
Department of Commerce
State Capitol, Rm. 108
Boise, ID 83720
(208) 334-2470

ILLINOIS
Bureau of Small Business
Department of Commerce and Community
  Affairs
620 E. Adams St.
Springfield, IL 62701
(217) 785-7500

INDIANA
Division of Small Business Expansion
Department of Commerce
1 N. Capital Ave., Ste. 700
Indianapolis, IN 46204
(317) 232-8800

IOWA
Small Business Section
Iowa Development Commission
200 E. Grand Ave.
Des Moines, IA 50309
(515) 281-8310
(800) 532-1216 (IA only)

KANSAS
Small Business Development Center
Wichita State University
021 Clinton Hall, Campus Box 148
Wichita, KS 67208
(316) 689-3193

KENTUCKY
Business Information Clearinghouse
Commerce Cabinet

Capitol Plaza Tower, 22d Floor
Frankfort, KY 40601
(502) 564-4252
(800) 626-2250 (KY only)

LOUISIANA
Department of Commerce
Office of Commerce and Industry
One Maritime Plaza
P.O. Box 94185
Baton Rouge, LA 70802-9185
(504) 342-5361

MAINE
Small Business Development Center
University of Southern Maine
246 Deering Ave.
Portland, ME 04102
(207) 780-4420

MARYLAND
Office of Business and Industrial Development
45 Calvert St.
Annapolis, MD 21404
(301) 269-2945

MASSACHUSETTS
Small Business Assistance Division
Department of Commerce
100 Cambridge St., 13th Floor
Boston, MA 02202
(617) 727-4005
(800) 632-8181 (MA only)

MICHIGAN
Local Development Service
Department of Commerce
P.O. Box 30225
Lansing, MI 48909
(517) 373-3530

MINNESOTA
Small Business Assistance Center
Department of Energy and Economic Development
900 American Center
150 E. Kellogg Blvd.
St. Paul, MN 55107
(612) 296-3871

MISSISSIPPI
Small Business Clearinghouse
Research and Development Center

3825 Ridgewood Rd.
Jackson, MS 39211-6453
(601) 982-6231
(800) 521-7258 (MS only)

MISSOURI
Small and Existing Business Development
  Office
Department of Economic Development
P.O. Box 118
Jefferson City, MO 65102
(314) 751-4982

MONTANA
Business Assistance Division
Department of Commerce
1424 Ninth Ave.
Helena, MT 59620
(406) 444-3923

NEBRASKA
Small Business Division
Department of Economic Development
P.O. Box 94666
301 Centennial Mall South
Lincoln, NE 68509
(402) 471-3111

NEVADA
Small Business Development Center
University of Nevada (Reno)
College of Business Administration
Business Bldg., Rm. 411
Reno, NV 89557-0016
(702) 784-1717

NEW HAMPSHIRE
Industrial Development Authority
4 Park St., Rm. 302
Concord, NH 03301
(603) 271-2591

NEW JERSEY
Office of Small Business Assistance
Department of Commerce and Economic
  Development
1 W. State St., CN 823
Trenton, NJ 08625
(609) 984-4442

NEW MEXICO
Business Development and Expansion
Department of Economic Development and
  Tourism

Joseph Montoya Bldg.
1100 St. Francis Dr.
Santa Fe, NM 87503
(505) 827-0300

NEW YORK
Small Business Division
Department of Commerce
230 Park Ave., Rm. 834
New York, NY 10169
(212) 309-0400

NORTH CAROLINA
Small Business Development Division
Department of Commerce
Dobbs Bldg., Rm. 282
430 N. Salisbury St.
Raleigh, NC 27611
(919) 733-6254

NORTH DAKOTA
Small Business Specialist
Economic Development Commission
Liberty Memorial Bldg.
Bismarck, ND 58505
(701) 224-2810

OHIO
Small Business Office
Department of Development
P.O. Box 1001
Columbus, OH 43266-0101
(614) 466-4945
(800) 848-1300 (OH only)

OKLAHOMA
Small Business Development Center
Station A
517 W. University
Durant, OK 74701
(405) 924-0277

OREGON
Economic Development Department
Lane Community College
400 E. 30th Ave.
Eugene, OR 97405
(503) 373-1205
(800) 547-7842

PENNSYLVANIA
Small Business Action Center
Department of Commerce
483 Forum Bldg.

Harrisburg, PA 17120
(717) 783-5700

RHODE ISLAND
Small Business Development Division
Department of Economic Development
7 Jackson Walkway
Providence, RI 02903
(401) 277-2601

SOUTH CAROLINA
Business Assistance Services and Informa-
tion Center
Industry-Business and Community Services
Division, State Development Board
P.O. Box 927
Columbia, SC 29202
(803) 734-1400

SOUTH DAKOTA
Small Business Development Center
University of South Dakota
414 E. Clark St.
Vermillion, SD 57069-2390
(605) 677-5272

TENNESSEE
Small Business Office
Department of Economic and Community
Development
320 Sixth Ave., N., 7th Floor
Nashville, TN 37219-5308
(615) 741-2626
(800) 251-8594 (TN only)

TEXAS
Small and Minority Business Assistance
Division
Economic Development Commission
P.O. Box 12728, Capitol Station
410 E. Fifth St.
Austin, TX 78711
(512) 472-5059

UTAH
Small Business Development Center
University of Utah
660 S. 200 East, Ste. 418

Salt Lake City, UT 84111
(801) 581-7905

VERMONT
Small Business Development Center
University of Vermont Extension
  Service
Morrill Hall
Burlington, VT 05405
(802) 656-2990

VIRGINIA
Small Business Coordinator
Department of Economic Development
1000 Washington Bldg.
Richmond, VA 23219
(804) 786-3791

WASHINGTON
Small Business Development Center
441 Todd Hall
Washington State University
Pullman, WA 99164-4741
(509) 335-1576

WEST VIRGINIA
Small Business Division
Governor's Office of Community and Indus-
  trial Development
Capitol Complex
Charleston, WV 25305
(304) 348-2960

WISCONSIN
Small Business Ombudsman
Department of Development
123 W. Washington Ave.
P.O. Box 7970
Madison, WI 53707
(608) 266-0562

WYOMING
Economic Development Division
Economic Development and Stabilization
  Board
Herschler Bldg., 3d Floor East
Cheyenne, WY 82002
(307) 777-7287

Business Plans

A business plan describes the company in terms of its history (product, experience, human resources) and its strategy for future growth. The business plan is a key element in raising venture capital.

MISCELLANEOUS SERVICES

The Robert Morris "Projection of Financial Statements" form is widely used by entrepreneurs in preparing financial statements for business plans. Contact the following source for more information.

Bankers' Systems, Inc.
P.O. Box 1457
St. Cloud, MN 56302
(612) 251-3060

I recommend Curtis & Gaj, a firm that specializes in writing business plans.

Carey Curtis
Curtis & Gaj
956 Chappel St.
New Haven, CT 06510
(203) 782-6659

PUBLICATIONS

The *Business Planning Guide,* by David Bangs and William Osgood, is one of the best documents available on the subject of business plans. It was originally offered to customers of the Federal Reserve Bank of Boston and has received wide distribution.

David Bangs
Upstart Publishing
50 Mill St.
Dover, NH 03820
(603) 749-5071

The following information on Business Plans is available from CEM, a membership association of small business presidents and entrepreneurs. It also offers an archive of the original business plans that launched many major U.S. businesses.

How to Prepare & Present a Business Plan, by Dr. Joseph R. Mancuso, is a 360-page guide to preparing a business plan that will attract venture or debt capital. ($20)

How to Write a Winning Business Plan, by Dr. Joseph R. Mancuso, is a comprehensive guide to preparing a business plan to raise venture capital. It includes the original business plans that launched Storage Technologies, *Venture* magazine, and Shopsmith. ($25)

How to Write a Winning Business Plan, a three-hour audio- and videotape program by Dr. Joseph R. Mancuso, offers a hands-on approach to writing business plans. ($100). It is also available as a four-hour audiotape program. ($60)

Contact either of the following sources for more information.
 Center for Entrepreneurial Management, Inc.
 180 Varick St., Penthouse
 New York, NY 10014-4606
 (212) 633-0060

 Prentice Hall Press
 Order Department
 200 Old Tappan Rd.
 Old Tappan, NJ 07675
 (201) 767-5937

Many accounting firms (*see also* Accounting) provide free booklets on business plans. One that I recommend is available from any of the regional offices of Arthur Young & Company.
 G. Steven Burrill, Partner
 Arthur Young & Co.
 One Post St., Ste. 3100
 San Francisco, CA 94104
 (415) 393-2731

SBA offers several excellent, inexpensive pamphlets on writing a business plan, including *Business Plans for Small Manufacturers* (Management Aid [MA] #2.007); *Business Plans for Small Construction Firms* (MA #2.008); *Business Plans for Retailers* (MA #2.020); *Business Plans for Small Service Firms* (MA #2.022).
 Small Business Administration
 P.O. Box 15434
 Fort Worth, TX 76119
 (800) 368-5855
 (Call this number to determine the price and then send payment to the Fort Worth address.)

Eliminates the tedium of preparing a full range of financial statements. The package is a software add-on for Lotus Development Corporation's 1-2-3, Symphony, or Jazz for the IBM PC and compatibles that lay the business plan out on a spreadsheet; the user merely adds the numbers. The cost is $69.95. It uses formulas and logic explained in *Develop Your Business Plan,* by Richard Leza and Joseph Plancencia, a how-to text provided with the software.

Emmet Ramey, Pres.
Develop Your Business Plan
Oasis Press
720 S. Hillview Dr.
Milpitas, CA 95035
(408) 263-9671

HOW TO FIND INVESTORS FOR YOUR BUSINESS PLAN

A clear, concise business plan is the key to starting a new business. Until the business is actually up and running, the plan is the only thing investors and lenders have available as a decision-making tool. Entrepreneurs often feel compelled to dress up their business plans in fancy, leatherbound covers and ship them via Federal Express. But the basic look of a plan doesn't change what's inside and has little, if any, effect on how an investor views it.

Other entrepreneurs choose to spend months in preparing their business plans, and then take only a few minutes in deciding how to deliver them. They usually opt for a mass mailing. Armed with a directory of venture capitalists and aided by a secretary, they send the plan, with a form letter, to as many venture capitalists as they can find. This isn't much of a strategy. It wastes everybody's time, particularly that of the entrepreneur.

Making a personal visit with the business plan tucked under an arm is another bad tactic. This humble, straightforward approach is like going to a doctor as an unreferred patient. The question everyone wants answered is, "Who sent you?" Furthermore, the key man is often away from his office or simply unable to see the unscheduled visitor, who then begins to feel like an intruder. Even if he does get a chance to talk to someone, he feels as if the game is already lost.

In talking with venture capitalists, I've discovered that they first look for names of companies when they are confronted with a stack of business plans. If they see something that sounds intriguing, they pick it up. The second critical element is the geographical location of the company; they may like to invest in certain parts of the country, either close by, or close to places where they have made other investments. The third critical element is the thickness of the plan: Shorter plans receive more attention.

The physical "look" of the plan is the least important element. In fact, it's not uncommon to walk into a venture capitalist's office and see a stack of unopened Federal Express packages on a credenza. Sending materials via an overnight delivery service used to be an effective attention getter, but it's so common today that the impact isn't worth the cost.

Getting Your Plan Read

Two key variables determine how closely a business plan is read by an investor. The first is the way an entrepreneur presents the plan: how he gets it into the hands of a venture capitalist. The second is the preselling: what goes on before the plan is presented.

The best method of delivering a business plan is through a third party. Unless the entrepreneur is already established and successful, a third-party referral adds credibility to the plan; as a result, the chances that it will be read increase. It's best to tap consultants, bankers, lawyers, accountants, and other entrepreneurs, as long as their reputations and ties with the venture capitalist are positive. A different person can be used for each potential investor.

Before handing your plan to a third party, be sure you haven't committed one grave error: numbering each plan. Entrepreneurs often send out their plans with numbers on the cover. Imagine the venture capitalist who gets plan no. 16. Even before he turns the cover page, he asks, "What happened to the first 15?" Number each plan discreetly on the last page or label all copies "Plan no. 1."

Preselling is invaluable if it's done correctly. If potential investors are told about an exciting company six months before they actually see the plan, and are kept up-to-date on the company's development once a month until the plan arrives, they will be more receptive when it finally reaches them. A well-managed company that hopes to expand should invest time and energy on preselling early and often. When the time comes to raise money, venture sources will be automatically interested. The preselling of a plan is as important as any aspect of the process.

The person who presells the plan should be the one who delivers it. With the company name, address, and location clearly spelled out on the cover page, the plan should be hand-carried by the preseller to a select group of venture capitalists.

This process may seem to be a roundabout way of doing things, but remember that the best business plans don't automatically raise money. The potential gain for venture capitalists is obviously great (that's why they are in business), but losing money is much more common. Businesses that never recover their initial investment outnumber the winners by more than three to one. And venture capitalists keep this statistic in mind as they examine every deal.

MINI–BUSINESS PLANS?

I wish I had a dollar for every person who has asked me if he could submit a "mini–business plan" to a lender or investor. Some people say that they want to raise only a small amount of money, like $100,000. Others explain that the deal's "all but done," so the plan isn't a central issue. A greater number claim that they don't have the time or money for a full-fledged business plan, or that they will do one at a later date. All of these explanations are cop-outs. There's no such thing as a mini–business plan.

A good business plan requires hard work. It takes months and sometimes thousands of dollars to complete. I should know. I've read thousands of plans: big money raisers and even bigger flops. The element common to all of the successful business plans I've read is completeness. They cover all the bases.

Entrepreneurial Planning

It's amusing to observe the entrepreneurial planning process. For instance, at CEM, we sell 150 books and tapes from our mail-order bookstore, including audiotapes of Peter Drucker's *Management By Objectives,* which sell for more than $300. When we ask the customer how he would like the Drucker tapes shipped, the almost universal response is "the cheapest way," which means via parcel post.

In contrast, our business-plan books sell for about $20. And how do budding entrepreneurs want them delivered? By Federal Express, of course, for 40 percent of our business-plan orders. These buyers will pay $35 to get the book by 10:30 A.M. the next day. The irony is that these books are about business *planning.* Apparently, entrepreneurs are willing to pay a penalty to be short-term planners. Why can't they buy the book a month in advance and save money?

In these situations my favorite three-word definition of an entrepreneur is particularly apropos: Ready—Fire—Aim.

Unlike income taxes, real planning can't be done on a short form. You wouldn't ask an artist to save time in painting a picture by omitting the background or leaving out the color. The picture needs all of its elements to be effective. So it is with nearly all creative endeavors. To have any real value, each has to be complete.

Telling someone that you're sending them a mini–business plan triggers the question, "Where's the complete plan?" or, "Who gets the full plan?" It's the kiss of death to hopes of getting financed. What you're telling potential investors is that your plans are half-baked at best and poorly done at worst.

So much for the notion of a shortcut to a valid document. The next alternative for frustrated writers of mini–business plans is the derivative route. They want to see a "perfect" business plan and copy it. This is like trying to paint the Mona Lisa with a paint-by-numbers kit. Each business plan is a separate and distinct piece of art. You can get good ideas by examining other solid plans, but you can't simply copy another plan's format and assume that yours will hold together.

Studying other plans to gain new ideas about what you might want to include in yours can be useful, however. The intent isn't to copy, but to gain some familiarity with the end results. It's like visiting art museums before attempting to paint. You won't automatically become a good painter, but you'll have a better idea of the standards of excellence.

WRITING A WINNING BUSINESS PLAN

Most entrepreneurs assume that there is a direct ratio between the time a venture source spends reading their business plan and the likelihood of that plan receiving funding. "If only they would read my plan," mumbles the unsuccessful entrepreneur, "they would be chasing me instead of vice versa." With that goal in mind, and assuming that the product is only as good as the package, business plans are often dressed in their Sunday best—leatherbound jackets costing $10 or more each.

As part of research over the past several years, I've conducted tests with venture capitalists to determine the method they used to select a single business plan out of a group of five or more. Several deals were randomly placed on a table, and the investors were asked to examine only the covers of the plans before selecting which one they would read first. The plans that received the most initial attention weren't the ones with the pretty covers: The company names were the most crucial factor. Next in importance was the geographic location of the company, followed by the thickness of the plan: Shorter plans received more attention.

In these tests, nothing was revealed about the business plans except what appeared on the cover. The order in which the plans were arranged on the table was completely random, and I observed each venture capitalist as he gave them a first look. I have ranked these variables in descending order of importance:

1. Company name
2. Geographic location
3. Length of the plan
4. Quality of the cover

The next question I explored was, "How can an entrepreneur increase the likelihood that a venture capitalist will *read* the business plan after he gets past the cover?" Should the entrepreneur send out a summary of his plan, or a summary and a few of the more enticing elements of the plan, to get the venture capitalist's attention? My research showed that summaries and "mini-plans" were not effective documents. A teaser summary that is not an integral part of a plan only delays the eventual reading of the entire plan, and the teaser is often vague or incomplete. It is much better to make the entire document available to each potential investor and to highlight the plan with a succinct, informative summary as the first page of the business plan.

Two additional variables help to determine if a plan will be read, thus raising its chances of being financed. The first is the entrepreneur's method of presenting the plan: how he actually gets the plan into the hands of a venture capitalist. The second is the preselling that precedes the plan. Months may be devoted to preparing the plan, but only a few minutes are devoted to deciding how to deliver it.

The naive entrepreneur follows a suicidal path of a blind mass mailing. Armed with a directory of venture capitalists, and aided by a secretary, he sends the plan, with a form letter, to as many venture capitalists as he can. But this strategy is really no strategy at all. It wastes everybody's time, and for the entrepreneur wasted time can be more significant than wasted money. This strategy never works.

Making a personal visit with the business plan tucked under an arm is another bad tactic. This humble, straightforward method is like going to a doctor as an unreferred patient. The question everyone wants answered is, "Who sent you?" Furthermore, the key man is often away from his office or simply unable to see the visitor, who then begins to feel like an intruder. Even if he does get a chance to talk to someone, he feels as if the game is already lost.

Third-Party Referral

The best method of delivering the business plan is through a third party. Unless the entrepreneur is already established and successful, a third-party referral adds credibility to the plan; as a result, the likelihood that it will be read increases. Anyone from the following group is acceptable, as long as his reputation and liaison with the venture capitalist is positive: consultants, bankers, lawyers, accountants, and other entrepreneurs. (You don't have to use the same person for each potential investor.)

Preselling is invaluable if it's done correctly. If potential investors are told about an exciting company six months before they actually see the plan, and are kept up-to-date on the company's development once a month until the plan arrives, they will be more receptive when it finally reaches them. After all, the best time to raise money is when you don't need it. The same holds true for arousing the interest of potential investors. A well-managed company planning to expand should invest time and energy on preselling early and often. When the time comes to actually raise money, venture sources automatically will be interested. The preselling of a plan is as important as any aspect of the process.

The person who presells the plan should be the one who delivers it. With the company name, address, and location clearly spelled out on the cover page, the plan should be hand-carried by the preseller to a select group of venture capitalists.

Nothing Is Automatic

This process may seem to be a roundabout way of doing things (even the best preselling job doesn't mean that investors will be lined up, checkbooks in hand, outside your office), but remember that the best business plans don't automatically raise money. In fact, the two most successful venture capital deals in the northeastern United States were turned down a number of times before receiving a "yes."

In 1958, Digital Equipment Corporation (now the second-largest computer company in the world) had to shop its plan around for quite a while before American Research and Development Corporation finally agreed to a $70,000 commitment. Rumor has it that the investment is now worth more than $300 million, but its value wasn't readily apparent to any of the investors who initially rejected it.

The second deal, a spin-off from Digital, occurred in 1968, when three engineers in their twenties approached Fred Adler, a New York attorney, who agreed to make a modest investment in a struggling start-up known as Data General Corporation. But the potential that the entrepreneurs thought was obvious wasn't apparent to the financial community at large until rumors circulated that the four principals in the deal each made in excess of $10 million within four years of their initial investments.

The potential gain for venture capitalists can be great (that's why they're in business), but losing money is much more common. Businesses that never recover their initial investments outnumber the winners by more than three to one. And every venture capitalist keeps this statistic in mind as he examines each deal.

In other words, although the preselling and presentation of the plan are both vitally important, they only serve to get an investor's attention. They get you in the door. Once you're in, you don't want to disappoint him. Let the plan speak to his needs and he'll speak to yours.

Canada

The Canadian Consulate General is an excellent source for general information on Canadian business.

John Morand
Senior Investment Adviser
Canadian Consulate General
1251 Ave. of the Americas
New York, NY 10020
(212) 586-2400

Quebec Economique International is a quarterly publication of the Department of External Trade (Government of Quebec). It has a circulation of 40,000 and is published in French, English, German, Spanish, Italian, and Japanese.

Quebec Economique International
770 rue Sherbrooke ouest
Place Mercantile, Septième Étage
Montreal, Que.
Canada H3A 1G1

The Department of External Affairs and Investment Canada are good sources for science, technology, and communications companies.

Michael Farley
Science, Technology & Communications Division
Department of External Affairs
Lester B. Pearson Bldg.
125 Sussex Dr.
Ottawa, Ont.
Canada K1A 0G2
(613) 992-8050

Investment Canada
P.O. Box 2800
Station D
Ottawa, Ont.
Canada K1P 6A5
Telex: 0534450

MEMBERS OF THE ASSOCIATION OF CANADIAN VENTURE CAPITAL COMPANIES OF (DECEMBER 31, 1986)

Aeonian Capital Corp.
602-12th Ave. S.W., Ste. 400
Calgary, Alta. T2R 1J3

Agence Quebeçois de Valorisation
1 Complexe Desjardins, Ste. 2204
Montreal, Que. H5B 1B3

Alexis Nihon Corp.
6380 Côte de Liesse
Montreal, Que. H4T 1E3

Alta-Can Telecom Inc.
411 First St. S.E., Floor 26H
Calgary, Alta. T2G 4Y5

Altamira Capital Corp.
475 Michel Jasmin
Dorval, Que. H9P 1C2

Atlantic Ventures Trust
1246 Hollis St.
Halifax, N.S. B3J 1T6

A.V.F. Investments Ltd.
1550-Eighth St. S.W., Ste. 300
Calgary, Alta. T2R 1K1

BG Acorn Capital Fund
141 Adelaide St. West, Ste. 601
Toronto, Ont. M5H 3L5

Boyd, Stott & McDonald Technologies Ltd.
55 York St., Ste. 1311
Toronto, Ont. M5J 2R7

Canada Overseas Investments Ltd.
P.O. Box 62
South Tower, Royal Bank Plaza
Toronto, Ont. M5J 2J2

Canadian Enterprise Development Corp.
  Ltd.
199 Bay St., Ste. 1100
Toronto, Ont. M5J 1L4

Canadian Pacific Ltd.
800-123 Front St. West
Toronto, Ont. M5J 2M8

Cavendish Investing Ltd.
2850 Bow Valley Sq. 2
205 Fifth Ave. S.W.
Calgary, Alta. T2P 2J7

Central Capital Management Inc.
1 First Canadian Pl.
P.O. Box 38
Toronto, Ont. M5X 1G4

Churchill Corp.
2300 Scotia Pl.
10060 Jasper Ave.
Edmonton, Alta. T5J 3R8

Citicorp Capital Investors Ltd.
123 Front St. West, Ste. 1900
Toronto, Ont. M5J 2M3

Commonwealth Development Finance Co.
  Ltd.
Colechurch House
1 London Bridge Walk
London SE1 2SS, England

Discovery Foundation/Enterprise Program
Ste. 220, Discovery Park
3700 Gilmore Way
Burnaby, B.C. V5G 4M1

Federal Business Development Bank
800 Place Victoria
Bureau 4600, C.P. 335
Tour de la Bourse
Montreal, Que. H4Z 1L4

First City Technology Ventures
35555 Curtis Blvd.
Eastlake, OH 44094

First Merchant Equities Inc.
122-First Ave., South, Ste. 305
Saskatoon, Sask. S7K 7E5

Fonds de Solidarity
505 E. Sherbrooke, Ste. 2440
Montreal, Que. H2L 1K2

Frandevcor Ventures Ltd.
612 St. Jacques St. West
Montreal, Que. H3C 1E1

Gold Bar Developments Ltd.
P.O. Box 3160
Edmonton, Alta. T5J 2G7

Gordon Capital Corp.
P.O. Box 67, Ste. 5401

Toronto-Dominion Centre
Toronto, Ont. M5K 1E7

Grayrock Shared Ventures Ltd.
150 King St. West
P.O. Box 12
Sun Life Tower, Ste. 1212
Toronto, Ont. M5H 1J9

Groupe Cantal Inc.
835 boul. des Recollets, Ste. 300
Trois-Rivières, Que. G8Z 3W5

Helix Investments Ltd.
401 Bay St., Ste. 2400
Toronto, Ont. M5H 2Y4

Hendron Holding Corp.
150 York St., Ste. 800
Toronto, Ont. M5H 3S5

Industrial Promotion Services Ltd.
797 Don Mills Rd., Ste. 904
Don Mills, Ont. M3C 1V2

Investissements NOVACAP Inc.
1981 McGill College Ave., Ste. 465
Montreal, Que. H3A 2W9

LavalinTech Inc.
1100 Dorchester Blvd., West, 24th Floor
Montreal, Que. H3B 4T3

Les Enterprises CGI Inc.
240 rue St. Jacques ouest
Montreal, Que. H2Y 1L9

Les Investissements Capidev Inc.
Bureau 400
370 Chemin Chambly
Longueuil, Que. J4H 3Z6

Manitoba Industry, Trade & Technology
Technology Commercialization Program
Bay 9, 1329 Niakwa Rd.
Winnipeg, Man. R2J 3T4

Maziv Industries
201 Consumers Rd., Ste. 105
Willowdale, Ont. M2J 4G8

Middlefield Capital Fund
1 First Canadian Place, Ste. 5850
P.O. Box 192
Toronto, Ont. M5X 1A6

MontRoyal Capital Inc.
1155 Dorchester Blvd. West, Ste. 3310
Montreal, Que. H3B 3Z6

National Bank, Merchant Banking Group
150 York St., 2d Floor
Toronto, Ont. M5H 3A9

Noranda Enterprise Ltd.
90 Sparks St., Ste. 1128
Ottawa, Ont. K1P 5T8

North American Ventures Fund
85 Bloor St., East, Ste. 506
Toronto, Ont. M4W 1A9

Northern Telecom Ltd.
33 City Centre Dr.
Mississauga, Ont. L5B 3A2

Ontario Centre for Resource Machinery
Technology
127 Cedar St., 4th Floor
Sudbury, Ont. P3E 1B1

Ontario Development Corp.
1200 Bay St., Sixth Floor
Toronto, Ont. M7A 2E7

Parcap Management Inc.
1000 Sherbrooke St., West, Ste. 2310
Montreal, Que. H3A 3G4

Royal Bank Venture Capital Ltd.
13th Floor, South Tower
Royal Bank Plaza
Toronto, Ont. M5J 2J5

RoyNat Inc.
P.O. Box 51
1 First Canadian Pl., Ste. 1040
Toronto, Ont. M5X 1B1

SB Capital Corp. Ltd.
85 Bloor St., East, Ste. 506
Toronto, Ont. M4W 1A9

Soccrent
3251 boul. St. François
C.P. 933
Janquiere, Que. G7X 7W8

Société D'Investissement Desjardins
Bureau 1717
2 Complexe Desjardins
C.P. 760
Montreal, Que. H5B 1B8

Soquia
2 Parc Samuel Holland, Ste. 824
Quebec City, Que. GI5 4S5

TD Capital Group
P.O. Box 1
Toronto-Dominion Centre
Toronto, Ont. M5K 1A2

Triarch Corp. Ltd.
120 Adelaide St., West,
    Ste. 1120
Toronto, Ont. M5H 1V1

Trucena Investments Ltd.
Exchange Tower, Ste. 1020
2 First Canadian Pl.
Toronto, Ont. M5H 1V1

Varity Enterprise Corp.
595 Bay St.
Toronto, Ont. M5G 2C3

Vencap Equities Alberta Ltd.
10180-101st St., Ste. 1980
Edmonton, Alta. T5J 3S4

VenGrowth Capital Funds
111 Richmond St., West, Ste. 805
Toronto, Ont. M5H 2G4

Ventures West Management Inc.
321 Water St., Ste. 400
Vancouver, B.C. V6B 1B8

FBDB BACKING INDEPENDENT BUSINESS

The Federal Business Development Bank (FBDB) is a Crown Corporation that exists to promote and assist businesses in Canada. It offers three principal services to Canada's business community: financial services, investment banking, and management services such as counseling, training, and information.

Financial Services

FBDB offers term loans to allow its customers to acquire fixed assets such as land, buildings, machinery, and equipment. Its term loans can also be used to finance many other business proposals such as a change in the ownership of a business, or the need to replenish or increase working capital. The bank also offers clients a Financial Planning Program which includes financial matchmaking, do-it-yourself kits on topics such as *Arranging Financing,* and a packaging service to develop proposals for loans or grants on behalf of clients.

Investment Banking

For businesses requiring equity financing, FBDB offers investment banking services through which it can purchase shares in a business or work with other financial institutions to obtain the risk capital required.

Management Services

Through its Management Services Division, FBDB offers a counseling program (CASE) that puts 1,500 business counselors at the service of small and medium-size businesses across Canada. It also offers full- and half-day seminars, management clinics, 30-hour business management courses, an information service on government business programs, a series of pocketbooks on management topics, and a newspaper on business in general.

Contact the following source for more information on FBDB.

Federal Business Development Bank
Investment Banking Division
800 Place Victoria, Ste. 4600
P.O. Box 335
Stock Exchange Station
Montreal, Que. H4Z 1L4
(514) 283-2252

FBDB BRANCHES

Atlantic Region

Regional Office:
Cogswell Tower, Ste. 1400
Scotia Sq.
P.O. Box 1656
Halifax, N.S. B3J 2Z7
(902) 426-7860

Branch and CASE Offices:

New Brunswick
270 Douglas Ave.
P.O. Box 780
Bathurst, N.B. E2A 4A5
(506) 548-3345

121 de l'Église St., Ste. 401
Edmundston, N.B. E3V 3L2
(506) 739-8311

King's Place Complex, Ste. 644
440 King St.
P.O. Box 1235
Fredericton, N.B. E3B 5C8
(506) 452-3030

(CASE office)
same address as above
Ste. 646
E3B 4Y3
(506) 452-3022

860 Main St.
P.O. Box 1090
Moncton, N.B. E1C 8P6
(506) 857-6120

(CASE office)
same address as above
Fourth Floor
E1C 1G2
(506) 857-6000

75 Prince William St.
P.O. Box 7173
Postal Station "A"
Saint John, N.B. E2L 4S6
(506) 648-4751

Newfoundland
Herald Tower
4 Herald Ave.
P.O. Box 790
Corner Brook, Nfld. A2H 6G7
(709) 637-4515

(CASE office)
4A, Herald Ave.
(709) 637-4513

Zenith 07082

42 High St.
P.O. Box 744
Grand Falls, Nfld. A2A 2M4
(709) 489-2151

Atlantic Pl., Fourth Floor
Water St.
P.O. Box 520
Postal Station "C"
St. John's, Nfld. A1C 5K4
(709) 772-5505

(CASE office)
same address as above
(709) 772-5515

Nova Scotia
655 King St.
P.O. Box 540
Bridgewater, N.S. B4V 2X6
(902) 543-7821

Scotia Sq.
Cogswell Tower, Ste. 1400

P.O. Box 1656
Halifax, N.S. B3J 2Z7
(902) 426-7850

(CASE office)
710 Cogswell Tower
Scotia Sq.
B3J 3K1
(902) 426-2474

48-50 Dorchester St.
P.O. Box 726
Sydney, N.S. B1P 6H7
(902) 564-7700

(CASE office)
same address as above
(902) 564-7710

802 Prince St., Ste. 202
P.O. Box 1378
Truro, N.S. B2N 5N2
(902) 895-6377

Prince Edward Island
137 Kent St.
P.O. Box 488
Charlottetown, P.E.I. C1A 7L1
(902) 566-7454

(CASE office)
same address as above
(902) 566-7460

Quebec Region

Regional Office:
800 Victoria Sq.
Place Victoria
Ste. 4600
P.O. Box 190
Montreal, Que. H4Z 1C8
(514) 283-3657

Branch and CASE Offices:
475 rue des Champs Élysées
Chicoutimi, Que. G7H 5V7
(418) 545-1580

(CASE office)
same address as above

1010 des Galeries
Drummondville, Que. J2C 5W4
(819) 478-4951

161 rue Principale
Granby, Que. J2G 2V5
(514) 372-5202

Plaza Val Tétreau
400 boul. Alexandre-Taché
Hull, Que. J9A 1M5
(819) 997-4434

2525 boul. Daniel-Johnson
Chomedey, Laval, Que. H7T 1S9
(514) 687-4121

(CASE office)
same address as above

Complexe Bienville
1000 rue de Sérigny, Ste. 500
Longueuil, Que. J4K 5B1
(514) 670-9550

(CASE office)
same address as above

800 Victoria Sq.
Place Victoria, Ground Floor
P.O. Box 187
Montreal,
    Que. H4Z 1C8
(514) 878-9571

(CASE office)
same address as above

6068 rue Sherbrooke est
Montreal, Que. H1N 1C1
(514) 255-2311

(CASE office)
same address as above

871 Chemin St-Louis
Québec, Que. G1S 1C1
(418) 648-3972

(CASE office)
same address as above

320 rue St-Germain est, Ste. 303
Rimouski, Que. G5L 1C2
(418) 722-3300

(CASE office)
same address as above
Ste. 702
(418) 722-3315

147 av. Mercier
Rouyn, Que. J9X 4X4
(819) 764-6701

Galeries des Laurentides
St-Antoine des Laurentides, Que. J7Z 5V3
(514) 432-7111

3100 Côte Vertu
St-Laurent, Que. H4R 2J8
(514) 334-6560

(CASE office)
same address as above
H4R 1P8

106 rue Napoléon, Ste. 305
Sept-Îles, Que. G4R 3L7
(418) 968-1420

2532 rue King ouest
Sherbrooke, Que. J1J 2E8
(819) 565-4740

(CASE office)
same address as above

1410 rue des Cyprès
Trois-Rivières, Que. G8Y 4S3
(819) 375-1621

(CASE office)
same address as above

Ontario Region

Regional Office:
777 Bay St., 29th Floor
Toronto, Ont. M5G 2C8
(416) 973-1141
(416) 973-0341

Branch and CASE Offices:
151 Dunlop St., East
P.O. Box 876
Barrie, Ont. L4M 4Y6
(705) 728-6072

8 Main St., East
P.O. Box 619
Hamilton, Ont. L8N 1E8
(416) 572-2954

(CASE office)
same address as above

20 Main St., South
Kenora, Ont. P9N 1S7
(807) 468-5575

Plaza 16
16 Bath Rd.
Kingston, Ont. K7L 1H4
(613) 545-8636

Commerce House
50 Queen St., North, Fourth Floor
N2H 6P4
P.O. Box 2667
Postal Station "B"
Kitchener, Ont. N2H 6N2
(519) 744-4186

(CASE office)
same address as above

197 York St., Ste. 1000
London, Ont. N6A 1B2
(519) 434-2144

(CASE office)
same address as above
(519) 432-6705

33 City Centre Dr., Ste. 145
(Square One, Northern
Telecom Bldg.)
Mississauga, Ont. L5B 2N5
(416) 273-9880

(CASE office)
same address as above
P.O. Box 43
Postal Station "A"
L5A 2Y9

Business Office to
St. Catharines
(416) 685-4804

205 Main St., East
P.O. Box 925
North Bay, Ont. P1B 8K2
(705) 476-4123

(CASE office)
same address as above

22 King St., West, Fifth Floor
Oshawa, Ont. L1H 1A3
(416) 576-6800

(CASE office)
same address as above
(416) 571-1355

280 Albert St.
Ottawa, Ont. K1P 5G8
(613) 995-0234

(CASE office)
same address as above
(613) 995-5068

340 George St., North
P.O. Box 1419
Peterborough, Ont. K9H 7H6
(705) 748-3241

43 Church St., Ste. 504
P.O. Box 1193
St. Catharines, Ont. L2R 7E1
(416) 685-4804

405 Queen St., East
Sault Ste. Marie, Ont. P6A 1Z5
(705) 949-3680

Canada Life Centre
55 Town Centre Ct., Ste. 516
Scarborough, Ont. M1P 4X4
(416) 296-0498

1036 Ontario St.
Stratford, Ont. N5A 6Z3
(519) 271-5650

1 Elm St., East
P.O. Box 820
Sudbury, Ont. P3C 1R6
(705) 674-8347

905 Victoria Ave., East
P.O. Box 878
Station "F"
Thunder Bay, Ont. P7C 1B3
(807) 623-2745

(CASE office)
same address as above

83 Algonquin Blvd., West
P.O. Box 1240
Timmins, Ont. P4N 7J5
(705) 267-6416

204 Richmond St., West
Toronto, Ont. M5V 1V6
(416) 973-0341

(CASE office)
same address as above
(416) 973-0075

7501 Keele St., Ste. 200
Concord, Ont. L4K 1Y2
(416) 738-1788

(CASE office)
same address as above

500 Ouellette Ave.
Windsor, Ont. N9A 1B3
(519) 254-8626

(CASE office)
same address as above

Prairie and Northern Region

Regional Office:
161 Portage Ave., Ste. 300
Winnipeg, Man. R3B 0Y4
(204) 949-7811

Branch and CASE Offices: Manitoba
940 Princess Ave.
Brandon, Man. R7A 0P6
(204) 727-8415

(CASE office)
same address as above

386 Broadway Ave., Stes. 101 & 105
Winnipeg, Man. R3C 3R6
(204) 949-7900

(CASE office)
same address as above

Saskatchewan
1100-First Ave., East
P.O. Box 520
Prince Albert, Sask. S6V 5R8
(306) 764-6448

Bank of Canada Bldg., Ste. 320
2220-12th Ave.
Regina, Sask. S4P 0M8
(306) 780-6478

(CASE office)
same address as above

105-21st St., East
Eighth Floor, Canada Bldg.
Saskatoon, Sask. S7K 0B3
(306) 975-4822

(CASE office)
same address as above

Alberta
3015-12th St., N.E., Ste. 170
Calgary, Alta. T2E 7J2
(403) 291-4700

(CASE office)
same address as above
(403) 230-5930

606 Principal Plaza
10303 Jasper Ave.
Edmonton, Alta. T5J 3N6
(403) 420-2277

(CASE office)
same address as above

10135-101st Ave.
P.O. Box 10
Grande Prairie, Alta. T8V 0Y4
(403) 532-8875

Professional Bldg., Ste. 500
740-4th Ave., South
Lethbridge, Alta. T1J 0N9
(403) 328-9681

Riverside Office Plaza, Ste. 100
4919-59th St.
Red Deer, Alta. T4N 6C9
(403) 343-3232

Northwest Territories
5202 Franklin Ave.
Yellowknife, N.W.T. X1A 1E2
(403) 873-3565

British Columbia and Yukon Region

Regional Office:
900 W. Hastings St.
Vancouver, B.C. V6C 1E7
(604) 666-7800

Branch and CASE Offices: British Columbia
2467 Pauline St.
Abbotsford, B.C. V2S 3S1
(604) 853-5561

1260 Island Hwy.
Campbell River, B.C. V9W 2C8
(604) 287-9236

Business Office to Campbell River
(604) 338-9245

30 S. 11th Ave.
Cranbrook, B.C. V1C 2P1
(604) 426-7241

(CASE office)
same address as above

Business Office to Nanaimo
(604) 748-5202

9900-100th Ave., Ste. 315
Fort St. John, B.C. V1J 5S7
(604) 787-0622

63 W. Victoria, Ste. 100
Kamloops, B.C. V2C 6L3
(604) 374-2121

(CASE office)
same address as above

260 Harvey Ave.
Kelowna, B.C. V1Y 7S5
(604) 762-2035

(CASE office)
same address as above

20316-56th Ave. #101
Langley, B.C. V3A 3Y7
(604) 533-1221

(CASE office)
same address as above

190 Wallace St.
Nanaimo, B.C. V9R 5B1
(604) 753-2471

(CASE office)
same address as above

227-Sixth St.
New Westminster, B.C. V3L 3A5
(604) 525-1011

(CASE office)
same address as above

6-221 W. Esplanade
North Vancouver, B.C. V7M 3J3
(604) 666-7703

(CASE office)
same address as above

299 Victoria St.
Prince George, B.C.
  V2L 5B8
(604) 563-0641

(CASE office)
same address as above

4641 Lazelle Ave.
Terrace, B.C. V8G 1S8
(604) 635-4951

900 W. Hastings St., 5th Floor
Vancouver, B.C. V6C 1E7
(604) 666-7850

(CASE office)
same address as above

3303-30th St.
Vernon, B.C. V1T 5E4
(604) 545-7215

990 Fort St.
Victoria, B.C. V8V 3K2
(604) 388-0161

(CASE office)
same address as above

94 N. First Ave.
Williams Lake, B.C. V2G 1Y6
(604) 398-8233

Yukon Territory
204 Lambert St.
Whitehorse, Y.T. Y1A 1Z4
(403) 668-4030

Chamber of Commerce

The U.S. Chamber of Commerce is the largest volunteer business federation in the world. The individuals, companies, associations, and chambers of commerce that comprise it represent all aspects of business in locations throughout the United States.

The Small Business Programs, part of the Office of Chamber of Commerce Relations, provide members with *Small Business Update,* an information exchange, and publications.

> U.S. Chamber of Commerce
> Small Business Programs
> 1616 H St., N.W.
> Washington, DC 20062
> (202) 463-5580

The Center for Small Business provides issue reports as well as staffing for the Council of Small Business. It is actively involved in representing small business before the government.

> U.S. Chamber of Commerce
> Center for Small Business
> 1615 H St., N.W.
> Washington, DC 20062
> (202) 463-5503

The North Central Regional Office serves Illinois, Indiana, Kentucky, Michigan, and Ohio.

> U.S. Chamber of Commerce
> North Central Regional Office
> 1200 Harger Rd., Ste. 606
> Oak Brook, IL 60521
> (312) 325-7818

The Northeastern Regional Office serves Connecticut, Delaware, Maine, Massachusetts, New Jersey, New Hampshire, New York, Pennsylvania, Rhode Island, and Vermont.

> U.S. Chamber of Commerce
> Northeastern Regional Office
> 711 Third Ave., Ste. 1702
> New York, NY 10017
> (212) 370-1440

The Northwestern Regional Office serves Colorado, Iowa, Kansas, Nebraska, Minnesota, Montana, North Dakota, South Dakota, Wisconsin, and Wyoming.

U.S. Chamber of Commerce
Northwestern Regional Office
Southdale Pl.
3400 W. 66th St., Ste. 300
Minneapolis, MN 55435
(612) 925-2400

The Southeastern Regional Office serves Alabama, the District of Columbia, Florida, Georgia, Maryland, Mississippi, North Carolina, South Carolina, Tennessee, Virginia, and West Virginia.

U.S. Chamber of Commerce
Southeastern Regional Office
223 Perimeter Center Pkwy., N.E.
Atlanta, GA 30346
(404) 393-0140

The Southwestern Regional Office serves Arkansas, Louisiana, Missouri, New Mexico, Oklahoma, and Texas.

U.S. Chamber of Commerce
Southwestern Regional Office
4835 LBJ Freeway, Ste. 750
Dallas, TX 75234
(214) 387-0404

The Western Regional Office serves Alaska, Arizona, California, Hawaii, Idaho, Nevada, Oregon, Utah, and Washington.

U.S. Chamber of Commerce
Western Regional Office
500 Airport Blvd., Ste. 240
Burlingame, CA 94010
(415) 348-4011

Clipping Services

Below is a partial list of services that will clip newspaper and magazine articles about your company or about a product area. This can be a valuable service to keep you posted on the advertising and public relations efforts of your competitors, and keep you up-to-date on your own company's programs. This list is not complete because no organization keeps this information on a national scale. Consult your local Yellow Pages for clipping services in your area.

Allen's Press Clipping Bureau
657 Mission St.
San Francisco, CA 94105
(415) 392-2353

Bacon's Clipping Bureau
332 S. Michigan Ave.
Chicago, IL 60604
(312) 922-8419

Luce Press Clipping Service
912 Kansas Ave.
Topeka, KS 66612
(913) 232-0201

New England Newsclip Service
5 Auburn St.
Framingham, MA 01701
(617) 879-4460

Burrelles Clipping Service
75–89 E. Northfield Ave.
Livingston, NJ 07039
(201) 992-6600
(800) 631-1160

American Press Clipping Service
119 Nassau St.
New York, NY 10038
(212) 962-3797

RESOURCES

The Competitor Intelligence Group specializes in obtaining detailed competitive information. They claim that this intelligence helps companies win in their respective markets.

The Competitor Intelligence Group
2021 Midwest Rd., Ste. 300
Oak Brook, IL 60521
(312) 953-8537

Small businesses can hardly afford to advertise in every available outlet, so they must pick and choose very carefully. SpaceTrak will analyze competitors' advertising strategies during a 24-month period and report on the areas in which they've maintained or increased their ad space (showing their most effective outlets) and areas in which their advertising has decreased or been dropped entirely (showing the least effective outlets).

Previously, to get this kind of information, small companies had to turn to either advertising agencies or to media consultants (or they had to do it themselves). SpaceTrak seems to be a cost-effective alternative. Contact the following source for more information.

Space Analysis Systems
1800 Byberry Rd., Ste. 711
Huntington Valley, PA 19006
(215) 938-0162

Computers in Small Businesses

ASSOCIATIONS

The Association of Data Processing Service Organizations (ADAPSO) was founded in 1960. Membership includes companies that perform data-processing services for the public for a fee. This is a very good trade association for software.

Association of Data Processing Service Organizations
1300 N. 17th St.
Arlington, VA 22209
(703) 522-5055

The Electronics Industry Association provides an excellent booklet for people interested in purchasing a computer. Send a 5″ x 7″ envelope with $3.00 for postage to the following address.

Electronics Industry Association
Consumer Electronics Group
P.O. Box 19100
Washington, DC 20036

MISCELLANEOUS SERVICES

Quantic Systems, Inc. is a firm of data-processing consultants.

Donald K. Royhl, Pres.
Quantic Systems, Inc.
3166 DesPlaines Ave., Ste. 24
Des Plaines, IL 60618
(312) 699-1169

Q Systems Research Corp. specializes in data processing, consulting, and home-based programming on microcomputers.

Thomas Dakow, Pres.
Q Systems Research Corp.
478 Morris Ave.
Summit, NJ 07901
(201) 522-1774

Elliot B. Nowak & Associates, Inc. is a firm of experts on computers for small businesses.

Elliot B. Nowak, Pres.
Elliot B. Nowak & Associates, Inc.
70½ West St. Plaza
Danbury, CT 06810
(203) 792-0503

Richmond Electronics specializes in the purchase/resale of computer peripherals.
Gregory B. Richmond, Pres.
Richmond Electronics
1471 Metcalf
San Jose, CA 95138
(408) 274-3432

McCabe & Associates is a firm of experts on computers for small businesses.
Thomas J. McCabe, Pres.
McCabe & Associates
5501 Twin Knolls Rd., Ste. 111
Columbia, MD 21045
(301) 596-3080

PUBLICATIONS

Major shakeouts in the field of computer magazines have paralleled those in the computer industry in general. The following magazines have survived because they are the best.
BYTE
McGraw-Hill Publishing
1 Phoenix Mill La.
Peterborough, NH 03458
(603) 924-9281
(monthly)

Infoworld
CW Communications
1060 Marsh Rd., Ste. C-200
Menlo Park, CA 94025
(415) 328-4602
(weekly)

PC Magazine
Ziff-Davis Publishing Co.
One Park Ave.
New York, NY 10016
(212) 503-5319
(biweekly)

CW Communications publishes about 80 magazines for the computer industry.
Computer World
CW Communications
375 Cochitute Rd.
P.O. Box 9171
Framingham, MA 01701
(617) 872-8200
(monthly)

Available monthly, *Publish! The Magazine of Desktop and Personal Computer Publishing* deals with personal computing technology and printing for businesses. Circulation is about 30,000.
Publish!
PC Communications, Inc.
501 Second St.
San Francisco, CA 94107
(415) 546-7722

The 1987 Encyclopedia of Information Systems and Services (seventh edition, three volumes, $370) is billed as "the world's leading guide to electronic information systems and services." It covers systems and services offered in the United States and overseas.
Gale Research Co.
Book Tower
Detroit, MI 48226
(800) 223-GALE

The Whole Earth Software Catalog compares and rates the best available software. The November 1985 edition is the most recent, but the quarterly *Whole Earth Software Review* serves as an update to the directory. The cost of the catalog is $17.00, postpaid.
Whole Earth Access
2990 Seventh St.
Berkeley, CA 94710
(415) 845-3000

Four issues of the *Whole Earth Software Review* cost $18 per year.
Whole Earth Software Review
27 Gate Five Rd.
Sausalito, CA 94965
(415) 332-1716

Updated annually, *Programmer's Market* lists 70 software buyers looking for free-lance microcomputer programs. It includes contract and payment advice as well as articles on writing and selling user-friendly software, game programs, and so on. The cost is $18.95. You can find it at many bookstores, or order it from the following source.

Writer's Digest Books
9933 Alliance Rd.
Cincinnati, OH 45242
(513) 984-0717

The Business Computer, by Franklin Peterson and Judi K. Turkel, is a syndicated column which appears in many newspapers. Reprints and other publications are available from the following source.

PK Associates
4343 W. Beltline Hwy.
Madison, WI 53711
(608) 271-0220

Consultants

Where can you find specialized professional management help? Directories of consultants are available from ACME, Inc., an association of management consulting firms. Founded in 1929, this organization screens companies for membership and holds them to a code of professional conduct. It has about 60 members.

ACME, Inc.
230 Park Ave., Ste. 544
New York, NY 10169
(212) 697-9693
(800) 221-2557

ASSOCIATION

The American Association of Professional Consultants is a national professional association that provides seminars, insurance programs, meetings, and publications on consulting.

American Association of Professional Consultants
9140 Ward Pkwy.
Kansas City, MO 64114
(816) 444-3500

A *Directory of Members,* with capsule descriptions of areas of competence/fields of practice is available from the Institute of Management Consultants. Because there are no company memberships in this organization, each member is qualified on his individual merits. There are about 2,000 members.

Institute of Management Consultants, Inc.
19 W. 44th St., Ste. 810
New York, NY 10036
(212) 921-2885

MISCELLANEOUS SERVICES

In addition to several good booklets on consulting and related subjects, SBA offers three consulting services for small businesses: The Service Corps of Retired Executives (SCORE), the Active Corps of Executives (ACE), and Management Assistance Officers (MAO). Consult your local telephone directory for the regional SBA office closest to you, or contact the Washington, DC headquarters.

Small Business Administration
1441 L St., N.W., Rm. 317

Washington, DC 20416
(202) 653-6881
(800) 368-5855 (SBA hotline number)

The Enterprise Forum at the Massachusetts Institute of Technology (MIT) offers
to companies asking advice and assistance an opportunity to present their case before
a panel of experts and entrepreneurial peers. Each month, the panel reviews a
company's history, its ongoing business situation, and its future plans, and then
offers constructive advice on resolving problems. There are MIT Forums in a dozen
locations throughout the United States. The Enterprise Forum also offers a monthly
newsletter.

Paul E. Johnson, Exec. Dir.
MIT Enterprise Forum
MIT Alumni Center, Rm. 10120
77 Massachusetts Ave.
Cambridge, MA 02139
(617) 253-8240

Time-Place is an on-line database of consulting professionals. Available through
subscription, database services, and the American Society for Training and Development, it accepts advertising from consultants on database.

Time-Place
460 Totten Pond Rd.
Waltham, MA 02154
(617) 890-4636

PUBLICATIONS

A free catalog is available from the Consultants Bookstore. Founder James Kennedy
also publishes *Consultants News,* a monthly newsletter with inside information on
the consulting industry. A directory of executive recruiters is also available.

James Kennedy
Consultants Bookstore
Templeton Rd.
Fitzwilliam, NH 03447
(603) 585-2000

The Consultants Library offers a large selection of books on consulting, as well as
a free catalog of its listings.

Herbert Bermont
The Consultants Library
P.O. Box 309
Glenelg, MD 21737
(301) 531-3560

Howard Shenson is widely known as the "consultant's consultant." His company offers books and seminar tapes, as well as a monthly newsletter, *The Professional Consultant.* Send for a free *Resource Guide.*

Howard L. Shenson, Inc.
20720 Ventura Blvd., Ste. 206
Woodland Hills, CA 91364
(818) 703-1415

Jeffrey Lant Associates offers books and seminars on consulting.

Jeffrey Lant
Jeffrey Lant Associates
50 Follen St., Ste. 507
Cambridge, MA 02138
(617) 547-6372

Credit and Collection

ASSOCIATION

The National Association of Credit Management is an excellent source of credit information and offers many publications.

National Association of Credit Management
520 Eighth Ave.
New York, NY 10018
(212) 947-5070

MISCELLANEOUS SERVICES

A good source of collection information is Mid-Continent Agencies, Inc., which publishes an excellent monthly newsletter.

Les J. Kirschbaum
Mid-Continent Agencies, Inc.
3703 W. Lake Ave.
Glenview, IL 60025
(312) 729-8300
(800) 323-1417

Revenue Service of America is an excellent collection agency.

Muriel Schulman, CEO
Revenue Service of America
10811 Washington Blvd., Ste. 301
Culver City, CA 90232
(213) 204-2044

Although smaller than Dun & Bradstreet, TRW Business Credit Services is a good source of credit information.

TRW Business Credit Services
505 City Pkwy., West, Ste. 100
Orange, CA 92668
(714) 937-2670

PUBLICATIONS

The Federal Reserve System publishes several books on the subject of credit, including the *Consumer Handbook to Credit Protection Laws.*

Federal Reserve System
Board of Governors
Publication Services, Rm. MP-510
Washington, DC 20551
(202) 452-3244

The Federal Trade Commission publishes *Facts for Consumers* and many free publications on related subjects.
Federal Trade Commission
6th St. & Pennsylvania Ave., N.W., Rm. B-3
Washington, DC 20580
(202) 523-3575

The Consumer Information Center publishes a listing of more than 200 reasonably priced consumer publications, including many on credit and collection that would be of interest to the small-business owner.
Consumer Information Center
P.O. Box 100
Pueblo, CO 81002

A subsidiary of Dun & Bradstreet (D&B), the National Credit Office (NCO) produces reports that are similar to D&B reports but are more effective for smaller companies. The information is compiled by telephone analysis.
National Credit Office
1290 Sixth Ave.
New York, NY 10019
(212) 957-3800

CHECKING YOUR OWN CREDIT

You have a right to know your credit history, even if you haven't been denied credit. To check your records, write to or visit the nearest credit bureau. If you go in person, be sure to carry proper identification to gain access to your file. Anyone who requests this information when a credit infraction is *not* pending against him may incur a charge for going through his file.

If you've been denied credit, the Fair Credit Reporting Act provides that you have a right to know why. To obtain this information, contact the company refusing credit; they will send you a letter explaining why they denied credit on the basis of information supplied to them by a credit-rating bureau.

You have a month after rejection of your credit to see the existing report at the cited credit bureau. If you find an error, the credit bureau is legally obligated to recheck the disputed information through the original source of information. If the credit source still holds to its original findings, you must untangle the mess with it. If you do not reach an agreement with the source, insert a letter into your credit record that states your side of the story. Potential lenders will be able to weigh both sides of the story through the letter.

PLUG UP THOSE CASH LEAKS

When the money starts rolling in, managing expenses is about the last thing an entrepreneur has on his mind. Unfortunately, this is the time when he most needs to check his spending, because it's the time when he's most likely to develop bad spending habits. For example, he may begin paying bills before they are due, instead of letting the company's cash pile up in a high-interest bank account. Or, he may slack off during negotiations and fail to cut the best deals. In short, he may lose the savvy that helped him found his business.

Bad spending habits can spring leaks in a company's cash flow. And even if the leaks go unnoticed at the beginning, they will eventually take their toll on the company's health. Nine simple but often overlooked ways to manage spending before damage is done are listed below.

1. Be a smart negotiator. You've arrived at a "final price" with one of your suppliers. Do you stop negotiating? Definitely not. The smart entrepreneur knows that he can negotiate for additional services and contract terms *after* the price has been set. Maybe the supplier will agree to quicker delivery, or maybe he'll reduce the amount of your deposit and let you pay the balance in installments.

2. Never passively accept a supplier's price increase. If the company representative can't justify a price hike, start looking for another supplier.

3. Trim your inventory. Warehousing, insurance, spoilage, obsolescence, and theft all drain enormous amounts of cash. Some entrepreneurs report that storing inventory costs one-third as much as manufacturing it. Although you can't simply discard inventory to cut storage costs, you *can* make sure you don't overstock slow-moving items. Categorize products in your warehouse as "Critical," "Major," or "Minor," depending upon how much revenue they bring in. This labeling will indicate where you can trim stock.

4. Listen to your accountant. Too many entrepreneurs view their accountants as adversaries. Instead, treat your accountant like a family doctor. Learn to level with him on all aspects of your business's finances so that he can give you the best advice possible.

5. Avoid across-the-board cost-cutting campaigns. Blanket cost-cutting is the easiest way to save money, but it often does more harm than good. A smart money manager examines the whole corporation to determine precisely how and where money is being wasted. For example, he might find that the purchasing department is overstaffed and overbudgeted, but the sales force is operating on an austerity budget. In this case, an across-the-board cut would practically destroy the sales staff.

6. Monitor mail-room spending. Everything you send does not absolutely, positively have to be there overnight. Many packages that are sent by expensive courier services can be shipped either by mail or by UPS Blue Label at a fraction of the costs.

7. Pay suppliers when invoices are actually due, not when it's convenient. Bookkeepers usually pay bills once a month when they have free time, especially in small businesses where one person does several jobs. Consequently, some bills are paid well before they are due. If you pay bills on time, not early, your money could be earning interest in the bank or in a money market fund for a few more days.

8. Be a smart shopper. Cheapest isn't always best when buying big-ticket items. Select items that will best suit your company's needs, even if they're more expensive. Then negotiate with the supplier for a better deal. Try using this strategy: Explain that you're taking bids on an in-house laser-printing system. Make your selection. Then call the supplier and announce that he "won" the bid, but that you can't pay what he's asking. See if he can put together a deal that will meet your budget. By that point, you will have piqued his interest, and he will probably find a way to work within your constraints and to sell you a quality system.

9. Impress upon your employees the importance of managing expenses. Cost-cutting is a company-wide endeavor, not a one-man crusade. Show your staff that most cost-cutting affects the bottom line immediately. If the company saves $2,000, for example, it will add $2,000 to the pretax profit that year. In a company with a 10-percent profit margin, that $2,000 savings is worth $20,000 in additional sales. And that's a fact with a lot of impact.

Databases

The Federal Database Finder is a guide to more than 4,200 federal databases and files that are available for either free use or for a nominal fee. It includes information on how a database is used, as well as the addresses, phone numbers, and all possible fees. A section on databases that are on magnetic tape is also included. The cost is $125.

Information USA, Inc.
4701 Willard Ave., Ste. 1707
Chevy Chase, MD 20815
(301) 657-1200

The following listing of databases is not complete. Consult your local library for more information on locating other databases.

BRS
BRS Marketing
1200 Rte. 7
Latham, NY 12210
(800) 227-5277

CompuServe
CompuServe Information Service
P.O. Box 20212
Columbus, OH 43220
(800) 848-8199

Delphi
3 Blackstone St.
Cambridge, MA 02139
(800) 544-4005

Dialog Information Services Inc.
3460 Hillview Ave.
Palo Alto, CA 94304
(800) 334-2564

Dow Jones News/Retrieval
Dow Jones and Co.
P.O. Box 300
Princeton, NJ 08543
(800) 257-5114

National Computer Network
1929 N. Harlem Ave.

Chicago, IL 60635
(312) 662-6666

Newsnet
945 Haversford Rd.
Bryn Mawr, PA 19010
(800) 345-1301

Schwab Technology Services
101 Montgomery St.
San Francisco, CA 94104
(415) 627-7000

Telescan
11011 Richmond Ave., #600
Houston, TX 77042
(713) 952-1060

The Source
1616 Anderson Rd.
McLean, VA 22102
(800) 336-3366
(703) 821-6666 (in VA)

Trade Plus
480 California Ave.
Palo Alto, CA 94306
(800) 952-9900

VU/TEXT
1211 Chestnut St.
Philadelphia, PA 19107
(800) 258-8080

Warner Computer Systems
1 University Plaza, Ste. 300
Hackensack, NJ 07601
(800) 626-4634

A different approach to conducting an information search is the "DowPhone," a service available from Dow Jones in New York. All that's needed to access this information service is a telephone. The information available includes stock market updates, company and industry news, late-breaking economic reports, and business indexes. Dow Jones charges a modest fee, which is based on the number of minutes spent on the phone. Call (800) 352-5378 to find out more.

Department of Commerce Services

MISSION AND FUNCTIONS OF THE U.S. DEPARTMENT OF COMMERCE

Office of the Secretary

The Office of the Secretary is the hub of the department, advising the president on policies and programs affecting industry and commerce, and providing essential services to keep the department operating smoothly. The Office of the Secretary includes the top managers of the department's bureaus and agencies, and several organizations—the Offices of Public Affairs, Business Liaison, Consumer Affairs, Congressional and Intergovernmental Affairs, General Counsel, and Inspector General.

Office of Business Liaison

The Office of Business Liaison (OBL) is a valuable resource for businesses, keeping you informed on department and administration resources, policies, and programs, and advising government officials of the interests and needs of the business world.

OBL's "ROADMAP" program is custom tailored to business needs. Just a phone call away, ROADMAP can guide you through the federal maze to the correct source for the information or assistance you need. ROADMAP can answer questions concerning government policies, programs, and services, and provide information on published materials dealing with a variety of business topics.

ROADMAP
Office of Business Liaison
Rm. H5898C
U.S. Department of Commerce
Washington, DC 20230
(202) 377-3176

Office of Small and Disadvantaged Business Utilization

The Office of Small and Disadvantaged Business Utilization (OSDBU) helps small and disadvantaged businesses to a fair share of the government procurement pie. If your business qualifies, send a statement of your firm's capabilities to OSDBU; it will provide nearly 100 Commerce program offices with copies. They use the statements to develop source lists for their future purchases, which could mean increased sales for your company.

Your capability statement can be brief—two to five pages is fine—but it should contain:

A statement of your firm's strategy, philosophy, or purpose
A list of past and present clients and references
A summary of your firm's marketing experience

It's also useful to include:

A list of your firm's principals and their resumes
A description of your firm's specialty areas
Commerce Department activities that especially interest you

Mail your capability statement to:
Office of Small and Disadvantaged Business Utilization
Rm. H6411
U.S. Department of Commerce
Washington, DC 20230

If you have questions, call (202) 377-5614.

Bureau of the Census

The world's largest statistical organization, the Bureau of the Census keeps count of America by tabulating data on important aspects of the U.S. population and economy. Its censuses of population, housing, manufacturing, agriculture, mineral industries, governments, construction industries, business, and transportation paint a detailed statistical picture of the United States.

Bureau of Economic Analysis

BEA develops and maintains the U.S. economic accounts, a primary tool for economic analysis and decision making by governments, businesses, universities, and research organizations.

Economic Development Administration

EDA helps America help itself by providing loans, grants, and technical assistance to aid depressed areas in combating unemployment and low family income.

International Trade Administration

ITA promotes exports of American products, and helps American businesses to increase their international sales. ITA also works to protect U.S. strategic materials and advanced technology from transfer to unfriendly nations, helps formulate foreign policy, and monitors international agreements. ITA's U.S. and Foreign Commercial Service operates in 47 U.S. cities and 68 countries to serve U.S. business worldwide.

Minority Business Development Agency

MBDA offers technical and management assistance to boost participation of minority-owned businesses in the American success story. Their six offices in major U.S. cities serve minority-owned firms from coast to coast.

National Bureau of Standards

NBS, one of the largest physical science, engineering, and computer laboratories in the United States, sets the measurement standards necessary to produce and sell U.S. products and services at home and overseas. NBS standards and measurement services provide the basis of quality control within industry.

National Oceanic and Atmospheric Administration

On land, in the skies, and at sea, NOAA is the department's largest operating unit, and a vital protector of lives, public safety, property, and endangered species. It's the home of the National Marine Fisheries Service, National Weather Service, National Ocean Service, National Environmental Satellite, Data, and Information Service, Office of Oceanic and Atmospheric Research, and the uniformed NOAA Corps.

National Technical Information Service

NTIS is the central source for public sale of U.S. government-sponsored research, development, and engineering reports, and other analyses by national and local governments, their contractors, or grantees. NTIS stocks more than 1 million titles, including more than 300,000 foreign technical reports, and ships about 23,500 information products daily. NTIS also manages the Federal Software Exchange Center.

National Telecommunications and Information Administration

NTIA is the president's main adviser on U.S. communications policy and deregulation of the nation's telecommunications industry. NTIA offers technical assistance to minorities in telecommunications, works to minimize unnecessary U.S. and foreign government interference in international telecommunications markets, and studies telephone systems and radio signal transmission in its internationally recognized telecommunications laboratory.

Patent and Trademark Office

PTO safeguards U.S. inventions and products and corporate identifications by issuing patents and trademarks, publishing patent and trademark information, maintaining public search files of domestic and foreign patents and trademarks, and providing copies of patents and trademarks to the public.

United States Travel and Tourism Administration

USTTA is a small agency with a major mission—encouraging travelers from other countries to visit the United States. Incoming travelers provide profits for U.S. businesses and help boost the U.S. GNP. USTTA's published statistics on tourist arrivals and departures provide essential research and marketing tools to governments and the U.S. travel industry.

U.S. DEPARTMENT OF COMMERCE PROCUREMENT OFFICES

Headquarters Procurement

(for all Washington, DC, area agencies not listed separately below)
Office of Procurement Operations (OPO)
Procurement Division
Rm. H6516
Washington, DC 20230
(202) 377-5555

Agency and Field Procurement

National Oceanic and Atmospheric Administration
National Capital Administrative Support Center
6010 Executive Blvd., WSC-5, Rm. 508
Rockville, MD 20852
(301) 443-8584

Bureau of the Census
Procurement Office
Federal Office Bldg. 3, Rm. 1556
Suitland, MD 20233
(301) 763-4550

National Bureau of Standards
NBS Contracting Office
Bldg. 301, Rm. B-117
Gaithersburg, MD 20899
(301) 921-2695

Patent and Trademark Office
Office Services Division
Crystal Plaza #1
Washington, DC 20231
(703) 557-0014

National Technical Information Service*
Contracting Service Division
Yorktowne Bldg., Rm. 209
5285 Port Royal Rd.
Springfield, VA 22161
(703) 487-4720

Eastern Administrative Support Center
Procurement Division, RAS/EC3
253 Monticello Ave., Rm. 403
Norfolk, VA 23510
(804) 441-6893

Central Administrative Support Center
Procurement Division, RAS/CC3
601 E. 12th St., Rm. 1758
Kansas City, MO 64106
(816) 374-7267

Mountain Administrative Support Center
Procurement Division, RAS/MC3
325 Broadway, Rm. 5536
Boulder, CO 80303
(303) 497-3515

Western Administrative Support Center
Procurement Division, RAS/WC3
7600 Sand Point Way, N.E.
Seattle, WA 98115
(206) 526-6032

*Purchases of more than $25,000 are handled by Headquarters Procurement.

SPECIAL PROCUREMENT PROGRAMS

The federal government is committed to helping small, minority- and women-owned, and labor surplus area businesses to a fair share of the government market. All government procurement requests are screened to determine if needed goods or services can be provided efficiently and economically by these types of firms.

Women-Owned Businesses

On June 22, 1983, President Reagan signed Executive Order 12426, which created the President's Advisory Committee on Women Business Ownership to focus the federal government's continuing interest in aiding women-owned businesses.

The Department of Commerce, through OSDBU, identifies women-owned businesses and their capabilities, provides this information to its procurement officers, and encourages them to buy from qualified women-owned firms.

Small-Business "Set-Asides"

Government purchases of certain classes of goods and services are "set aside" exclusively for competition by small businesses. Other procurements are individually set aside when adequate competition and economical and efficient supply can be expected from small businesses.

Small-Business Innovation Research Programs

In October 1982, Congress passed Public Law 97-219, the Small Business Innovation Development Act, to increase small business participation in federal R&D.

The Department of Commerce responded by establishing the Small Business Innovation Research (SBIR) program, and annually issues an SBIR solicitation to small businesses describing the department's R&D needs and inviting them to submit proposals.

Contact the following source to be placed on the mailing list for SBIR solicitations.

Office of Small and Disadvantaged Business Utilization
Rm. H6411
U.S. Department of Commerce
Washington, DC 20230
(202) 377-5614

SBA 8(a) Program

Under Section 8(a) of the Small-Business Act [Title 15 of the U.S. Code, 637(a)], the federal government helps socially or economically disadvantaged small businesses to obtain government contracts. The "8(a) contracts" are awarded to SBA, which then subcontracts to the approved firms. These 8(a) contracts can extend for several years to allow firms to become commercially competitive.

For more information on the 8(a) program, contact your nearest SBA Field Office (see page 92).

Labor Surplus Area Concerns

Businesses in areas designated by the Department of Labor as "labor surplus areas" are given preference in contract awards when costs are equal and the procurement meets the requesting agency's needs. Labor surplus areas are identified in the Department of Labor's monthly publication, *Area Trends in Employment and Unemployment,* which is available for $32 per year, $4.75 single copy, from the following source.

Superintendent of Documents
U.S. Government Printing Office
Washington, DC 20402
(Stock Number 029-014-80002-3)

Subcontracts for Small and Disadvantaged Businesses

Federal agencies are required by Public Law 95-507 to ensure that prime contractors for contracts of $500,000 or more ($1 million for construction) submit subcontracting plans with percentage goals for small and disadvantaged-business subcontracting, and details on how the goals will be met.

Minority-Owned Businesses

Federal agencies, in addition to soliciting bids from known small firms, also refer to SBA procurement requirements which the agencies believe can be competently filled by minority-owned businesses. If your firm qualifies, contact your nearest SBA office (see page 92) to let them know of your interest and describe the capabilities of your business.

U.S. DEPARTMENT OF COMMERCE ITA DISTRICT OFFICES

ITA serves businesses through the district offices of its U.S. and Foreign Commercial Service. Although services are mainly export oriented, trade specialists in your district office are experts on the business conditions in your geographic region, and can advise you and direct you to sources of additional information and assistance.

Each district office maintains a business reference library open to the public. Your trade specialist can provide you with a guide to this collection, *Selected Publications to Aid Business and Industry.*

You can meet potential buyers by attending a Federal Procurement Conference coproduced by the U.S. and Foreign and Commercial Service and the Department of Defense. These conferences, sponsored by members of Congress, unite buyers and sellers under one roof so they may become acquainted. Contact your trade specialist to learn of conferences planned for your area.

Northeastern Region I

CONNECTICUT
Federal Office Bldg., Rm. 610B
450 Main St.
Hartford, CT 06103
(203) 244-3530

MAINE
Casco Bank Bldg.*
1 Memorial Circle
Augusta, ME 04330
(207) 622-8249

MASSACHUSETTS
441 Stuart St., 10th Floor
Boston, MA 02116
(617) 223-2312

NEW HAMPSHIRE
Serviced by Boston District Office

NEW YORK
1312 Federal Bldg.
111 W. Huron St.
Buffalo, NY 14202
(716) 846-4191

183 E. Main St., Rm. 666*
Rochester, NY 16404
(716) 263-6480

Federal Office Bldg., Rm. 3718
26 Federal Plaza
Foley Sq.
New York, NY 10278
(212) 264-0634

RHODE ISLAND
7 Jackson Walkway*
Providence, RI 02903
(401) 277-2605

VERMONT
Serviced by Boston District Office

Mid-Atlantic Region II

DELAWARE
Serviced by Philadelphia District Office

DISTRICT OF COLUMBIA
Serviced by Baltimore District Office

*Trade Specialist at duty station only.

MARYLAND
415 U.S. Customhouse
Gay & Lombard Sts.
Baltimore, MD 21202
(301) 962-3560

101 Monroe St., 15th Floor*
Rockville, MD 20850
(301) 251-2345

NEW JERSEY
Capitol Plaza, Eighth Floor
240 W. State St.
Trenton, NJ 08608
(609) 989-2100

PENNSYLVANIA
9448 Federal Bldg.
600 Arch St.
Philadelphia, PA 19106
(215) 597-2866

2002 Federal Bldg.
1000 Liberty Ave.
Pittsburgh, PA 15222
(412) 644-2850

Appalachian Region III

KENTUCKY
U.S. Post Office and Courthouse Bldg., Rm.
  636B
Louisville, KY 40202
(502) 582-5066

NORTH CAROLINA
203 Federal Bldg.
W. Market St.
P.O. Box 1950
Greensboro, NC 27402
(919) 378-5345

Dobbs Building*
430 N. Salisbury St., Rm. 294
Raleigh, NC 27611
(919) 755-4687

SOUTH CAROLINA
Strom Thurmond Federal Bldg., Ste. 172
1835 Assembly St.
Columbia, SC 29201
(803) 765-5345

505 Federal Bldg.*
334 Meeting St.
Charleston, SC 29403
(803) 677-4361

P.O. Box 5823*
Station B
Greenville, SC 29606
(803) 235-5919

TENNESSEE
One Commerce Pl., Ste. 1427
Nashville, TN 37239
(615) 251-5161

3693 Central Ave.*
Memphis, TN 38111
(901) 521-4826

VIRGINIA
8010 Federal Bldg.
400 N. Eighth St.
Richmond, VA 23240
(804) 771-2246

8100 Oak St., Ste. 32*
Fairfax County, VA 22027
(703) 573-9460

WEST VIRGINIA
3000 New Federal Bldg.
500 Quarrier St.
Charleston, WV 25301
(304) 343-6181

Southeastern Region IV

ALABAMA
908 S. 20th St., Ste. 200–201
Birmingham, AL 35205
(205) 254-1331

FLORIDA
Federal Bldg., Ste. 224
51 S.W. First Ave.
Miami, FL 33130
(305) 350-5267

128 N. Osceola Ave.*
Clearwater, FL 33515
(813) 461-0011

3 Independent Dr.*
Jacksonville, FL 32202
(904) 791-2796

75 E. Ivanhoe Blvd.*
Orlando, FL 32802
(305) 425-1247

Collins Bldg., Rm. G-20*
Tallahassee, FL 32304
(904) 488-6469

GEORGIA
1365 Peachtree St., N.E., Ste. 600
Atlanta, GA 30309
(404) 881-7000

27 E. Bay St.
P.O. Box 9746
Savannah, GA 31401
(912) 944-4204

MISSISSIPPI
Jackson Mall Office Center,
Ste. 3230
300 Woodrow Wilson Blvd.
Jackson, MS 39213
(601) 960-4388

PUERTO RICO
Federal Bldg., Rm. 659
San Juan, PR 00918
(809) 753-4555

Great Lakes Region V

ILLINOIS
1406 Mid Continental Plaza Bldg.
55 E. Monroe St.
Chicago, IL 60603
(312) 353-4450

W.R. Harper College*
Algonquin & Roselle Rd.
Palatine, IL 60067
(312) 397-3000, ext. 532

INDIANA
357 U.S. Courthouse & Federal Office Bldg.
46 E. Ohio St.
Indianapolis, IN 46204
(317) 269-6214

MICHIGAN
445 Federal Bldg.
231 W. Lafayette
Detroit, MI 48226
(313) 226-3650

300 Monroe, N.W., Rm. 409*
Grand Rapids, MI 49503
(616) 456-2411

MINNESOTA
108 Federal Bldg.
110 S. Fourth St.
Minneapolis, MN 55401
(612) 349-3338

OHIO
9504 Federal Office Bldg.
550 Main St.
Cincinnati, OH 45202
(513) 684-2944

666 Euclid Ave., Rm. 600
Cleveland, OH 44114
(216) 522-4750

WISCONSIN
Federal Bldg.
U.S. Courthouse
517 E. Wisconsin Ave.
Milwaukee, WI 53202
(414) 291-3473

Plains Region VI

IOWA
817 Federal Bldg.
210 Walnut St.
Des Moines, IA 50309
(515) 284-4222

KANSAS
P.O. Box 48*
Wichita State University
Wichita, KS 67208
(316) 269-6160

MISSOURI
120 S. Central Ave.
St. Louis, MO 63105
(314) 425-3302/4

601 E. 12th St., Rm. 1840
Kansas City, MO 64106
(816) 374-3142

NEBRASKA
Empire State Bldg., First Floor
300 S. 19th St.

Omaha, NE 68102
(402) 221-3664

NORTH DAKOTA
Serviced by Omaha District Office

SOUTH DAKOTA
Serviced by Omaha District Office

Central Region VII

ARKANSAS
Savers Federal Bldg., Ste. 635
320 W. Capitol Ave.
Little Rock, AR 72201
(501) 378-5794

LOUISIANA
432 International Trade Mart
No. 2 Canal St.
New Orleans, LA 70130
(504) 589-6546

NEW MEXICO
505 Marquette Ave., N.W., Ste. 1015
Albuquerque, NM 87102
(505) 766-2386

OKLAHOMA
4024 Lincoln Blvd.
Oklahoma City, OK 73105
(405) 231-5302

440 S. Houston St.*
Tulsa, OK 74127
(918) 581-7650

TEXAS
1100 Commerce St., Rm. 7A5
Dallas, TX 75242
(214) 767-0542

2625 Federal Courthouse Bldg.
515 Rusk St.
Houston, TX 77002
(713) 229-2578

Rocky Mountain Region VIII

ARIZONA
Valley Bank Center, Ste. 2750
201 N. Central Ave.
Phoenix, AZ 85073
(602) 261-3285

*Trade Specialist at duty station only.

COLORADO
U.S. Customhouse, Rm. 119
721 19th St.
Denver, CO 80202
(303) 837-3246

IDAHO
Statehouse*
Boise, ID 83720
(208) 334-2470

MONTANA
Serviced by Denver District Office

NEVADA
1755 E. Plumb Lane, #152
Reno, NV 89502
(702) 784-5203

UTAH
U.S. Courthouse
350 S. Main St.
Salt Lake City, UT 84101
(801) 524-5116

WYOMING
Serviced by Denver District Office

Pacific Region IX

ALASKA
701 C St.
P.O. Box 32
Anchorage, AK 99513
(907) 271-5041

CALIFORNIA
11777 San Vicente Blvd., Rm. 800

Los Angeles, CA 90049
(213) 209-6707

Port Administration Bldg., Second Floor*
3165 Pacific Hwy.
San Diego, CA 92101
(619) 293-5395

Federal Bldg.
P.O. Box 36013
450 Golden Gate Ave.
San Francisco, CA 94102
(415) 556-5860

111 W. Saint John St., Rm. 424*
San Jose, CA 95113
(408) 275-7648

HAWAII
4106 Federal Bldg.
P.O. Box 50026
300 Ala Moana Blvd.
Honolulu, HI 26850
(808) 546-8694

OREGON
1220 S.W. Third Ave., Rm. 618
Portland, OR 97204
(503) 221-3001

WASHINGTON
Lake Union Bldg., Rm. 706
1700 Westlake Ave., North
Seattle, WA 98109
(206) 442-5616

P.O. Box 2170*
Spokane, WA 99210
(509) 838-8202

SELLING THROUGH THE GENERAL SERVICES ADMINISTRATION

Many government purchases must be made from a General Services Administration (GSA) "schedule"—a list of vendors from whom agencies can directly buy. Supplies on the GSA schedule range from pencils and paper clips to expensive electronic equipment, with many thousands of items in between. Services on the schedule include typewriter repair, maintenance of data-processing equipment, copier repair, and cafeteria operations.

If the products or services you sell are on a GSA schedule, your firm must also be listed before you can sell to the government. If you are new to the government market, contact the GSA Business Service Center nearest you to see if they have schedule contracts for the goods or services you offer. If they do, you can ask GSA to negotiate a schedule contract with you. The schedule contract will set the unit prices and terms and conditions under which you can sell to any agency of the government. Your government customers can then issue a simple purchase order to buy what you sell.

GSA schedules benefit both you and your government customer: They allow purchases to be made quickly, they ensure consistent quality and price of goods and services, and they save tax dollars and money in the procurement process.

GSA gives particular attention to small, disadvantaged, and minority- and women-owned businesses.

GSA Business Service Centers

Just getting started or need additional help with the federal procurement process? Call, write, or visit your nearest GSA Business Service Center. Their knowledgeable counselors can give you details on federal purchasing and contracting opportunities, copies of bid abstracts, solicitation mailing list applications, and publications on how to do business with the federal government. If your business qualifies, be sure to ask about small business "set-aside" contracts, and the small and disadvantaged-business subcontracting program. Special efforts are being made to identify these businesses as potential government suppliers and subcontractors.

DISTRICT OF COLUMBIA AND NEARBY MARYLAND AND VIRGINIA
7th & D Sts., S.W., Rm. 1050
Washington, DC 20407
(202) 472-1293/1804

MAINE, VERMONT, NEW HAMPSHIRE, MASSACHUSETTS, CONNECTICUT, RHODE ISLAND
John W. McCormack Post Office and Courthouse
Boston, MA 02109
(617) 223-2868

NEW YORK, NEW JERSEY, PUERTO RICO, VIRGIN ISLANDS
26 Federal Plaza
New York, NY 10278
(212) 264-1234

PENNSYLVANIA, DELAWARE, WEST VIRGINIA, MARYLAND, VIRGINIA
9th & Market Sts., Rm. 5142
Philadelphia, PA 19107
(215) 597-9613

NORTH CAROLINA, SOUTH CAROLINA, GEORGIA, TENNESSEE, KEN-

TUCKY, FLORIDA, ALABAMA, MISSISSIPPI
Richard B. Russell Federal Bldg. and Courthouse
75 Spring St.
Atlanta, GA 30303
(404) 221-5103/3032

OHIO, INDIANA, ILLINOIS, MICHIGAN, MINNESOTA, WISCONSIN
230 S. Dearborn St.
Chicago, IL 60604
(312) 353-5383

MISSOURI, IOWA, KANSAS, NEBRASKA
1500 E. Bannister Rd.
Kansas City, MO 64131
(816) 926-7203

ARKANSAS, LOUISIANA, TEXAS, NEW MEXICO, OKLAHOMA
819 Taylor St.
Fort Worth, TX 76102
(817) 334-3284

GULF COAST FROM BROWNSVILLE, TX, TO NEW ORLEANS, LA
Federal Office Bldg. and Courthouse

515 Rusk St.
Houston, TX 77002
(713) 226-5787

COLORADO, NORTH DAKOTA, SOUTH DAKOTA, UTAH, MONTANA, WYOMING
Bldg. 41
Denver Federal Center
Denver, CO 80225
(303) 234-2216

NORTHERN CALIFORNIA, HAWAII, ALL OF NEVADA EXCEPT CLARK COUNTY
525 Market St.

San Francisco, CA 94105
(415) 556-0877/2122

LOS ANGELES, SOUTHERN CALIFORNIA, ARIZONA, CLARK COUNTY, NV
300 N. Los Angeles St.
Los Angeles, CA 90012
(213) 688-3210

WASHINGTON, OREGON, IDAHO, ALASKA
440 Federal Bldg.
915 Second Ave.
Seattle, WA 98174
(206) 442-5556

GOVERNMENT-WIDE PROCUREMENT NEWS

Wouldn't it be nice to know—every work day—what the government wanted to buy and planned to sell? You can find out, with a subscription to *Commerce Business Daily*. This indispensable sales tool will tell you which government agencies are planning to buy products or services that you could supply, and whom to contact for more information.

Since it is impossible for the Commerce Department to notify the thousands of firms on its Solicitation Mailing List each time it plans a procurement, a subscription to *Commerce Business Daily* is the surest way you can keep up with what the Commerce Department—and the rest of the government—is buying. You'll find:

Requests for bids and proposals for planned civilian and military purchases of $10,000 or more
Procurements reserved for small businesses
Contractors seeking subcontractors
Upcoming sales of surplus property, including real estate, machinery, equipment, and supplies
R&D leads and foreign government procurement in the United States

Commerce Business Daily annual subscriptions are $160 for first-class mail or $81 for second-class mail. (If ordering after January 1, 1985, check prices with your nearest ITA District Office.) *Commerce Business Daily* is available for inspection at ITA District Offices and SBA Field Offices. You can order from the following source.
Superintendent of Documents
U.S. Government Printing Office
Washington, DC 20402

Other publications of interest include the following:

SBA's *U.S. Government Purchasing and Sales Directory,* $7 from the Superintendent of Documents, U.S. Government Printing Office, Washington, DC 20402, Stock Number 045-000-00153-9.

Selling to the Federal Government, free from SBA Field Offices or the Small Business Administration, 1441 L St., N.W., Washington, DC 20416, (202) 653-6938.

Doing Business with the Federal Government, free from GSA Business Service Centers (see page 135), SBA Field Offices, or the General Services Administration, Rm. 1050, 7th & D Sts., S.W., Washington, DC 20407, (202) 472-1804.

PROCUREMENT AUTOMATED SOURCE SYSTEM

If your firm qualifies as a small business, it's a good idea to apply to SBA's Procurement Automated Source System (PASS) program. A computerized matching system, PASS puts government procurement sources and major corporations in touch with small businesses capable of filling their contract and subcontract requirements.

More than 110,000 small firms are listed with PASS, more than 16,000 of them minority-owned and more than 19,000 women-owned. When you register with PASS, your firm's capabilities will be identified by key words in the PASS database. Whenever a government agency or major corporation asks for a firm with your capabilities, the computer printout provided to them will include your company's name.

PASS can be searched for firms by geographic location, type of ownership, labor surplus area, and other data elements. PASS can expand your network of contacts by putting your firm's data on-line in SBA Field Offices nationwide.

Registration is simple. Pick up, write, or phone for the simple one-page, self-mailer registration form, available from any SBA Field Office. The form is easy to understand and fill out.

Apply to both PASS and individual government agency procurement offices. The personal contact with people actually buying and using goods and services is indispensable in selling to the U.S. government—or any potential buyer.

SBA FIELD OFFICES

MAINE, NEW HAMPSHIRE, RHODE ISLAND, MASSACHUSETTS, VERMONT, CONNECTICUT
60 Batterymarch, Tenth Floor
Boston, MA 02110
(617) 223-3162

NEW YORK, NEW JERSEY, PUERTO RICO, VIRGIN ISLANDS
26 Federal Plaza
New York, NY 10278
(212) 264-7770

PENNSYLVANIA, MARYLAND, WEST VIRGINIA, VIRGINIA, DELAWARE, DISTRICT OF COLUMBIA
W. Lobby, Ste. 646

231 St. Asaphs Rd.
Bala Cynwyd, PA 19004
(215) 596-1072

NORTH CAROLINA, SOUTH CAROLINA, GEORGIA, FLORIDA, MISSISSIPPI, ALABAMA, KENTUCKY, TENNESSEE
1375 Peachtree St., N.E., Fifth Floor
Atlanta, GA 30367
(404) 881-7587

OHIO, ILLINOIS, INDIANA, WISCONSIN, MICHIGAN, MINNESOTA
219 S. Dearborn St., Rm. 838
Chicago, IL 60604
(312) 886-4727

TEXAS, LOUISIANA, ARKANSAS, OKLAHOMA, NEW MEXICO
1720 Regal Row
Dallas, TX 75235
(214) 767-7639

KANSAS, MISSOURI, NEBRASKA, IOWA
911 Walnut St., 23rd Floor
Kansas City, MO 64106
(816) 374-5502

COLORADO, WYOMING, UTAH, MONTANA, NORTH DAKOTA, SOUTH DAKOTA
1405 Curtis St., 22d Floor
Denver, CO 80202
(303) 837-5441

SOUTHERN CALIFORNIA (ZIP Codes 90000–93599), **ARIZONA**
350 S. Figueroa St., Sixth Floor
Los Angeles, CA 90071
(213) 688-2946

NORTHERN CALIFORNIA (ZIP Codes 93600–95999), **HAWAII, NEVADA, GUAM**
P.O. Box 36044
450 Golden Gate Ave.
San Francisco, CA 94102
(415) 556-9616

OREGON, IDAHO, WASHINGTON, ALASKA
Dexter-Horton Bldg.
710 Second Ave.
Seattle, WA 98104
(206) 442-0390

Directories of Telephone Numbers, Addresses, and Zip Codes

The telephone company now charges you for every long-distance information call. Using *The National Directory of Addresses and Telephone Numbers* saves money as well as time.

General Information
401 Park Pl., Ste. 305
Kirland, WA 98033
(206) 828-4777

You may need a second directory of zip codes. I recommend the *Zip Code Directory,* which costs $30.

National Information Data Center
P.O. Box 2977
Washington, DC 20013
(301) 565-2539

A complete directory of zip codes (about the size of the Manhattan Yellow Pages) is available from any U.S. Post Office. This is the best and cheapest ($9) source of zip-code information.

Superintendent of Documents
Government Printing Office
Washington, DC 20402
(202) 783-3238

The Postal Service offers a toll-free number for the new nine-digit zip codes. Operators will provide zip codes for up to 25 different addresses per call and will also verify the spelling of street names.

Zip-Code Hotline: (800) 228-8777

The 1987 second edition of the *Telephone Services Directory* lists 800 and 900 numbers and local numbers. The three-issue set costs $160. Also from the Postal Service. The 1985 second edition of the *Telecommunications Systems and Services Directory* contains descriptions and contact information on high-technology communications systems and services, covering the range of modern voice and data communications, long-distance telephone services, teleconferencing, and electronic mail. The 975-page directory costs $250. Supplements are issued frequently at a cost of $170.

Gale Research Co.
Book Tower

Detroit, MI
(800) 223-GALE

The *AT&T Consumer Toll-Free Directory* has both Yellow and White Pages. The
8½" × 11" telephone book costs $10.
AT&T 800 Directory
P.O. Box 44068
Jacksonville, FL 32232
(800) 562-2255 (subscriptions)

Janan Weber
AT&T 800 Numbers
Toll-Free Directory
295 N. Maple Ave., Rm. 5237a3
Basking Ridge, NJ 07920
(publisher)

Teleprofessional is the quarterly forum for professionals doing business by phone.
Teleprofessional
Winthrop-Ward, Inc.
1049-J Camino Del Mar
P.O. Box 123
Del Mar, CA 92014
(619) 755-6500

You might want to consider contacting the following dialing companies. Also, note
the address of *The 800 Report.*
The 800 Report
353 Lexington Ave.
New York, NY 10016
(212) 683-9070

Jay Leonard
American Discount Dialing Service
1810 Salvio St.
Concord, CA 94520
(800) 227-1617

Brent Rasmussen
Automated Phone Exchange, Inc.
P.O. Box 16048
Salt Lake City, UT 84116
(800) 654-8000

Robert Rudolph
Call Center Services, Inc.
302 Knickerbocker Rd.
Cresskill, NJ 07626

(800) 238-CALL
(800) 238-2254 (in NJ)

Barbara Benthin
National Switchboard
2150 E. Thomas Rd.
Phoenix, AR 85016
(800) 262-5389

Wats Marketing of America
18681 Cornett Rd.
Brookings, OR 97415
(800) 351-1000
(800) 469-7459

Directors and Advisers

The National Association of Corporate Directors is oriented primarily toward middle-size companies. A membership association (formerly owned by the American Management Association), this group offers informative seminars and books.

    John Nash, Dir.
    National Association of Corporate Directors
    1707 L St., N.W., Ste. 560
    Washington, DC 20036
    (202) 775-0509

The Institute of Internal Auditors is an international association of about 30,000 auditors.

    Institute of Internal Auditors
    249 Maitland, Box 1119
    Altamonte Springs, FL 32715
    (305) 830-7600

The Securities and Exchange Commission offers information on public companies.

    Securities and Exchange Commission
    Public Information Office
    450 Fifth St., N.W.
    Washington, DC 20001
    (202) 272-7450

The National Association of Security Dealers offers good material for going public and for public companies.

    National Association of Security Dealers
    1511 K St., N.W.
    Washington, DC 20036
    (202) 728-8000

Directors & Boards is a good newsletter with information on directors.

    Directors & Boards
    Boards of Directors of City Trust
    21 S. 12th St.
    Philadelphia, PA 19107
    (215) 568-0440

Edward P. Mattar III wrote and edited an excellent reference book on the subject for McGraw-Hill Publishing Company: *The Corporate Directors Handbook.*

Edward P. Mattar III, CEO
Effective Management Systems
768 Main St.
Worcester, MA 01608
(617) 755-4314

Korn/Ferry International publishes an excellent 26-page booklet, *Boards of Directors—Fourteenth Annual Study,* February 1987, which costs $20. It has offices all over the world and is an excellent source of information.
Korn/Ferry International
237 Park Ave.
New York, NY 10017
(212) 687-1834

Educational Sources

ASSOCIATIONS

The Association of Collegiate Entrepreneurs is a national group of student and future entrepreneurs. Based in Wichita, Kansas, it has chapters at leading business schools around the United States. Fran Jabara is the most effective academic who teaches entrepreneurship.

Fran Jabara, Dir.
Association of Collegiate Entrepreneurs
Wichita State University
P.O. Box 40A
Wichita, KS 67208
(316) 689-3000

The Association of MBA Executives is a 20,000-member association for MBAs; it is a powerful network for business school alumni. Membership is $55 per year ($25 for students) and includes a subscription to *MBA Executive,* the bimonthly news-letter.

Association of MBA Executives
227 Commerce St.
East Haven, CT 06512
(203) 467-8870

The Institute for Business and the International Council for Small Business are composed mostly of academics who work with small businesses. There are about 500 U.S. members, 160 international members, and 160 Canadian members.

Vivian B. Edwards
The Institute for Business
Chicoppe Bldg.
University of Georgia
1180 E. Broad St.
Athens, GA 30602
(404) 542-5760

Donald Myers
The International Council for Small Business
University of Missouri at Rolla
304 Harris Hall
Rolla, MO 65401
(314) 341-4568

MISCELLANEOUS SERVICES

The Small Business High Technology Institute is a political group founded by an old friend of small business, Milton Stewart, to promote high technology among entrepreneurs. It is especially active in the SBIR programs and in innovation networks across the United States.

Milton Stewart
Small Business High Technology Institute
3300 N. Central Ave., Ste. 1740
Phoenix, AZ 85102
(602) 277-6603

The Enterprise Forum at MIT offers companies seeking advice and assistance an opportunity to present their case before a panel of experts and entrepreneurial peers. Each month, the panel reviews a company's history, its ongoing business situation, and its future plans. It then offers constructive advice on resolving problems. There are MIT Forums in a dozen locations throughout the United States. The Enterprise Forum also offers a monthly newsletter.

Paul E. Johnson, Exec. Dir.
MIT Enterprise Forum
MIT Alumni Center
77 Massachusetts Ave.
Cambridge, MA 02139
(617) 235-8240

The Entrepreneurial Studies Program at Babson College has periodic conferences on entrepreneurship and an academy of distinguished entrepreneurs—an Entrepreneurial Hall of Fame.

Professor Jeffery Timmons
Center for Entrepreneurial Studies
Babson College
Tamasso Hill
Wellesley, MA 02157
(617) 235-1200

Resources for Entrepreneurship Education is a good source of vocational educational training.

Resources for Entrepreneurship Education
Occupational Curriculum Laboratory
East Texas State University
Commerce, TX 75428
(214) 886-5623

Achieving Success in Small Business: an Educational Program for New Small Business Owners-Managers is presented in learning modules and is available from the following source.

Wisconsin Vocational Studies Center
Educational Sciences Bldg. Rm. 964
W. Johnson St.
Madison, WI 53706
(608) 263-3696

Karl Vesper is the most knowledgeable person in the entire academic community on the subject of entrepreneurship. His books and research on entrepreneurs are fundamental. His wife, Joan, also teaches courses in entrepreneurial communications.

Professor Karl Vesper
School of Business Administration
University of Washington
Seattle, WA 98195
(206) 543-6737

Donald Sexton is an expert on entrepreneurship.

Donald Sexton
Baylor University
Hankamer School of Business
Waco, TX 76706
(817) 755-1211

Cliff Baumback's textbooks on small-business management are simply the best.

Professor Cliff Baumback
College of Business Administration
University of Iowa
Iowa City, IA 52242
(319) 353-5379

The Harvard Business School is the greatest promoter of the case study method and has one of the largest case-study collections.

Intercollegiate Case Clearing House
Morgan Hall
Harvard Business School
Soldiers Field Rd.
Boston, MA 02163
(617) 495-6117

The Foresight Group is the only school in the world for corporate entrepreneurs.

Sven Atterhead
Gustaf Delin
Sefram-Gruppen (The Foresight Group)
Uppsalavagen Z5
S-19300 Sigtuna, Sweden
076 575-14

Howard Ruff, the famous financial adviser, conducts a unique one-week "boot camp" for entrepreneurs and investors several times each year. It's a worthwhile experience, and the location is spectacular.

Howard J. Ruff, Chairman
Mark J. Staddard, Pres.
Jefferson Institute
757 S. Main St.
Springville, UT 84663
(801) 489-3691

PUBLICATION

The *Journal of Small Business Management* is an academic journal that publishes observations and research on small business. I especially recommend its resource section.

Journal of Small Business Management
Small Business Development Center
West Virginia University
Morgantown, WV 26506
(304) 293-0111

Employee Stock Ownership Programs

There are many advantages available to entrepreneurs who elect to sell their business to their employees by using employee stock ownership programs (ESOPs): The new tax laws of 1986 strengthen this option even further, although less than 10,000 companies have taken advantage of ESOPs to date. This program was created by lawyer-economist Louis O. Kelso and was sponsored by Russell B. Long, the Democratic senator from Louisiana.

The National Center for Employee Ownership is a nonpolitical association that provides information on ESOPs.

Carey Rosen
Karen Young
National Center for Employee Ownership
426-17th St., Ste. 650
Oakland, CA 94612
(415) 268-6850

The ESOP Association is an industry trade organization that is active in making ESOPs more attractive via legislation.

ESOP Association
1725 DeSalle St., N.W., Ste. 401
Washington, DC 20036
(202) 293-2971

Benefits Concepts Inc. is a group that is very active on the east coast in establishing ESOPs

Don Israel
Benefits Concepts Inc.
101 Park Ave., 26th Floor
New York, NY 10178
(212) 682-9480

Kelso & Co. are the pioneers in the field.

Louis Kelso
Kelso & Co.
505 Sansome St., Ste. 1005
San Francisco, CA 94111
(415) 788-7454

Entrepreneurship

THE ENTREPRENEURS' QUIZ

Who is the entrepreneur? What molds him and what motivates him? How does he differ from the nine-to-fiver, and where are those differences most telling? Why will one brother set out to build a business while another aspires to promotions and perks? Why does one stay up nights working on a business plan while the other brags about his pension plan? Is it brains? Luck? Hard work? Or is it something else altogether?

When most people think of entrepreneurs, such names as Henry Ford and Edwin Land or Apple Computer's Steven Jobs come to mind. But, in fact, American entrepreneurs number in the millions. Of the 16 million businesses in the United States, more than 12 million are operated as sole proprietorships. And although not all of those businesses can be labeled "entrepreneurial ventures," *Webster's Dictionary* defines an entrepreneur as "one who manages, organizes and assumes the risk of a business or enterprise."

Why, then, do we think of the entrepreneur in almost mythical terms? The answer is easy. Like the cowboys of the old West, the entrepreneur represents freedom: freedom from the boss, freedom from the time clock, and—with a lot of hard work and more than a little luck—freedom from the bank.

So who is the entrepreneur? Anyone who has ever looked at a problem and seen it as an opportunity is a likely prospect. The same goes for anyone who feels his ambition is being held in check by corporate red tape. But it takes more than just cleverness and frustration to get an entrepreneurial venture off the ground. It takes guts, an indefatigable personality, and nothing short of total dedication to a dream. In fact, it's often said that an entrepreneur is someone who works 90 hours a week for himself so he doesn't have to work 40 hours a week for someone else.

There is no single entrepreneurial archetype, but certain character traits indicate an entrepreneurial personality. This quiz, developed from a series of questionnaire analyses performed by CEM, concentrates on more indicators. If you've ever wondered whether or not you have what it takes to be an entrepreneur, here's your chance to find out.

1. How were your parents employed?
    a. Both worked and were self-employed for most of their working lives.
    b. Both worked and were self-employed for some part of their working lives.
    c. One parent was self-employed for most of his or her working life.
    d. One parent was self-employed at some point in his or her working life.
    e. Neither parent was ever self-employed.

2. *Have you ever been fired from a job?*
   a. Yes, more than once.
   b. Yes, once.
   c. No.
3. *Are you an immigrant, or were your parents or grandparents immigrants?*
   a. I was born outside of the United States.
   b. At least one of my parents was born outside of the United States.
   c. At least one of my grandparents was born outside of the United States.
   d. Does not apply.
4. *Your work career has been:*
   a. Primarily in small business (100 or fewer employees).
   b. Primarily in medium-size business (101 to 500 employees).
   c. Primarily in big business (more than 500 employees).
5. *How many businesses did you operate before you were 20?*
   a. Many.
   b. A few.
   c. None.
6. *What is your present age?*
   a. 21–30.
   b. 31–40.
   c. 41–50.
   d. 51 or over.
7. *You are the ——— child in the family.*
   a. Oldest.
   b. Middle.
   c. Youngest.
   d. Other.
8. *What is your marital status?*
   a. Married.
   b. Divorced.
   c. Single.
9. *Your highest level of formal education is:*
   a. Some high school.
   b. High school diploma.
   c. Bachelor's degree.
   d. Master's degree.
   e. Doctorate.
10. *What is your primary motivation in starting a business?*
    a. To make money.
    b. I don't like working for someone else.
    c. To be famous.
    d. To have an outlet for excess energy.
11. *Your relationship with the parent who provided most of the family's income was:*
    a. Strained.
    b. Comfortable.
    c. Competitive.
    d. Nonexistent.
12. *If you could choose between working hard and working smart, you would:*
    a. Work hard.
    b. Work smart.
    c. Both.

13. *On whom do you rely for critical management advice?*
   a. Internal management teams.
   b. External management professionals.
   c. External financial professionals.
   d. No one except myself.

14. *If you were at the racetrack, which of these would you bet on?*
   a. The daily double—a chance to make a killing.
   b. A ten-to-one shot.
   c. A three-to-one shot.
   d. The two-to-one favorite.

15. *The only ingredient that is both necessary and sufficient for starting a business is:*
   a. Money.
   b. Customers.
   c. An idea or product.
   d. Motivation and hard work.

16. *If you were an advanced tennis player and had a chance to play a top pro like Jimmy Connors, you would:*
   a. Turn it down because he could easily beat you.
   b. Accept the challenge, but not bet any money on it.
   c. Bet a week's pay that you would win.
   d. Get odds, bet a fortune, and try for an upset.

17. *You tend to "fall in love" too quickly with:*
   a. New product ideas.
   b. New employees.
   c. New manufacturing ideas.
   d. New financial plans.
   e. All of the above.

18. *Which of the following personality types is best suited to be your right-hand person?*
   a. Bright and energetic.
   b. Bright and lazy.
   c. Dumb and energetic.

19. *You accomplish tasks better because:*
   a. You are always on time.
   b. You are superorganized.
   c. You keep good records.

20. *You hate to discuss:*
   a. Problems involving employees.
   b. Signing expense accounts.
   c. New management practices.
   d. The future of the business.

21. *Given a choice, you would prefer:*
   a. Rolling dice with a one-in-three chance of winning.
   b. Working on a problem with a one-in-three chance of solving it in the allotted time.

22. *If you could choose among the following competitive professions, your choice would be:*
   a. Professional golf.
   b. Sales.

    c. Personnel counseling.

    d. Teaching.

23. If you had to choose between working with a partner who is a close friend and working with a stranger who is an expert in your field, your choice would be:

    a. The close friend.

    b. The expert.

24. You enjoy being with people:

    a. When you have something meaningful to do.

    b. When you can do something new and different.

    c. Even when you have nothing planned.

25. In business situations that demand action, will clarifying who is in charge help produce results?

    a. Yes.

    b. Yes, with reservations.

    c. No.

26. When playing a competitive game, you are concerned with:

    a. How well you play.

    b. Winning or losing.

    c. Both of the above.

    d. Neither of the above.

SCORING

1.	a = 10	6.	a = 8	11.	a = 10	16.	a = 0	21.	a = 0
	b = 5		b = 10		b = 5		b = 10		b = 15
	c = 5		c = 5		c = 10		c = 3		
	d = 2		d = 2		d = 5		d = 0	22.	a = 3
	e = 0								b = 10
		7.	a = 15	12.	a = 0	17.	a = 5		c = 0
2.	a = 10		b = 2		b = 5		b = 5		d = 0
	b = 7		c = 0		c = 10		c = 5		
	c = 0		d = 0				d = 5	23.	a = 0
				13.	a = 0		e = 15		b = 10
3.	a = 5	8.	a = 10		b = 10				
	b = 4		b = 2		c = 0	18.	a = 2	24.	a = 3
	c = 3		c = 2		d = 5		b = 10		b = 3
	d = 0						c = 0		c = 10
		9.	a = 2	14.	a = 0				
4.	a = 10		b = 3		b = 2	19.	a = 5	25.	a = 10
	b = 5		c = 10		c = 10		b = 15		b = 2
	c = 0		d = 8		d = 3		c = 5		c = 0
			e = 4						
5.	a = 10			15.	a = 0	20.	a = 8	26.	a = 8
	b = 7	10.	a = 0		b = 10		b = 10		b = 10
	c = 0		b = 15		c = 0		c = 0		c = 15
			c = 0		d = 0		d = 0		d = 0
			d = 0						

The scoring is weighted to determine your Entrepreneurial Profile. The rating guide appears after the analysis quiz.

QUIZ ANALYSIS

The following percentages are based on a survey given to the 2,500 members of CEM.

1. How were your parents employed?
   a. Both worked and were self-employed for most of their working lives. (4%)
   b. Both worked and were self-employed for some part of their working lives. (10%)
   c. One parent was self-employed for most of his or her working life. (36%)
   d. One parent was self-employed at some point in his or her working life. (16%)
   e. Neither parent was ever self-employed. (34%)

The independent way of life is not so much genetic as it is learned, and the first school for any entrepreneur is the home. It's only natural that a child who has grown up in a home where at least one parent is self-employed is more likely to try his hand at his own business than a child whose parents were in, say, the civil service. Research has shown that to be the case more than two-thirds of the time.

2. Have you ever been fired from a job?
   a. Yes, more than once. (17%)
   b. Yes, once. (34%)
   c. No. (49%)

This question is tricky because the independent-thinking entrepreneur will very often quit a job instead of waiting around to get fired. However, the dynamics of the situation are the same: The impasse results from the entrepreneur's brashness and his almost compulsive need to be right. Steven Jobs and Steven Wozniak went ahead with what would become Apple Computer when their project was rejected by their respective employers, Atari and Hewlett-Packard. And when Thomas Watson was fired by National Cash Register in 1913, he joined the Computer-Tabulating-Recording Company and ran it until a month before his death in 1956. He also changed the company's name to International Business Machines (IBM). The need to be right very often turns rejection into authority.

3. Are you an immigrant, or were your parents or grandparents immigrants?
   a. I was born outside of the United States. (7%)
   b. At least one of my parents was born outside of the United States. (10%)
   c. At least one of my grandparents was born outside of the United States. (36%)
   d. Does not apply. (47%)

America is still the land of opportunity and a hotbed for entrepreneurship. The displaced people who arrive here every day (Cubans, Koreans, Vietnamese, and so on) can still turn hard work and enthusiasm into successful business enterprises. Although it is far from a necessary ingredient for entrepreneurship, the need to fit into society often plays a role.

4. *Your work career has been:*
   a. Primarily in small business (100 or fewer employees). (62%)
   b. Primarily in medium-size business (101 to 500 employees). (15%)
   c. Primarily in big business (more than 500 employees). (23%)

It's been said that "inside every corporate body, there's an entrepreneur struggling to escape." However, small-business management is more than just a scaled-down version of big-business management. The skills needed to run a big business are altogether different from those needed to orchestrate an entrepreneurial venture. The professional manager is skilled at protecting resources, but the entrepreneurial manager is skilled at creating them.

5. *How many businesses did you operate before you were 20?*
   a. Many. (24%)
   b. A few. (49%)
   c. None. (27%)

The enterprising adult first appears as the enterprising child. Mowing lawns, shoveling snow, and promoting rock concerts are common examples of early business ventures. And although every kid who runs a lemonade stand won't necessarily grow up to be an entrepreneur, a kid who runs a *chain* of lemonade stands is a good bet.

6. *What is your present age?*
   a. 21–30. (18%)
   b. 31–40. (38%)
   c. 41–50. (26%)
   d. 51 or over. (18%)

The average age of entrepreneurs has been falling steadily since the late 1950s and early 1960s, when it was found to be between 40 and 45. Our most recent research puts the highest concentration of entrepreneurs in their thirties, but such people as Jobs and Wozniak, Ed DeCastro and Herb Richman of Data General, and Frederick Smith of Federal Express all got their businesses off the ground when still in their twenties. Although we look for these data to stabilize around age 30, there are always exceptions that leave us wondering. Computer whiz Jonathan Rotenberg is such an exception. He currently presides over the 10,000-member Boston Computer Society, is the publisher of the slick magazine *Computer Update,* and earns up to $1,500 a day as a consultant. In 1978, his advice was solicited by the promoter of an upcoming public computer show. After conferring with him several times on the phone, the promoter suggested they meet for a drink to continue their discussion. "I can't," Rotenberg replied. When asked "Why not?" he answered, "Because I'm only 15." An established entrepreneur, Rotenberg is now approaching his mid-twenties.

7. *You are the ——— child in the family.*
   a. Oldest. (59%)
   b. Middle. (19%)
   c. Youngest. (19%)
   d. Other. (3%)

An entrepreneur is most commonly the oldest child in a family. With an average of 2.5 children per American family, the chances of being the first child are around 40 percent. However, entrepreneurs tend to be the oldest child more than 60 percent of the time.

8. *What is your marital status?*
   a. Married. (76%)
   b. Divorced. (14%)
   c. Single. (10%)

Our research concluded that the vast majority of entrepreneurs are married. But most men in their thirties are married, so that alone isn't a significant finding. However, follow-up studies have shown that most successful entrepreneurs have exceptionally supportive wives. (Our results didn't provide conclusive results on women entrepreneurs, but we suspect that their husbands would have to be doubly supportive.) A supportive mate provides the love and stability necessary to balance the insecurity and stress of the job. A divorce or a strained marriage or love life will simply add too much pressure to an already strained business life.

It's also interesting to note that bankers and venture capitalists look a lot more favorably on entrepreneurs who are married than on those living with their mates without the benefit of clergy. As one venture capitalist told us, "If an entrepreneur isn't willing to make a commitment to the woman he loves, then I'll be damned if I'm going to make any financial commitment to him."

9. *Your highest level of formal education is:*
   a. Some high school. (1%)
   b. High school diploma. (17%)
   c. Bachelor's degree. (43%)
   d. Master's degree. (30%)
   e. Doctorate. (9%)

The question of formal education among entrepreneurs has always been controversial. Studies in the 1950s and 1960s showed that many entrepreneurs, like W. Clement Stone, had failed to finish high school, not to mention college. And Polaroid's founder, Edwin Land, has long been held up as an example of an "entrepreneur in a hurry" because he dropped out of Harvard in his freshman year to get his business off the ground.

However, our data conclude that the most common educational level achieved by entrepreneurs is the bachelor's degree, and the trend seems headed toward the M.B.A. Few entrepreneurs have the time or patience to earn a doctorate. (Notable exceptions include An Wang of Wang Laboratories, Robert Noyce and Gordon Moore of Intel, and Robert Collings of Data Terminal Systems.)

10. *What is your primary motivation in starting a business?*
    a. To make money. (34%)
    b. I don't like working for someone else. (56%)
    c. To be famous. (4%)
    d. To have an outlet for excess energy. (6%)

Entrepreneurs don't like working for anyone but themselves. Money is always a consideration, but there are easier ways to make money than by going it alone. More often than not, money is a by-product of an entrepreneur's motivation rather than the motivation itself.

11. Your relationship with the parent who provided most of the family's income was:
    a. Strained. (29%)
    b. Comfortable. (53%)
    c. Competitive. (9%)
    d. Nonexistent. (9%)

The results surprised us because past studies, including our own, have always emphasized the strained or competitive relationship between the entrepreneur and the income-producing parent (usually the father). However, our latest study showed that a surprising percentage of the entrepreneurs we questioned had what they considered to be a comfortable relationship with that parent. To a large extent, we think that is directly related to the changing ages and educational backgrounds of the new entrepreneurs, who are children of the 1950s and 1960s, not children of the Depression. In most cases, they were not forced to drop out of high school to help support the family, but had the luxury of a college education; therefore, the entrepreneur's innate independence hasn't come into such dramatic conflict with the father as it might have in the past. In our opinion, a strained or competitive relationship best fits the entrepreneurial profile, although the nature of that relationship is no longer black-and-white.

12. If you could choose between working hard and working smart, you would:
    a. Work hard. (0%)
    b. Work smart. (47%)
    c. Both. (53%)

The difference between the hard worker and the smart worker is the difference between the hired hand and the boss. What's more, the entrepreneur usually enjoys what he's doing so much that he rarely notices how hard he's working. A decision can be thought of as an action taken by an executive when the information he has is so incomplete that the answer doesn't suggest itself. The entrepreneur's job is to make sure the answers always suggest themselves.

13. On whom do you rely for critical management advice?
    a. Internal management teams. (13%)
    b. External management professionals. (43%)
    c. External financial professionals. (15%)
    d. No one except myself. (29%)

Entrepreneurs seldom rely on internal people for major policy decisions, because employees very often have pet projects to protect or personal axes to grind. And outside financial sources simply lack the imagination that characterizes most entrepreneurs: The most noble ambition of most bankers and accountants is to maintain the status quo. When it comes to critical decisions, entrepreneurs most often rely on outside management consultants and on other entrepreneurs.

14. If you were at the racetrack, which of these would you bet on?
    a. The daily double—a chance to make a killing. (22%)
    b. A ten-to-one shot. (23%)

    c. A three-to-one shot. (40%)
    d. The two-to-one favorite. (15%)

Contrary to popular belief, entrepreneurs aren't high-risk takers. They tend to set realistic and achievable goals, and when they do take risks, they're usually calculated ones. Entrepreneurs are very confident in their own skills and are much more willing to bet on their tennis or golf game than they are to buy lottery tickets or to bet on spectator sports.

15. The only ingredient that is both necessary and sufficient for starting a business is:
    a. Money. (3%)
    b. Customers. (44%)
    c. An idea or product. (25%)
    d. Motivation and hard work. (28%)

All businesses begin with orders. And orders come from customers. You may think you're in business when you've developed a prototype or after you've raised capital, but bankers and venture capitalists are only buying potential. It takes customers to buy a product.

16. If you were an advanced tennis player and had a chance to play a top pro like Jimmy Connors, you would:
    a. Turn it down because he could easily beat you. (4%)
    b. Accept the challenge, but not bet any money on it. (78%)
    c. Bet a week's pay that you would win. (14%)
    d. Get odds, bet a fortune, and try for an upset. (4%)

This question narrows the focus on the risk-taking concept, and the results emphasize what we have already stated: Entrepreneurs are not high-rollers. What is interesting about this response is that more than three-quarters of our respondents would accept the challenge, not so much on the off-chance of winning, but for the experience. And experience is what entrepreneurs parlay into success.

17. You tend to "fall in love" too quickly with:
    a. New product ideas. (40%)
    b. New employees. (10%)
    c. New manufacturing ideas. (4%)
    d. New financial plans. (13%)
    e. All of the above. (33%)

One of the biggest weaknesses that entrepreneurs face is their tendency to "fall in love" too easily. They go wild over new employees, products, suppliers, machines, methods, and financial plans. Anything new excites them. But those love affairs usually don't last long; many of them are over almost as suddenly as they begin. The problem is that while they're going on, entrepreneurs can quite easily alienate their staffs, become stubborn about listening to opposing views, and lose their objectivity.

18. Which of the following personality types is best suited to be your right-hand person?
  a. Bright and energetic. (81%)
  b. Bright and lazy. (19%)
  c. Dumb and energetic. (0%)

The answer to this question is easy: "Bright and energetic," right? Wrong. That describes a personality like your own. But stop and think a minute. You're the boss. Would you be happy—or for that matter, efficient—as someone else's right-hand man? Probably not. And you don't want to hire an entrepreneur to do a hired hand's job.

That's why the "bright and lazy" personality makes the best assistant. He's not out to prove himself, so he won't be butting heads with the entrepreneur at every turn. And although he's relieved at not having to make critical decisions, his delegating ability makes him a whiz when it comes to implementing them.

19. You accomplish tasks better because:
  a. You are always on time. (24%)
  b. You are superorganized. (46%)
  c. You keep good records. (30%)

Organization is the key to an entrepreneur's success. It is the fundamental principle on which all entrepreneurial ventures are based. Without it, no other principles matter. Some entrepreneurs keep lists on their desks, always crossing things off the top and adding to the bottom. Others use note cards, keeping a file in their jacket pockets. Organizational systems may differ, but you'll never find an entrepreneur who's without one.

20. You hate to discuss:
  a. Problems involving employees. (37%)
  b. Signing expense accounts. (52%)
  c. New management practices. (8%)
  d. The future of the business. (3%)

The only thing an entrepreneur likes less than discussing employee problems is discussing petty-cash slips and expense accounts. Solving problems is what an entrepreneur does best, but problems involving employees seldom require his intervention, so discussing them is just an irritating distraction. Expense accounts are even worse. What an entrepreneur wants to know is how much his salespeople are selling, not how much they're padding their expense accounts.

21. Given a choice, you would prefer:
  a. Rolling dice with a one-in-three chance of winning. (8%)
  b. Working on a problem with a one-in-three chance of solving it in the allotted time. (92%)

Entrepreneurs are participants, not observers; they are players, not fans. And to be an entrepreneur is to be an optimist, to believe that you can do anything with the right amount of time and money. Of course, luck—being in the right place at the right time—plays a part in anyone's career, but entrepreneurs have a tendency to make their own luck. There's an old story about a shoe manufacturer who sent his two sons to the Mediterranean to scout out new markets. One wired back, "No point in staying on. No one here wears shoes." The other son wired back, "Terrific opportunities. Thousands still without shoes." Who do you think inherited the business?

22. If you could choose among the following competitive professions, your choice would be:
   a. Professional golf. (15%)
   b. Sales. (56%)
   c. Personnel counseling. (8%)
   d. Teaching. (21%)

Sales give an instant feedback on your performance; it the easiest job for measuring success. How does a personnel counselor or a teacher ever know if he's winning or losing? Entrepreneurs need immediate feedback and are always capable of adjusting their strategies in order to win. Some entrepreneurs brag that they play by the rules when they're winning and change the rules when they're losing. Although we don't endorse it (look what happened to John DeLorean), when it works, it's known as the win/win strategy.

23. If you had to choose between working with a partner who is a close friend and working with a stranger who is an expert in your field, your choice would be:
   a. The close friend. (13%)
   b. The expert. (85%)

Although friends are important, solving problems is clearly more important. Often the best thing an entrepreneur can do for a friendship is to spare it the extra strain of a working relationship.

24. You enjoy being with people:
   a. When you have something meaningful to do. (32%)
   b. When you can do something new and different. (25%)
   c. Even when you have nothing planned. (43%)

Like billionaire Daniel Ludwig, many entrepreneurs will state, categorically, that they have no hobbies. But that doesn't mean they have no social life. In fact, the entrepreneur is a very social person and, more often than not, a very charming one. (Remember, an entrepreneur is someone who gets things done, and getting things done often involves charming the right banker or supplier.) And although he will often have difficulty talking about things other than himself or his business, his enthusiasm is such that whatever he talks about sounds interesting.

25. In business decisions that demand action, will clarifying who is in charge help produce results?
   a. Yes. (66%)
   b. Yes, with reservations. (27%)
   c. No. (7%)

Everyone knows that a camel is a horse that was designed by a committee, and unless it's clear that one person is in charge, decisions are bound to suffer from a committee mentality.

26. *When playing a competitive game, you are concerned with:*
   a. How well you play. (19%)
   b. Winning or losing. (10%)
   c. Both of the above. (66%)
   d. Neither of the above. (5%)

Vince Lombardi was famous for saying, "Winning isn't everything, it's the only thing," but a lesser-known quote is closer to the entrepreneur's philosophy. Looking back at a season, Lombardi remarked, "We didn't lose two games, we just ran out of time twice." Entrepreneurship is a competitive game, and an entrepreneur has to be prepared to run out of time occasionally.

YOUR ENTREPRENEURIAL PROFILE	
235–285	Successful entrepreneur
200–234	Entrepreneur
185–199	Latent entrepreneur
170–184	Potential entrepreneur
155–169	Borderline entrepreneur
154 and below	Hired hand

QUESTIONS YOU MUST ANSWER BEFORE STARTING A BUSINESS

Have you thought about customers, marketing plans, tax reports . . . ? In most cases, people start out in a business with just a concept or product idea, and not much more. And although some entrepreneurs have the energy and motivation to handle any kind of problem as it emerges, others like to have some idea of what they're getting into before they begin.

To give potential entrepreneurs an idea of the sort of questions they must face when entering business for themselves, I've prepared the following checklist:*

BEFORE YOU START

What About You?

- Are you the kind of person who can get a business started and make it go? (The first question is really the last, so before you answer, study the rest of this checklist.)
- Do you want your own business badly enough to work long hours without knowing how much money you'll end up with?
- Have you ever worked in a business like the one you want to start?
- Have you worked for someone else as a foreman or manager?
- Do you have any business-school training?
- Do you have previous experience being in business for yourself?

*This checklist was prepared with help from SBA. Established in 1953, SBA provides a full range of services to small business, from loans and grants to management training and advice. To determine how SBA can help you start a new business, check the Yellow Pages for the regional office nearest you, or contact the Office of Public Communications, Small Business Administration, 1441 L St., N.W., Washington, DC 20416; (202) 653-6832.

What About the Money?

- Do you know how much money you will need to get your business started?
- Have you figured out how much money of your own you can put into the business versus how much money is needed?
- Will you need a partner who can supply money?
- Do you know how much credit you can get from your suppliers—the people you will buy from?
- Do you know where you can borrow the rest of the money you need to start your business?
- Have you figured out the annual net income that you expect to get from the business? (Count the interest you would expect from the money you put into the business as well as your salary.)
- Can you live on less than this so that you can use some of it to help your business grow?

What About a Partner?

- If you need a partner with money or know-how, do you know someone who will fit—someone you can get along with?
- Do you know the good and bad points about going it alone, having a partner, and incorporating your business?
- Have you ever worked closely with someone else on a long-term project?

What About Your Customers? (for retail businesses)

- Do most businesses in your community seem to be doing well?
- Have you tried to find out whether stores like the one you want to open are doing well in your community and in the rest of the United States?
- Do you know what kind of customers will want to buy what you plan to sell?
- Are there enough customers of this kind in the area where you want to open your store?
- Do they need a store like yours? If not, have you thought about opening a different kind of store or going to another neighborhood?

GETTING STARTED

Your Building

- Have you found a good building for your business?
- Did you evaluate several locations before making your final selection?
- Will you have enough room when your business gets better?
- Can you outfit the building the way you want without spending too much money?
- Is the location convenient for parking and/or public transportation?
- Have you made a scaled layout of your office or work area in order to study and/or plan customer flow?
- Have you had a lawyer check the lease and zoning?

Equipment and Supplies

- Do you have an idea of what the equipment and supplies will cost?
- Can you save money by buying second-hand equipment?
- Have you considered the advantages of leasing versus buying?

Your Merchandise
(for retail businesses)

- Have you decided what things you will sell?
- Do you know how much or how many of each you will need to open your store?
- Have you found suppliers who will sell you merchandise at a good price?
- Have you compared the prices and credit terms of different suppliers?

Your Records

- Have you worked out a record-keeping system to keep track of your income and expenses—what you owe people and what they owe you?
- Have you determined a plan to control your inventory so that you will always have enough on hand for your customers but not more than you can sell?
- Have you figured out how to keep your payroll records and take care of tax reports and payments?
- Do you know what financial statements you will need to prepare and how to use them?
- Do you know an accountant who will help with your records and financial statements?
- Do you know what licenses and permits you need?

Protecting Your Store
(for retail businesses)

- Have you made plans for protecting your store against thefts of all kinds, e.g., shoplifting, robbery, burglary, employee theft?
- Have you asked an insurance agent about what kinds of insurance you need?

Buying a Business

- Have you made a list of what you like and don't like about buying a business instead of starting your own?
- Are you sure you know the real reason the owner wants to sell his business?
- Have you compared the cost of buying the business with the cost of starting a new business?
- Are the fixtures, machinery, and/or stock up-to-date and in good condition?
- Is the building in good condition?
- Will the owner of the building be able to transfer the lease to you?

- Have you asked other businessmen in the area and in the industry what they think of your business?
- Have you talked to the company's suppliers?

MAKING IT GO

Advertising and Marketing

- Have you decided how you will market and/or advertise your products?
- Do you know how to prepare a marketing plan?
- Do you know where to get help with your ads?
- Have you observed what other stores and manufacturers do to get people to buy?
- Have you considered direct mail as an alternative or an adjunct to your marketing strategy?
- Do you have a good mailing list, or do you know how and where to purchase mailing lists?

Pricing

- Do you know how to figure what you should charge for each of the products you will sell?
- Do you know what other stores, services, or manufacturers charge for goods like yours?
- Have you considered the advantages of being a price leader rather than a price follower?
- Have you considered competitors' reactions to your pricing policies?
- Will your pricing allow you to make a profit on each of the products you sell?

Buying (for retail businesses)

- Do you have a strategy for finding out what your customers want?
- Will your plan for controlling inventory tell you when it's time to reorder and how much you should reorder?
- Do you plan to buy most of your stock from primarily a few suppliers in order to get more favorable terms?

Selling (for retail businesses)

- Have you decided whether you will have sales clerks or self-service?
- Do you know how to get customers to buy?
- Have you thought about why you like to buy from some salespeople, when others turn you off?

Your Employees

- Do you know what kind of people you need?
- Do you have particular people lined up to fill certain positions?

- Do you know how much to pay?
- Do you have a plan for training your employees?

Credit for Your Customers

- Do you plan to let customers buy on credit?
- Do you know how to set up an efficient invoicing system?
- Do you know the good and bad points about joining a credit card plan?

More Questions

- Have you figured out whether you could make more money working for someone else?
- Does your family go along with your plan to start a business of your own?
- Do you know where to find out about new ideas and new products?
- Do you have a work plan for yourself and your employees?
- Have you discussed your plans thoroughly with a lawyer? With an accountant? With a commercial banker?

Now, go back and answer the first question. If the answer is yes, I wish you the best of luck in getting your new business off the ground, because luck is the one intangible factor which, added to good planning and hard work, will make your business go.

LESSONS TO LEARN FROM TWO-TIMING ENTREPRENEURS

In the mid-1960s, engineer J. Reid Anderson decided to try his hand as an entrepreneur. Using the technical experience he gained at Bell Laboratories and Stanford Research Institute, he developed the Tempo Tuner, an electronic metronome that he successfully sold to music stores.

Buoyed by his first venture, he then teamed up with a marketing and financial consultant to make and distribute an acoustic data coupler, a device used to transfer computer data over telephone lines. Again, success followed.

Two years later, Anderson launched Verbatim Corp. to produce magnetic tape data-storage devices for computers. Four years later, the company began producing floppy disks to replace magnetic tape. The change in product generated sales of $7 million in 1975. By 1984, Verbatim's sales had grown to $171 million. The next year, Anderson agreed to sell Verbatim to Eastman Kodak Co. for $175 million.

What makes an entrepreneur look for a second business venture when his first is still thriving?

The reasons are as different as the individuals themselves, but in nearly every case the formation of a second company gives the founder a chance to build on his small business experience to create an even bigger challenge for himself.

Like J. Reid Anderson, entrepreneurs who have already founded and developed a company often produce superior results in their second and third ventures. These entrepreneurs usually bring three strengths to their subsequent companies:

A product orientation
A higher level of capitalization
A balance of business skills

Generally, the second start-up company is a spin-off venture that is product oriented. First-time ventures, in contrast, are often based on contract work, where the entrepreneur concentrates on developing a new process or technology.

The primary focus of the second venture is often on a new product. The entrepreneur usually reduces the time it takes to get a product launched by transferring some of the development and production technology from the first company. Often, the products marketed through the new company are improved versions of items marketed by the original company. This translates into superior sales performance, which is the key to success in any new venture.

Most first-generation start-up companies are undercapitalized because entrepreneurs without a track record have little more than an interesting idea to sell to potential investors. Second-time entrepreneurs can present a much more convincing story. The proven success allows them to tap a wider group of investors, including venture capitalists. This, in turn, gives them leverage in negotiating the most favorable financing terms. In fact, some venture capitalists have committed funds to second-time entrepreneurs with hot track records in less than 24 hours.

Finally, second-time entrepreneurs possess a better-balanced set of business skills. Not only have they increased their business savvy from lessons learned in their first venture but they also tend to recognize the limits of their own expertise. To compensate for their deficiencies, they build a management team that possesses complementary skills. Unlike first ventures, second ventures are more inclined to have production, general management, and marketing talent in place from the start.

Entrepreneurs with small business experience under their belts bring valuable market knowledge to the new firm. They have a keen awareness of specific business opportunities and know where the sales will have to come from to reach a break-even level. This direct knowledge eliminates the need for expensive and time-consuming market research.

For example, J. Reid Anderson's second company succeeded by using an existing device, the acoustic data coupler that had been developed by Stanford Research Institute (SRI). He saw how the product could be marketed effectively and produced inexpensively, so he started his new company by obtaining a license for the device from SRI.

Second start-up companies also benefit from an owner who knows the specific cash requirements for product development and working capital. They have learned to match their financing needs to funding sources, such as proprietary product sales and progress payments from contracts. They also know when to use other sources of external funds, such as loans from price investors' stock sales, credit lines, and short-term trade credit.

Some of the smarter entrepreneurs I've known have made the time to interact with the larger business community, thereby opening access to other business leaders and potential management recruits. This approach also provides a talent pool from which to draw when selecting outside members for the board of directors. Many companies also select outside advisers to sit on the executive committee along with corporate management. This broadens the scope of management's experience and allows the group to meet more frequently and with less formality than the full board of directors.

The dream of many successful entrepreneurs is to do it all over again despite their age or the odds. They like the journey better than the final destination. The second start-up provides a new challenge and an opportunity to use the knowledge gained the first time around.

Family Businesses

ASSOCIATION

The Dealer Management Association offers useful advice on family businesses in the automotive industry.

Richard M. Caravati, Pres.
Dealer Management Association
Garrison La., P.O. Box 1000
Exeter, NH 03833
(603) 772-1000

MISCELLANEOUS SERVICES

The problems involved in running a family-owned business are becoming a much discussed topic. The best source of books, information, and seminars on this subject is the Family Business Institute, founded by Leon Danco. Personal consultations are also available.

Leon Danco
Center for Family Business
P.O. Box 24268
5862 Mayfield Rd.
Cleveland, OH 44124
(216) 442-0800

The Independent Business Institute publishes information on family businesses and does consulting in the same field.

Frank Butrick, Managing Dir.
Independent Business Institute
P.O. Box 159
Akron, OH 44309
(216) 253-1757

The National Family Business Council (NFBC) is a source of family-owned businesses and of speakers on the subject.

John Messervey, Exec. Dir.
National Family Business Council
60 Revere Dr., Ste. 500
Northbrook, IL 60062
(312) 480-9574

Wharton School, led by Peter Davis, offers extensive family business services.

Ian McMillian, Dir.
Bernie Tannebaum, Assoc. Dir.
Family Business Center
Wharton School of Business
Snider Entrepreneurial Center
3620 Locust Walk
Steinberg-Dietrich Hall
Philadelphia, PA 19104
(215) 898-4856 (general)
(215) 898-1278 (direct)
(215) 898-6848 (Peter Davis, Family Business Expert)

PUBLICATIONS

Success & Survival in the Family-Owned Business, by Pat B. Alcorn, is a good source. The 1986 paperback edition costs $9.95 and is available from the following source.

Warner Books, Inc.
666 Fifth Ave.
New York, NY 10103
(212) 484-2900

The Family in Business Series (1985), by Paul C. Rosenblatt and associates, is interesting and informative, despite its academic approach to psychological interaction of family members in *Family Businesses and Business Families.* Josscy-Bass Publishers produce several good books on this subject.

The Family in Business Series
Jossey-Bass Publishers
433 California St.
San Francisco, CA 94104
(415) 433-1740 (editorial)
(415) 433-1767 (customer service)

Family Pride: Profiles of Five of America's Best Run Family Businesses, by Thomas Goldwasser, profiles Hallmark, Noxell, Marriott, H & R Block, and Johnson Wax, and includes a chapter on "Strategies for Success." The book is interesting, although it lacks some "how-to" advice. Other companies mentioned are Anheiser-Busch, Control Data, Federal Express, Levi Strauss, The Limited, Nike, Toys "R" Us, Wendy's, and Wang Laboratories.

Dodd, Mead & Co.
71 Fifth Ave.
New York, NY 10003
(212) 627-8444

Family Business, Risky Business: How to Make It Work, by David Block, is an inside look at the trials and triumphs of America's 13 million family businesses. Contact the following source for more information.

AMACOM
135 W. 50th St.
New York, NY 10020
(212) 586-8100

MINDING THE FAMILY'S BUSINESS

You may not realize it, but family-owned businesses are an extremely powerful force in the U.S. economic structure. In fact, a recent study posited that family-held businesses account for as many as one-half of the jobs in the United States. And that's the single best argument I've heard for keeping them viable.

A family business always starts out auspiciously—with an entrepreneur. The entrepreneur builds the business from the ground up, and as the children come of age, it's often his dream to bring them into it. Even though he may have the ability to build a business, he's not necessarily capable of transferring his skills and enthusiasm to his children. Blue eyes or curly hair may pass through the genes; business acumen does not.

Victims of Affluence

It's not uncommon, in successful family businesses, for the children to fall victim to the family's growing affluence. I'm reminded of a story about the great hotelier Conrad Hilton and his son Nicky. Nicky came home one day with an expensive pair of shoes. His father protested, "I've never paid that much for a pair of shoes in my life." To which Nicky replied, "Ah! But you never had a rich father." And if Conrad had had a rich father, would he have had the drive to build a chain of hotels? The success of the first generation breeds the complacency of the second.

Furthermore, it's not unusual for a father to inadvertently poison the business for the children. Leon Danco, founder and president of the Cleveland-based Center for Family Business, describes a typical scenario: "Dad comes home and over a drink tells the kids how the competitors are no damn good, the suppliers won't deliver, the customers won't pay, and how the government is taking what little he has left. Then Dad puts his arm around his kid and says, 'And someday, Son, this will all be yours.' "

What Dad usually neglects to say is that he loves the business, that the kids could too, and that all the aggravation is just part of being successful. And it's that love for the business that he must pass on to his children if it is to survive. With that in mind, let me offer three suggestions for perpetuating growth and entrepreneurship in a family-owned and -managed business.

1. Develop an organizational chart for the business. Let people know where they stand. This is important, both for family members and for managers outside the family. Entrepreneurs are usually excellent decision makers, but when it comes to family, they often lose their objectivity completely. For example, they may have a difficult time promoting one child over another, even when merit demands the promotion. For management to be effective, the structure has to be stable and unwaffling. It can't be "what I say it is, when I say it."

2. Let the kids make mistakes. A powerful father often so dominates the business and the family that the children are reluctant to compete with him. The problem is further compounded when, after they make one or two minor mistakes, he snatches back what little authority he may have ceded. By allowing the children to make mistakes and find out how they can correct them on their own, he's letting them learn to run the business the way he learned to run it.

3. Establish clear and consistent boundaries between business issues and emotional issues within the family. This is easier said than done. Keep issues of the home at home and issues of the office at the office. Lines must be drawn and agreed upon *before* a problem occurs; otherwise, valuable time and energy will be taken away from the business—typically, when you need it most.

Nonfamily Input

Establish a board of directors that includes directors from outside the family. In a privately held business, entrepreneurs like to control everything. This approach is fine in the beginning, when tunnel vision is required just to get the business off the ground. But as the business grows, the market climate changes, and outside advice can be the key to a broad view. Also, the objectivity of outside directors is often necessary for setting up a pattern of succession.

Choosing a successor is, without question, the most painful subject that will ever come up in a family business. For one thing, entrepreneurs simply don't want to admit that they're mortal; their families, too, may feel ghoulish about planning for the patriarch's death. So they'll all put off choosing a successor for as long as possible. But by not choosing a successor (and setting up a clear timetable for turning over the controls), an entrepreneur is doing his family and business a double disservice. First, his refusal to admit that one of his children is ready to take over may become a self-fulfilling prophecy. By keeping a good kid down, he's stifling his child's ability to become a good decision maker and manager. Second, by not deciding, he's ensuring someone else will choose his successor, and, in many cases, it's not the person he would have chosen.

According to Leon Danco, the chief tragedy in family-operated businesses is that "a man with courage and guts and the dream to build a business may destroy it by refusing to yield power."

A Conflict of Cousins

Even if succession has been planned, there can be problems. One of my consulting assignments will illustrate this point. In the early 1900s, two brothers started a small paint company in Quincy, Mass. The company survived the Depression and provided "a good living for our families." The children of these two families included two sons on one side and one son on the other, an arrangement which became the core of a knotty problem when it came time for succession.

When the two brothers left their sons in control, what had been a workable 50-50 partnership became a 25-25-50 partnership. Now, any business without firmly established controls ends up with management by compromise, not management by objectives or by one man. And whenever there was a 50-50 vote, one of the brothers would usually throw up his hands and side with his cousin to avoid a protracted conflict.

But in avoiding one problem, they created a more difficult one. The brothers resented the cousin for long-standing personal reasons. Wives and children were recruited into the feud, and the bitterness increased.

Obviously, some changes were long overdue, and I came up with this solution: For decisions to be made, one member or preferably two members of the management had to be taken out of the loop. I proposed a rotating scheme whereby one of the sons took a nine-month sabbatical while the other two ran the business. Brother number one left while brother number two and the cousin ran the business. Then brother number two took a sabbatical. Then the cousin did the same. Over a 27-month period, each combination had a chance to work. All three sons also got a chance to find out what the world was like outside of the family business.

Instead of the business being sold off and everyone going away mad, as had been threatened, each of the two brothers decided he'd be happier running his own company. The cousin was happy to buy them out. The original company survived intact, two new companies were formed, and nobody came away with hard feelings.

Diluted Ownership

The above example illustrates a common occurrence in family businesses that survive for two generations or more: the dilution of ownership. As the stock becomes more dispersed, those most concerned with running the business lose more control. In turn, the stockholders, often no longer just two or three close families, get upset about how the company is being managed and try to force a sellout to a third party. Therefore, it may become necessary for key members of the family to continually prune the stock structure by buying out family members who aren't active participants in the business.

Foundations and Grants

The Foundation Centers offer comprehensive information on all aspects of grant writing; seminars, computer searches, and extensive libraries are available in their regional offices. Foundation Center Directories are also available in most libraries.

The Foundation Center
79 Fifth Ave.
New York, NY 10003
(212) 620-4230
(Headquarters)

The Foundation Center
Hanna Bldg.
1422 Euclid Ave.
Cleveland, OH 44115
(216) 861-1933

The Foundation Center
1001 Connecticut Ave., N.W.
Washington, DC 20036
(202) 331-1400

The Foundation Center
312 Sutter St., Ste. 312
San Francisco, CA 94108
(415) 397-0902 (tape message)
(415) 397-0903 (general information)

The number to call to get access to libraries not in the four cities above is (800) 424-9836.

The Grantsmanship Center offers periodicals and arranges seminars on getting grants.

The Grantsmanship Center
650 S. Spring St., Ste. 507
Los Angeles, CA 90014
(213) 689-9222

Four government publications are good sources for contracts and grants: *The Federal Register, The Commerce Business Daily, The Congressional Record,* and the

Catalog of Federal Domestic Assistance. All of these documents are available from public libraries or local legislators. You may also contact the following source.

Superintendent of Documents
U.S. Government Printing Office
Washington, DC 20402
(202) 783-3238

The Gale Research Company offers several good directories for grants and foundations.

Gale Research Co.
Book Tower
Detroit, MI 48226
(800) 223-GALE

Franchising

Franchising exists in many industries: fast foods, motels, automobiles and parts, infrared heating, business services, dry cleaning, home repair, health clubs, industrial supplies, building products, schools, vending operations, and so on. Although franchise operations are not new, they have expanded greatly since the mid-1970s. Millions of outlets now exist in all fields, accounting for more than $800 billion in annual sales.

A franchising operation is a legal contractual relationship between a franchisor (the company offering the franchise) and a franchisee (the individual who will own the business). Usually the franchisor is obligated to maintain a continuing interest in the business of the franchisee in such areas as site location, management training, financing, marketing, promotion, and record keeping. In addition, the franchisor offers the use of a store motif, standardized operating procedures, prescribed territory, and a trade name. The franchisee, in return, agrees to operate under the conditions set forth by the franchisor. For the help and services provided, the franchisee is usually expected to make a capital investment in the business. In addition, the franchisee agrees to buy all of his products from the franchisor.

Franchising allows a manufacturer to conserve capital and to simultaneously establish a distribution system in the shortest possible time. It takes many dollars and much time to develop a major distribution system. Using franchises may reduce both expenditures because the franchisee finances part of the system through his initial franchise fee and because it is many times easier and faster to enlist independent firms. Also, franchising makes lower marketing costs a possibility for the manufacturer. Franchising substantially cuts down on the subsequent commitment to fixed overhead expenses like personnel administration. For the franchisee, a franchise may facilitate going into business because it cuts down on the amount of capital required and provides a sense of security through the guidance offered by the franchisor. Franchising is a way for small business owners to avoid problems that can ruin a business.

MISCELLANEOUS SERVICES

Francorp is an excellent Chicago-based consulting organization.
Donald Boroian, Chairman
Francorp, Inc.
20200 Governors Dr.
Olympia Field, IL 60461
(312) 481-2900

The Franchise Consulting Group is a fine group of experts on franchising.
Edward Kushell
The Franchise Consulting Group
2049 Century Park East, Ste. 2290
Los Angeles, CA 90067
(213) 552-2901

PUBLICATIONS

Contact Pilot Books for a complete list of titles on franchising, including the *Directory of Franchising Organizations* and *Franchise Investigation & Contract Negotiation.*
Pilot Books
103 Cooper St.
Babylon, NY 11702
(516) 422-2225

The International Franchise Association offers information and publications on franchising, including the quarterly *Franchising World.*
International Franchise Association
1350 New York Ave., Ste. 900
Washington, DC 20005
(202) 628-8000

Venture magazine publishes an annual "Franchise 100," a compilation of information on the top franchises in the United States.
Arthur Lipper III, Chairman
Venture
521 Fifth Ave.
New York, NY 10175
(212) 682-7373

Entrepreneur magazine offers an annual "Franchising Directory" issue.
Entrepreneur
2311 Pontius Ave.
Los Angeles, CA 90064
(213) 477-1011

The following books on the subject of franchising are well worth reading.

The 1985 second edition of the *Handbook of Successful Franchising,* by M. Freidlander, is available from following source. The cost is $40.
Van Nostrand Reinhold
115 Fifth Ave.
New York, NY 10003
(212) 254-3232

The *Source Book of Franchise Opportunities* by J. Bond, published in 1985, is available from the following source. The cost is $20.

Richard D. Irwin, Inc.
1818 Ridge Rd.
Homewood, IL 60430
(312) 798-6000

The *Franchise Opportunities Handbook* (1986 edition, order no. 003-008-00201-3), published by the U.S. government, is the most complete reference book of its kind. It gives information on the number of franchise outlets, length of time the franchise has been in business, start-up capital required, and assistance given by franchisors to franchisees. The cost is $15.

Superintendent of Documents
U.S. Government Printing Office
710 N. Capital St., N.W.
Washington, DC 20402-9325
(202) 783-3238

Franchise Magazine is a new monthly that covers the topic.

Franchise Magazine
PG Communications
747 Third Ave., 34th Floor
New York, NY 10017
(212) 319-2200

Information Press has published a directory of about 3,000 franchise listings for 18 years.

Information Press
728 Center St.
P.O. Box 550
Lewiston, NY 14092
(716) 754-4669

The Department of Commerce offers the following tips for investing in a franchise:*

THE FRANCHISE

1. Did your lawyer approve the franchise contract you are considering after studying it paragraph by paragraph?

2. Does the franchise call upon you to take any steps that are, according to your lawyer, unwise or illegal in your state, county, or city?

*Source: *Franchise Opportunities Handbook,* Department of Commerce. A comprehensive list of U.S. companies that sell franchises, with a brief description of each business and the start-up capital required to get in franchising, is available from the Department of Commerce. For a copy of *Franchise Opportunities Handbook,* send $15 to the U.S. Government Printing Office, Washington, DC. The Stock Number is 003-008-00201. To charge the purchase, call (202) 783-3238.

3. Does the franchise give you an exclusive territory for the length of the franchise, or can the franchisor sell a second or third franchise in your territory?

4. Is the franchisor connected with any other franchise company handling similar merchandise or services?

5. If your answer to question four is "yes," what is your protection against this second organization?

6. Under what circumstances can you terminate the franchise contract, and at what cost to you, if you decide for any reason at all that you wish to cancel it?

7. If you sell your franchise, will you be compensated for your goodwill, or will you lose the goodwill you have built into the business?

THE FRANCHISOR

1. How many years has the firm offering you a franchise been in operation?

2. Has it a reputation for honesty and fair dealing among the local firms holding its franchise?

3. Has the franchisor shown you any certified figures indicating exact net profits of one or more going firms that you personally checked yourself with the franchise?

4. Will the firm assist you with a management training program, an employee training program, a public relations program, capital, credit, or merchandising ideas?

5. Will the firm help you find a good location?

6. Is the franchising firm adequately financed so that it can carry out its stated plan of financial assistance and expansion?

7. Is the franchisor a one-man company or a corporation with an experienced, well-trained management (so that there will always be an experienced leader)?

8. Exactly what can the franchisor do for you that you cannot do for yourself?

9. Has the franchisor investigated you carefully enough to assure itself that you can successfully operate one of its franchises at a profit to both you and it?

10. Does your state have a law regulating the sale of franchises, and has the franchisor complied with that law?

11. How much equity capital will you need in order to purchase the franchise and operate it until your income equals your expenses? Where will you get it?

12. Are you prepared to give up some independence of action to secure the advantages offered by the franchise?

13. Do you believe you have the innate ability, training, and experience to work smoothly and profitably with the franchisor, your employees, and your customers?

14. Are you ready to spend much or all of the remainder of your business life with this franchisor, offering the product or service to your public?

15. Have you made any study to determine if the product or service that you propose to sell under franchise has a market in your territory at the prices you must charge?

16. Will the population in your territory increase, remain static, or decrease during the next five years?

17. Will the product or service you are considering be in greater demand, about the same, or in less demand five years from now?

18. What competition already exists in your territory for the product or service you contemplate selling? Nonfranchise firms? Franchise firms?

DO SOME CHECKING BEFORE YOU TAKE THE PLUNGE

- Be aware of risks. The risk of buying a franchise is related to the track record of the franchise. The highest-risk franchises usually are offered by new companies without a proven track record. When buying a franchise, you depend not only on your own business experience and aptitude but also on the business skills of the franchisor.
- Protect yourself by self-evaluation. Are you willing to make personal sacrifices, work long hours, and deal with financial uncertainty? A reputable franchisor usually will help you in this process; after all, his profit is determined by your continued success. Friends and family can make an important contribution to your self-evaluation, too, providing answers that may be more objective than those from a franchisor.
- Investigate the franchise. Compare it with other franchises in the same line of business. Call or write to those other franchises; you may discover that some offer benefits not available from your chosen franchise.
- Study disclosure statements. If the initial information you receive from a franchisor doesn't include a disclosure statement, ask for one. Among the subjects covered in the disclosure statement are names and addresses of other franchisees, business experience of the franchisor, lawsuits involving the franchisor, and the initial franchise fee.
- Check out the disclosures. After reading the disclosure statement, you should check the accuracy of the information. A good way to start is to contact several of the franchisees listed and ask them about their experience in the business. Be sure to talk to more than one franchisee—no single franchisee can be an accurate representative of the franchise program. Also, look for franchisees who have been in the business for at least a year. Older franchises are less risky than one just starting out.
- Question earnings claims. If a franchisor makes any claims about the sales or income you can expect from the franchise, carefully examine the claims—and demand written substantiation. If you do nothing else, be sure to check what percentage of the franchisor's present franchisees actually have had sales or income that equaled or exceeded the amount claimed.
- Get professional advice. Professional help is especially important in reviewing the financial statements of the franchise and the franchise agreement that you'll have to sign. A lawyer's advice could be the most important professional assistance you'll get before investing in a franchise. Don't assume that the disclosure statement tells you all you need to know about the consequences of signing a franchise agreement and related contracts.

Government Information

A great deal of information about small businesses is available from the federal government. However, getting that information is sometimes more difficult than tackling the original problem the information was intended to solve. There are a number of organizations and associations that help small business owners. This chapter lists some of the fundamental sources of help. Also, try contacting your local, state, and city governments; the chamber of commerce in each of these areas is especially important. Moreover, state and regional government associations can also provide some of this information.

Information about selling your product overseas or about buying products from overseas markets is equally important. The Yellow Pages of New York City and Los Angeles list most of the import-export offices of major companies. These directories are invaluable.

SBA is the arm of the federal government charged with helping entrepreneurs.

- SBA Hotline: (800) 368-5855
- Small Business Development Center coordinates SBA-sponsored groups: (202) 653-6768
- Financial Assistance includes banks in local areas that are participants in PLP: (202) 653-6574
- SBIR Program coordinates all SBIR grants: (202) 653-7875

Much of this wealth of information is not used because too few small business owners know about it. The next time you need information or are trying to solve a problem, call the National Referral Service of the Library of Congress at (202) 426-5467; it is a good starting point for most information searches. The Library of Congress routinely conducts searches free of charge and handles most queries in less than five days. The Federal Information Center can direct you to the right government agency to get the information you need; call (202) 755-8660. The Commerce Department's ITA will compile business profiles on your foreign competitors at a cost as low as $25; call (202) 377-2000.

AGENCIES

GSA arranges for the purchase of billions of dollars of items that civilian agencies need, such as computers, automobiles, and office supplies. It provides two broad procurement services for small businesses: First, GSA provides specifics on what it is buying and whether individual small businesses might qualify as suppliers; second, it disseminates information and advice on selling to other federal agencies.

GSA provides its services through Business Service Centers in each of its 13 regional offices (Atlanta, Boston, Chicago, Denver, Fort Worth, Houston, Kansas City, Los Angeles, New York, Philadelphia, San Francisco, Seattle, Washington, D.C.) According to a GSA booklet, the centers "exist primarily to serve entrepreneurs in their search for government contracts." For businesses located outside the 13 metropolitan areas with Business Service Centers, the GSA operates a "Circuit Rider Program"; GSA counselors visit outlying cities periodically.

General Services Administration
18th & F Sts., N.W.
Washington, DC 20405
(202) 472-1082
(202) 566-1231 (Public Information)
(703) 557-7901 (Procuring Information)
(202) 535-7662 (Freedom of Information)

SBIR offers seed money grants to small businesses for R&D. Phase I grants range between $25,000 and $50,000. Phase II follow-up grants range between $250,000 and $500,000. Grants are administered by 11 different government agencies.

Office of Innovation, Research and Technology
Small Business Administration
1441 L St., N.W.
Washington, DC 20416
(202) 653-6938

The following sources can provide information on grant solicitations from individual agencies within the SBIR program.

Dr. W. R. Murphey
Office of Grants and Program Systems
Department of Agriculture
West Auditors Bldg., Rm. 112
15th St. & Independence Ave., S.W.
Washington, DC 20251

James P. Maruca, Dir.
Office of Small and Disadvantaged Business
    Utilization
Department of Commerce
14th St. & Constitution Ave., N.W., Rm. 6411
Washington, DC 20230

Horace Crouch, Dir.
Small Business and Economic Utilization
Office of Small and Disadvantaged Business
    Utilization
Office of the Secretary of Defense
The Pentagon, Rm. 2A340
Washington, DC 20301

Dr. Edward Esty, SBIR Program Coordinator
Office of Educational Research and Improvement
Department of Education
Brown Bldg., Rm. 717
Mail Stop 40
Washington, DC 20208

Gerry Washington
c/o SBIR Program Manager
Department of Energy
Washington, DC 20545

Richard Clinkscales, Dir.
Office of Small and Disadvantaged Business
    Utilization
Department of Health and Human Services
200 Independence Ave., S.W., Rm. 513D
Washington, DC 20201

Dr. Thomas Henrie, Chief Scientist
Bureau of Mines
Department of the Interior
2401 E St., N.W.
Washington, DC 20241

George Kovatch, SBIR Program Manager
Transportation Systems Center
Department of Transportation
Kendall Sq.
Cambridge, MA 02142

Walter H. Preston
Office of Research and Development
Environmental Protection Agency
410 M St., S.W.
Washington, DC 20460

Dr. Carl Schwenk
SBIR Office Code RB
National Aeronautics and Space Administration
600 Independence Ave., S.W.
Washington, DC 20546

Roland Tibbetts, SBIR Program Manager
Ritchie Coryell, SBIR Program Manager
National Science Foundation
1800 G St., N.W.
Washington, DC 20550

Wayne Batson
Office of Nuclear Regulatory Research
Nuclear Regulatory Commission
Washington, DC 20555

Maintained by the SBA Office of Advocacy, the SBA Answer Desk is a toll-free information and referral service to assist small business owners in matters relating to the government and their businesses. It refers callers to the appropriate agency, trade association, or office.

U.S. Small Business Administration Answer Desk
(800) 368-5855

The Office of Business Liaison serves as liaison between the Department of Commerce and the business community. Its free publication, *Business Services Directory,* is aimed at making the government more accessible to small businesses. Also available is the ROADMAP Program service, which provides information about government procurement, exporting, statistical sources, marketing, and regulatory matters.

Office of Business Liaison
U.S. Department of Commerce
Washington, DC 20230
(202) 377-3176

There are 38 Federal Information Centers located throughout the United States. Their job is to personally assist the public in using the federal government as a source of information. To find a center near you, check the White Pages of your telephone book under "U.S. Government."

Your congressman's office is a good place to turn to when all else fails. Remember, your congressman works for you in Washington. He can be reached by contacting his local district office or by writing to him at the following address.

c/o U.S. Capitol
Washington, DC 20515
(202) 224-3121

The Chamber of Commerce is an excellent source of data on both large and small businesses throughout the United States.

Chamber of Commerce USA
1615 H St., N.W.
Washington, DC 20062
(202) 659-6000

SBA's Office of Procurement and Technical Assistance maintains capability profiles on small businesses interested in federal government procurement opportunities. PASS is used by federal agencies and major prime contractors to identify the capabilities of individual small businesses. Appropriate forms for participating in PASS are available from any SBA office, or from the following source.

Diane Thompson
General Information
Procurement Automated Source System
Procurement Assistance
Small Business Administration
1441 L St., N.W., Rm. 628
Washington, DC 20416
(202) 653-6938
(202) 653-6586

MISCELLANEOUS SERVICES

The Washington Researchers are an excellent source of government information. They offer many books, tapes, and directories that are designed to answer questions about government services and programs.

Washington Researchers
2612 P St., N.W.
Washington, DC 20007
(202) 333-3499

Matthew Lesko, founder of the Washington Researchers, has compiled a one-volume guide to "the largest source of information on Earth," the U.S. government. Titled *Information U.S.A.,* this guide provides names, addresses, and phone numbers for more than 3,000 government data experts, as well as access to more than a million free and low-cost government publications. The cost is $23 for the softcover edition, $50 for the hardcover edition.

Viking Penguin Books
299 Murray Hill Pkwy.
East Rutherford, NJ 07073
(201) 933-1460

CEM offers a four-hour audiotape program on "How to Win an SBIR Grant" ($59), as well as *Writing SBIR Proposals,* a comprehensive 328-page book on the who, what, where, and how of writing SBIR proposals ($87).

Center for Entrepreneurial Management
180 Varick St., Penthouse
New York, NY 10014-4606
(212) 633-0060

SCORE is an organization of retired businesspeople that provides actual or potential entrepreneurs with free advice. It operates an answer desk that provides information on all government agencies: (800) 368-5855.

Service Corps of Retired Executives
1129-20th St., N.W.
Washington, DC 20416
(202) 653-6279

PUBLICATIONS

The U.S. Government Printing Office is one of the best sources of information around. For a small fee, you can get many booklets on business management and basics, such as *Doing Business with the Federal Government.*

Superintendent of Documents
U.S. Government Printing Office
Washington, DC 20402
(202) 783-3238

The U.S. Product Safety Commission offers publication lists and pamphlets on product safety.

U.S. Consumer Product Safety Commission
Washington, DC 20207

PTO offers several booklets on patents and trademarks.

U.S. Department of Commerce
Patent and Trademark Office
Washington, DC 20231

FDA statute and regulation guides are available from the Public Health Service of the Food and Drug Administration.

U.S. Department of Health and Human Services
Public Health Service
Food and Drug Administration
Rockville, MD 20857

Booklets that examine the role of women in business are available from the Department of Labor.

U.S. Department of Labor
Office of the Secretary
Women's Bureau
200 Constitution Ave., N.W.

Washington, DC 20210
(202) 523-6653

The 1,000-page *Catalog of Federal Domestic Assistance* is the most complete source
of information on government programs. It is published by the Office of Management and Budget once a year with updates. Subscriptions are $32.
    Superintendent of Documents
    U.S. Government Printing Office
    Washington, DC 20402
    (202) 783-3238

The Federal Assistance Programs Retrieval Systems (FAPRS) is a computerized
information system which contains much of the same information found in the
Catalog of Federal Domestic Assistance. It is designed to identify quickly specific
federal assistance programs for which applicants are eligible. It can be accessed
through computer terminals in many government regional offices and in university
libraries. The price of a search varies with the request. Contact the following source
for an access point near your location.
    Federal Program Information Branch
    Budget Review Division
    Office of Management and Budget
    17th & Pennsylvania Aves., N.W.
    Washington, DC 20503
    (202) 395-6182

The Directory of State and Federal Funds is a single source for basic data on the
financial assistance programs for the 50 states and 12 federal agencies. It can help
you to shop, compare, select, and/or discard a wide range of aid programs without
having to sort through mountains of government literature. The cost is $6.
    Pilot Books
    103 Cooper St.
    Babylon, NY 11702
    (516) 422-2225

The *Catalog of Federal and Domestic Assistance* is one of the best books available
that discusses doing business with the government. The Stock Number is 941-001-
000009; the cost is $30. You can purchase a copy via credit card by contacting the
following source.
    Superintendent of Documents
    26 Federal Plaza, Rm. 110
    New York, NY 10278
    (212) 264-3825

The Small Business Subcontracting Directory contains the names and addresses of
prime Department of Defense contractors and their products or services, as well as
the phone numbers of small business liaison officers who can provide purchasing

information. Specify Stock Number 008-040-00190-3 when ordering. The cost is $6.50, postpaid.

Superintendent of Documents
Department 36-TC
Washington, DC 20402-9325
(202) 783-3238 (to order by VISA, Choice, or Mastercard)

Senate Select Small Business Committee
Russell Senate Office Bldg., SR-428a
Washington, DC 20515
(202) 224-5175

U.S. House of Representatives
Small Business Committee
2361 Rayburn House Office Bldg.
Washington, DC 20515
(202) 225-5821

Home-Based Businesses

Millions of Americans are finding that there is no place like home to work. It not only cuts down on commuting time but it also offers a number of financial incentives. Recent estimates indicate that there are more than 14 million home-based businesses in the United States. As a result, a number of associations, newsletters, and books have sprung up to help the home-based entrepreneur.

ASSOCIATIONS

The American Home Business Association is a new association for home-based business owners and operators. It publishes *Home BusinessLine,* a monthly newsletter.

American Home Business Association
60 Arch St.
Greenwich, CT 06830
(203) 661-0105
(800) 433-6361

A division of the Small-Business Development Center, the Center for Home-Based Businesses is a clearinghouse for information on home-based businesses. It offers "Organizations for Home-Based Businesses," a comprehensive list of organizations of interest to home businesses.

Center for Home-Based Businesses
Truman College
1145 W. Wilson
Chicago, IL 60640
(312) 989-6112

Founded in 1981, the National Alliance of Home-Based Businesswomen (NAHB) is a 1,000-member national support group for home-based businesswomen. NAHB publishes *Alliance,* a bimonthly newsletter, holds an annual meeting, and provides discounts on insurance, car rentals, and hotels.

National Alliance of Home-Based Businesswomen
P.O. Box 306
Midland Park, NJ 07432
(201) 423-9131

Founded in 1982, the National Association for the Cottage Industry acts as an advocacy system for cottage workers. This 30,000-member group publishes a bimonthly newsletter, *Mind Your Own Business at Home,* and holds two meetings a year.

National Association for the Cottage Industry
P.O. Box 14460
Chicago, IL 60614
(312) 472-8116

Founded in 1981, the National Association for the Self-Employed (NASE), a 350,000-member organization, analyzes issues and provides information on the needs of self-employed and independent businesspersons. NASE publishes brochures and pamphlets, as well as *Small Business America,* a monthly newsletter.

National Association for the Self-Employed
P.O. Box 612067
Dallas, TX 76118
(800) 433-8004

The National Association of Home-Based Businesses was founded in 1984. This 500-member group holds an annual meeting and offers a number of publications on operating a home-based business.

National Association of Home-Based Businesses
P.O. Box 30220
Baltimore, MD 21270
(301) 466-8070

PUBLICATIONS

Alliance is a bimonthly newsletter on home-based business issues.

Alliance
National Alliance of Home-Based Businesswomen
P.O. Box 306
Midland Park, NJ 07432
(201) 423-9231

Home BusinessLine is a new monthly newsletter with tips on taxes, marketing, and promotion, as well as information on issues specific to home-business entrepreneurs.

Home BusinessLine
60 Arch St.
Greenwich, CT 06830
(203) 661-0105
(800) 433-6361

Home Business News is a bimonthly magazine for home-based entrepreneurs; it features articles on marketing, mail order, and computers.

Home Business News
12221 Beaver Pike
Jackson, OH 45640
(614) 988-2331

Mind Your Own Business at Home is an informative bimonthly newsletter for home-business entrepreneurs.

> *Mind Your Own Business at Home*
> P.O. Box 14460
> Chicago, IL 60614
> (312) 470-8116

Mothers' Home Business Network is a networking newsletter for mothers who work at home.

> *Mothers' Home Business Network*
> P.O. Box 423
> East Meadow, NY 11554
> (516) 997-7394

Barbara Brabec Productions publishes *National Home Business Report,* a quarterly newsletter which contains a wide range of information and advice on operating a home business. Also available is *Homemade Money: The Definitive Guide to Success in a Home Business,* by Barbara Brabec. The cost is $16.45 postpaid.

> *National Home Business Report*
> Barbara Brabec Productions
> P.O. Box 2137
> Naperville, IL 60566
> (Requests for information by mail only.)

Office at Home, by Robert Scott, is an informative guide. Published by Scribners, it is available for $16.95 postpaid from the following source.

> Macmillan Publishing
> Order Department
> Front & Brown Sts.
> Riverside, NJ 08075
> (800) 257-5755

Small Business America is a monthly newsletter for self-employed and independent businesspeople.

> *Small Business America*
> National Association for the Self-Employed
> P.O. Box 612067
> Dallas/Ft. Worth, TX 76118
> (800) 433-8004

Starting and Managing a Business from Your Home is a 48-page booklet from SBA, which discusses the pluses and minuses of home-based businesses, including how to get started, record keeping, taxes, and pertinent laws. The cost is $1.75.

> *Starting and Managing a Business from Your Home*
> Department 146-R
> Consumer Information Center
> Pueblo, CO 81009

Working at Home, by Paul and Sara Edwards, offers advice for the home-based businessperson. The cost is $12.95 plus $1.25 shipping and handling.

St. Martins Press
175 Fifth Ave.
New York, NY 10010
(212) 674-4141, ext. 577

The Worksteader News is a newsletter for people who work at home. The New Career Center also offers *The Work-at-Home Sourcebook,* by Lynie Arden, which provides information on home work and the law. *The Whole Work Catalog* provides more information. The cost is $1.00 postpaid.

The Worksteader News
c/o The New Career Center
6003 N. 51st St.
Boulder, CO 80301
(303) 530-1087

Import-Export

Most of America's smaller firms overlook their export options. Only 10 percent of the more than 300,000 U.S. companies with export capabilities actively sell their products overseas. Furthermore, small and medium-size companies account for only 10 percent of U.S. exports.

Many smaller firms overlook the potential benefits of exporting, such as expanding the company's customer base, and thus opening new markets for extra production capacity; eliminating seasonal sales fluctuations; and extending a product's life. To determine whether the company can export profitably, top management should evaluate the following five factors.

1. Financing: To obtain export funding, companies must be able to demonstrate a good credit record, strong internal cash flow, and sufficient management depth. Sources of export financing include state governments, SBA, and the Export-Import Bank of the United States (Eximbank).

2. Production: Schedules and processes should be flexible enough to accommodate, if necessary, shorter production runs and nonstandard items.

3. Distribution: Consider the extent to which the company would have to rely on the assistance of foreign sales representatives and distributors.

4. Sales: Domestic sales should be above the "break-even point" given current investment levels.

5. Market: SBA, the Department of Commerce, and international banks can furnish information on existing competition, potential market size, and current overseas markets for products similar to those you intend to export.

PUBLICATIONS

An affiliate of the International Chamber of Commerce, the ICC Publishing Corporation of Paris, France, is an excellent source of publications on doing small business internationally.

Rachelle Bijou
ICC Publishing Co.
156 Fifth Ave., Ste. 820
New York, NY 10010
(212) 206-1150

The *World Guide to Foreign Services 1986/87,* 1st edition, contains 170 country sections and 18,400 entries. It is a directory of ministries of foreign affairs, embassies, consulates, high commissions, missions, legations, and so on. The cost is $155.

Basic Guide to Exporting
Department of Commerce Publication

U.S. Government Printing Office
Washington, DC 20402
(202) 783-3238

The Department of Commerce and SBA offer weekly listings of up-to-date export trade leads developed and reported by more than 200 U.S. posts. Contact the following sources for free information and a sample.

TOP Bulletin
Trade Opportunities Program
U.S. Department of Commerce
Industry and Trade Administration, Rm. 2323
Washington, DC 20230

Market Overseas with U.S. Government Help
Small Business Administration
P.O. Box 15434
Fort Worth, TX 76119
(800) 424-5201

The latest edition (1981) of the International Trade Commission's 130-page *A Guide to Exporting* contains new facts and marketing strategies for successful exporting, as well as many sources to contact for free information. The book (Stock Number 003-009-00487-0) is available for $8.50 from the following source.

Superintendent of Documents
U.S. Government Printing Office
Washington, DC 20402
(202) 783-3238

ASSOCIATIONS AND AGENCIES

SBA has a toll-free "hotline" number for import/export questions.
(202) 653-7561
(800) 424-5201

The National Association of Export Companies (NEXCO) seeks to foster the expansion of U.S. trade through independent export firms. There are about 100 members who benefit from the shipping association and consulting services. NEXCO keeps its members up-to-date via a monthly bulletin.

National Association of Export Companies
17 Battery Pl., Ste. 1425
New York, NY 10004
(212) 809-8023

The International Traders Association publishes *Trade Opportunities Magazine* and teaches import-export programs. It also puts members in touch with overseas contacts.

International Traders Association
c/o The Mellinger Co.
6100 Variel Ave.
Woodland Hills, CA 91367
(818) 884-4400

The American Association of Exporters and Importers publishes *International Trade Alert Newsletter* and has about 1,000 members.
Eugene Milosh, Pres.
American Association of Exporters and Importers
11 W. 42d St.
New York, NY 10036
(212) 944-2230

The World Trade Institute runs seminars on exporting.
Director
Export Development & Information Group
The World Trade Institute
One World Trade Center, 55th Floor
New York, NY 10048
(212) 466-3248
Telex: 427346 NYANDNJ
Cable: WORLDTRADENEW YORK

ITA has an excellent library of import-export information.
Department of Commerce
International Trade Administration
26 Federal Plaza
New York, NY 10278
(212) 264-0630

The National Council on International Trade Documentation is a nonprofit organization dedicated to the elimination of excess paperwork. It sells books and offers seminars.
National Council on International Trade Documentation
350 Broadway, Ste. 1200
New York, NY 10013
(212) 925-1400

National Foreign Trade is a nonprofit trade association of more than 500 members.
National Foreign Trade
100 E. 42d St., 9th Floor
New York, NY 10017
(212) 867-5630

The Overseas Private Investment Corporation is a federal agency that encourages American businesspeople to invest overseas. They provide market-evaluation assistance, support feasibility studies, and offer direct and guaranteed loans and insurance protection.

Overseas Private Investment Corp.
1615 M St., N.W.
Washington, DC 20527
(202) 457-7000
(800) 424-6742

Eximbank provides services, including the following, which can be very helpful.

1. Conferences on small business exporting: Eximbank, in coordination with the Department of Commerce and SBA, sponsors one-day conferences throughout the United States to inform smaller firms about opportunities available in foreign trade and what government services can do to help.

Eximbank Marketing Division
811 Vermont Ave., N.W., Rm. 1278
Washington, DC 20571
(202) 566-8873

2. Feasibility studies: Eximbank will support U.S. firms that undertake studies of overseas projects.

Business Advisory Service
Export-Import Bank of the United States
811 Vermont Ave., N.W., Rm. 1275
Washington, DC 20571
(202) 566-8860
(800) 424-5201

3. Hotline service: A counseling service, set up by Eximbank, can answer questions that small-business exporters may have concerning assistance in financing goods and/or services for sale to foreign countries. It can also offer information on the various programs that exist to help small exporters, including the small-business advisory service, briefing programs, financial support programs, and export credit insurance.

Business Advisory Service
Export-Import Bank of the United States
811 Vermont Ave., N.W., Rm. 1275
Washington, DC 20571
(202) 566-8860

Incorporating and Forming Partnerships

One of the first steps in setting up a business is to decide the form it will take: sole proprietorship, partnership, limited partnership, or corporation.

PUBLICATIONS

How to Incorporate for under $75.00 Without a Lawyer, by Ted Nicholas, is worthwhile reading for anyone considering incorporation. Enterprise Publishing can also provide forms for incorporation in any of the 50 states.

Ted Nicholas
Enterprise Publishing Co.
725 Market St.
Wilmington, DE 19801
(302) 656-0110
(800) 533-2665

Investigate the benefits of incorporating in the state of Delaware. *Incorporating in Delaware,* published by the Gauge Corporation, is an informative booklet which lists the advantages of Delaware incorporation and all of the forms necessary for setting up a Delaware corporation. The cost is $5.

Gauge Corp.
1300 N. Market St.
Wilmington, DE 19801
(302) 658-8045

The Partnership Book: How to Write Your Own Small Business Partnership Agreement, 3rd edition (revised to cover new tax rules), was written by Dennis Clifford and Ralph Warner. Nolo Press also offers books for Texas, Florida, New York, and California incorporations.

Nolo Press
950 Parker St.
Berkeley, CA 94710
(415) 549-1976

AGENCIES

Corporate Agents, Inc., a group of corporate register agents, will provide information on how to incorporate in Delaware.

Corporate Agents, Inc.
P.O. Box 1281
Wilmington, DE 19899
(800) 441-4303

Delaware Business Incorporators will help you to incorporate in Delaware and then help you to file to do business in your home state.

Lori M. Smith, General Manager
Delaware Business Incorporators
1001 Jefferson Plaza, Ste. 112
Wilmington, DE 19801
(800) 423-2993

MISCELLANEOUS SERVICES

If you want to purchase a corporate kit and stock certificates (including seal and by-laws) and don't want to pay a lawyer to do it for you, go directly to their source, the Corpex Bank Note Company, Inc.

Corpex Bank Note Co., Inc.
480 Canal St.
New York, NY 10013
(212) 925-2400 (New York City)
(800) 221-8181
(800) 522-7299 (in NY)

Incubators

According to the Humphrey Institute at the University of Minnesota, the number of "incubators for small businesses" more than doubled nationally in 1986. But this trend is so new that many small business owners don't even know what incubators are.

In brief, incubators, which are most often run by nonprofit corporations, are designed to help start-ups get off the ground by providing low rent, business and financial advice (including advice on business plans and SBA loans), as well as secretarial and computer services. Moreover, studies show that start-ups in incubators fail only 50 percent of the time, compared with an 80-percent failure rate for businesses started on the outside.

ASSOCIATIONS

An industry trade association for incubators, the National Business Incubation Association is very effective in helping areas with high unemployment to create new business centers.

Carlos Morales
National Business Incubation Association
114 N. Hanover St.
Carlisle, PA 17013
(717) 249-4508

MISCELLANEOUS SERVICES

David Allen is a good source of incubator information.

Dr. David Allen
Business Administrative Bldg.
Penn State University
University Park, PA 16802
(814) 865-4700 (general)
(814) 863-0815 (direct line)

Mark Weinberg is an expert in urban incubators.

Dr. Mark Weinberg
Institute for Local Government and Rural Development
Bentley Hall
Ohio University
Athens, OH 45701
(614) 593-4388

John Mullen is an expert in rural incubators.

Dr. John Mullen
Landscape Architecture
University of Massachusetts
Hills-North
Amherst, MA 01003
(413) 545-2255

PUBLICATIONS

The November 1984 issue of *Venture* magazine lists 50 incubators in California, Colorado, Connecticut, Georgia, Illinois, Indiana, Iowa, Maryland, Massachusetts, Michigan, Minnesota, New York, Ohio, Pennsylvania, Rhode Island, South Carolina, Utah, Vermont, and Wisconsin. A capsule summary of specific services is also provided. You can find the November 1984 issue of *Venture* in your local library, or contact the following source.

Venture
521 Fifth Ave.
New York, NY 10175
(212) 682-7373

The New Business Incubator: 1986, by Raymond Smilor and Michael Doud Gill, Jr., is an excellent book published by IC². Contact the following sources for more information.

Lexington Books
D. C. Heath & Co.
125 Spring St.
Lexington, MA 02173
(617) 862-6850

Dr. George Kozmetsky
IC² Institute
University of Texas at Austin
2815 San Gabriel
Austin, TX 78705
(512) 478-4081

Incubator Times, a quarterly newsletter published by SBA, keeps entrepreneurs up-to-date on the activities of business incubators around the United States. For information contact the following source.

Office of Private Initiatives
Small Business Administration
1441 L St., N.W., Rm. 720-A
Washington, DC 20416
(202) 653-7880

IDEAS ARE THE ROOTS OF SUCCESSFUL VENTURES

Having a business of your own is like having a child. You experience many of the same emotions and problems. And, as with having a child, getting started is a large part of the fun. The point of conception for any new business is the idea stage. Of all the stages in the development of a business, the idea stage is probably the most interesting and rewarding. The world is your oyster and the opportunities seem to be endless. And they are.

Every business starts with an idea. Successful businesses start with good, workable ideas. And entrepreneurs always seem to generate more ideas than nonentrepreneurs. They're not all good ideas, and for every entrepreneur who builds a business around a good idea, there are dozens of other men or women who have had that same idea. The entrepreneur, however, has the drive and the ability to follow through. He sees an idea *and* sees how to make it work. Other people see only the idea, if that much.

But where do good ideas come from? Why do some people have better ideas than other people? And what is creativity? Why are some people more creative than others? These are universal questions, and there are no universal answers. But there are some clues. Few thoughts and ideas are actually "new." In fact, it is shocking to find out how many are just the same old ideas warmed over and served up in a new package.

Schools of Thought

There are two schools of thought about entrepreneurial creativity. The philosophy of the first school is, "Let's think hard and long for something truly new; let's make a significant breakthrough and be the only ones with our device." The second school is more realistic. It tends more toward repackaging: "A widget works fine in such and such a case; let's see if we can apply it here in a new situation." It focuses more on a process of transferring techniques, products, or services from one specific area of use to another. The first computer dating service, for example, was not a new invention. Computers weren't new and dating services weren't new. The computer dating service was simply a new application of technology—a new way to pursue an old idea.

So what, in fact, is a "new" idea? Let's look at the technological breakthrough that may have the largest impact on our lives: the microprocessor. Surely it must be a new idea if it's so powerful. But, in fact, it isn't a new idea at all. It's simply an efficient repackaging of an old idea: the circuit board. And all of the innovations that have stemmed from the circuit board aren't actually new ideas, just refinements and new applications.

Let's face reality: How frequently does the opportunity arise to do something really "new"? I claim that if you were to examine the new technology companies, you would find that few are based on new ideas. Most are simply in the business of repackaging old ideas.

But that's doesn't mean you can't do something so substantially different that it seems like a brand new idea. Huge breakthroughs have come out of companies as varied as Polaroid, McDonald's, Xerox, and Kentucky Fried Chicken. Each of these companies introduced dramatically new concepts into old markets. When you look at any fast-growth company, you'll find unique ideas; sometimes the ideas show up in product development, sometimes in marketing. The ideas may be unique, but are they really new? And is it really necessary that they be new?

Whenever you come up with an idea for a new business, honestly ask yourself whether it's a new idea or just a reworked version of someone else's basic concepts. Then identify the similarities among your product and existing products. Furthermore, identify just what is new and different about your idea and examine exactly how that difference will open up existing market positions.

At the same time, bear in mind that good ideas are often killed by purely logical reasoning. For every new or unique idea that's ever existed, there have been dozens of logical reasons why it would never succeed. The airplane, the automobile, and the telephone were all ideas that were condemned as impractical, for any number of reasons, by many reasonable people. Your prior training can destroy many wonderful ideas if you don't watch out, especially if you are an engineer or a scientist. Remember, our biggest scientific breakthroughs have been a *combination* of intuition and cold reason.

Allow for Emotion

Avoid automatically applying logical reason to new business ideas: It isn't fair to the ideas. And don't try to make them stand up to the test of time from day one. In the beginning stages, ideas are still gaining strength. After all, it's unlikely that anyone would ever marry if purely logical reasoning were the sole criterion. Most people base their marriage plans primarily on emotion, with a little logic thrown in.

Starting a business is like starting a marriage (and just slightly more risky). Let a little emotion enter into the decision. Keep your mind open to all kinds of new applications and original thoughts. There's plenty of time for cold logic later, after the idea gets to the start-up stage and becomes a business.

In the development stage, you may discover that what you thought was your best idea is seriously flawed, and that a related idea, which you thought was only marginal, measures up to all the tests. So always keep an open mind. Just because you're engaged to an idea doesn't mean you have to marry it.

And if you insist on developing "new" ideas, don't rule out the possibility of developing new ways to apply existing high-tech or low-tech ideas. Remember, Ford didn't invent the automobile, and he wasn't the first person to experiment with an assembly-line system. But he was the first person to manufacture cars on an assembly line. And Jobs and Wozniak of Apple Computer didn't invent the microprocessor; they simply envisioned its possibilities before anyone else did.

Moreover, a "new" marketing idea can do wonders for an old product. For example, Amway built a billion-dollar business because it thought of a new way to sell soap—through multilevel marketing. So, perhaps the best advice I can offer to anyone still in the idea stage is to study the market carefully, have fun, and don't rule anything out.

Industry-by-Industry Studies

MISCELLANEOUS SERVICES

FIND/SVP is a business research source which offers reports, studies, and surveys. Their free information catalog is a wonderful source of market studies.

FIND/SVP
500 Fifth Ave.
New York, NY 10110
(212) 354-2424
(800) 346-3787

Standard & Poors Corporation is a good source of statistical financial information.

Standard & Poors Corp.
25 Broadway
New York, NY 10004
(212) 208-8000

Theta Technology publishes market research reports on the medical and electronics fields. They also produce customized reports.

Theta Corp., Inc.
Theta Bldg.
Middlefield, CT 06455
(203) 349-1054

SRI is a major source of technical information and studies.

Stanford Research Institute
333 Ravenswood Ave.
Menlo Park, CA 94025
(415) 326-6200

Venture Development Corporation provides data specifically relating to the electronics industry.

Venture Development Corp.
One Apple Hill, Ste. 206
Natick, MA 01760
(617) 653-9000

Dun & Bradstreet is a good primary source for industry lists and directories.

Dun & Bradstreet
99 Church St.

New York, NY 10007
(212) 285-7000

Morton Research Corporation and Frost & Sullivan are two sources of industry-by-industry data.

Morton Research Corp.
P.O. Box 375
Merrick, NY 11566
(516) 378-1066

Frost & Sullivan
106 Fulton St.
New York, NY 10038
(212) 233-1080

Predicasts, headquartered in Cleveland, produces the Predicasts Terminal System (PTS), a series of ten on-line databases used by the international business community. PTS is the largest on-line source of business information of its kind, with more than 5 million entries prepared from worldwide business, trade, defense, and government publications.

Gordon Lensner
Predicasts
11001 Cedar Ave.
Cleveland, OH 44106
(216) 795-3000
(800) 321-6388

PUBLICATIONS

State-by-state directories of manufacturers in the northeastern United States are available from the following source:

Commerce Register
190 Godwin Ave.
Midland Park, NJ 07432
(201) 445-3000

Manufacturers News Inc. is a good source of state-by-state directories of manufacturers.

Manufacturers News Inc.
4 E. Huron St.
Chicago, IL 60611
(312) 337-1084

The Standard Industrial Classification Code Manual is a widely used four-digit code for classifying manufacturing and nonmanufacturing businesses. These SIC codes are excellent tools for obtaining industry-by-industry statistics. The Stock Number is 041-001-00314-2; the cost is $24.

U.S. Government Printing Office
710 N. Capitol St., N.W.
Washington, DC 20402-9325
(202) 783-3238

Harris Publishing Company is the largest publisher of state-by-state industrial directories.

Harris Publishing Co.
2057-2 Aurora Rd.
Twinsburg, OH 44087
(800) 321-9136

To find out if a state government offers an industrial directory, contact the secretary of state's office or the Office of Corporation for that state.

UPDATE OF THE STANDARD INDUSTRIAL CLASSIFICATIONS

The Technical Committee on Industrial Standards has recently completed an update of the Standard Industrial Classification (SIC) codes, the first update in 15 years. The new codes cover 1,006 industry categories.

SIC is a four-digit classification developed by the government for the government; it is specifically designed to define the activities of businesses. Its primary purposes are to help the Internal Revenue Service (IRS), the Census Department, and the Department of Labor in their record keeping and in tracking business and labor trends.

Private enterprises have found ways to use SIC codes for their own purposes. List compilers, such as Dun & Bradstreet and Market Data Retrieval, use them to generate mailing lists by industry in order to provide accurate market targeting for business-to-business marketing. Trade journals and market forecasters have long relied on SIC codes for surveys and statistical studies. As the ability to reach target markets via new technology increases, the SIC codes have become increasingly important to business-to-business marketers.

The revisions, which reflect the changing economy, dropped (or merged into existing SIC codes) 78 of the classifications. Seventy-nine new SIC codes were added. Service businesses showed the largest increase; manufacturing and wholesaling categories showed modest increases. All other general categories were reduced.

Order hardbound copies of the *Standard Industrial Classification Code Manual 1987* from the National Technical Information Service. The Order Number is PB87-100012/HCQ; the cost is $30. A computer tape version, including documentation (9-track, 1600 or 6250 bpi) may be ordered as PB87-100020/HCQ. The cost is $175. It is also available on diskettes by special request. Add $3 per order for handling costs.

Clara Gannon, Product Mgr.
U.S. Department of Commerce
National Technical Information Service
5285 Port Royal Rd.
Springfield, VA 22161
(703) 487-4929

Insurance and Financial Planning

ASSOCIATIONS

NASE is an association of small businesses. It offers excellent insurance plans for small companies with only a few employees.

National Association for the Self-Employed
2121 Precinct Line Rd.
Hurst, TX 76054
(817) 656-6313

Support Services Alliance, Inc. is a cooperative for people who are self-employed or who work in small groups. It offers many services, including insurance and a publication list.

Support Services Alliance, Inc.
P.O. Box 547
Nanuet, NY 10954
(914) 623-8665

MISCELLANEOUS SERVICES

Thomas Financial & Insurance, Inc. specializes in executive compensation plans.

Leo Thomas, Pres.
Thomas Financial & Insurance, Inc.
5900 Wilshire Blvd., #17
Los Angeles, CA 90036
(213) 937-9400

Oland International is an insurance broker.

James H. Butler, Pres.
Oland International
489 Fifth Ave.
New York, NY 10017
(212) 916-3001

Access America, Inc. provides travel assistance and insurance for travel.

Edward Shulman, CEO
Access America, Inc.
600 Third Ave.
New York, NY 10016
(212) 490-4061

Century Financial Group offers tax preparation and planning services and financial planning.

Charles Putney, Pres.
Century Financial Group
1705 N. California Blvd.
Walnut Creek, CA 94596
(415) 932-4700

The Regan Group is a life insurance company that offers state-of-the-art products.

John D. Regan, Pres.
The Regan Group
475 Gate Five Rd.
Sausalito, CA 94965
(415) 331-6275

Financial Planning Concepts, Inc. provides investment, tax, and estate planning.

Richard J. Berher, Pres.
Financial Planning Concepts, Inc.
P.O. Box 30510
Bethesda, MD 20814
(301) 460-9022

Cigna offers financial counseling.

Thomas F. Clark, F.C.
Cigna
8200 Greensboro Dr.
McLean, VA 22102
(703) 821-1685
(703) 442-0711

Williams & Dubin, Inc. offers advisory and investment services.

Steven H. Dubin, Principal
Williams & Dubin, Inc.
1266 Furnace Brook Pkwy.
Quincy, MA 02169
(617) 786-1625

John J. Shortmann Insurance Agency is a total insurance facility.

John J. Shortmann, Jr.
John J. Shortmann Insurance Agency
1424 Highland Ave.
Needham, MA 02192
(617) 444-7011

Shea Financial Corporation specializes in fire and casualty, life and employee benefits, counseling, syndicating and merger and acquisitions.

Robert Shea, Pres.
Shea Financial Corp.
225 Friend St.
Boston, MA 02114
(617) 720-2800

The Lubin-Bergman Organization, Inc. provides insurance and financial services.
Robert Lubin, Pres. & CEO
The Lubin-Bergman Organization, Inc.
7101 N. Cicero Ave.
Lincolnwood, IL 60646
(312) 673-4900

The Gallop Group, Inc. specializes in executive compensation and financial planning.
Gerald D. Gallop, Pres.
The Gallop Group, Inc.
10960 Wilshire Blvd., Ste. 2380
Los Angeles, CA 90024
(213) 477-3952

Cal-Surance Group specializes in executive and employee benefits.
Donald H. Melig, Pres.
Cal-Surance Group
2790 Skypark Dr.
Torrance, CA 90505
(213) 543-1660

Corroon & Black is a good source of insurance information.
Larry R. Thompson, CEO
Corroon & Black
50 California St.
San Francisco, CA 94111
(415) 981-0600

The Small Business Service, Inc. offers many insurance-based services for small businesses, including a "New Business Survival Kit," an easy-to-use guide for starting and managing your business.
Small Business Service, Inc.
544 Main St.
P. O. Box 1411
Worcester, MA 01608
(800) 343-0939

PUBLICATION

To assist policyholders with filing an insurance claim, the insurance industry has prepared a pamphlet, *How to File an Insurance Claim.* To receive a free copy, send a stamped, self-addressed envelope to the following source.

Insurance Information Institute
Publications Service Center
110 William St.
New York, NY 10038
(212) 669-9200

Lawyers and Legal Self-Help

ASSOCIATIONS

Used for a wide range of conflicts, including construction warranties, dissolution of partnerships, cost overruns, and consumer complaints, the American Arbitration Association offers a good alternative to the court process.

American Arbitration Association
140 W. 51st St.
New York, NY 10020
(212) 484-4000

The American Bar Association maintains a legal referral service.

American Bar Association
750 N. Lake Shore Dr.
Chicago, IL 60611
(312) 988-5000

MISCELLANEOUS SERVICES

The firm of Fishman & Merrick, P.C. is knowledgeable about the corporate securities field.

Karen Carasik, Partner
Fishman & Merrick, P.C.
30 N. LaSalle St., Ste. 3600
Chicago, IL 60602
(312) 726-1224

Sachnoff, Weaver & Rubenstein, Ltd. is a large multiservice legal firm.

Georgia A. Vinyard, Managing Partner
Sachnoff, Weaver & Rubenstein, Ltd.
30 S. Wacker Dr., 29th Floor
Chicago, IL 60606
(312) 207-6406

Friedman & Ginsberg is a small firm specializing in business law.

Lawrence J. Friedman, Partner
Friedman & Ginsberg
14755 Preston Rd.
424 Signature Pl.

Dallas, TX 75240
(214) 788-1400

Baker and Botts is one of the best-known legal firms in Texas.
W. John Glancey, Partner
Baker and Botts
2020 LTV Center
2001 Ross Ave.
Dallas, TX 75201
(214) 953-6501

Rhodes, Maloney, Hart, Mullen, Jakle, & Watters is a general business firm.
Thomas L. Watters, Pres.
Rhodes, Maloney, Hart, Mullen, Jakle, & Watters
919 Santa Monica Blvd., Third Floor
Santa Monica, CA 90401
(213) 393-0174

Donohue & Donohue is an excellent New York–based legal firm.
William Phelan, Partner
Donohue & Donohue
26 Broadway
New York, NY 10004
(212) 269-2330

Dennis O'Conner offers both legal and business experience.
Dennis O'Conner
O'Conner Bourde & Snyder
950 Winter St., Ste. 2300
Waltham, MA 02154
(617) 890-6600

The Practicing Law Institute, a nonprofit organization founded in 1933, conducts seminars and offers excellent audiotapes and videotapes on a wide range of legal subjects.
Practicing Law Institute
810 Seventh Ave.
New York, NY 10019
(212) 765-5700

Widely used by the legal profession, Browne & Company is a financial and legal printer with offices throughout the United States.
Browne & Co.
345 Hudson St., 10th Floor
New York, NY 10014
(212) 924-5500

Horwich & Warner is a good business/legal firm.
William E. Horwich
Horwich & Warner
353 Sacramento St., 19th Floor
San Francisco, CA 94111
(415) 956-5410

PUBLICATIONS

The Martindale-Hubbell Law Directory (1987 edition, 8 volumes) lists every attorney able to practice law in the United States. An excellent source of legal reference, the *Directory* costs $160.
The Martindale-Hubbell Law Directory
Martindale-Hubbell, Inc.
P.O. Box 1001
Summit, NJ 07901
(201) 464-6800

Enterprise Publishing is an excellent source of legal self-help information. A looseleaf book titled *The Complete Set of Corporate Forms* is highly recommended.
Ted Nichols
Enterprise Publishing
725 Market St.
Wilmington, DE 19801
(302) 654-0110
(800) 533-2665

Nolo News is a 16-page quarterly self-help law newspaper. It provides good advice on a variety of topics, including collecting on bad checks, evaluating cases, filing and serving papers, and deciding who, where, and why to sue.
Nolo Press
950 Parker St.
Berkeley, CA 94710
(415) 549-1976
(800) 992-NOLO
(800) 445-NOLO (in CA)

SMALL BUSINESS LEGAL STRUCTURES

The popular view of the entrepreneur is that of a high flyer, a person who's going to start the next General Motors or Apple Computer. But in the early stages of any enterprise—I'm thinking in particular of garage operations that have launched multimillion-dollar businesses—the last thing on the entrepreneur's mind is an elaborate corporate structure.

For example, you've started a little company in your garage—making widgets in your spare time. A distributor calls you with a sizable order. You decide to quit your job and work full time at your own company. You're not sure the company will take off, so you don't bother to incorporate. One year later, your orders total $200,000 a month. The continued growth of the business seems imminent.

But there's a problem. Because you didn't bother to incorporate, you're in a much higher personal tax bracket. As a result, your taxes have gone through the roof. And when you go to the bank for a loan, the bank refuses because the limit for personal loans is too low for your needs. So you look for an investor, but you don't have a vehicle for giving up equity—if you aren't a corporation you can't sell stock.

The time to incorporate has long since passed. Now, you must spend valuable time with accountants and lawyers to straighten out the transfer of liabilities and assets. In addition to the cost, the time spent away from your business could prove devastating.

The legal structure you choose for your business can make a crucial difference in your ability to raise money and to expand. The decision you make at the start of your business will influence future expansion and financing alternatives. And if you put off making that decision at the outset ("I just want to concentrate on my business"), you are accepting the sole proprietorship structure by default. That's fine for a mom-and-pop type of operation, but if you find you need to restructure at a later date in order to grow, the process will take critical time away from running your business when you need it most. Therefore, careful consideration of the pros and cons of the basic available legal structures is very important. Discuss the specific implications of each option with an attorney and an accountant.

There are three principal legal structures to consider: proprietorships, partnerships, and corporations. Understanding how choosing one of these structures will affect your long-term goals may seem as complex as the business venture itself. Therefore, the first consideration in choosing a legal structure should be the goals of the business, as well as your individual goals. If you want a small, quiet, mom-and-pop operation, a simple proprietorship may be your best bet.

Proprietorships

A proprietorship is basically an extension of the individual. It is the easiest and cheapest of the three legal structures. (It is essentially the absence of a specialized form of business.) Record keeping for a proprietorship is relatively simple. In addition, a proprietorship is not required to pay business taxes, so the owner's income is taxed only once—on his 1040 federal tax form. Traditionally, it is an effective legal structure until your income from the business exceeds $65,000.

On the negative side, a proprietorship offers only minimal opportunities for tax planning, and it cannot offer tax breaks on fringe benefits, such as sick pay or medical, dental, and life insurance. Furthermore, the business is automatically dissolved on the death of the proprietor, and the assets are tied up in the estate. No allowances can be made for succession or for transferring the business. And perhaps most important, because a proprietorship is basically an extension of the individual, the owner is exposed to unlimited personal liabilities and has no protection against creditors.

Partnerships

There are two kinds of partnerships: limited and general. These forms of business have generally been effective for real estate, accounting, and legal firms, and they are becoming serious competitors to the more popular corporate form of business, especially with regard to the accelerating payroll tax-related expenses involved in doing business as a corporation. Partnerships and proprietorships face these problems to a lesser extent, or not at all.

In a general partnership, partners share operating responsibility and decision-making authority, as defined in the Uniform Partnership Act (unless otherwise negotiated in advance). Partners may also deal with the enterprise as a separate legal entity, i.e., they may sell or lease property or loan money to the partnership, with reasonably controllable consequences. However, there are serious drawbacks to the general partnership. General partners are responsible for any debts or obligations of the partnership; any partner can contractually bind the enterprise, since each is its agent; and, by definition, a partnership is dissolved by the death or withdrawal of one of the partners. Furthermore, no new partners may be added without the approval of all the partners. Because of these strictures, the general partnership may often look fragile to potential backers and employees.

In a limited partnership, one or more general partners manage the day-to-day operations of the business and are personally responsible for its debts. Limited partners are liable for business debts only to the extent of their investments. They have no rights in management and may transfer their interests without dissolving the partnership. Limited partnerships are frequently chosen for real estate and other tax shelters.

As with proprietorships, partnerships offer the advantage of not suffering double taxation. For example, if an equal five-person partnership made $10,000 in one year, each partner would claim $2,000 on his or her personal income tax. Losses are likewise deductible from personal income.

Corporations

The corporation is the most common and best-known form of business enterprise. There are several good reasons for this. A corporation is the only business structure that is legally recognized as a totally separate legal entity, apart from its investors. In effect, it's an artificial person; as such, the corporation, and not its owners, is liable for its debts and must file its own tax returns and pay its own taxes. Furthermore, the corporation has the right to sue and be sued in its own name.

Insulation from personal liability can be especially important in high-risk situations. And although shareholders in the corporation may be called on to sign personal guarantees for business loans, other creditors, including suppliers and employees with wage claims, can have no legal claim to an investor's personal assets.

Also, there are no present limits to the life of a corporation. Unlike partnerships and proprietorships, corporations do not automatically dissolve when the owner dies or when one or more investors decide to leave the enterprise. And the corporate legal structure offers its owners the widest range of estate-planning possibilities.

Another important advantage is that a corporation offers the opportunity for centralized management. Unlike partners, a corporation's shareholders can appoint directors to set basic company policy; those directors, in turn, appoint corporate officers. The corporate form allows for systematic delegation of responsibility even if, in many cases, shareholders, directors, officers, and management may be made up of the same small group.

By electing to go under Subchapter S, a corporation's owners can let business losses flow through to their personal income, thus allowing them direct tax deductions. Furthermore, no corporate tax is paid as long as Subchapter S is in effect. Five requirements must be met before a corporation can elect Subchapter S.

1. A corporation cannot have more than 35 shareholders.
2. All shareholders must be individuals, not other corporations or trusts.
3. All shareholders must be U.S. citizens or resident aliens.
4. Only one class of stock is allowed.
5. All shareholders must consent, in writing, to having the corporation elect Subchapter S.

Know Your Options

Many years of legal rules and exceptions have gone into defining how you may or may not do business in the United States, and each case must be considered separately. But no matter what form you choose for your business, you should discuss the full implications with both your accountant and your lawyer. In addition, many hybrid legal structures exist that offer various advantages to the savvy businessperson. (One example is forming a limited partnership with a corporation serving as the general partner: This choice offers tax advantages and protection against liability.) But the more complicated the legal structure you choose, the more time you will have to spend with it, not only when setting up the business, but during the life of the business.

In any event, by knowing what your options are going in, you will be better able to shape your business to suit your goals. And that's what business is all about.

Libraries

The *Directory of Special Libraries and Information Centers* is a good but expensive reference; however, it is available in most libraries.

Gale Research Co.
Book Tower
Detroit, MI 48226
(313) 961-2242
(800) 223-GALE

The Association of College and Research Libraries can help you find college and research libraries that cover your area of interest.

Association of College and Research Libraries
American Library Association
50 Huron St.
Chicago, IL 60611
(312) 944-6780

The goal of the Special Libraries Association is to find a library with information that you need. Ask for the information specialist.

Special Libraries Association
1700-18th St., N.W.
Washington, DC 20009
(202) 234-4700

The Strand Bookstore specializes in hard-to-find books. It has an inventory of 2.5 million books, the majority of which are out of print.

Strand Bookstore
828 Broadway
New York, NY 10003
(212) 473-1452

The National Referral Center is a free service which directs you to organizations that can provide answers on virtually any subject. Most inquiries are handled within five days.

National Referral Center
Library of Congress, LA 5122
10 First St., S.E.
Washington, DC 20540
(202) 287-5670

DOCUMENT RETRIEVAL

"There's nothing more frustrating than to turn up the citation to an article or study that fills the gap in your market research project, and then be unable to obtain the actual document," says Georgia Finnigan, publisher of the *Document Retrieval Sources & Services Directory*. It identifies more than 200 document-retrieval organizations, some of which provide their services on-line.

Listed in the directory are libraries that have retrieval services outside their immediate localities; information centers at nonprofit organizations; trade groups and research institutes with services for nonmembers; commercial information firms; and so on. The firms are indexed by types of information, locations, whether or not copyright compliance is offered, and whether or not on-line ordering is provided.

Contact the following source for more information. The cost is $50.

Document Retrieval Sources & Services Directory
The Information Store
140 Second St.
San Francisco, CA 94105
(415) 543-4636

Lobbying

The actions of the federal, state, and local governments can affect your business in many ways. These actions can be influenced by a well-planned lobbying campaign to explain the needs of your business to lawmakers. Many organizations exist to present the concerns of businesses to government officials. The best political lobbying groups for small businesses are listed below.

With more than 600,000 dues-paying members, the National Federation of Independent Business (NFIB) provides a strong voice for small business interests. NFIB publishes a newsletter, the *NFIB Mandate,* eight times a year through which it polls its membership to determine lobbying positions.

> John Sloan, Pres.
> National Federation of Independent Business
> 150 W. 20th Ave.
> San Mateo, CA 94403
> (415) 341-7441

> John J. Motley III, Dir. Federal Legislation
> National Federation of Independent Business
> Capital Gallery East, Ste. 700
> 600 Maryland Ave., S.W.
> Washington, DC 20024
> (202) 554-9000

National Small Business United has about 50,000 members.

> National Small Business United
> 1155-15th St., N.W., Ste. 710
> Washington, DC 20005
> (202) 293-8830

The Small Business Center coordinates efforts of regional chambers of commerce and helps businesspeople deal with regulatory agencies.

> Ivan C. Elmer, Mgr.
> Small Business Center
> U.S. Chamber of Commerce
> 1615 H St.
> Washington, DC 20062
> (202) 659-6000

The 2,500 members of the Smaller Business Association of New England, the oldest regional association of small business owners, are very active politically.

Lewis A. Shattuck
Smaller Business Association of New England
69 Hickory Dr.
Waltham, MA 02154
(617) 890-9070

Neece, Cator Associates is the legal firm which supports National Small Business United.

Thomas Cator, Counsel
National Small Business United
c/o Neece, Cator Associates
1050-17th St. N.W., Ste. 810
Washington, DC 20036
(202) 887-5599

SBA is the government agency which supports small businesses.

Frank Swain
Office of Advertising
Small Business Administration
1441 L St., N.W., Ste. 1012
Washington, DC 20416
(202) 653-6808 (direct)
(800) 368-5855 (answer desk)

The United Shareholders Association was formed to protect shareholder rights.

T. Boone Pickens, Jr.
United Shareholders Association
1667 K St., N.W., Ste. 770
Washington, DC 20006
(202) 393-4600

COMMITTEES ON SMALL BUSINESS

The Committees on Small Business shape the government's policies on small business. If you have questions, comments, or complaints about government policies and regulations, call your congressman. (If your state or district isn't represented in the following lists, call the committee chairmen.) Let Congress know which small business policies are working and which aren't; make suggestions. It's the only way to keep Congress informed about the needs of the small-business owner.

MEMBERS OF THE FULL COMMITTEE ON SMALL BUSINESS OF THE U.S. SENATE

Dale Bumpers, Ark., *Chairman,* 44843*
Sam Nunn, Ga., 43521
James R. Sasser, Tenn., 43344

*Telephone extensions are for internal use only.

Max Baucus, Mont., 42651
Carl Levin, Mich., 46221
Alan J. Dixon, Ill., 42854
David L. Boren, Okla., 44721
Tom Harkin, Iowa, 43254
John F. Kerry, Mass., 42742
Barbara A. Mikulski, Md., 44654
Lowell Weicker, Jr., Conn., 44041
Rudy Boschwitz, Minn., 45641
Warren Rudman, N.H., 43324
Alfonse M. D'Amato, N.Y. 46542
Bob Kasten, Wisc., 45323
Larry Pressler, S.D., 45842
Malcolm Wallop, Wyo., 46441
Christopher S. Bond, Mo., 45721

SUBCOMMITTEES

Export Expansion

Mr. Sasser, *Chairman*
Mr. Bumpers
Mr. Nunn
Mr. Harkin
Mr. Boschwitz
Mr. D'Amato
Mr. Wallop

Rural Economy and Family Farming

Mr. Baucus, *Chairman*
Mr. Nunn
Mr. Levin
Mr. Dixon
Mr. Boren
Mr. D'Amato
Mr. Boschwitz
Mr. Kasten
Mr. Pressler

Government Contracting and Paperwork Reduction

Mr. Dixon, *Chairman*
Mr. Sasser
Ms. Mikulski
Mr. Kasten
Mr. Rudman

Innovation, Technology, and Productivity

Mr. Levin, *Chairman*
Mr. Baucus
Mr. Boren
Mr. Kerry
Mr. Rudman
Mr. Weicker
Mr. Bond

Competition and Antitrust Enforcement

Mr. Harkin, *Chairman*
Mr. Bumpers
Mr. Wallop

Urban and Minority-Owned Business Development

Mr. Kerry, *Chairman*
Ms. Mikulski
Mr. Bond

MEMBERS OF THE COMMITTEE ON SMALL BUSINESS OF THE U.S. HOUSE OF REPRESENTATIVES, 100TH CONGRESS*

John J. LaFalce, N.Y. (32d), Chairman, Rm. 2367, 53231†
Neal Smith, Iowa (4th), Rm. 2373, 54426
Henry B. Gonzalez, Tex. (20th), Rm. 2413, 53236
Thomas A. Luken, Ohio (8th), Rm. 2368, 52216
Ike Skelton, Mo. (4th), Rm. 2453, 52876
Romano L. Mazzoli, Ky. (3d), Rm. 2246, 55401
Nicholas Mavroules, Mass. (6th), Rm. 2432, 58020
Charles Hatcher, Ga. (2d), Rm. 405, 53631
Ron Wyden, Oreg. (3rd), Rm. 1406, 54811
Dennis E. Eckart, Ohio (11th), Rm. 1210, 56331
Gus Savage, Ill. (2d), Rm. 1121, 50773
Buddy Roemer, La. (4th), Rm. 103, 52777
Norman Sisisky, Va. (4th), Rm. 426, 56365
Esteban Edward Torres, Calif. (3d), Rm. 1740, 55256
Jim Cooper, Tenn. (4th), Rm. 125, 56831
Jim Olin, Va. (6th), Rm. 1238, 55431
Richard Ray, Ga. (3d), Rm. 425, 55901
Charles A. Hayes, Ill. (1st), Rm. 1028, 54372
John Conyers, Jr., Mich. (1st), Rm. 2313, 55126
James H. Bilbray, Nev. (1st), Rm. 1431, 55965

*As of April 1987. Located at 2361 Rayburn House Office Bldg.; (202) 225-5821.
†Telephone extension.

Kweisi Mfume, Md. (7th), Rm. 1107, 54741
Floyd H. Flake, N.Y. (6th), Rm. 1427, 53461
H. Martin Lancaster, N.C. (3d), Rm. 1408, 53415
Ben Nighthorse Campbell, Colo. (3d), Rm. 1724, 54761
Peter A. DeFazio, Oreg. (4th), Rm. 1729, 56416
David Price, N.C. (4th), Rm. 1223, 51784
Matthew G. Martinez, Calif. (30th), Rm. 109, 55465
Joseph M. McDade, Pa. (10th), Rm. 2370, 53731
Silvio O. Conte, Mass. (1st), Rm. 2300, 55335
William S. Broomfield, Mich. (18th), Rm. 2306, 56135
Andy Ireland, Fla. (10th), Rm. 2416, 55015
John Hiler, Ind. (3d), Rm. 407, 53915
David Dreier, Calif. (33d), Rm. 410, 52305
D. French Slaughter, Jr., Va. (7th), Rm. 319, 56561
Jan Meyers, Kans. (3d), Rm. 315, 52865
Dean A. Gallo, N.J. (11th), Rm. 1318, 55034
J. Alex McMillan, N.C. (9th), Rm. 401, 51976
Stewart B. McKinney, Conn. (4th), Rm. 237, 55541
Larry Combest, Tex. (19th), Rm. 1529, 54005
Richard H. Baker, La. (6th), Rm. 506, 53901
John J. Rhodes, III, Ariz. (1st), Rm. 510, 52635
Joel Hefley, Colo. (5th), Rm. 508, 54422
Frederick S. Upton, Mich. (4th), Rm. 1607, 53761
Elton Gallegly, Calif. (21st), Rm. 1020, 55811

Magazines

Black Enterprise is a useful and highly respected monthly business magazine. The June flagship issue lists the top 100 black-owned U.S. businesses. The cost is $15 per year for 12 issues.

   Black Enterprise
   Earl G. Graves Publishing Co., Inc.
   295 Madison Ave.
   New York, NY 10017-6304
   (212) 242-8000
   (800) 247-5470 (subscriptions)

A weekly with a circulation of more than 800,000, *Business Week* is primarily for big business.

   Business Week
   1221 Avenue of the Americas
   New York, NY 10020-1001
   (212) 997-1221
   (800) 635-1200 (subscriptions)

Folio is the magazine for magazine management. It is a good source for information on magazines.

   Folio Magazine
   Six River Bend
   Box 4949
   Stamford, CT 06907
   (203) 358-9900

Forbes is the capitalist's tool. Its up-and-coming section is particularly interesting.

   Forbes
   60 Fifth Ave.
   New York, NY 10011
   (212) 620-2200

The *Fortune 500* issue of this bimonthly is published on the last Monday of April. Standard rates are $44.50 for 27 issues. The magazine is primarily for big business.

   Fortune
   1270 Avenue of the Americas
   New York, NY 10020
   (212) 586-1212
   (800) 621-8200 (subscriptions)

In Business is written for owners of very small businesses with less than $1 million of annual sales. Strong emphasis is placed on the relationship of the business with its community. The September/October Small Business Management issue is an annual highlight. *In Business* also profiles successful small alternative businesses. The cost is $18 for six issues. Circulation is about 200,000.

> *In Business*
> JG Press, Inc.
> Box 323
> 18 S. Seventh St.
> Emmaus, PA 18049
> (215) 967-4135

Inc. focuses on growing businesses with more than $1 million of annual sales. It is a good ongoing reference source of information on regulatory, tax, and political developments affecting small businesses. Editorial policy favors positive profiles of successful companies. The cost is $24 for 12 issues. Circulation is about 625,000.

> *Inc. Magazine*
> 38 Commercial Wharf
> Boston, MA 02110-3801
> (617) 227-4700
> (800) 525-0643 (subscriptions)

The quarterly *Journal of Small Business Management* devotes each issue to a specific area of interest to the small-business owner.

> Linda Hastings
> *Journal of Small Business Management*
> National Council for Small Business Management and the
> Small Business Development Center
> P.O. Box 6025
> West Virginia University
> Morgantown, WV 26506
> (304) 293-5837

Nation's Business is a publication of the U.S. Chamber of Commerce. The cost is $22 for 12 issues.

> *Nation's Business*
> 1615 H St., N.W.
> Washington, DC 20062
> (202) 463-5650
> (800) 638-6582

Success Magazine is an upscale monthly which has a circulation of more than 400,000. Shifting its appeal from positive mental attitudes to more entrepreneurial focus, it features good articles on short, specific topics.

Success Magazine
342 Madison Ave.
New York, NY 10173
(212) 503-0700

Venture is the magazine for entrepreneurs and entrepreneurial investors. It has a history of solid editorial information, particularly on the subjects of money and capital sources. Circulation is about 400,000. The cost is $18 per year.

Venture
521 Fifth Ave.
New York, NY 10175
(212) 682-7373
(800) 247-5470

COMPREHENSIVE SOURCES

The best listing of publications of all kinds is the *Gale Directory of Publications: An Annual Guide to Newspapers, Magazines, Journals and Other Serials* (formerly the *Ayer Directory of Publications*). Available in many libraries, it has 1,500 pages and 23,000 entries. The cost is $115.

To locate articles on specific subjects in past issues of magazines, ask a librarian about the *Business Periodicals Index* (which also has an on-line counterpart). To key in on a specific company, go to the *Business Index,* which lists articles from more than 300 journals, and to the *Predicasts F & S Index,* which also has European and international editions.

Mail-Order Marketing

ASSOCIATIONS AND AGENCIES

The National Mail Order Association is an industry group which offers newsletters, books, and directories on mail-order marketing.

Paul Muchnick
National Mail Order Association
5818 Venice Blvd.
Los Angeles, CA 90019
(213) 934-7986

The Direct Marketing Association offers seminars and books, as well as a free weekly newspaper that is informative and widely read.

Direct Marketing Association
6 E. 43d St.
New York, NY 10017
(212) 689-4977

All mail-order marketers need to know the rules established by the Federal Trade Commission. This office offers a publications list, "Facts for Consumers," as well as the following free publications.

Federal Trade Commission
6th St. & Pennsylvania Ave., N.W., Rm. B-3
Washington, DC 20580
(202) 523-3575

MISCELLANEOUS SERVICES

The American List Counsel is a good source of small business mailing lists.

Liza Price
American List Counsel
88 Orchard Rd., CN-5219
Princeton, NJ 08540
(201) 874-4300
(800) 526-3973

Concord Mail Marketing is an excellent source of all mail-order marketing and offers consulting help.

Louis J. Leber, Pres.
Concord Mail Marketing

61 Domino Dr.
Concord, MA 01742
(617) 369-1904

Standard Rate & Data Service, Inc. is an industry information service.
Standard Rate & Data Service, Inc.
3004 Glenview Rd.
Wilmette, IL 60091
(800) 323-4588

Direct Media, Inc. is a major list broker.
David Florence, Chairman
Direct Media, Inc.
220 Grace Church St.
P.O. Box 1151
Port Chester, NY 10573
(914) 937-5600

PUBLICATIONS

Selling by Mail Order contains more than 800 directory titles, with business names, addresses, zip codes, phone numbers, affiliation or professional specialty, and year of first appearance in the Yellow Pages. Compiled from current Yellow Pages, covering every city and town in the United States, it offers sales, telemarketing, and direct-mail leads.

Selling by Mail Order
SBA Bibliography #3
Small Business Administration
Washington, DC 20416
(800) 358-5855

Maxwell Sroge Publishing, Inc. publishes three newsletters covering mail order, telephone selling, and direct selling, one of which is *Non-store Marketing Report.* It also publishes a book, *Inside the Leading Mail Order Houses.*

Maxwell Sroge Publishing, Inc.
731 N. Cascade Ave.
Colorado Springs, CO 80903
(303) 633-5556

Mail Order Moonlighting, which contains 125 stories of what works, how to do it, and a detailed list of 900 books, tapes, newsletters, seminars, and articles on selling by mail, is available from the following source.

Ten-Speed Press
P.O. Box 7123
900 Modock St.
Berkeley, CA 94707
(415) 845-8414

John Jay Daly Associates has prepared a series of booklets and other information on various types of services offered to businesspeople. One such booklet is *Twenty-Four Principles of Direct Marketing*. It covers the various types of direct-mail and direct-marketing techniques. Another booklet is titled *108 Questions to Ask When Planning an Event*.

> Daly Associates, Inc.
> World Center Bldg., Ste. 702
> 918-16th St., N.W.
> Washington, DC 20006
> (202) 659-2925

Friday Report is a weekly newsletter-type publication of direct-marketing information.

> *Friday Report*
> Henry R. Hoke, Jr., Publisher
> Hoke Communications, Inc.
> 224 Seventh St.
> Garden City, NY 11530
> (516) 746-6700

Catalog Age Publishing Corporation produces a major catalog for direct marketing.

> Charles F. Tanner, Publisher
> Catalog Age Publishing Corp.
> Six River Bend
> P.O. Box 4949
> Stamford, CT 66907-0949

DM News is a tabloid newspaper for direct mail/marketing industry.

> Ray Schultz, Editor
> *DM News*
> 19 W. 21st St.
> New York, NY 10010
> (212) 741-2905

TESTING YOUR HUNCHES

If you've got enough money, a market-research firm will tell you which women in Dallas wear red shoes with spiked heels on Thursdays, how many pairs they are likely to buy during the second week of February 1988, and how much they'll pay for them. But for small businesses with tight budgets, "market research" usually amounts to little more than an entrepreneur's gut feeling that his product will sell.

In the competitive business world, however, playing a mere hunch is far too risky. Entrepreneurs need substantial data about the appeal of their products to make informed marketing decisions. Three marketing techniques will provide that essential market information at a very low cost.

1. Space advertising: Many entrepreneurs test the waters for new products and services by placing ads in regional editions of magazines and newspapers. The simplest (and cheapest) approach is to compose the ad yourself, although most publications will help you design it for a small fee. The ad must be large enough (at least one-quarter page) to include four essential elements: a block of text, a picture, a caption, and, of course, an order form.

The text is your sales pitch. Explain the benefits your product will bring to the buyer: "Save money!" "Relax!" "Save time!" The picture illustrates what the buyer will receive, and, more important, it draws his attention to the accompanying caption, which restates the benefits you've outlined in the text and makes your strongest sales pitch. If you include an 800 number with the order form, your response rate will greatly increase.

Joe Sugarman, president of JS&A National Sales, a mail-order company in Northbrook, Illinois, is a firm believer in this technique. The key to an accurate test, he says, is locating publications with active readers: people who are willing to fill out order forms and dial 800 numbers. "Look for publications that carry a lot of mail-order ads," he says. "That indicates that other entrepreneurs are having success."

2. Direct mail: Once considered a slightly sleazy, plain-brown-wrapper business, direct mail has come a long way in recent years. Essentially, it's an inexpensive way to reach target markets. Using list brokers, you can locate people who would be most interested in your product. Clubs and trade associations rent membership lists. Specialty magazines rent subscription lists. You might even be able to rent the customer lists of your top competitors.

A simple but effective direct-mail package includes a number-ten business envelope, a two-color flier, and a one-page letter introducing your product. Avoid lavish prose, just explain the benefits. Consider using a copy of your print ad for a flier. A 5,000-piece mailing will provide accurate results and will cost about $2,500. For a few cents more per letter, you can enclose a business-reply envelope and greatly increase your response.

3. Distributors: National distributors won't invest in a large quantity of your product if you have no sales record. You might have a shot, however, if you approach regional companies that sometimes take small quantities of new products on consignment. Work backward to locate possible distributors: Find retailers who sell products like yours and ask which distributors they use.

Once you've found a willing company, you can create a demand for your product by placing print ads in local shopping guides and newspapers. You might even want to purchase time on a regional radio station.

Don't be discouraged by early test-market results. You may have to run three or four tests before you hit pay dirt. But once you find your market, you can use the test data to accurately predict the response that a full-scale campaign will generate. Sugarman, for instance, says his margin of error is only 5 percent. "The results of the product rollout," he says, "more than cover the cost of the market tests."

Manufacturers' Agents and Representatives

ASSOCIATIONS

The Direct Selling Association provides assistance for home-based salespeople, focusing on door-to-door selling.

Direct Selling Association
1776 K St., N.W., Ste. 600
Washington, DC 20006
(202) 293-5760

Founded in 1947, the Manufacturers' Agents National Association, an association of manufacturers' representatives, has about 10,000 members. The organization publishes *Agency Sales,* a monthly magazine.

James J. Gibbons, Pres.
Manufacturers' Agents National Association
P.O. Box 3467
Laguna Hills, CA 02654
(714) 859-4040

An association of industrial and consumer products manufacturers' agents, the United Association of Manufacturers' Representatives publishes a monthly bulletin for its members.

Keith Kittrell, Dir.
United Association of Manufacturers' Representatives
P.O. Drawer 6266
Kansas City, KS 66106
(913) 268-9466

An association of manufacturers' agents for electrical manufacturers, the National Electrical Manufacturers' Representatives Association has a membership that includes about 800 representatives and 250 manufacturers.

National Electrical Manufacturers' Representatives Association
222 W. Chester Ave., Ste. 330
White Plains, NY 10604
(914) 428-1307

A group of about 2,300 manufacturers' agents who serve the electronics industry, the Electronic Representatives Association is an excellent source of books and seminars.

Electronic Representatives Association
20 E. Huron St.
Chicago, IL 60611
(312) 649-1333

MISCELLANEOUS SERVICES

The Manufacturers Representative Educational Research Foundation supports academic research projects on the use of manufacturers' representatives, such as case studies at business schools.

Marilyn Stevens
Manufacturers Representative Educational Research Foundation
P.O. Box 8541
Rolling Meadows, IL 60008
(312) 991-8500

Representative Resources, Inc. is a specialized firm which helps manufacturers locate representatives.

Representative Resources, Inc.
P.O. Box Drawer A
Thorndale, PA 19372
(215) 383-1177

PUBLICATIONS

An advertisement in the *Manufacturers' Agents Newsletter* reaches both agents and manufacturers in the United States and Canada. You can let them know who you are, where you are, and what territories you cover or wish to cover.

Manufacturers' Agents Newsletter
23573 Prospect Ave.
Farmington, MI 48024
(313) 474-7383

Albee Campbell, a good source for industrial original equipment manufacturers, publishes *Rep World,* a quarterly newsletter.

Albee Campbell
806 Pennsylvania Ave.
Sinking Springs, PA 19608
(215) 678-3361

The National Council of Salesman's Organizations offers an excellent directory.

National Council of Salesman's Organizations
255 Broadway
New York, NY 10007
(212) 349-1707

DON'T COMPLAIN: COME UP WITH THREE SOLUTIONS

When the bottom fell out of the domestic petroleum industry, oil producers were not the only people who got hurt. Businesses manufacturing products used in exploration and refining suddenly found that their markets, which had risen so precipitously, were declining at an alarming rate. One of the companies that felt the pinch was Magnetrol International, a manufacturer of industrial instrumentation based in Downers Grove, Illinois, which was founded in 1932 to manufacture boiler controls.

The word *Magnetrol* has become an almost generic term used in industry circles for magnetic level and flow controls. But in recent years, the company's growth (sales are about $23 million) has come to a virtual standstill. As her competitors have watched their sales decline, or have been swallowed up by larger companies, Judy Stevenson, Magnetrol's president, has been looking for ways to get her company back on the growth track.

One solution has been to develop products for a more diversified market. "We want to be a part of an industry that's growing, not one that's going down," explained Stevenson. Among other things, Magnetrol has developed new products for use in waste-water treatment, as well as an ultrasonic device for measuring dry-bulk storage. But new products in industrial markets are often a "long sell." So Stevenson started a reevaluation of Magnetrol's traditional market, looking for new voids to fill. And the void she found concerned the overall effectiveness of her sales representatives (reps) in a changing market.

The company currently uses 63 different sales-rep firms (about 300 sales reps, altogether) to cover the U.S. market. The past practice had been to employ two regional sales managers to coordinate and work with the reps. But as Magnetrol's products have become more sophisticated, more "high-tech," Stevenson has observed that the reps can't give the customers the service they need. "We had a real scare when customers called and said a new product didn't work," she said. "We brought the products back and found that they worked fine. They just hadn't been installed correctly." She also found that, even if Magnetrol's instruction manuals were well written, they still didn't solve all the problems. Her customers needed hands-on help.

Stevenson considered going to direct sales—developing her own sales force, which would be willing and able to spend more time with each customer. But in the end, she decided it wasn't practical for Magnetrol. "We're not a sales company, and we decided we didn't want to be a sales company," Stevenson explained, adding, "I'm a firm believer in doing what you do best. What the reps do best is selling. What we do best are engineering and manufacturing."

She still had an important void to fill. If Magnetrol was to hold on to its traditional customer base, and perhaps to grab some business from the competition, the company would have to make an extra effort to keep its customers satisfied. Stevenson, now 49 years old, is an old hand at filling voids. Hired by Magnetrol in 1964 as a part-time bookkeeper, she discovered there was a void in the accounting department. Within three months, she became the department's manager. Eighteen months later, she was promoted to treasurer. As she continued to find and fill important voids in the company, she continued to move up. In 1975, Stevenson was named as the company's president, and in 1978, she bought out the previous owner. When faced with a problem, her philosophy is, "Don't complain. Come up with three solutions." So it goes without saying that when her customers needed help, she came up with a solution.

Stevenson decided to expand from two regional sales managers to six traveling sales managers. The sales managers (compensated with salary and bonus, but no commissions) don't do any actual selling. They provide a support service for the reps, visiting customers before the rep makes a call and making sure the customers understand the advantages of Magnetrol's new lines and products. The rep then comes in to make the sale, and the managers come back to do the follow-up. Of course, the managers aren't needed for every sale, but when they're needed, they're available. "Many of the smaller companies we sell to don't have large technical staffs," explained Stevenson. "We have to fill that void for them."

Early signs show that the plan is already working. And by the end of the year, when Magnetrol has all six traveling sales managers in the field, Stevenson will be able to get a clear picture as to whether that void has been filled. And if it hasn't, you can bet that she won't complain. She'll just come up with three more solutions.

WHAT TO LOOK FOR IN A SALES REPRESENTATIVE

Sales reps offer entrepreneurial companies an effective way to build sales and increase market penetration. But getting the most out of a sales rep means starting out right—with a rep who's a perfect match for your company's product.

Although each firm has its own requirements for selling its products or services, the following criteria can be applied to sales-rep searches in any type of firm:

Customer base. The sales rep should currently be selling to the same customers that the company wants to reach with its products.

Territory. The sales rep's current territory should include markets the company would like to enter or develop.

Compatibility. The sales rep should be selling a product line that is compatible, but not competitive, with the company's products.

Style. The sales rep's selling style must match the company's style. For example, if the firm's strongest selling point is state-of-the-art technology, the sales rep's selling style should complement this strength. A selling style that promotes low price would be unacceptable.

Lead time. The lead time between when orders are generated and when the company pays commissions should be similar to the lead time required for the sales rep's current accounts. For example, a firm selling capital equipment for long-term projects would not select a sales rep accustomed to receiving quick commissions.

Financial status. The sales rep's financial status must be compatible with the turnaround time on commissions.

Staff size. When considering a sales-rep agency, the agency's staff size should match the company's potential demands in terms of product lines, territory size, and market density.

Personal drive. Sales reps must be self-motivated.

Continuity and tenure. Reps should have several years of service with their client base. Look for minimum turnover when dealing with an agency.

High standards. Sales reps should possess high ethical and professional standards.

Chemistry. Personal chemistry may be a hard thing to define, but it is crucial to a company's relationship with its sales reps.

Marketing and Selling

This chapter offers sources of marketing information that fall into several categories: marketing directories and publications, organizations that exist to help the entrepreneur with the marketing function, and marketing research agencies.

The directories listed in this chapter offer statistics and information of markets and market sizes. In addition, SBA offers a guidebook titled *Library Sources for Information that You May Want to Look At,* which lists many of the marketing directories. It is available at any of the regional SBA offices. Your local library will be helpful in locating marketing directories for you. College libraries should be investigated as well.

The organizations and publications listed in this chapter can be helpful in either selling your product or in understanding how your product is sold. On the premise that all entrepreneurial problems will vanish if you sell enough of your product at the right price, these journals and organizations focus on how to expand your sales. You should also examine other marketing categories and marketing information available from manufacturers' representatives.

Several national agencies specialize in marketing research for small companies. These agencies and informational sources are listed in this chapter. They provide information on an industry-by-industry basis to help you to locate a specific source of help within your industry. (This information is particularly vital to the new-product decision process.)

ASSOCIATIONS

The American Marketing Association has 68 local chapters, mostly in larger cities, and offers conferences, seminars, and a wide range of services to marketing professionals. It is one of the most broadly based and wide-ranging associations with 233 collegiate chapters. Several publications are produced.

American Marketing Association
250 S. Wacker Dr., Ste. 200
Chicago, IL 60606
(312) 648-0536

The Direct Marketing Association is a very good source of mail-order marketing information.

Direct Marketing Association
6 E. 43d St.
New York, NY 10017
(212) 689-4977

MISCELLANEOUS SERVICES

Standard Rate and Data Service (SRDS) is one of the fundamental services for the advertising industry because it provides all of the information necessary for placing advertisements. SRDS also offers market data summaries and Standard Metropolitan Statistical Area (SMSA) rankings.

Standard Rate & Data Service, Inc.
3004 Glenview Rd.
Wilmette, IL 60091
(312) 256-6067

Washington Researchers, Ltd. teaches companies how to gather competitor intelligence by using legal and ethical methods. Competitor intelligence training, guidebooks, and customized studies especially effective for government information are available.

Washington Researchers, Ltd.
2612 P St., N.W.
Washington, DC 20007
(202) 333-3499

PUBLICATIONS

Dun & Bradstreet's *Million Dollar Directory* contains marketing information on approximately 45,000 businesses, each with a net worth of $1 million or more.

Dun & Bradstreet
99 Church St.
New York, NY 10007
(212) 285-7000

The *Guide to American Directories* is a comprehensive directory of directories. Indexing is by name, and directory listings are broken down by industry and associated categories. Klein Publishing also offers an excellent mail-order directory.

B. Klein Publishing Inc.
P.O. Box 8503
Coral Springs, FL 33065
(305) 752-1708

Sales & Marketing Management Magazine, published 16 times per year, provides estimates for populations, effective buying income, and retail sales for U.S. states, counties, and cities, as well as per capita and per household incomes. It is also the best source of marketing maps.

Sales & Marketing Management Magazine
Bill Communications
633 Third Ave.
New York, NY 10017
(212) 986-4800

Rand McNally is an excellent source of maps of all kinds, including marketing and manufacturing.

Rand McNally
8255 N. Central Park Ave.
Skokie, IL 60076
(312) 673-9100

Folio, published by a subsidiary of the Hanson Publishing Group, is devoted to magazine management. Each issue provides marketing data for specialty markets.

Folio
Folio Publishing
P.O. Box 4949
6 River Bend
Stamford, CT 06907
(203) 358-9900

The Zig Ziglar Corporation is an excellent source of books and tapes on selling. Consulting services are also available.

The Zig Ziglar Corp.
3330 Earhart Dr., Ste. 204
Carrollton, TX 75006
(214) 233-9191

Hoke Communications publishes two excellent resources, the *Friday Report* and *Direct Marketing Magazine.*

Hoke Communications
224 Seventh St.
Garden City, NY 11530
(516) 746-6700

WHAT BUSINESS ARE YOU REALLY IN?

It's often said that if you don't know where you're going, any road will take you there. And nowhere is this more apparent than in small business.

Although no one knows for sure what makes one business strategy work and another fail, it's often assumed that the companies that succeed have better strategies than the ones that fail. Consequently, when I counsel entrepreneurs on developing long-term strategies, I offer advice on how to avoid ineffective strategies, as well as how to identify the one right road to take.

Corporate strategies are usually set by groups of executives whose principal job is to monitor the thousands of variables that go into any business decision. In a smaller venture, however, making strategy is the exclusive responsibility of the entrepreneur. The entrepreneur is like the lead dog in a sled team, accepting an unobstructed view of what lies ahead in addition to the responsibility for establishing the correct course. Only he can determine the direction of the business.

Don't confuse short-term strategies with long-term strategies. Short-term strategies aren't really strategies at all; they're more like tactics. Long-term strategies answer the fundamental question: "What business am I in?"

Consider, by way of analogy, a computer. It will never lose a game of checkers, even when playing the world's greatest checker player. That's because checkers is a game of tactics, not of strategies. A computer has the capacity to handle the finite number of moves necessary to constitute a tactic; therefore, it can be programmed to always gain at least a draw.

But in the more complex game of chess, a chess master can often beat the most sophisticated computer. Computers still are unable to outthink the chess master at all of the levels necessary to develop an effective winning strategy. A computer, by definition, is limited to a redundant step-by-step pattern of reasoning, and there are literally thousands of variables to consider before a single move can be made on the chessboard, and that's before the strategy even begins. Computers are still unable to make the intuitive leaps that the human mind is capable of. And long-term strategies require not only solidly reasoned projections, but also intuitive leaps. An entrepreneur must answer the question "What business am I in?" before attempting to formulate a long-term strategy.

Coke's Secret

Let's look at some examples. In the late 1920s, the leading manufacturer of soft drinks was Moxie, a Boston-based company. Its share of the market was larger than that of Coca-Cola. But Moxie determined that it was in the business of marketing "herblike" soft drinks; Coca-Cola assumed a broader-based marketing strategy. Moxie, today headquartered near Atlanta, still sells several million dollars' worth of its unusual drink annually; Coca-Cola has long since become an international giant. Why didn't Moxie hold on to a larger share of the market? Because Moxie's answer to the question "What business am I in?" was much too narrow.

The railroad industry took the same approach as Moxie. As Theodore Levitt, a professor of marketing at the Harvard Business School, puts it, "The problem with the railroad industry was that it defined its mission too narrowly." Its owners answered the question of what business they were in with one word: *railroads.* A sounder choice would have been "the transportation industry." The lead dogs didn't see the course was changing, and they wound up in the snowbank, where they remain today.

In another case, when deregulation came to the airline industry, two similar airlines, Braniff and Continental, chose to confront the situation very differently. Braniff expanded its routes and tried to grab a bigger market share. What it failed to observe was that the expanding share of the market wasn't at the high end. It was at the low end, with the new airlines like People's Express. And that failure to respond to the changes in the market cost Braniff dearly.

Continental saw right away that if it was to survive, it would have to cut costs drastically and come in at the low end. The new airlines springing up in the wake of deregulation were able to attract customers on price alone, because they weren't saddled with costly union contracts. Continental saw that the only way to survive was to bite the bullet and bite it hard. It eliminated the union contracts by filing

Chapter 11 and repositioned itself as a low-cost carrier. When faced with a new and changing set of circumstances, Continental saw that it couldn't continue to give the same answer to the question "What business am I in?" It had to adapt.

Braniff has continued to compound its troubles since its reorganization. When it reentered the market, it came back with the same "me too" marketing plan that had been used before. In answer to the question "What business am I in?" its response was, "The same business as American Airlines." Despite past difficulties, it continued to view the low-cost strategy only as a fallback position. But now that it has fallen back on the low-cost strategy to attract a market, the public really doesn't know what business Braniff is in, or even if it's still in business. Consumers just can't handle that kind of corporate transition.

The typewriter business of the early 1950s provides another noteworthy example. The major companies in the business were Olivetti Typewriter, Underwood Typewriter, Royal Typewriter, and International Business Machines (IBM). The difference in how each answered the question "What business am I in?" was reflected in the names of the companies. And over the past 30 years, the difference between the typewriter business and the business-machine business has turned out to be substantial. IBM positioned itself in the international business market and set out to capture it. Today, IBM continues to hold an edge in the office typewriter market, but typewriters are only a small part of its total business. The other companies wound up with small shares of only the typewriter market.

The point is that a commitment to marketing is essential in any business, small or large. And that commitment must be one that permeates the entire organization. All too often, an entrepreneur assumes that marketing falls under the heading of selling and advertising. In fact, it's the other way around. Selling and advertising are key elements in a marketing plan, but on their own they are only tactics. And with tactics alone, entrepreneurs may win the early battles (as Moxie did with Coke), but wind up losing the war. The following five steps can help entrepreneurs in mapping out a total marketing strategy:

1. Define the target market area(s).
2. Research the customers' needs.
3. Develop and/or redevelop the product or service to meet the customers' needs.
4. Recruit and/or train personnel to deliver effectively the product/service to the defined marketplace.
5. Develop the necessary sales approach and advertising support.

Adapt to the Market

Above all, marketing plans must be flexible. Observe the way Continental adapted to the changing marketplace. And just as every young man must wrangle with the question "Who am I?" the entrepreneur must wrangle with the question "What business am I in?" Although conventional wisdom dictates that entrepreneurs should always go with their strengths, the very act of developing a marketing plan can help to define those strengths. Without this exercise, strengths and weaknesses will not always be apparent. The strength of the railroad industry was its iron grip on the transportation industry. Its weakness was its inflexibility.

In order to succeed, a marketing strategy must not only define today's market but also be able to anticipate and adapt to future markets. So the question "What business am I in?" cannot be answered once. It must be answered continuously in a process that will help to keep the business operating and to open doors to future opportunities.

FINDING A MARKET NICHE

Think small—that's the advice I've often given to entrepreneurs. By finding an area of the market that has been ignored because it seems too small, you can often carve out a profitable niche for yourself with a minimum of marketing effort and expense. What are some secrets to identifying and exploiting market niches?

Look for a market that's growing rapidly and try to identify a portion of it that's being neglected. For example, one of the fastest-growing markets in the United States today is videotape rentals. In New York City alone, hundreds of video stores have sprung up in the past few years. Ninety percent of the VCRs currently being sold are VHS, so hundreds of entrepreneurs are slugging it out for a share of that market. However, 10 percent of the VCRs are Beta, and this market is underserviced. A "Beta Only" store (and as far as I can tell, no such thing currently exists in New York City) offers a doubly inviting niche: The market is out there just waiting to be tapped, and it's small enough that one or two outlets could easily control it without inviting competition.

Defining the market is crucial. I can't tell you how often someone has told me the potential market for his product idea was "every man, woman, and child." The funny thing is, I've never seen one of these products make it to market. The problem is that the market hasn't been defined. It's better to find an existing need and fill it. For example, Tom Drewes, president of Quality Books in Lake Bluff, Illinois, has done just that. His company distributes books by small publishers to the library market. "Libraries are a $2-billion market," Drewes says, "and most of that market is covered by the large wholesalers and the publishers themselves." Drewes estimates that as little as *one-tenth of 1 percent* of sales to libraries are small press books. That's a mighty small niche, but it's worth millions a year to his company. And "while the publishing market is growing incrementally," Drewes says, "our company is growing like wildfire. Sales have gone up 20 percent and profits have increased 100 percent in the last year."

Price alone isn't a niche. If all you offer is a cheap price, then someone else is going to come along and knock you off. Consider the personal-computer market. A quick glance at any computer magazine will show you that there are dozens of mail-order companies selling no-name IBM PC clones at rock-bottom prices. Twenty small companies competing for the low end of the market hardly qualifies as finding a niche.

Once you've got a niche, service the hell out of it. When you've got a good niche, you'll get business just by being there. But if you don't do a good job, your customers might be willing to look elsewhere. On the other hand, if you service it well, you might find yourself with a permanent niche.

Here's Drewes's approach: "We listen to our customers. We sell millions of books—one at a time. That requires patience and hard work, and maybe that's why no one else has come into the market to compete with us directly."

Be aware of your product's life cycle. There are four phases in the life of a product or a service: start-up, growth, maturity, and decline. At the start-up phase the market hasn't yet developed, so the chance of finding a viable niche is limited. In the growth stage the market is blossoming with niches. When the market reaches the mature stage, the niches tend to diminish. But niches sometimes reappear when a product's life cycle begins its decline. In fact, they occur whenever significant change occurs in the market structure.

Don't get too comfortable. A successful niche doesn't always last forever. Markets change, as do customers' needs and attitudes. Keep your eye on your own market, and on other markets, for opportunities. And be prepared to make changes if you see the market beginning to dwindle. One percent of a thriving market can be very profitable; 5 percent of a fading market can leave you awash in red ink.

Minority-Owned Businesses

ASSOCIATIONS AND AGENCIES

Minority Enterprise Small Business Investment Companies (MESBICs) provide venture capital to minority-owned small businesses. Lists of the 140 MESBICs are available at SBA branch and district offices, or from the following source.

Office of Investment
Small Business Administration
1441 L St., N.W., Eighth Floor
Washington, DC 20416
(202) 653-6584

A listing of all MESBICs is also available through the National Association of Investment Companies, which provides assistance to minority-owned businesses.

National Association of Investment Companies
915 15th St., N.W., Ste. 700
Washington, DC 20005
(202) 347-8600

The Minority Business Development Agency provides management, marketing, and technical assistance to new and developing minority-owned businesses. They can also provide help in obtaining procurement and construction contracts.

Director's Office
Minority Business Development Agency
U.S. Department of Commerce, Rm. 5053
Washington, DC 20230
(202) 377-3163

The U.S. Hispanic Chamber of Commerce represents the interests of 400,000 businesses; it has 200 chapters nationwide. Publications are also available.

U.S. Hispanic Chamber of Commerce
4900 Main St.
Kansas City, MO 64112
(816) 531-6363

Started in 1900 by Booker T. Washington, the black educator-writer, the National Business League is the oldest organization devoted to promoting minority causes in Congress. A business development lobby, small-business assistance, and publications, such as *The Corporate Guide to Minority Vendors,* are available.

National Business League
4324 Georgia Ave., N.W.
Washington, DC 20011
(202) 829-5900

The Bureau of Indian Affairs makes loans available to Indians on federal reservations to start or acquire businesses, or to expand existing businesses. It is also a good
source for information on minority-owned businesses.

Director
Office of Tribal Resources Development
Bureau of Indian Affairs
18th & C Sts., N.W., Rm. 4513
Washington, DC 20245
(202) 343-3600
(202) 343-3657

MISCELLANEOUS SERVICES

The National Minority Supplier Development Council will supply addresses, phone
numbers, and contacts for its local councils to minority entrepreneurs who contact
its main office in New York.

Alphonso Whitfield, Jr.
National Minority Supplier Development Council
1412 Broadway, 11th Floor
New York, NY 10018
(212) 944-2430

A nonprofit organization, the National Minority Business Directory publishes directories and booklets for minority-owned businesses.

National Minority Business Directory
65-22d Ave.
Minneapolis, MN 55418
(612) 781-6819

The Minority Business Exchange is a database that contains more than 10,000
minority suppliers.

Wendell L. Crosswhite
Minority Business Exchange
Univex, Inc.
One Madison Ave.
New York, NY 10010
(212) 684-7722

PUBLICATIONS

Black Enterprise is the most influential business magazine for black and minority business owners and executives. It sponsors a Minority Business Institute Library, which is an excellent resource. Circulation is more than 236,000.

> Earl Graves, Publisher
> *Black Enterprise*
> 130 Fifth Ave.
> New York, NY 10011
> (212) 242-8000

Samuel D. Ewing and Clifton H. Maloney are the authors of *Minority Capital Resource Handbook: A Guide to Raising Capital for Minority Entrepreneurs.* Contact the following source for more information.

> Securities Industry Minority Capital Formation
> 490 L'Enfant Plaza East, S.W.
> Washington, DC 20024

A free, two-volume guide providing technical assistance to minority business entrepreneurs interested in the energy industry is available from the National Minority Energy Information Clearinghouse. The publication focuses on new product development, market research, finance, commercialization, and marketing. Additional information in *The Guide* applies to residential, commercial, industrial, and transportation sectors of the energy industry.

> National Minority Energy Information Clearinghouse
> Office of Minority Economic Impact
> U.S. Department of Energy
> Washington, DC 20805
> (202) 252-5876

DIRECTORY OF MINORITY BUSINESS DEVELOPMENT AGENCY OFFICES

Established in the U.S. Department of Commerce by Executive Order 11458 in 1969, and expanded by Executive Order 11625 in 1971, the Minority Business Development Agency (MBDA) promotes and encourages business ownership by minorities. Originally known as the Office of Minority Business Enterprise, it was renamed in 1979 and redirected in support of larger minority-owned firms in growth industries.

MBDA coordinates and monitors support for minority-owned businesses in the public and private sectors, and sponsors a national network of Minority Business Development Centers (MBDCs) offering management counseling to minority entrepreneurs. The centers receive operating funds from MBDA and report client services to MBDA.

MBDC counselors advise minority owners in areas such as marketing, accounting, personnel management, and business training. They help owners to secure government and private procurement contracts and to assemble financial packages for submission to lenders. MBDA itself does not make loans. Business services are offered for a nominal fee to current operators of minority-owned businesses and to those considering starting a business.

Executive Order 11625 defines a minority business enterprise as follows:

> "Minority business enterprise" means a business enterprise that is owned or controlled by one or more socially or economically disadvantaged persons. Such disadvantage may arise from cultural, racial, chronic economic circumstances or background or other similar cause. Such persons include, but are not limited to, Negroes, Puerto Ricans, Spanish-speaking Americans, American Indians, Eskimos, and Aleuts.

Contact the following source for more information.

U.S. Department of Commerce
Minority Business Development Agency
Information Clearinghouse, Rm. 6708
Washington, DC 20230
(202) 377-2414

REGIONAL OFFICES

Xavier Mena, Dir.
San Francisco Regional MBDA
  Office
221 Main St., 12th Floor
San Francisco, CA 94105
(415) 974-9597
FTS-454-9597*
(Alaska, American Samoa, Arizona, California, Hawaii, Idaho, Nevada, Oregon, Washington)

Willie Williams, Dir.
Washington Regional MBDA Office
14th & Constitution Ave., N.W., Rm. 6711
Washington, DC 20230
(202) 377-8275
FTS-377-8275
(Delaware, Maryland, Pennsylvania, Virginia, Washington, DC, West Virginia)

Carlton Eccles, Dir.
Atlanta Regional MBDA Office
1371 Peachtree St., N.E., Ste. 505
Atlanta, GA 30309
(404) 347-4091
FTS-257-4091
(Alabama, Florida, Georgia, Kentucky, Mississippi, North Carolina, South Carolina, Tennessee)

David Vega, Dir.
Chicago Regional MBDA Office
55 E. Monroe St., Ste. 1440
Chicago, IL 60603
(312) 353-0182
FTS 353-0182
(Illinois, Indiana, Iowa, Kansas, Michigan, Minnesota, Missouri, Nebraska, Ohio, Wisconsin)

Georgina A. Sanchez, Dir.
New York Regional MBDA Office
26 Federal Plaza, Rm. 3720
New York, NY 10278
(212) 264-3262
FTS-264-3262
(Connecticut, Maine, Massachusetts, New Hampshire, New Jersey, Puerto Rico, Rhode Island, Vermont, Virgin Islands)

Melda Cabrera, Acting Dir.
Dallas Regional MBDA Office
1100 Commerce St., Rm. 7B19
Dallas, TX 75242
(214) 767-8001
FTS-729-8001
(Arkansas, Colorado, Louisiana, Montana, New Mexico, North Dakota, South Dakota, Oklahoma, Texas, Utah, Wyoming)

*FTS stands for Federal Telephone System.

DISTRICT OFFICES

Rudy Guerra
Joseph Galindo
District Officers
2500 Wilshire Blvd., Ste. 908
Los Angeles, CA 90057
(213) 688-7157
FTS-798-7157

Rudy Suarez, District Officer
Federal Office Bldg., Rm. 930
51 S.W. First Ave.
Miami, FL 33130
(305) 350-5054
FTS-350-5054

R. K. Schwartz, District Officer
10 Causeway St., Rm. 418
Boston, MA 02222-1041
(617) 565-6850
FTS-835-6850

Alfonso C. Jackson, District
  Officer
Federal Office Bldg.,
  Rm. 9436
600 Arch St.
Philadelphia, PA 19106
(215) 597-9236
FTS-597-9236

STATE AND LOCAL OFFICES

Rose Newsome, Project Dir.
City of Phoenix
Equal Opportunity Department
251 W. Washington, 3d Floor
Phoenix, AZ 85003-2299
(602) 262-7716

Elizabeth A. Moore, Project Dir.
City of San Diego
202 C St., M.S.9A
San Diego, CA 92101
(619) 236-6945

Adelbert L. Campbell, Project Dir.
City of San Francisco State & Local Govern-
  ment
City Hall, Rm. 284
San Francisco, CA 94102
(415) 554-6748

Elaine T. Williams, Project Dir.
City of Hartford State & Local Government
Finance Department
550 Main St.
Hartford, CT 06103
(203) 722-6608

Bob Revelle, Project Dir.
City of Wilmington
City County Bldg.
800 French St., 5th Floor

Wilmington, DE 19801
(302) 571-4323

Lamar Green, Project Dir.
State of Illinois
Small Business Assistance Bureau
100 W. Randolph St., Ste. 3-400
Chicago, IL 60601
(312) 917-3263

David H. Swanson, Project Dir.
Iowa State University
205 Engineering Annex
Ames, IA 50011
(515) 294-3420

Bill McCray, Project Dir.
Kansas Department of Economic Development
Capitol Towers
400 W. Eighth St., 5th Floor
Topeka, KS 66603-3957
(913) 296-3583

Dennis C. Brownlee, Project Dir.
Prince George's County Government
County Administration Bldg., Rm. L-22
Upper Marlboro, MD 20772
(301) 952-4413

Otha Burton, Acting Dir.
City of Jackson
201 S. President St.

P.O. Box 17
Jackson, MS 39205
(601) 960-1594

Mark Miller, Dir.
State of Missouri/MBDO
Truman State Office Bldg.
301 W. High St.
P.O. Box 809
Jefferson City, MO 65102
(314) 751-2249

Kenneth Johnson, Project Dir.
City of Omaha
Mayor's Office of Economic
  Development
1819 Farnam St., Ste. 304
Omaha, NE 68102
(402) 444-5036

Larry Hicks, Project Dir.
City of Atlantic City
City Hall, Rm. 706
Atlantic City, NJ 08401
(609) 347-6483

Borden R. Putnam, Commissioner
State of New Jersey
1 W. State St., CN823
Trenton, NJ 08625
(609) 292-2444

Steve Griego, Acting Dir.
New Mexico State MBDA
Joseph Montoya Bldg.
1100 St. Francis Dr., Rm. 2150
Santa Fe, NM 87503
(505) 827-0425

Jim Miles, Project Dir.
Oklahoma State MBDA
Oklahoma Department of Commerce
6601 Broadway Extension
Oklahoma City, OK 73116
(405) 521-2401

Elena Morgan, Project Dir.
City of Harrisburg
10 N. Market Sq.

Harrisburg, PA 17101
(717) 255-3027

Manuel Dones Piner, Project Dir.
Municipality of Ponce
City Hall
P.O. Box 1709
Ponce, PR 00731
(809) 840-4141

Sanoya Cruz, Project Dir.
Municipality of San Juan
Call Box 857
Hato Rey, PR 00919
(809) 756-5080

Juan Vicens, Project Dir.
Chamber of Commerce of Ponce
Franchise Ownership Development
  Program
10 Salud St., Ste. 512
Ponce, PR 00731
(809) 844-4400

Dr. Tonia Richardson, Dir.
City of Charleston
701 E. Bay St., Ste. 301
Charleston, SC 29403
(803) 723-9600

Dana Nelson, Project Dir.
South Dakota State MBDA
Government Operations
State Capitol Bldg.
500 E. Capitol
Pierre, SD 57501
(605) 773-3661

Troy Lynn, Project Dir.
City of Nashville
1001 Stahlman Bldg.
Nashville, TN 37201
(615) 259-6581

Ricardo Gomez, Project Dir.
City of San Juan
709 S. Nebraska
San Juan, TX 78589
(512) 787-9923

TRADE ASSOCIATION OFFICES

Richard L. McCline, Exec. Pres.
Golden State Business League, Inc.
333 Hegenberger Rd., Ste. 315
Oakland, CA 94621
(415) 635-5900

Malcolm R. LaPlace II, Project Dir.
National Association of Blacks
654 13th St.
Oakland, CA 94612
(415) 451-9231

Gloria Valencia, Project Dir.
The Mexican & American Foundation, Inc.
1446 Front St., Ste. 200
San Diego, CA 92101
(619) 232-1010

Irma Burks, Project Dir.
American Association of Community and
    Junior Colleges
One Dupont Circle, Ste. 410
Washington, DC 20036
(202) 293-7050

Benjamin Maynigo, Project Dir.
Asian Pacific American Chamber of Com-
    merce
1118 22d St., N.W., Ste. 300
Washington, DC 20037
(202) 659-4037

Linda L. Lee, Pres.
Coalition of Minority Women in Business
624 H St., N.W.
Washington, DC 20001
(202) 393-1375

Tom Mcclimon, Dir.
Conference of Mayors Research & Education
    Foundation
Institute of Urban & Regional Economic
    Analysis
1620 Eye St., N.W., 4th Floor
Washington, DC 20006
(202) 293-7330

Jose Antonio Font, Pres.
Greater Washington Ibero-American
2100 M St., N.W., Ste. 607

Washington, DC 20037
(202) 296-0335

Stephen Denlinger, Pres.
Latin American Manufacturers Association
419 New Jersey Ave., S.E.
Washington, DC 20003
(202) 546-3803

Ralph Thomas, Exec. Dir.
National Association of Minority Contrac-
    tors
806 15th St., N.W., Ste. 340
Washington, DC 20005
(202) 347-8259

John P. Kelly, Jr., Pres.
National Bankers Association
122 C St., N.W., Ste. 240
Washington, DC 20001
(202) 783-3200

Nancy Brailsford, Exec. Dir.
National Business League
4324 Georgia Ave., N.W.
Washington, DC 20011
(202) 829-5900

Ana C. O'Brien, Pres.
National Council of Hispanic Women
815 C St., S.E.
P.O. Box 1655
Washington, DC 20003
(202) 639-8823
(202) 789-3718

Sybil Mobley, Dean
Florida A&M University
College of Business and Industry
Tallahassee, FL 32307
(904) 599-3589

Cassandra Redd, Deputy Dir.
Cosmopolitan Chamber of Commerce
1326 S. Michigan Ave., Ste. 100
Chicago, IL 60605
(312) 786-0212

Edward C. Grant, Project Dir.
Neighborhood Development Collaborative
326 First St.

Annapolis, MD 21403
(301) 261-1787

Hanford Jones, Project Dir.
Maryland Minority Contractor's Association, Inc.
P.O. Box 1677
Baltimore, MD 21203
(301) 675-2149

Marcos Rincon, Exec. Dir.
United States Hispanic Chamber of Commerce
Board of Trade Center
4900 Main, Ste. 700
Kansas City, MO 64112
(816) 531-6363

William H. Bailey, Pres.
NEDCO Inc.
701 E. Bridger, Ste. 701
Las Vegas, NV 89101
(702) 384-3293

John Garcia, Pres
Albuquerque Hispano Chamber of Commerce
1520 Central, S.E.
Albuquerque, NM 87106
(505) 842-9003

Michael Nunez, Pres.
Bronx Venture Corp.
2804 Third Ave., Seventh Floor
Bronx, NY 10454
(212) 665-7170

Malcolm Corrin, Pres.
Interracial Council for Business
  Opportunity
800 Second Ave., Ste. 307
New York, NY 10017
(212) 599-0677

Alfonso Whitfield, Project Dir.
National Minority Supplier Development
  Council
1412 Broadway, 11th Floor

New York, NY 10018
(212) 944-2430

Luis E. Mora-Rechnitz, Acting Dir.
Spanish Merchants Association of
  Philadelphia, Inc.
2825 N. Fifth St.
Philadelphia, PA 19133
(215) 739-2915

Juan Vicens, Project Dir.
Chamber of Commerce of Ponce
10 Salud St., Ste. 512
Ponce, PR 00731
(809) 844-4400

Juan Woodroffe, Project Dir.
Caribbean Marketing Overseas Corp.
P.O. Box 6338
Loiza St. Station
Santurce, PR 00914
(809) 728-1240

Joe Morin, Exec. Dir.
Texas Association of Mexican American
  Chamber of Commerce
P.O. Box 3628
2211 S. IH35, Ste. 103
Austin, TX 78741
(512) 447-9821

John Charles, Procurement Specialist
South Texas Private Industry Council, Inc.
P.O. Box 1757
4217 N. Bartlett Ave.
Laredo, TX 78044-1757
(512) 722-3973

Tito Palacios, Pres.
Lower Rio Grande Valley Conference of
  Mayors
P.O. Box 744
Pharr, TX 78577
(512) 783-0711

Jude Valdez, Exec. Dir.
UTSA Center for Economic Development
University of Texas at San Antonio
San Antonio, TX 78285-0660
(512) 224-1945

MINORITY BUSINESS DEVELOPMENT CENTERS

Harold Gilchrist, Project Dir.
Birmingham MBDC
2000 First Ave. North, Ste. 722
Birmingham, AL 35203
(205) 252-3682

Tony Carter, Project Dir.
Mobile MBDC
4321 Downtowner Loop North, Ste. D
Mobile, AL 36609
(205) 344-9650

Bernell Mapp, Project Dir.
Montgomery MBDC
503 S. Court St., Ste. 210
Montgomery, AL 36104
(205) 263-0818

Francis Gallela, Project Dir.
Alaska MBDC
1011 E. Tudor Rd., Ste. 210
Anchorage, AK 99503
(907) 562-2322

Robert Franco, Project Dir.
Phoenix MBDC
5050 N. 19th Ave., Ste. 405
Phoenix, AZ 85015
(602) 433-0153

Lawrence P. Cooper, Project Dir.
American Indian Consultants MBDC
2070 E. Southern Ave.
Tempe, AZ 85282
(602) 945-2635

Nelson Bia, Project Dir.
Arizona Indian MBDC
2111 E. Baseline Rd., Ste. F-8
Tempe, AZ 85283
(602) 831-7524

Evelia M. Bierner, Project Dir.
Tucson MBDC
181 W. Broadway
Tucson, AZ 85701
(602) 629-9744

Lewis Cole, Project Dir.
Little Rock MBDC
One Riverfront Pl., Ste. 415

North Little Rock, AR 72114
(501) 372-7312

Andrew Delgado, Project Dir.
Anaheim MBDC
2700 N. Main St., Ste. 810
Santa Ana, CA 92701
(714) 667-8200

Manuel Lerma, Project Dir.
Bakersfield MBDC
1308 Chester Ave.
Bakersfield, CA 93301
(805) 328-1111

Walter Hare, Project Dir.
California Indian MBDC
9650 Flair Dr., Ste. 303
El Monte, CA 91731-3008
(818) 442-3701

Amer Makki, Project Dir.
Fresno MBDC
NEDA San Joaquin Valley
2010 N. Fine, Ste. 103
Fresno, CA 93727
(209) 252-7551

Philip Vasquez, Project Dir.
Los Angeles North MBDC
3460 Wilshire Blvd., Ste. 1006
Los Angeles, CA 90010
(213) 382-5032

Cleveland O. Neil, Project Dir.
Los Angeles South MBDC
3807 Wilshire Blvd., Ste. 700
Los Angeles, CA 90010-3108
(213) 380-9541

Victor Fontaine, Project Dir.
Oxnard MBDC
451 W. Fifth St.
Oxnard, CA 93030
(805) 483-1123

Charles West, Project Dir.
Riverside MBDC
3601 University Ave., Ste. 200
Riverside, CA 92501
(714) 788-9777

Melissa Cadet, Project Dir.
Sacramento MBDC
530 Bercut Dr., Ste. C
Sacramento, CA 95814
(916) 443-0700

Diane Skidmore, Project Dir.
Salinas MBDC
137 Central Ave., Ste. 1
Salinas, CA 93901
(408) 422-3701

Charles Shockley, Project Dir.
San Diego MBDC
6363 Alvarado Court, Rm. 225
San Diego, CA 92120
(619) 265-3684

Duane Okamoto, Project Dir.
San Francisco/Oakland MBDC
One California St., Ste. 2100
San Francisco, CA 94111
(415) 989-2920

Maria Acosta, Project Dir.
Santa Barbara MBDC
829 De La Vina, Ste. 300
Santa Barbara, CA 93101
(805) 564-2414

Martha Villarreal, Project Dir.
Stockton MBDC
37th W. Yokuts, Ste. C-4
Stockton, CA 95207
(209) 957-5721

Michael Juarez, Project Dir.
Denver/Colorado Springs MBDC
428 E. 11th Ave.
Denver, CO 80203
(303) 832-2228

Cynthia Cooper, Project Dir.
Connecticut MBDC
410 Asylum St., Ste. 243
Hartford, CT 06103
(203) 246-5371

Gabriel Santiago, Acting Project Dir.
Washington MBDC
4301 Connecticut Ave., N.W.
Third Floor, Ste. 136
Washington, DC 20008
(202) 362-3882

Jean Pettis, Project Dir.
Jacksonville MBDC
333 N. Laura St., Ste. 465
Jacksonville, FL 32202-3508
(904) 353-3826

Ricardo Martinez, Project Dir.
Miami/Fort Lauderdale MBDC
7925 N.W. 12th St., Ste. 117
Miami, FL 33126
(305)591-7355

Jack Perkins, Project Dir.
Orlando MBDC
132 E. Colonial Dr., Ste. 211
Orlando, FL 32801
(305) 422-6234

George Powell, Project Dir.
Tampa MBDC
315 E. Madison St.
Sun Bank Bldg., Ste. 617
Tampa, FL 33602
(813) 273-9145

Rodney Smith, Project Dir.
West Palm Beach MBDC
1675 Palm Beach Lakes Blvd.,
Tower A, Ste. 1002
West Palm Beach, FL 33401
(305) 683-4400

Charles Blackmon, Project Dir.
Atlanta MBDC
75 Piedmont Ave., N.E., Ste. 256
Atlanta, GA 30303
(404) 586-0973

Harvey Johnson, Project Dir.
Augusta MBDC
1208 Laney Walker Blvd.
P.O. Box 1283
Augusta, GA 30901
(404) 722-0994

Rudolph Quarterman, Project Dir.
Savannah MBDC
31 W. Congress St., Ste. 201
Savannah, GA 31401
(912) 236-6708

John C. Overton, Project Dir.
Honolulu MBDC
1001 Bishop St., Rm. 1340

Honolulu, HI 96813
(808) 533-4401

Brian LaPerriere, Project Dir.
Chicago South MBDC (1)
35 E. Wacker Dr., Ste. 790
Chicago, IL 60601
(312) 977-9190

Joe Laredo, Project Dir.
Chicago North MBDC (2)
600 Prudential Plaza, 6th Floor
130 E. Randolph
Chicago, IL 60601
(312) 565-4710

Jeffrey Williams, Project Dir.
Gary MBDC
567 Broadway, Ste. 4
P.O. Box 9007
Gary, IN 46402
(219) 883-5802

William A. Youck, Project Dir.
Indianapolis MBDC
1201 Merchants Plaza
101 W. Washington St.
Indianapolis, IN 46204
(317) 636-5592

Robert L. Tinnin, Project Dir.
Louisville MBDC
835 W. Jefferson St., Ste. 103
Louisville, KY 40202
(502) 589-7401

Bonnie Jackson, Project Dir.
Baton Rouge MBDC
2036 Wooddale Blvd., Ste. D
Baton Rouge, LA 70806
(504) 924-0186

Melvet Dangerfield, Project Dir.
New Orleans MBDC
1440 Canal St., Ste. 1619
New Orleans, LA 70112
(504) 529-5157

Richard C. Costello, Project Dir.
Shreveport MBDC
4050 Linwood Ave., Ste. 206
Shreveport, LA 71108-2430
(318) 636-6969

Hallot Watkin, Acting Project Dir.
Baltimore MBDC
2901 Druid Park Dr., Ste. 203
Baltimore, MD 21215
(301) 462-3700

Laura Junglas, Project Dir.
Boston MBDC
Twin City Office Plaza
264 Monsignor O'Brien Hwy.
Cambridge, MA 02141
(617) 776-8980

Joseph Harris, Project Dir.
Detroit MBDC
65 Cadillac Sq., Ste. 2215
Detroit, MI 48226-2822
(313) 961-2100

Brian Kerfoot, Project Dir.
Minnesota Chippewa Tribe MBDC
Rte. 2, Facility Center
P.O. Box 217
Cass Lake, MN 56633
(218) 335-2252

Laura Theroux, Project Dir.
Minneapolis/St. Paul MBDC
950 E. Hennepin Ave.
Minneapolis, MN 55414
(612) 623-3977

Robert Funches, Project Dir.
Jackson MBDC
1350 Livingston La., Ste. A
Jackson, MS 39206
(601) 362-1631

Stan Peeples, Project Dir.
Bennett Levy, Manager
Kansas City MBDC
1550 Boatmen's Center
920 Main St.
Kansas, MO 64105
(816) 221-6500

Douglas Archibald, Project Dir.
St. Louis MBDC
500 Washington Ave., Ste. 1200
St. Louis, MO 63101
(314) 621-6232

Ernest Fountain, Project Mgr.
Las Vegas MBDC
618-20 E. Carson

Las Vegas, NV 89101
(702) 384-3293

William Doneghy, Project Dir.
New Brunswick MBDC
134 New St., Rm. 102
New Brunswick, NJ 08901
(201) 247-2000

James H. Blow, Jr., Project Dir.
Newark MBDC
60 Park Pl., Ste. 1604
Newark, NJ 07102
(201) 623-7710

Teri Carpenter, Project Dir.
Albuquerque MBDC
718 Central St., S.W.
Albuquerque, NM 87102
(505) 843-7114

Robert Johnson, Project Dir.
New Mexico Indian MBDC
1015 Indian School Rd., N.W.
P.O. Box 6507, Station B
Albuquerque, NM 87197-6507
(505) 242-4774

Delores McCarley, Project Dir.
Buffalo MBDC
523 Delaware Ave.
Buffalo, NY 14202
(716) 885-0336

Celia Cadiz, Project Dir.
Bronx MBDC
349 E. 149th St., Ste. 702
Bronx, NY 10451
(212) 665-8583

Henry Snead, Exec. Dir.
Brooklyn MBDC
50 Court St., Ste. 304
Brooklyn, NY 11201
(718) 797-9224

Rabbi Zvi Kestenbaum, Exec. Dir.
Opportunity Development Association
  MBDC
12 Heyward St.
Brooklyn, NY 11211
(718) 522-5620

Fernando Gainza, Project Dir.
Queens MBDC

110-29 Horace Harding Expressway
Corona, NY 11368
(718) 699-2400

Rogelio Ramos, Exec. Dir.
Nassau/Suffolk MBDC
555 Broadhollow Rd., Ste. 230
Melville, NY 11747
(516) 420-4090

Tony Janniere, Project Dir.
Manhattan MBDC
551 Fifth Ave., Ste. 320
New York, NY 10176
(212) 661-8044

Stephen M. Ash, Project Dir.
Rochester MBDC
One Marine Midland Plaza, Ste. 1400
Rochester, NY 14604
(716) 454-1644

Troy Watson, Project Dir.
Charlotte MBDC
230 S. Tryon St., Ste. 810
Charlotte, NC 28202
(704) 334-7522

Ronald Blythe, Acting Project Dir.
Cherokee MBDC
Qualla Boundary
P.O. Box 1200
Cherokee, NC 28719
(704) 497-9335

Andrew McCall, Project Dir.
Fayetteville MBDC
114 1/2 Anderson St.
P.O. Box 1387
Fayetteville, NC 28302
(919) 483-7513

Richard Hunter, Project Dir.
Raleigh/Durham MBDC
114 W. Parrish St.
P.O. Box 1088
Durham, NC 27702
(919) 683-1047

David Gipp, Project Dir.
Bismarck IBDC
3315 University Dr.
Bismarck, ND 58501
(701) 255-3285

Robert L. Hall, Project Dir.
Cincinnati/Dayton MBDC
113 W. Fourth St., Ste. 600
Cincinnati, OH 45202
(513) 381-4770

Tanya Allmond, Project Dir.
Cleveland MBDC
601 Lakeside Ave., Rm. 335
Cleveland, OH 44114
(216) 664-4152

Charles H. Williams, Project
  Dir.
Columbus MBDC
815 E. Mound St., 2d Floor
Columbus, OH 43205
(614) 252-0197

Marilyn Murrell, Project Dir.
Oklahoma City MBDC
1500 N.E. Fourth St., Ste. 101
Oklahoma City, OK 73117
(405) 235-0430

Ted Bryant, Project Dir.
Oklahoma Indian MBDC
1600 19th St., S.E., Ste. 501
Edmond, OK 73013
(405) 341-5047

Margaret Garza, Project Dir.
Portland MBDC
8959 S.W. Barbur Blvd., Ste. 102
Portland, OR 97219
(503) 245-9253

Gualberto Medina, Project Dir.
Philadelphia MBDC
30 S. 15th
1 Penn Sq., 14th Floor
Philadelphia, PA 19102
(215) 561-7300

Eustace O. Uku, Project Dir.
Pittsburgh MBDC
1040 Fifth Ave.
Pittsburgh, PA 15219
(412) 261-3073

Yolanda V. Garcia, Project Dir.
Mayaguez MBDC
P.O. Box 3146
Marina Station

Mayaguez, PR 00709
(809) 833-7783

Manual L. Prats, Project Dir.
Ponce MBDC
19 Salud St.
Ponce, PR 00731
(809) 840-8100

Oscar Prieto, Project Dir.
San Juan MBDC
207 O'Neill St.
P.O. Box 3631
San Juan, PR 00936
(809) 753-8484

Ellis Mack, Project Dir.
Charleston MBDC
701 E. Bay St., Ste. 539
Charleston, SC 29403
(803) 723-2771

Milton A. Smalls, Project Dir.
Columbia MBDC
2700 Middleburg Dr., Ste. 208
P.O. Box 5915
Columbia, SC 29250
(803) 256-0528

Orlando Wright, Project Dir.
Greenville/Spartanburg MBDC
300 University Ridge, Ste. 110A
Greenville, SC 29601
(803) 271-8753

Gary Rowe, Project Dir.
Memphis MBDC
Five N. Third St., 2d Floor
Memphis, TN 38103
(901) 527-2298

Marilyn Robinson, Project Dir.
Nashville MBDC
404 James Robertson Pkwy., Ste. 1920
Nashville, TN 37219
(615) 255-0432

Rojelio Rice, Project Dir.
Austin MBDC
2009B E. Riverside Dr.
Austin, TX 78741
(512) 448-4101

Lucy Pelaez, Project Dir.
Beaumont MBDC

3155 Executive Blvd., Ste. 210
Beaumont, TX 77705
(409) 842-1958

Hernan Orellana, Project Dir.
Brownsville MBDC
855 W. Price Rd., Ste. 6
Brownsville, TX 78520
(512) 544-7173

Tom Wattley, Project Dir.
Dallas/Fort Worth/Waco MBDC
800 Allied Bank Tower
Dallas, TX 75202
(214) 855-7373

Pete Barrez, Project Dir.
El Paso MBDC
3707 Admiral, Ste. A
El Paso, TX 79925
(915) 592-2020

James J. Smith, Project Dir.
Houston MBDC
2870 Citicorp Center
1200 Smith St.
Houston, TX 77002
(713) 650-3831

Arturo Meraz, Project Dir.
Laredo MBDC
800 E. Mann Rd., Ste. 101
Laredo, TX 78041
(512) 742-8305

Gabe Garcia, Project Dir.
McAllen MBDC
4307 N. Tenth St., Ste. F
McAllen, TX 78501
(512) 687-8336

Rudy Ramirez, Project Dir.
San Antonio MBDC
Business Development Center
College of Business Administration
University of Texas at San Antonio

San Antonio, TX 78285
(512) 224-1945

Andrew Gallegos, Project Dir.
Salt Lake City MBDC
350 E. 500 South, #101
Salt Lake City, UT 84111
(801) 328-8181

Charles Aughtry, Project Dir.
Newport News MBDC
2600 Washington Ave., Ste. 502
Newport News, VA 23607
(804) 928-2222

Daniel Bailey, Project Dir.
Norfolk MBDC
One Main Plaza, Ste. 801
Norfolk, VA 23510
(804) 627-5254

William Harvey, Project Dir.
Richmond MBDC
Heritage Bldg.
1001 E. Main St., Ste. 525
Richmond, VA 23219
(804) 648-0200

La Verne Esquilin, Project Dir.
U.S. Virgin Island MBDC
P.O. Box 838
St. Thomas, VI 00801
(809) 774-7215

Jay Takemura, Project Dir.
Seattle MBDC
North Gate Executive Center One
155 N.E. 100th, Ste. 401
Seattle, WA 98125
(206) 525-5617

Eric Rautenberg, Project Dir.
Milwaukee MBDC
135 W. Wells St., Ste. 428
Milwaukee, WI 53203
(414) 272-8300

Naming a Business

More than 52,000 new and renewed trademarks were added to the 29th edition of the *Trademark Register of the United States, 1881 to 1987.* The 700,000 currently registered trademarks (U.S. and international classes) in use are listed.

> The Trademark Register
> 300 Washington Sq.
> 1050 Connecticut
> Washington, DC 20036

COPYRIGHTS

Copyright for the Eighties: Cases and Materials, 2d Edition, by Alan Latman and Robert A. Gorman is available from the following source. The cost is $50.

> Michie Co.
> P.O. Box 7587
> Charlottesville, VA 22906
> (804) 972-7600

Copyright Laws and Treaties of the World is one of the better reference works on the subject.

> Bureau of National Affairs
> 1231-25th St., N.W.
> Washington, DC 20037
> (202) 452-4200
> (800) 372-1033

The following services provide indexing and actual texts of legal cases, statutes, orders, and opinions from 1938 to the present. Inquire as to on-line cost and availability.

> LEXIS
> Mead Data Central
> P.O. Box 933
> Dayton, OH 45401
> (800) 227-4908
> (annual)

> *Catalog of Copyright Entries*
> U.S. Library of Congress, Copyright Office
> U.S. Government Printing Office
> Washington, DC 20402

(202) 783-3238
(quarterly)

Copyright Clearance Center
27 Congress St.
Salem, MA 01970
(617) 744-3350
(quarterly)

Copyright Society of the United States of America
40 Washington Sq., South
New York University School of Law
New York, NY 10012
(212) 598-2280
(quarterly)

International Copyright Information Center
Association of American Publishers
2005 Massachusetts Ave., N.W.
Washington, DC 20036
(202) 232-3335
(quarterly)

Copyright Law Reports are published in two looseleaf volumes and supplemented periodically. The cost is $295 per year.
Copyright Law Reports
Commerce Clearing House, Inc.
4025 W. Peterson Ave.
Chicago, IL 60646
(312) 583-8500

TRADEMARKS AND TRADE NAMES

General Information Concerning Trademarks, 1987
U.S. Government Printing Office
Washington, DC 20402
(202) 783-3238
(irregularly published)

The *Index of Trademarks* issues annually from the United States Patent and Trademark Office.
Index of Trademarks
U.S. Government Printing Office
Washington, DC 20402
(202) 783-3238

Brand Names: Who Owns What, a source of product and company information, by George and Diane Frankenstein, is available from the following source.

Facts on File
460 Park Ave., South
New York, NY 10016
(212) 683-2244

Published annually, *Macrae's Blue Book* lists manufacturers and industrial firms
with their financial ratings. The cost is $125.
Macrae's Blue Book
Macrae's Blue Book Co.
817 Broadway
New York, NY 10003
(212) 673-4700

Published annually, the *Thomas Register of American Manufacturers* and the
Thomas Register Catalog File comprise 18 volumes and an index. The cost is $175.
Thomas Register of American Manufacturers and Thomas Register Catalog File
Thomas Publishing Co.
One Penn Plaza
New York, NY 10119
(212) 695-0500

The *Trade Names Dictionary: Company Index* is an alphabetical list of companies
appearing in the basic *Trade Names Dictionary*, with products and trade names for
each firm. The 1987 edition costs $275.
Donna Wood, Editor
Trade Names Dictionary: Company Index
Gale Research Co.
Book Tower
Detroit, MI 48226
(313) 961-2242
(800) 223-GALE

The International Patent and Trademark Association is the trade association for
those involved in and concerned with patents and trademarks.
International Patent and Trademark Association
33 W. Monroe
Chicago, IL 60603
(312) 641-1500

Trademark, by John Oathout, is the best book on the subject.
Charles Scribner & Sons
115 Fifth Ave.
New York, NY 10003
(212) 614-1300

The U.S. Patent and Trademark Office publishes a list of 13,000 attorneys registered
to practice before PTOs.

U.S. Patents and Trademarks Office
2021 Jefferson Davis Hwy.
Washington, DC 20231

Ira Bachrach makes a full-time business out of naming a business. He named
Compaq Computer Corporation.
Ira Bachrach
NameLab, Inc.
711 Marina Blvd.
San Francisco, CA 94123
(415) 563-1639

Attorneys and trademark owners are members of the U.S. Trademark Association.
U.S. Trademark Association
6 E. 45th St.
New York, NY 10017
(212) 986-5880

Compumark
1333 F St., N.W.
Washington, DC 20005
(202) 937-7900

Thomson & Thomson is the largest search firm for names.
Thomson & Thomson
120 Fulton St.
Boston, MA 02109
(617) 479-1600

An Intellectual Preparatory Law Primer, by Earl Kinter, is a layman's survey of the
law of patents, trademarks, and names.
Clark Boardman Publishing
435 Hudson St.
New York, NY 10014
(212) 645-0215
(800) 221-9428

WHAT TO NAME YOUR COMPANY

One of my favorite pastimes when traveling to other cities is to pick up the Yellow
Pages and start reading, just to see the inventive (or uninventive) names that people
have given their companies. In fact, a fresh set of Yellow Pages can often hold my
attention longer than a good novel. I've also shown up late for appointments because
I lingered in a building's lobby reading the floor directory.

I've come to classify the names people choose for their businesses into four
groups. They are, in reverse order of their effectiveness:

1. Ego Trippers
2. Modest Ego Trippers
3. Nonsense Names
4. Names That Work

Ego Trippers

Ego Trippers are the people who name a business after themselves because they want fame; they see their businesses as the primary vehicle toward achieving it. This almost always proves disastrous, and not just because those people's priorities are mixed up. Remember that many entrepreneurial ventures fail. If a business named after you doesn't make it, your name fails too. Consider the failure of the Osborne Computer Corporation (OCC). Although Adam Osborne invented the first low-cost portable computer, his name will still be associated with failure. Under new management, OCC has bounced back from Chapter 11, and Osborne has a new software publishing company.

Another example that comes to mind is a product, not a business, but it illustrates the danger of ego-tripping better than any other example I can think of. It's the Edsel. Even if you don't remember the car, you automatically equate the name with failure, because the Edsel—named for the son of Henry Ford I—was one of the biggest marketing failures in American business history. And when I met Edsel Ford II at a cocktail party in the mid-1970s, the whole story flashed through my mind before I'd even finished shaking his hand. That's a tough history to carry around.

So it's a good idea to isolate your name from your business in much the same way that you protect personal assets by incorporating. Also, if your business goes bust and your name is on it, it's much easier for the creditors to look you up in the local telephone directory and pester you at home with calls.

But the possibility of failure isn't the only argument against naming a business after yourself. The venture may succeed—without you. Royden Sanders is founder and former president of Sanders Associates, a multimillion-dollar electronics company in Nashua, New Hampshire. When the board of directors fired Sanders as head of the company, he petitioned the board to change its name. They voted him down. Sanders called his new company S.D.I. He's learned his lesson.

Modest Ego Trippers

The Modest Ego Trippers know enough not to name the company after themselves, but they still want to grab a little glory. So they name the company after the street they live on, as Howard Freeman did with the Jamesbury Corporation, which manufactures valves in Worcester, Massachusetts, or after their wife's middle name, like Freeman's son Jack, who named his computer-oriented business Stewart Systems Company. Names like these don't really contribute much to the business.

There are exceptions, of course. A few years ago, Doug Greene changed the name of his company from Greene Communications to New Hope Communications, ostensibly after New Hope, Pennsylvania, where the company is located. But the name has a much broader meaning. In addition to publishing both trade and consumer magazines (the *Natural Foods Merchandiser* and *Delicious*), New Hope Communications puts on the annual Natural Foods Expo and is sponsoring "How to Do Business," a series of seminars promoting the rebirth of free enterprise in Grenada. Says Greene, "We wanted a broad name that would reflect a broad meaning, but that would not be so esoteric as to turn off people in the marketplace who are leery of that sort of thing." Greene freely acknowledges that "new hope is what the company is all about, bringing positive products to the marketplace." Yet if conservative businesspeople look askance upon hearing the name, he can defuse their skepticism by saying, "We're located in New Hope, Pa."

Nonsense Names and No-Nonsense Neologisms

Nonsense Names are tags like the XYC Corporation or Widget, Inc. My opinion is that naming a company is like naming a child: The name lasts forever, so make the right choice. Remember, the name will probably be the first impression customers, suppliers, stockholders, and employees have of the business. If it's nonsense, it may have a negative effect on them.

Some names may look like nonsense at first glance, but actually are carefully constructed. Ira Bachrach, founder of NameLab, uses constructional linguistics to create names that express an attribute of the product or business. His San Francisco firm is perhaps best known for "inventing" the name Compaq for Compaq Computer Corporation (previously known as Gateway Technologies). NameLab creates new names by putting together morphemes, words or parts of words that cannot be broken down into smaller units. "There are 6,200 morphemes in the English language," says Bachrach. "Their computer was a portable, so we focused on morphemes that conveyed the sense of a small integral object—like *pod* and *pack*. The *com* conveys computers." The *q* was a surprising ending to arrest the eye on a page. Bachrach goes on to explain NameLab's inventions: "We deal primarily in neologisms [new words] and another type of method for naming—symbolism."

Names that Work

Apple has been one of the most effective company names in recent history. Consumers need a name and trademark they can remember. For IBM, they were built in. But Apple's name may have just been a matter of good luck. The company's co-founder, Steven Jobs, didn't have much of an idea of how to start a business, but he did have a computer to sell. The name "Apple" came off the top of his head; it was simple and first-in-the-book, an apt symbol for their personal computer. The company's name distinguished it from a pack of competitors with names based on words like *digital, data,* and *electronic.* Couple the catchy name with a strong product, and you've got a $1½ billion company.

Says Steven Levy, author of *Hackers: Heroes of the Computer Revolution,* "It used to be that all a computer company had to do was call itself by its initials and call its products by a bunch of numbers." But when affordable PCs entered the consumer marketplace, all that changed for good. Adds Bachrach, "If Texas Instruments hadn't insisted on calling its home computer the 99/4, the company might still be in the home computer business."

Also in the category of "Names that Work" is a company my brother John Mancuso started in 1980. Originally called Tremon, Inc., John's company was forced to change its name in response to a trade secrets legal action initiated by his previous employer, Transamerica Delaval. So he renamed his firm Equal, Inc., because so many of the engineering blueprints requiring the custom-designed, electromechanical components specified "Transamerica or equal."

Finally, the name you choose should say something about the business you are in, without being *too* generic. Let's say you manufacture shoes. You don't want to saddle your company with a name like "The Shoe Company" for two important reasons. First, although the name tells people what business you're in, it does nothing to distinguish you from the rest of the industry. Even if your business succeeds with a generic name, you'll have no legal way of protecting it. If someone else wants to trade using the name "The Shoe Company," you'll find that the courts won't let you stop them.

Whatever name you choose, make it one that your customers will understand with ease and one that will fit your company as it grows. Then, it's not just a name, but a valuable asset.

Negotiations

Harvard Law School's Program on Negotiation is one of the better academic programs on the topic.

Jeff Rubin
Roger Fisher
The Program on Negotiation
Harvard Law School
Pound Hall, Rm. 513
Cambridge, MA 02138
(617) 495-1684

The Negotiation Institute offers a wide range of excellent books and tapes on the subject. Videos and software are also available.

Gerard Nierenberg
The Negotiation Institute
230 Park Ave.
New York, NY 10169
(212) 986-5555

Herb Cohen is an effective and entertaining public speaker. His book, *You Can Negotiate Anything,* is a classic.

Herb Cohen
The Power Negotiation Institute
633 Skokie Blvd.
Northbrook, IL 60062
(312) 564-9155

Karras Negotiations is a father and son team that conducts a wide range of public seminars.

Chester Karras
Karras Negotiations
1633 Stanford St.
Santa Monica, CA 90404
(213) 453-1806

Newspapers and Newsletters

NEWSPAPERS

Steve Galente's widely read column on small business appears every Monday in the *Wall Street Journal,* on the second front page. Sanford "Sandy" Jacobs, now a staff specialist, used to write this column. He often writes small business features for the *Wall Street Journal.*

> Steve Galente
> *Wall Street Journal*
> Second Front
> World Financial Center
> 200 Liberty St.
> New York, NY 10281
> (212) 416-2000

NEWSLETTERS

NEWSNET is an on-line database for newsletters. Some wire services are on-line, and it is a useful source of information via computer searching.

> NEWSNET
> 945 Haversford Rd.
> Bryn Mawr, PA 19010
> (215) 527-8030

Newsletter: NASBIC News is a semimonthly newsletter of current information on government activity of concern to small businesses seeking venture capital.

> *Newsletter: NASBIC News*
> National Association of Small Business Investment Companies
> 512 Washington Bldg.
> Washington, DC 20005
> (202) 638-3411

Published biweekly, *Owner & Manager* is an excellent guide for the closely held business. The cost is $96 per year.

> *Owner & Manager*
> National Institute of Business Management
> 90 Fifth Ave.
> New York, NY 10011
> (212) 971-3300

Publishing Newsletters, by Howard Penn Hudson, is the newsletter industry's venerable guide to all aspects of the trade and is a good source for spotting trends. It is available in many bookstores or from the following source.

Charles Scribner & Sons
115 Fifth Ave.
New York, NY 10003
(212) 614-1300

The Newsletter Clearinghouse publishes *The Newsletter on Newsletters,* which is a good source for spotting trends.

The Newsletter Clearinghouse
44 W. Market St.
P.O. Box 311
Rhinebeck, NY 12572
(914) 876-2081

Success in Newsletter Publishing: A Practical Guide, by Frederick G. Goss, is an authoritative guide to getting and keeping subscriptions, setting subscription rates, and selling subscriptions. It is available from the Newsletter Association of America, an association of newsletter publishers.

Mike Kibler
Newsletter Association of America
1401 Wilson Blvd., Ste. 403
Arlington, VA 22209
(703) 527-2333

Patents, Trademarks, and Inventions

Patents, copyrights, and trademarks are the legal protections that exist for a new product; they give an inventor or a firm the chance to recoup the costs of research and development and to make a profit.

ASSOCIATIONS

Founded in 1935, the Inventors Club of America has 60 local groups and about 6,000 members nationwide. Among other functions, it seeks to prevent abuses to the individual inventor, such as theft of ideas.

Inventors Club of America
4229 First Ave., Ste. A
Tucker, GA 30084
(404) 938-5089

The Minnesota Inventors Congress is a nonprofit group that specializes in patent law in Minnesota.

Eugene Malecha, Exec. Dir.
Minnesota Inventors Congress
P.O. Box 71
Redwood Falls, MN 56283
(507) 637-2828

The Inventors Association is a regional group of investors.

Roberta Toole, Exec. Dir.
Inventors Association
P.O. Box 16544
St. Louis, MO 63105
(314) 534-2677

The Inventors Council is a regional group of inventors.

Don Moyer
Inventors Council
53 W. Jackson, Ste. 1041
Chicago, IL 60604
(312) 939-3329

The Tampa Bay Inventors is a regional group of inventors.

Renee Keller
Tampa Bay Inventors

P.O. Box 2254
Largo, FL 34294
(813) 681-0010

The Inventors Association of New England publishes a good resource book.
Inventors Association of New England
P.O. Box 335
Lexington, MA 02173
(617) 862-5008

MISCELLANEOUS SERVICES

The National Inventors Foundation coordinates information relating to inventor education and serves as a clearinghouse for inventors and those seeking inventions. It also conducts national innovation workshops and publishes a monthly newsletter and a bulletin. Three services are offered by three separate nonprofit businesses at the following location.
Ted DeBoer
National Inventors Foundation
Inventors Assistance League
National Inventors Museum and Hall of Fame
345 W. Cypress St.
Glendale, CA 91204
(818) 246-6540

Patent Attorney Joseph Iandorio publishes a newsletter and specializes in patents, trademarks, and copyrights.
Joseph Iandorio, Patent Attorney
260 Bear Hill Rd.
Waltham, MA 02154
(617) 890-5678

Entrepreneurs seeking assistance with inventions and patents can contact Invention Management Group, a large, well-known management consulting firm.
Walter J. Cairns
Invention Management Group
Arthur D. Little, Inc.
20 Acorn Park
Cambridge, MA 02140
(617) 864-5770

The search room at Crystal Plaza is open to the public. For information on how you can conduct a patent search, or on the Commerce Department's patent publications (*The Gazette,* the *Index of Patents,* and the *Index of Trademarks)* contact one of the following three sources.
Department of Commerce
Patent Office

2021 Jefferson Davis Hwy., Bldg. 3
Arlington, VA 20231
(703) 557-5168

Department of Commerce
Trademark Office
2011 Jefferson Davis Hwy. Bldg. 2
Arlington, VA 20231
(703) 557-3268

Copyright Office
(202) 479-0700
(202) 287-9100 (to order copyright forms)

The nine-year-old Technology Transfer Society publishes a newsletter.
Vid Beldavs, Exec. Dir.
Technology Transfer Society
611 N. Capitol Ave.
Indianapolis, IN 46204
(317) 262-5022

The Trade Marketing Group is a trademark search organization with an excellent group of paralegals.
Judith Weintraub
Trade Marketing Group
P.O. Box 30535
Bethesda, MD 20814
(301) 229-7777

PUBLICATIONS

Contact the Consumer Information Center for a free copy of the booklet *How to Get a Patent* (booklet #172p, $4.25, postage).
Consumer Information Center
Pueblo, CO 81009
(303) 948-3334

The U.S. Department of Commerce NTIS publishes a series of newsletters with one-paragraph summaries of the latest government-sponsored research in 28 technical fields. The *NTIS Abstract Newsletters* provide a great opportunity to keep up with government-sponsored R&D projects. Contact the following source for more information and a descriptive listing of each of the newsletters.
National Technical Information Service
U.S. Department of Commerce
5285 Port Royal Rd.
Springfield, VA 22161
(703) 487-4600

The fifth edition of *The Trade Names Dictionary 1986–87* is an 1,800-page list of trade names, trademarks, and brand names of consumer-oriented products and their manufacturers. It is available in libraries or from the following source.

Gale Research Co.
Book Tower
Detroit, MI 48226
(800) 223-GALE

Pamphlets on projects are available from the Superintendent of Documents and the U.S. Patent Office.

Superintendent of Documents
U.S. Government Printing Office
Washington, DC 20402
(202) 783-3238

U.S. Patent Office
Washington, DC 20231

The U.S. Department of Commerce publishes the *Guide to the Public Patent Search Facilities* and *What You Need to Know of the U.S. Patent and Trademark Office.*

Commissioner of Patents and Trademarks
U.S. Department of Commerce
Washington, DC 20231
(703) 557-2276

The Copyright Office offers circular R-2, a publication on copyrights.

Copyright Office
Library of Congress
Washington, DC 20559
(202) 287-9100

MY FAVORITE ENTREPRENEUR

As the founder and president of CEM and the CEO Club, I've probably met more entrepreneurs than anyone in the world. And as I travel around the United States, people always ask me who I think is the greatest entrepreneur of all.

To single out one as the greatest would downgrade the achievements of many others: Henry Ford, David Rockefeller, Ted Turner, H. Ross Perot, and so on. Instead of trying to rank the best of the best, I prefer to name my *favorite* entrepreneur.

And that person is Frederick W. Smith, founder, chief executive, and chairman of Federal Express Corporation. There are ten reasons why Smith is my favorite entrepreneur.

1. Smith wasn't a high-tech genius. And although the concept of delivering packages overnight was a great idea, it wasn't a new one. It took Fred Smith to make it work.

2. He didn't have an M.B.A. or an engineering degree. He was an ex-marine who had flown reconnaissance missions in Vietnam before starting Federal Express. (No doubt this experience was valuable training for the ordeal of raising venture capital.)

3. Federal Express started with just a business plan and raised more money than any company ever had from the hard-nosed venture capital community.

4. In the early days, Smith ran out of money all the time, including his own personal fortune of several million dollars. It seemed as if he sometimes made payroll on little more than a prayer; in fact, he once won enough gambling in Las Vegas to make a payroll. I like that.

5. He never thought of quitting—it just wasn't an option. This is my best reason for liking him.

6. He has run Federal Express from the beginning. And somehow he has successfully made the transition from entrepreneur to professional manager.

7. Before Federal Express, air express meant piggybacking packages on commercial airlines, which wasn't always a reliable proposition. Smith saw the need for truly reliable overnight package service and devised a way to serve that need. The idea of flying all packages to a central location (Memphis, Tenn.) for sorting and then rerouting them to their final destination is a brilliant spoke-and-hub concept. Smith clearly showed the wisdom of shipping a package originating in Newark, N.J., through Memphis, on its way to its final destination in New York City.

8. Building an idea into a $9-billion business is the mark of an inspired entrepreneur *and* manager. Although this feat is often referred to as the "impossible transition," Smith told the CEO Club of New York that being a successful entrepreneur and a successful professional manager are not mutually exclusive talents. "It's like being a great runner and speaking a foreign language," he said, "there's no reason why one person can't do both."

9. The Federal Express concept was conceived for a term paper while Smith was an undergraduate at Yale University. His professor gave him a "C" for the project. I'd like to see all the "A's" in that class.

10. While addressing the CEO Club of New York, Smith relished the now-famous story of his "C" term paper. But he also confided that he was so pleased with the grade that he rushed to call home, bragging, "I've gotten my second 'C' at Yale, and now I'm on my way!"

Sure, you could say that Fred Smith was a rich kid who parlayed a small fortune into a large one. And many people feel that way. "If I had several million dollars I could have done it, too" is the common sentiment. But it's an entrepreneurial decision to invest every penny of your fortune in an idea regardless of whether it is $100 or $1 million.

In the end, Smith was not out to make money. He already had wealth. He was out to make his dream come true. He wanted to show the wisdom of his new package-delivery system and his daring airplane schedules. He was a pilot who wanted to own and operate a "neat" airplane-business for a profit.

At first he thought the government's Federal Reserve Board would like the quick delivery concept of Federal Express enough to give his fledgling company a lot of business. He reasoned that a quicker method of delivering Federal Reserve checks would appeal to the banking system. He justified the quick delivery of checks by showing how much one day's "float" within the Federal Reserve banking system was worth. And then he showed that his system saved money for everyone.

It was perfectly logical, he reasoned—and that's why he named his company "Federal" Express. But he was wrong. The Federal Reserve System trades checks among each of its separately managed districts. And without unanimous cooperation from all districts (which he couldn't obtain), the idea wouldn't work.

But that didn't stop him. It only made him work harder at refocusing his business to save the company. He never considered quitting as an option. And that's why, when all is weighed, he is my favorite entrepreneur.

PATENT RESOURCES

A few basic resources in this field are listed below. A list of patent attorneys or agents registered with PTO is available. The cost is $9.

Superintendent of Documents
U.S. Government Printing Office
Washington, DC 20402

A good book for inventors is *A Handbook for Inventors,* by Calvin D. MacCracken. The cost is $17.95.

Charles Scribner & Sons
115 Fifth Ave.
New York, NY 10003

A free consultation with a good patent attorney for a half hour is available through the American Intellectual Property Law Association's Inventor Consultation Service. The application form is included in its book *How to Protect and Benefit from Your Ideas.* The cost is $9.95.

The American Intellectual Property Law Association
2001 Jefferson Davis Hwy., Ste. 203
Arlington, VA 22202

A filing fee of $175 with the PTO will give you 20 years of protection for your trademark; it may be renewed for 20-year periods indefinitely. Before filing, it's advisable to hire a lawyer to do a clearance search for you to make sure the trademark is not being presently used. A helpful free booklet, *General Information Concerning Trademarks,* is available from PTO.

Commissioner of Patents and Trademarks
Patent and Trademark Office
Washington, DC 20231

A copyright protects written material for the life of the author plus 50 years. If it is a collaboration, the 50-year period starts after the demise of the last collaborator. Place the notice "Copyright 1985 John Smith" on all of your work that you send out or distribute. Usually this notice is enough to discourage would-be plagiarizers;

for official protection, register your work with the Copyright Office; the cost is $10. Send for the government's useful "Copyright Kit #118."

Register of Copyrights
Library of Congress
Washington, DC 20559

The congressional office responsible for advising Congress on new technologies and their potential impact on the marketplace provides free executive summaries of its reports. Topics include commercial biotechnology, international competitiveness in electronics, technology and aging in America, forecasts of physician supply and demand, and effects of information technology on financial services.

Publishing Office
Office of Technology Assessment-Congress
600 Pennsylvania Ave., S.E.
Washington, DC 20510
(202) 224-8996

ADVICE FOR INVENTORS

If you have a new invention and you're not quite sure what to do next, you may want to contact the Innovation Evaluation Program. This university-based program provides inventors with sales, technical, and manufacturing advice, as well as warnings of potential liability and patent infringement. (A legal patent search is up to you.) The evaluation fee is a modest $100.

However, Don Sexton, head of the program at Baylor University, cautions inventors against requesting evaluations for faddish ideas like toys, games, or foods. Furthermore, he advises, up front, that no more than 7 percent of the ideas that he sees seem commercially feasible.

For the location of the Innovation Evaluation Program near you, contact the following source.

The Center for Entrepreneurship
Hankamer School of Business
Waco, TX 76798

When it comes time for a patent search, the U.S. government provides help, much of it at no cost. A list of patent attorneys is available from the the following source.

Office of Enrollment and Discipline
Patent and Trademark Office
Department of Commerce
Washington, DC 20231
(703) 557-1728

For $10, inventors can officially record evidence of the date they conceived an invention. A "Disclosure Document" is filed, which will be kept in confidence by PTO.

Commissioner of Patents and Trademarks
Patent and Trademark Office
Department of Commerce
Washington, DC 20231
(703) 557-3225

If you'd like to do your own patent search, the Department of Commerce publishes a *Guide to the Public Patent Search Facilities of the U.S. Patent & Trademark Office.* It explains the jargon used by the office, as well as types and locations of available documents. It also tells how to conduct your own patent search.

Commissioner of Patents and Trademarks
Department of Commerce
Bldg. 3, Rm. 1 A02
Washington, DC 20231
(703) 557-2276

If you're anxious to get started, contact the Patent Search Division of PTO. They will provide you with the necessary documentation and the location of the patent depository near you.

Patent Search Division
Patent and Trademark Office
Department of Commerce
Washington, DC 20231
(703) 557-2219

SOME THINGS YOU SHOULD KNOW ABOUT COPYRIGHT PROTECTION

What is copyright? To obtain copyright is to gain guaranteed rights from the federal government, exclusive only to you or to your heirs, to print, reprint, publish, copy in any form, and sell. It includes rights to translate into other languages and dialects. Copyright, by preventing mere duplication, tends to encourage the independent creation of competitive works.

President Gerald R. Ford signed a bill for the general revision of the U.S. copyright law on Oct. 19, 1976. The new law went into effect on Jan. 1, 1978, and superseded the old act of 1909. For works already protected, the new law retains the present term of copyright of 28 years from the first publication (or from registration in some cases), renewable by certain persons for a second period of protection, but it increases the length of the second period to 47 years. For works created after Jan. 1, 1978, the new law provides a term lasting for the author's life, plus an additional 50 years after the author's death. For works made for hire, and for anonymous and pseudonymous works (unless the author's identity is revealed in Copyright Office records), the new term will be 75 years from publication or 100 years from creation, whichever is shorter.

How to Register a Copyright

The procedure is simple and painless. Write to:
The Register of Copyrights
Copyright Office
The Library of Congress
Washington, DC 20559

Ask for the proper forms to be filled out and returned. Specify if it is a printed work as opposed to an audiotape or videotape. Fill out the forms in duplicate and return along with two copies of the work and the $10 registration fee. The fee is only for filing the application. It will not buy you information about whether or not you are trespassing on someone else's copyright. It is very important that you print the copyright notice on printed works or audio labels or video labels *before* you apply for the copyright. Notice comprises the *C* inside a circle, or the word *Copyright*, followed by the name of the copyright owner and the year of the first distribution. Copyright notice in printed works should appear on the title page, reverse of title page, first page of text, or title heading.

What Is "Fair Use" or "Infringement"?

1. Infringement of copyright is *not* limited to verbatim copying of the whole or a large part of the copyrighted work. It includes paraphrasing and even the appropriation of the literary work, labor, and ideas of another, such as arrangements and selection of materials, as well as mere language.
2. Extracts and quotations may be used to a limited extent for purposes of illustration of criticism.
3. If there is no copying, there is no infringement.
4. News, as such, cannot be copyrighted.

The unchecked spread of photocopying, audiotaping, videotaping, and other technological developmental equipment has brought pressure for change in the U.S. intellectual property system. One way to stay abreast of developments is to request a free Copyright Information Kit from the Copyright Office. The Copyright Office will answer your specific questions. It will *not* provide legal advice!
Copyright Office
Library of Congress
Washington, DC 20559
(202) 287-5000

You Can't Copyright an Idea

It is totally impossible for an agency to grant unquestionable ownership of an idea to one person. Therefore the Copyright Office does not attempt to offer idea protection to a writer. Editors and writers are constantly inserting material into their own work that has been contributed by other writers and is offered as original work. Often, it is not, and they have inadvertently plagiarized. Actually, no one can claim copyright to an idea. Ideas can be used by anyone at any time as long as treatment of the idea is not identical to its treatment by someone else, in copyrighted form. However, unauthorized copying of any substantial part of a work is infringement. Mere acknowledgment of a copyrighted source may not be taken as license for substantial use. What is considered fair? No more than a paragraph from a newspaper or magazine article or several paragraphs from a book (with full credit in each case, of course). If you wish to use more of the material, write to the copyright holder and request specific permission.

Personnel

ASSOCIATIONS

The American Society for Personnel Administration is a trade association for the U.S. personnel industry.

American Society for Personnel Administration
606 Washington
Alexandria, VA 22314
(713) 549-7100

The International Personnel Management Association is a trade association with an international focus.

International Personnel Management Association
1617 Duke St.
Alexandria, VA 22314
(710) 549-7100

MISCELLANEOUS SERVICES

Will G. Bowman is an unusual talent. He runs an excellent executive search firm.

Dr. Will G. Bowman, Pres.
Will G. Bowman, Inc.
560 Wellesley St.
Weston, MA 02193
(617) 431-1939

PDS Technical Services is an excellent source of temporary personnel in technical fields.

Arthur R. Janes, CEO
PDS Technical Services
P.O. Box 619820
8925 Sterling
Dallas, TX 75261
(214) 621-8080

Staffing by Priority is a good source of temporary medical personnel.

Leona Schultze, CEO
Staffing by Priority

91-31 Queens Blvd.
Elmhurst, NY 11373
(718) 779-3700

V. J. Pappas is the editor of the best source of jobs and career information in the United States.
V. J. Pappas, Editor
National Business Employment
Dow-Jones
P.O. Box 300
Princeton, NJ 08540
(609) 452-2754

Korn/Ferry International is one of the best worldwide executive search firms.
Korn/Ferry International
237 Park Ave.
New York, NY 10017
(212) 687-1834

JAI Press offers a research service, and is a good source of studies on human behavior.
Kendrith M. Rowland
Gerald D. Ferris
Research in Personnel and Human Resources Management
JAI Press
36 Sherwood Pl.
Greenwich, CT 06836
(203) 661-7602

PUBLICATIONS

The U.S. Office of Personnel Management provides an abstract service with indexes.
Personnel Literature
U.S. Office of Personnel Management
U.S. Government Printing Office
Washington, DC 20402
(202) 783-3238

The University of Michigan's Graduate School of Business Administration provides an abstract service with indexes.
Personnel Management Abstracts
University of Michigan
Graduate School of Business Administration
Ann Arbor, MI 48109
(313) 475-1979

Information Coordinators, Inc. provides an abstract service with indexes.

Work-Related Abstracts
Information Coordinators, Inc.
1435-37 Randolph St.
Detroit, MI 48226
(313) 962-9720

The *Personnel and Training Management Yearbook* is a good source of information on training worldwide.

Personnel and Training Management Yearbook
International Publications Service
Division of Taylor & Francis
242 Cherry St.
Philadelphia, PA 19106
(800) 821-8312

NBA's Employee Relations Weekly is an expensive but informative weekly newsletter.

NBA's Employee Relations Weekly
Bureau of National Affairs, Inc.
1231-25th St., N.W.
Washington, DC 20037
(202) 258-9401
(800) 372-1033

Employment Alert, a biweekly newsletter, is a best buy for less than $100 annually.

Employment Alert
Research Institute of America, Inc.
589 Fifth Ave.
New York, NY 10017
(212) 755-8900
(800) 431-2057

Personnel Administrator is a monthly newsletter which keeps you up-to-date on the activities of the American Society for Personnel Administration.

Personnel Administrator
American Society for Personnel Administration
30 Park Dr.
Berea, OH 44017
(216) 826-4790

Personnel Journal is a monthly newsletter.

Personnel Journal
245 Fischer Ave., B-2
Costa Mesa, CA 92626
(714) 751-1883

Personnel Guidelines is an excellent report on the topic by one of the better sources of small business information. Volume 14, number 2, 1988 costs $2.

Personnel Guidelines
Small Business Reporter
Bank of America
P.O. Box 37000
San Francisco, CA 94137

Interviewing skills are crucial; we recommend the fourth edition (1985) of *Interviewing Principles and Practices,* by Charles J. Stewart.

Interviewing Principles and Practices
William C. Brown, Co.
2460 Kerper Blvd.
Dubuque, IA 52001
(319) 588-1451

Sweaty Palms: The Neglected Art of Being Interviewed, by H. Anthony Medley, acquaints you with the other side of the interview process.

Sweaty Palms: The Neglected Art of Being Interviewed
Ten Speed Press
P.O. Box 7123
Berkeley, CA 94707
(415) 845-8414

INTERVIEW QUESTIONS

The following "Suggested Interview Questions" were formulated by Alan Glou Associates, Inc., management consultants of Needham, Massachusetts. They are guidelines for the hiring process. To quote Mr. Glou: "If you hire efficient people, you make your job easier. If you hire inadequate people, you make your job impossible."

1. How is your present company as a place to work? Why?
2. What would you rather have done more of in your last position?
3. What aspects of your last job did you like least? Why?
4. If you could have made one suggestion to management in your last job, what would it have been?
5. Would you tell me about the best boss you ever had? About the worst boss?
6. What's the hardest thing you've ever done? Why?
7. If you could have any job you wanted, what would you do?
8. What qualities do you think this company should look for in a person for this position?
9. Describe your personality: work traits, energy level.
10. If you could live your life over again, what changes would you make? Why?
11. What do you think is likely to make the difference between success and failure in this position?
12. What type of problems were you faced with at your previous company? What areas did you attack to become successful?

13. What do you feel has been your greatest accomplishment in life?

14. What have been your three most noteworthy accomplishments in the past year? Why?

15. What has been your greatest disappointment? Why?

16. As an employee, what can management do to assist you in functioning effectively?

17. What have you done in the past year to improve yourself?

18. How does your spouse feel about your application for this job?

19. If you are hired, how do you visualize your future with this company?

20. What do you consider to be your greatest strengths and greatest weaknesses? Why?

21. What are your "pet peeves"—the things that upset you most? Why?

22. How does this position compare with others you may now be considering?

23. What is your criterion for your own success? Why?

24. What do people most often criticize you for?

25. What do you most often criticize others for?

26. What factors in your past have contributed most to your development?

27. What factors would you say may have been handicaps in preventing you from moving ahead more quickly?

28. If your boss were promoted tomorrow, and you were given his job, what would you do to improve the department? Why?

29. What goals have you set for yourself to accomplish at your present employer for the next year?

30. What goals did you set for yourself this year and how well have you done toward accomplishing them?

Premiums and Incentives

There are many products that can be sold to people or organizations that will use them as premiums or give-aways, or in incentive buying programs. Perhaps your product(s) could be used in this way. Several sources offer a list of such buyers and sellers.

Salesman's Guide Nationwide Directory: Gift and Housewares Buyers is an annual listing of catalog showrooms and coordinators, trading-stamp houses, mail-order companies, jack jobbers, and retail stores having houseware and gift departments. The address of buying headquarters, type of store, number of stores, sales volume, and names of key managers are included. Salesman's Guide, Inc. also publishes a directory of premium and incentive buyers. This is published annually with 3 supplements for $95.

Salesman's Guide, Inc.
1140 Broadway
New York, NY 10001
(212) 684-2985

Incentive Marketing is a good annual directory of supply sources.

Incentive Marketing
Bill Publications
633 Third Ave.
New York, NY 10017
(212) 986-4800

Premium/Incentive Business is a monthly magazine.

Premium/Incentive Business
1515 Broadway
New York, NY 10036
(212) 869-1300

The *NPSE Newsletter* is published periodically and provides information on premium sales.

Andy Bopp, Editor
NPSE (National Premium Sales Executives) Newsletter
1600 Rte. 22
Union, NJ 07083
(201) 687-3090

Potentials in Marketing is a short synopsis of fundamental marketing functions.
   Potentials in Marketing
   Lakewood Publications, Inc.
   731 Hennepin Ave.
   Minneapolis, MN 55403
   (612) 333-0471

Incentive Manufacturers' Representatives is a group of sales agents.
   Incentive Manufacturers' Representatives
   110 Pennsylvania Ave.
   Oreland, PA 19075
   (215) 572-1010

Publicity

The entrepreneur's strategy is to obtain as much *free* advertising and public relations as possible before spending money on them. The nagging problem is how to get this free publicity. One enterprising company had a fascinating and successful philosophy: It was determined to obtain every ounce of free advertising possible before placing a single paid advertisement. During its first $1 or $2 million of sales, nothing was paid out. The company hired an individual to research all of the trade journals and various media to secure new-product releases, new-literature releases, and news stories. That person was paid about $25,000 annually (this was in 1980) and obtained close to $1 million of free publicity and information.

Instead of launching a marketing program with a series of paid advertisements, you may want to consider a free publicity release program first. Your firm may be eligible for news releases or product releases, or literature releases, all of which are free. Doesn't it make sense to have all initial effort directed toward using free material?

ASSOCIATIONS

The American Advertising Federation is a trade association for the advertising industry.

American Advertising Federation
251 Post St., Ste. 302
San Francisco, CA 94108
(415) 421-6867

The American Association of Advertising Agencies, Inc. is a trade association of advertising agencies.

American Association of Advertising Agencies, Inc.
8383 Wilshire Blvd., Ste. 342
Beverly Hills, CA 90211
(213) 658-5750

The American Business Press, Inc. is a trade association of members of more than 500 specialized periodicals and publications.

American Business Press, Inc.
205 E. 42d St.
New York, NY 10017
(212) 661-6360

The Direct Marketing Association is a good source of direct-mail information.
Direct Marketing Association
6 E. 43d St.
New York, NY 10017
(212) 689-4977

MISCELLANEOUS SERVICES

Kanan, Corbin, Schupak & Aronow is a full-service public relations firm.
Theodore Cott, Managing Partner
Kanan, Corbin, Schupak & Aronow
99 Park Ave.
New York, NY 10016
(212) 682-6300

The Blaine Group is a full-service public relations firm.
Devon Blaine
The Blaine Group
7465 Beverly Blvd.
Los Angeles, CA 90036
(213) 938-2577

PUBLICATIONS

The procedure for contacting trade journals varies from industry to industry. Some journals require black-and-white photographs; others require color photographs; others accept no photographs. To obtain specific information on how to obtain publicity and to obtain a list of relevant trade journals, the following sources offer directories and publicity release programs.
Gale Research Co.
Book Tower
Detroit, MI
(800) 223-GALE

Bacon's Publicity Checker
332 S. Michigan Ave.
Chicago, IL 60604
(312) 922-2400
(800) 621-0561

The Public Relations Publishing Co., Inc. is a good source of specialized directories for public relations, such as military colleges, business news, and investment letters.
Richard Weiner
Public Relations Publishing Co., Inc.
888 Seventh Ave.

New York, NY 10106
(212) 582-7373

An overall list of periodicals, the *Standard Periodical Directory* is published by Oxbridge Communications, Inc.

Oxbridge Communications, Inc.
150 Fifth Ave.
New York, NY 10011
(212) 741-0231

Ulrich's Directory of Periodicals is published by R. R. Bowker Company.

R. R. Bowker Co.
1180 Avenue of the Americas
New York, NY 10036
(212) 645-9700

Real Estate

The trouble with "real estate" as a listing in this book is that the topic is too broad. Most information on real estate that is available is localized, and it is beyond the scope of this book to offer a complete listing of regional sources of help. Instead, consider the following as a useful starting base: use of the local Yellow Pages, contacts with local real estate brokers, local real estate associations, and local real estate magazines and newsletters.

ASSOCIATIONS

The National Association of Real Estate Appraisers is a trade association of appraisers.

National Association of Real Estate Appraisers
853 Broadway
New York, NY 10003
(212) 673-2300

The Real Estate Research Center offers good information.

Real Estate Research Center
University of Florida
College of Business Administration
Gainesville, FL 32611
(904) 392-0157

A trade association of realtors.

National Association of Realtors
430 N. Michigan Ave.
Chicago, IL 60611
(312) 329-8200

A trade association of industrial realtors.

Society of Industrial Realtors
777-14th St., N.W.
Washington, DC 20005
(202) 383-1150

The Building Owners and Managers Association International can help with the purchase or subleasing of buildings.

Building Owners and Managers Association International
1250 I St., N.W., Ste. 200
Washington, DC 20005
(202) 298-7000

MISCELLANEOUS SERVICES

Genealogical Search, Inc. finds missing heirs of real estate properties. William J. Devine is an expert consultant on land acquisition.
William J. Devine, Pres.
Genealogical Search, Inc.
11 Beacon St., Ste. 327
Boston, MA 02108
(617) 367-6750

First Winthrop Corporation is a real estate expert.
Frank J. Rimkus, CEO
First Winthrop Corp.
5761 Buckingham Pkwy.
Culver City, CA 90230
(213) 215-3016

Waterfront Investments, Inc. is a very successful real estate developer.
Peter Fioretti, CEO
Waterfront Investments, Inc.
313 First St.
Hoboken, NJ 07030
(201) 792-7104

Goldsmith Murphy, Inc. is a quality real estate firm serving New York.
Robert J. Murphy, CEO
Goldsmith Murphy, Inc.
104 E. 40th St., Ste. 807
New York, NY 10016
(212) 687-6111

PUBLICATIONS

Bradley K. Haynes's book on real estate is one of the best; send for it!
Bradley K. Haynes, CEO
B. K. Haynes Corp.
Haynes Bldg.
501 S. Royal Ave.
Front Royal, VA 22630
(703) 635-7135

Warren, Gorham & Lamont publishes several periodicals on real estate.
Real Estate Outlook
Warren, Gorham & Lamont, Inc.
210 South St.
Boston, MA 02111
(617) 423-2020

A good source of published reports.
Essentials of Real Estate Finance, by David Sirota.
Real Estate Education Co.
500 N. Dearborn St.
Chicago, IL 60610
(312) 836-0466

Foreclosures often offer good values for entrepreneurs. A good reference is the *Law of Distressed Real Estate: Foreclosure, Workouts, and Procedures* by Baxter Dunaway.
Clark Boardman Co., Ltd.
435 Hudson St.
New York, NY 10014
(212) 929-7500
(800) 221-9428

The *Journal of Property Management* is a source of good periodicals.
Journal of Property Management
Institute of Real Estate Management
430 N. Michigan Ave.
Chicago, IL 60611
(312) 661-1930

Real Estate Forum is a monthly publication. The cost is less than $100 per year.
Real Estate Forum
12 W. 37th St.
New York, NY 10018
(212) 563-6460

JAI Press publishes *Research in Real Estate,* an almanac of research edited by C. F. Sirmans.
JAI Press
36 Sherwood Pl.
Greenwich, CT 06836
(203) 661-7602

Real Estate Books and Periodicals in Print is a source of good bibliographies on real estate.

Real Estate Books and Periodicals in Print
Real Estate Publishing Co.
P.O. Box 41177
Sacramento, CA 95841
(916) 677-3684

Real Estate Industry Sources is a good source of all small business information, especially real estate.

Real Estate Industry Sources
Baker Library/Publications
Harvard Graduate School of Business Administration
Soldiers Field
Boston, MA 02163
(617) 495-6405

The Commercial Real Estate Brokers Directory contains facts on firms and individuals specializing in large-scale transactions. They offer good directories.

Commercial Real Estate Brokers Directory
Whole World Publishing, Inc.
P.O. Box 665
Deerfield, IL 60015
(312) 945-8050
(800) 323-4305

The American Society of Real Estate Counselors offers a good directory of real estate counselors.

American Society of Real Estate Counselors Directory
American Society of Real Estate Counselors
430 N. Michigan Ave.
Chicago, IL 60611
(312) 329-8427

Reference Books

Business Information Sources
University of California Press
2223 Fulton St.
Berkeley, CA 94720-3104
(415) 642-6682

Business Organizations and Agencies Directory
Gale Research Co.
Book Tower
Detroit, MI 48226
(313) 961-2242
(800) 223-GALE

The Business Periodicals Index is a good listing of all recent articles on small business.
Business Periodicals Index
H. W. Wilson Co.
950 University Ave.
Bronx, NY 10452-4224
(212) 588-8400

The Directory of Directories and the *Directory of Industry Data Sources* are musts for any library.
Directory of Directories
Gale Research Co.
Book Tower
Detroit, MI 48226
(313) 961-2242
(800) 223-GALE

Directory of Industry Data Sources
Harfax Database Publishing
54 Church St.
Cambridge, MA 02138-3730
(617) 492-0670

The following are excellent sources of information.
Encyclopedia of Associations
Gale Research Co.
Book Tower

Detroit, MI 48226
(313) 961-2242
(800) 223-GALE

Encyclopedia of Business Information Sources
Gale Research Co.
Book Tower
Detroit, MI 48226
(313) 961-2242
(800) 223-GALE

Guide to American Directories
B. Klein Publications
P.O. Box 8503
Coral Springs, FL 33075-8503
(305) 752-1708

The *Million Dollar Directory* and *Sources of State Information on Corporations* are two good sources of middle-market U.S. companies.
Million Dollar Directory
Dun & Bradstreet
99 Church St.
New York, NY 10007-2701
(212) 285-7000

Sources of State Information on Corporations
Washington Researchers
918-16th St., N.W.
Washington, DC 20006-2901
(202) 333-3499

Standard & Poor's Corp. Records is a good information source for public companies.
Standard & Poor's Corp. Records
Standard & Poor's
25 Broadway
New York, NY 10004-1010
(212) 248-2525

A good source of marketing and sales information is the *Survey of Buying Power.*
Survey of Buying Power
Data Service Sales & Marketing Management
633 Third Ave.
New York, NY 10017-6706
(212) 986-4800

Thomas Register of American Manufacturers is a classic directory (series of books) which lists products and manufacturers.

Thomas Register of American Manufacturers
Thomas Publishing Co.
One Penn Plaza
New York, NY 10119-0001
(212) 695-0500

Marquis Who's Who, Inc. offers many *Who's Who* directories.
Who's Who in Finance & Industry
Marquis Who's Who, Inc.
200 E. Ohio St.
Chicago, IL 60611-3203
(312) 787-2008

Regional Small Business Associations

The Smaller Business Association of New England is the oldest small business association in the United States. It has several thousand members and is very active politically.

Lewis Shattuck
Smaller Business Association of New England
69 Hickory Dr.
Waltham, MA 02254-9117
(617) 890-9070

Founded in 1945, the Smaller Manufacturers Council has about 1,200 members.

Smaller Manufacturers Council
339 Boulevard of the Allies
Pittsburgh, PA 15222
(412) 391-1622

A division of the U.S. Chamber of Commerce, the Council of Smaller Enterprises has about 4,000 members.

Council of Smaller Enterprises
690 Huntington Bldg.
Cleveland, OH 44115
(216) 621-3300

The Independent Business Association of Wisconsin is a strong regional group which was founded in 1970 and has about 1,000 members.

Independent Business Association of Wisconsin
100 N. Hamilton St., #2600
Madison, WI 53703
(608) 251-5546
                or
7635 Bluemound Rd.
Milwaukee, WI 53214
(414) 258-7055

A group of several hundred high-tech executives from companies in the Los Angeles area, the Southern California Technology Executives holds seminars and monthly meetings.

Steven Panzer, Ph.D., Exec. Dir.
Southern California Technology Executives

12011 San Vicente Blvd., Ste. 401
Los Angeles, CA 90049
(213) 476-0618

Founded by Ray Stata (Analog Devices), the Massachusetts High Technology Council is a group of high-tech businesses with a strong lobbying arm for Massachusetts small businesses.

Massachusetts High Technology Council
164 Northern Ave.
World Trade Center, #315
Boston, MA 02210
(617) 227-4855

The New York Association of Small Business Councils is a federation of small business groups in upstate New York.

New York Association of Small Business Councils
1500 One MONY Plaza
Syracuse, NY 13202
(315) 422-1343

The Pittsburgh High Technology Council is a group of high-tech businesses in western Pennsylvania.

Timothy Parks, Exec. Dir.
The Pittsburgh High Technology Council
4516 Henry St.
Pittsburgh, PA 15213
(412) 687-2700

Retail

ASSOCIATIONS

The National Retail Merchants Association is the industry trade association.
National Retail Merchants Association
100 W. 31st St.
New York, NY 10001
(212) 244-8780

The National Association of Chain Drug Stores is a trade association that provides valuable listings of distribution by types of retail outlets.
National Association of Chain Drug Stores
Box 1417-D49
Alexandria, VA 22314
(703) 549-3001

PUBLICATIONS

Chain Store Age offers a national overview of chain-store operations.
Chain Store Age
Lebhar-Friedman
425 Park Ave.
New York, NY 10022
(212) 371-9400

Discount Merchandise focuses on overall discounting trends.
Discount Merchandise
641 Lexington Ave.
New York, NY 10022
(212) 872-8430

Merchandising provides good data on the electronics and appliance industries.
Merchandising
Gralla Publications
1515 Broadway
New York, NY 10036
(212) 869-1300

Supermarket News is a frequent source of industry changes and current hot topics.

> *Supermarket News*
> Fairchild Publications
> 7 E. 12th St.
> New York, NY 10003
> (212) 741-4000

Progressive Grocer is a source of information on all food products.

> *Progressive Grocer*
> 708 Third Ave.
> New York, NY 10017
> (212) 490-1000

Restaurants & Institutions is a good source of industry statistics.

> *Restaurants & Institutions*
> Cahner Publishing Co.
> 221 Columbus Ave.
> Boston, MA 02116
> (617) 536-7780

Phelan's Discount & Sheldon's Jobbing highlights jobbers, rack jobbers, and catalog showrooms.

> *Phelan's Discount & Sheldon's Jobbing*
> Phelan, Sheldon & Marsar
> 32 Union Sq.
> New York, NY 10003
> (212) 473-2590

Securities and Exchange Commission

The Securities and Exchange Commission (SEC) is the governmental watchdog agency overseeing the public stock market. An excellent source of information on public companies, the SEC also provides information to companies considering initial public offerings (IPOs). Writing to the SEC is the slowest but least expensive route you can take. For no more than the cost of a postage stamp, you can receive as many reports as you wish; however, the order may take weeks to arrive.

Securities and Exchange Commission
1100 L St., N.W.
Washington, DC 20549

If you are in Washington, you can pore over SEC documents at the SEC reference room.

Securities and Exchange Commission Bldg.
Public Reference Room
500 N. Capitol St., N.W.
Washington, DC 20549

Regional SEC offices have limited collections that are available for public inspection.

Everett McKinley Dirksen Bldg.
219 S. Dearborn St.
Chicago, IL 60604
(312) 353-7433

29 Federal Plaza, Rm. 1100
New York, NY 10007
(212) 264-1614

10960 Wilshire Blvd.
Los Angeles, CA 90024
(213) 473-4511

Disclosure, Inc. is a private company which is the SEC's sole vendor for the private reproduction and distribution of its report filings. This company has made SEC reports easy to find and easy to retrieve. The service's features include the following:

- An 800 number, to check where and when a particular SEC report was filed. Disclosure's operators are extremely helpful and will answer your questions almost immediately.

- Disclosure will either make paper copies of the report for you at a cost of less than 35 cents per page or accept an order for the entire filing on microfiche for $10 per report.
- For even faster service, you can retrieve the 10-K and 10-Q financials and company descriptions on-line, through Disclosure's database.

Disclosure, Inc.
5161 River Rd.
Bethesda, MD 20816
(800) 638-8241
            or
161 Williams St.
New York, NY 10038
            or
5757 Wilshire Blvd.
Los Angeles, CA 90036

Seminars

Seminars are an increasingly popular method of both disseminating and gathering information on topics of rapidly changing dimensions. Check your local college, university, SBA office, and chamber of commerce for regional programs and seminars.

The American Society for Training and Development is a national professional association for trainers. Strong local organizations provide assistance and help for professionals in the field. It publishes the *Training and Development Journal.*

    American Society for Training and Development
    1630 Duke St.
    Arlington, VA 22313
    (703) 683-8100

The Bureau of Business and Technology, Inc. distributes publications on continuing education and training. It publishes *Dean & Director,* a newsletter targeted for university continuing-education administrators.

    Bureau of Business & Technology, Inc.
    2472 Fox Ave.
    Baldwin, NY 11510
    (516) 868-5757

A national clearinghouse for information, the Council on Continuing Education is a communicator of standards for offering continuing-education credit for seminars and workshops.

    Council on Continuing Education
    1101 Connecticut Ave., N.W.
    Washington, DC 20036
    (202) 857-1122

Gale Research Company publishes numerous directories of benefit to individuals in the seminar business, as well as a directory of available training programs.

    Gale Research Co.
    Book Tower
    Detroit, MI 48226
    (313) 961-2242
    (800) 223-GALE

Howard L. Shenson offers how-to publications and seminars on marketing of seminars, competitive and market analysis/research, and consulting on marketing of seminars. He publishes a newsletter, *The Professional Consultant & Seminar Business Report.*

> Howard L. Shenson
> 20750 Ventura Blvd.
> Woodland Hills, CA 91364
> (818) 703-1415

Learning Resources Network offers publications, seminars, and a newsletter on development of continuing-education programs.

> Learning Resources Network
> P.O. Box 1448
> Manhattan, KS 66502
> (913) 539-5376

The Marketing Federation specializes in seminars, consulting services on marketing of conferences, and workshops.

> Marketing Federation
> 7141 Gulf Blvd.
> St. Petersburg Beach, FL 33706
> (813) 367-5629

Time-Place is an on-line database of seminars conducted by more than 6,000 providers. It is available by subscription, through database services, and through the American Society for Training and Development.

> Time-Place
> 460 Totten Pond Rd.
> Waltham, MA 02154
> (617) 890-4636

Publications of *Training Magazine* include the annual *Training Marketplace Directory.*

> *Training Magazine*
> 50 S. Ninth St.
> Minneapolis, MN 55402
> (612) 333-0471

University Associates produces numerous publications, resource documents, and training programs on the design and development of adult learning programs. Limited publications on marketing and promotion of seminars and workshops are available.

> University Associates
> 8535 Production Ave.
> San Diego, CA 92121
> (619) 578-5900

Small Business Answer Desk Directory

Finding the answer to a small business question can mean searching through a maze of federal, state, and private sector information sources. In October 1982, in an effort to assist small business owners and prospective entrepreneurs with their business questions, SBA's Office of Advocacy established a toll-free hotline, the Small Business Answer Desk.

In the course of responding to more than 200,000 inquiries, the Answer Desk staff has developed several tools to aid small business owners in their information search. One of these tools is the *Small Business Answer Desk Directory,* which includes lists of key federal and state agencies that provide help to businesses, a list of business and trade organizations, and a glossary of small business terms and programs.

I hope this compilation will be especially useful to members of the small business community. The Small Business Answer Desk is open for telephone inquiries on weekdays from 9:00 A.M. to 5:00 P.M., eastern standard time; call (800) 368-5855.

Office of the Chief Counsel for Advocacy
Small Business Administration
1441 L St., N.W.
Washington, DC 20416
(202) 653-7561 (in Washington, DC)
(800) 368-5855

GLOSSARY OF KEY SMALL BUSINESS TERMS

Accountants: All small businesses need accounting services periodically or full time. Referrals can be found through accountants' associations, chambers of commerce, the Yellow Pages, or the recommendations of other small businesses.

Artists: SBA, in affiliation with the National Endowment for the Arts, has sponsored special publications and seminars to educate visual artists in business practice. Artists may contact SBA district offices to get reference materials and for other management assistance. SBA contact: Charles Liner, (202) 653-2369.

Bankruptcy: A process in which a business that cannot meet its debt obligations petitions a federal district court for either reorganization of its debts or liquidation. Small businesses should seek legal assistance if considering bankruptcy.

Business Development Assistance Program (Training classes and printed publications): Call the SBA district office to ask for a starter kit, SCORE counseling, and a schedule of classes and workshops. (See also listings for Small Business Development Centers, Small Business Institute Program, SCORE.)

Many states also sponsor their own programs. Contact the state small business office.

Business License/Permit: A legal authorization in document form issued by municipal and state governments required for business operations. Contact city hall, county court, state small business program office, or SBA district office (which may have local numbers if you cannot find them in government sections of local telephone book) for assistance. This registration is generally made in the county in which the business operates. For corporations, registration is with the state's secretary of state.

Business Name: Businesses must register their business name usually on a "doing business as . . ." (d.b.a.) form with the local governments. This name is sometimes referred to as a *fictional name.* Part of the business-licensing process, this procedure prevents any other business from using the same name for a similar business in the same locality. (See also Trademark and Business License/Permit.)

Caribbean Basin Initiative (CBI): An interdisciplinary program to support commerce among the businesses in the nations of the Caribbean Basin and the United States. Agencies involved include the Agency for International Development (AID), SBA, and ITA of the Department of Commerce. Also included are private sector groups. The CBI information office at ITA is (202) 377-0703; the Eastern Caribbean Desk at AID is (202) 647-2116.

Certified Development Corporation (Fixed Asset Financing): A local area or statewide corporation or authority—for profit or nonprofit, depending on the situation—that packages SBA, bank, state, and/or private money into a financial assistance package for *existing business capital improvement.* SBA holds the second lien on its maximum share of 40-percent involvement. Each state has at least one certified development corporation. This program is called the "503 Program." Call SBA district offices for more information.

Certified Lenders: These banks participate in SBA's guaranteed loan program and have a good track record with SBA, and agree to certain conditions set forth by SBA. In return, SBA agrees to process any guaranteed loan application within three business days. District offices of SBA can provide lists of certified banks in a geographical area.

Congress: All members of Congress have state offices that are listed in the *Congressional Yellow Book.* For the member's Washington office, Constituents should contact the Capitol Hill Operator ([202] 224-3121), and ask for the office by member's name.

Consumer Price Index: A measure of the fluctuation in prices between two points in time. It is computed by the Bureau of Labor Statistics; call (202) 272-5160.

Consumer Protection: Call the consumer complaint number for your state given in the list of SBA offices which follows this section. Help is available from the state's attorney general's office, state or local consumer protection offices, better business bureaus, professional licensing and accreditation societies, and state and local business permit offices. Businesses are generally not defined as consumers and therefore have no recourse to consumer protection laws and must resort to civil tort action through legal recourse.

Copyright: A copyright is an intangible right granted by statute to the author or originator of certain literary or artistic productions. With a copyright, the owner is vested for a limited time period with the sole and exclusive privilege of reproducing copies of the work for publication and sale. Copyrights can be acquired for works of art, sculpture, music, and published or unpublished manuscripts. All copyrights *should* be registered by the Copyright Office of the Library of Congress. To obtain forms, call (202) 287-8700, or contact the reference desk of large libraries.

Corporation: A body of persons granted a charter legally recognizing them as a separate entity having its own rights, privileges, and liabilities distinct from those of its members. The process of incorporating should be completed with the state's secretary of state or state corporate counsel. It usually requires the services of an attorney. Contact the state small business program office and SBA district offices for pamphlets on corporate structure.

Disaster Loans: Various types of physical and economic loan assistance are available to individuals and businesses. This is the only SBA loan program available for residential purposes. See fact sheet on disaster loans on page 336.

Employer I.D. Number: It is assigned by the IRS, and is the business equivalent of a social security number. For more information, call or visit the IRS near you and ask for form SS-4. Also request publication number 15, *Employer's Tax Guide (Circular E),* and the "Small Business Tax Kit."

Employment Regulations: If you have questions about employment regulations, call the Department of Labor Wage/Hour Offices for your state given in the list of SBA offices which follows this section, or the state Employment Security Office, as identified in commercial telephone listings.

Equal Access to Justice: The Equal Access to Justice Act permits the award of attorneys' fees to individuals or businesses that prevail in civil litigation with the federal government. Many states have now enacted state versions of the Equal Access to Justice Act covering local situations.

Export: See the listing for International Trade.

Export License: A government document which permits "licensee" to engage in the export of designated goods to certain destinations. All exporters of goods will need an export license, granted by the Department of Commerce. The license may be either general or specific, depending on the article being exported. Some restricted articles will need Department of State, Defense, or Energy approval. Contact district offices of ITA for your state given in the list of SBA offices which follows this section, or call (202) 377-4811.

Farm/Rural Development Loans: Obtained through the Farmers' Home Administration (FmHA), The National Rural Development and Finance Corporation, the Cooperative League of the United States, the National Marine Fisheries Service, the National Cooperative Bank, or the Farm Credit Administration. SBA can make loans only in special circumstances. Call the FmHA number for your state given in the list of SBA offices which follows this section. For disaster assistance, contact disaster area offices if the loan assistance is needed as a result of a disaster or a government action, such as the Payment in Kind program.

F.O.B. (Free on Board): A pricing term indicating that the quoted price includes the cost of loading goods into transport vessels at the specified place.

Franchising: Franchising is a form of licensing by which the owner (the franchisor) distributes or markets a product, method, or service through affiliated dealers (the franchisees). The holder of the right is often given exclusive access to a defined geographical area. The product, method, or service being marketed is identified by a brand name, and the franchisor maintains control over the marketing methods employed. SBA district offices can provide generic information; the SBA publication *Evaluating Franchise Opportunities* is recommended.

The *Franchising Opportunities Handbook,* Stock Number 003-008-00198-0, published by the Department of Commerce, is the most complete handbook on franchising operations, including descriptions of rights and responsibilities of both franchisor and franchisee, as well as a description of hundreds of various franchise businesses. It is available from the Government Book Store (see page 138) for $15.00; call (202) 377-0342.

The International Franchise Association has a similar publication, as well as a code of conduct its members subscribe to.

International Franchise Association
1350 New York Ave., N.W.
Washington, DC 20005
(202) 628-8000

Garment Registration Number: A number that must appear somewhere on every garment sold in the United States; it indicates the manufacturer of the garment, which may not be the same as the label under which the clothing is sold. Numbers are assigned to manufacturers by the Federal Trade Commission. Contact Earl Johnson, (202) 376-2891.

Handicapped Assistance Loan Program: SBA district offices can be of help to sheltered workshops as well as to handicapped individuals who want to go into business for themselves. SBA has a low-interest (3 percent, set by law), direct loan program for disabled persons. However, SBA requires handicapped persons to demonstrate that their disability is such that it is impossible for them to secure employment, thus making it necessary to go into their own business to make a living. Contact state rehabilitation and/or state small business program offices for additional information.

High Tech (SBIR Program Grants and Venture Capital Financing): The Small Business Innovation Research (SBIR) program requires federal agencies with external research and development budgets of more than $100 million to set aside a fixed percentage of their awards for small firms. Each year, 12 participating federal agencies publish solicitations that describe their R&D needs, and whether they are to be awarded on a competitive basis. For additional information, call SBA/SBIR at (202) 653-6458.

Venture capital companies and other sources of capital interested in identifying SBIR award winners within particular technology or geographical areas can participate in the matching system by writing to the following source.

Commercialization Matching System
Small Business Administration
Office of Innovation, Research, and Technology
1441 L St., N.W., Rm. 500
Washington, DC 20416

Many states have special high-tech programs. Check the state lists that follow this section under the heading "State Offices."

Incubators: A concept in which many small businesses share one facility and common support activities, such as mailing, computer, and legal services, to lower costs. Incubators have been developed in several parts of the United States. SBA's Office of Private Sector Initiatives has several publications and is cosponsoring conferences. Contact the office at (202) 653-7880.

Insurance: All businesses should carry insurance. The best source of information will be insurance agents in the community where the business is located. Most carry general business owners' policies. Many businesses provide health insurance as an employee benefit; this is expensive and it will pay the business owner to shop around for the best plan. All states require some kind of workers' compensation insurance. State small business program offices can be helpful in providing information concerning workers' compensation policies.

Interest Rates   (current as of Oct. 1, 1986):

New York Prime Rate: 7½ percent;
SBA Guaranteed Loans: 2¼ to 2¾ percent over the prime rate;
SBA Direct Loans: 8¼ percent;
SBA Disaster Loans: 8 percent if money is available elsewhere; 4 percent if no other funds are available (call appropriate disaster area office listed on page 337);
Federal prompt pay interest rate: 8½ percent (see also prompt pay).

International Trade: SBA has a $500,000 guaranteed export revolving line of credit. SBA and Eximbank have joint programs that provide for up to 90-percent guaranty for loans ranging from $200,000 to $1 million, as well as a business development assistance program. Call your SBA district office for information.

A vital primer for the new exporter is *A Basic Guide to Exporting*, sold by U.S. Government Printing Office bookstores. The publication Stock Number is 003-009-00349-1; the cost is $6.50.

For more information, call the Department of Commerce's International Trade Administration Office. See also the state lists that follow this section. If no office is listed, contact your state commerce department. In addition, there is a general export counseling office in Washington, D.C. at (202) 377-3181. Many states offer help for small businesses; see the listing for ITA.

Call the toll-free number for the Overseas Private Investment Corporation: (800) 424-6742. Eximbank conducts regional conferences. Call the Eximbank (800) 424-5201 hotline for the schedule.

Export management companies (EMCs) and export trading companies (ETCs) are private entities that assist smaller firms with export paperwork and regulations. EMCs and ETCs can be located by contacting the ETC office of ITA at (202) 377-5131.

Labor Surplus Area: In procurement, extra points are given to firms in counties that are designated labor surplus (high unemployment) areas. This information is requested on procurement bid sheets. Contact Marie Gupta at the Department of Labor ([202] 376-6185) with the name of the *county* and *state* in which your business is either located or where the work is to be substantially done to find out if it is in a labor surplus area.

Loans: Many businesses obtain financing by borrowing money. Basic information on what information is received in a loan application should be obtained from banks or other lending institutions. SBA programs include the following.

Guaranteed loans are loans made by lending institutions in which SBA will pay a prior agreed-upon percentage of the outstanding principal in the event the borrower of the loan defaults. The terms of the guaranteed loan and the interest rate are negotiated between borrower and lending institution, within the following parameters: operating capital—up to 2¼ percent over the New York prime interest rate up to 7 years; investment capital—up to 2¾ percent over the New York prime interest rate from 7 to 25 years.

Direct loans are made directly by SBA. Monies for direct loans come from funds appropriated specifically for this purpose. They are available only to applicants unable to secure private financing or an SBA-guaranteed loan. Call SBA district offices for information. (Currently only handicapped, disabled and Vietnam veterans, and businesses located in depressed areas may apply, when funds are available.)

Special lending institution categories include certified banks for which the SBA has promised a 72-hour turnaround in giving its approval for the loan, and preferred lenders in a pilot program that allows banks to write SBA loans without seeking prior SBA approval. Other sources of small business financing include state and local economic development agencies, SBICs, and certified development corporations.

SBA requires all businesses seeking loans to contact commercial lending institutions. The business should also contact the SBA Office of Business Development in the local district office early for guidance.

Minority Businesses: SBA defines minorities as those who are "socially and economically disadvantaged." The regulations are complicated and applicants usually must fulfill all of the various criteria. Social disadvantage has to do with membership in one of several different racial or ethnic categories as defined by regulation, or on a case-by-case basis for others who feel they are socially disadvantaged (the physically handicapped, for example). Economic disadvantage has to do with the barriers that social disadvantage has placed in the way of an individual's participation in business and employment. SBA district offices have minority-business specialists who can help with the definitions. In most cases, being a woman does not by itself qualify as minority status.

For more information contact your SBA district office's minority-business representatives. SBA no longer has minority-business loans, although all of its loans are equal opportunity. Many states have small- and minority-business offices; see the state lists that follow this section.

One federal minority procurement program is called the SBA Act, Section 8(a) program. Call your SBA district office procurement specialist for details.

MBDA has contracted with private firms throughout the United States to sponsor MBDCs to provide minority firms with advice and technical assistance on a fee basis.

Nonprofit Corporations: A familiar form of nonprofit corporation is the religious, charitable, or educational corporation. Its purpose is not to make a profit, but it is permitted to do so if the profit is left within the corporation. By law, SBA can help nonprofit organizations only to the extent that some SBA management assistance programs offer general assistance on how to run a nonprofit organization.

Office of Small and Disadvantaged Business Utilization: Each agency of the federal government has an office located in Washington, DC that is responsible for assuring that the agency complies with federal regulations to purchase a certain percentage of products and services from small and minority-owned and -operated businesses. Small businesses with procurement problems or questions are advised to first contact a procurement center representative, a GSA business service center, or agency contracting officers. If the small firm cannot receive help, however, it can contact the OSDBU in Washington, DC; see the listing on page 81 of this directory.

Patent: A patent is a grant from the government that conveys and secures to an inventor the exclusive right to make, use, and sell an invention for 17 years. Inventors need to contact the Patent Office of the Department of Commerce. Getting a patent is a relatively time-consuming, somewhat expensive process, often necessitating the employment of a consultant or attorney. Special publications are available from both SBA and the Superintendent of Documents for a nominal fee. See the Government Printing Office bookstore listing on page 341. The telephone number of the Patent Office is (703) 557-3158.

Preferred Lenders Program: Preferred lenders are banks in a program under a written agreement with SBA that can write a guaranteed SBA loan without prior SBA approval. The business must already exist, and the loan must be between $100,000 and $1 million. SBA is at risk for 75 percent of any outstanding balance on one of these loans if it defaults. Call your SBA district office for more information.

Procurement Assistance (Contract from the Government): Procurement can be a good source of income for the small-business owner if the business has a product or service of interest to federal agencies. The procurement process is complicated, but not impossibly so. Small businesses should be particularly interested in two types of procurement: small business set-asides, which are procurement opportunities required by law to be on all contracts exceeding $10,000 or a certain percentage of an agency's total procurement expenditure; and the SBA 8(a) program, in which minority-owned and -operated small businesses are admitted to the program and can negotiate on special contracts. Sources for procurement information include your SBA district and regional office, the GSA Business Service Center; procurement center representatives of SBA; and agency offices of OSDBU. Many states have their own programs; check the state program lists that follow this section.

Prompt Pay: If federal government agencies do not pay invoices for goods and services within 45 days of billing, they have to pay interest to the vendor on any amount due over 30 days. Previous rates include:

> July to December 1984: $10\frac{3}{8}$ percent
> January to June 1985: $12\frac{1}{8}$ percent
> July to December 1985: $10\frac{3}{8}$ percent
> January to June 1986: $9\frac{3}{4}$ percent
> July to December 1986: $8\frac{1}{2}$ percent

The procurement office of the contracting agency can explain how the program will affect a particular vendor.

Publications: SBA publishes more than 140 separate publications, many at cost. The low-cost (25–50 cents) pamphlets are available by contacting your SBA district office or by writing to the SBA distribution center at P.O. Box 30, Denver, Colo. 80201-0030. There is no longer a toll-free service to order SBA publications. For-sale documents are available from the Government Printing Office bookstores listed on page 341, and can be ordered by calling (202) 783-3238. Publication lists of all SBA books are available from your SBA district office.

Residential Property: By law, SBA does not make loans for residential or investment property (even though running an apartment building is a business) unless the residential property is involved in a disaster declaration. Several other federal agencies do have programs. Call local lending firms (banks and savings and loan associations) for information.

Score/Ace: The Service Corps of Retired Executives (SCORE) and the Active Corps of Executives (ACE) are volunteer business-development programs of SBA. SCORE and ACE volunteers provide one-on-one counseling and teach workshops and seminars for small firms. Contact your SBA district office for an application for counseling. More than 400 chapters exist throughout the United States. Call your nearest SBA office or consult your local telephone directory under SCORE.

Secondary Market: There is a growing market for SBA-guaranteed loans sold as government securities. These are of primary interest to institutional investors, although individuals may also participate. Contact Jim Ramsey, at (212) 264-5877, in SBA's New York City office for more information. Major brokerage firms also have specialists in government securities that can provide information to both banks and individuals interested in participating in the secondary market for SBA-guaranteed loans.

Securities and Exchange Commission (SEC): See the listing for Stock.

Security Clearance: To bid on many Department of Defense and defense-related contracts and subcontracts, a security clearance is needed. Information on security clearances is available from Phillmar Tenney, Defense Investigative Service, Department of Defense at (202) 475-0906.

Size Standards: Measurements of business size that determine whether a business is "small" by the definitions of SBA (primarily as related to SBA programs). The size standard for an individual business is based on its particular type of business and the number of employees or gross annual sales it averages over a three-year period. The District Counsel in each SBA district office makes the initial certification of whether a business is small or not, but this decision can be appealed to the Regional Counsel or to the SBA Board of Hearings and Appeals in Washington, DC; a rule-of-thumb definition of a small firm is one that is independently owned and operated, not dominant in its field, and with fewer than 500 employees. For more information, contact the SBA Size Standard Office at (202) 653-7481.

Small Business Development Centers: SBDCs draw from resources of local, state, and federal government programs, the private sector, and university facilities to provide managerial and technical help, research studies, and other types of specialized assistance of value to small businesses. These university-based centers provide individual counseling and practical training for small-business owners. See the state listings that follow this section for local contacts.

Small Business Innovation Research Program (SBIR): See the listing for High Tech.

Small Business Institute (SBI) Program: Cooperative arrangements are made by SBA district offices and local colleges and universities to provide small businesses with graduate students to counsel them without charge. Contact your district office for more information.

Small Business Investment Company (SBIC): SBICs are licensed by SBA as federally funded private venture capital firms. Money is available to small businesses under a variety of agreements. This money is usually, but not always, limited to capital expansion for newer, riskier, or high-tech firms. SBA's Office of Investment publishes a directory of SBICs, what they fund and where they operate. Call the SBA Office of Investment at (202) 653-6584, or see the listing for Washington contacts on page 415.

Standard Industrial Classification Code (SIC Code Number): Generally, a four-digit number is assigned to identify a business based on the type of business or trade involved. The first two digits correspond to major groups such as construction and manufacturing; the next two digits correspond to subgroups such as constructing homes versus constructing highways. A business can determine its SIC number by looking it up in a directory published by the Department of Commerce, or by checking in the SIC book in the reference section of a local library. SBA size standards are based on SIC codes.

Standard Metropolitan Statistical Area (SMSA): A means that the government uses to define large population centers that may transverse different governmental jurisdictions. For example, the Washington, DC, SMSA includes the District of Columbia and contiguous parts of Maryland and Virginia because all of these geopolitical areas comprise one population and economic operating unit. SMSAs are set by the Department of Commerce.

Stock: A certificate of equity ownership in a business. Many small businesses at some point want to sell stock in their company to raise capital. When this happens, federal and state laws may require registration. Business owners should check with the SEC on the federal level and the state securities commission. Call the SEC small business office at (202) 272-2644, and your state small business program office.

Student Loans: The student-aid information clearinghouse in the Department of Education is at (301) 241-4710.

Surety Bond Guarantees: Surety bonds provide reimbursement to an individual, company, or the government if a firm fails to complete a contract. SBA guarantees surety companies administered by SBA regional offices. A list of regional surety bond contacts is on page 340.

Taxes: Small businesses should contact the IRS and state revenue office, both of which are given in the state lists that follow this section. A helpful IRS publication is the *Tax Guide for Small Business,* publication 334.

Tax Number (State Sales Tax): A number assigned to a business by a state revenue department that enables the business to buy wholesale without paying sales tax on goods and products. Contact your state Department of Revenue given in the state lists that follow this section. See also Employer I.D. Number.

Trademark: A trademark is a distinctive mark, model device, or emblem that manufacturers stamp, print, or otherwise affix to the goods they produce so that the goods can be identified in the market and their origin can be vouched for. Federal statute allows a trademark to be registered by its owner or user. Exclusive use of the trademark can be perpetual. All trademarks should be registered with the Trademark Office of the Department of Commerce at (703) 557-3268.

Trucking License for Interstate Carriers (ICC MC): Contact the Interstate Commerce Commission, Small Business Assistance Office at (202) 275-7597.

Uniform Product Code: A label comprised of ten digits and stripes that automatic checkout computers can use to determine what a product is and how much it costs. The first five numbers are assigned by the Uniform Product Code Council, and the last five digits by the individual manufacturer. For additional information, contact the following source.
Universal Code Council
7051 Corporate Way, Ste. 106
Dayton, OH 45459
(513) 435-3870

Veterans (Vietnam Era): Veterans have a preference on all SBA loans. This means the application should be processed more quickly, but no other requirements for a loan are waived. In some cases, money may be available from a direct loan program; most SBA district offices have Veterans' Affairs Coordinators. Call this individual, or the financial assistance number given in the state lists that follow this section.

Withholding: All employers are required to withhold certain taxes from employees' wages, including federal and state, social security, and unemployment taxes. Employers are liable for these taxes and the corporate umbrella and bankruptcy will not exonerate an employer from paying back payroll withholding. Employers should escrow these funds in a separate account and disperse them quarterly to withholding authorities. Employers should contact the SBA, IRS, local Social Security office, the Wage and Hour Office of the Labor Department, and the state Employment Security Office for information and forms.

Women: Most SBA offices have Women's Business Coordinators; contact these individuals using the direct phone number given in the state lists that follow this section.

Women, per se, are not classified as minorities for federal SBA programs; however, some states do class women as minorities for state programs. Call your state Small Business Program office. All SBA programs are *equal opportunity.*

Workers' Compensation: All employers must provide workers' compensation coverage for job-related accidents. In some states, the state is the insurer; in other states, insurance must be acquired from commercial insurance firms. Insurance rates are based on a number of factors, including salaries, firm history, and risk of occupation.

SMALL BUSINESS ADMINISTRATION OFFICES

Alabama Region IV

Small Business Administration
District Office
2121 Eighth Ave., North, Ste. 200
Birmingham, AL 35203-2398

Business Development	(205) 731-1338	
Financial Assistance	(205) 731-1344	
Veterans' Affairs Officer	(205) 731-1338	James W. Allen
Women's Business Ownership	(205) 731-0706	Donna Glenn
Disaster Home Loan Servicing Centers 4 and 7	(205) 731-0441	Dennis Bayles
Small Business Development Centers		
	(205) 826-4030	Auburn
	(205) 934-6760	Birmingham
	(205) 895-6407	Huntsville
	(205) 895-6407	High-Tech
	(205) 231-5271	Jacksonville
	(205) 652-9661, ext. 439	Livingstone
	(205) 293-4137	Montgomery
	(205) 859-7481	Normal
	(205) 566-3000	Troy
	(205) 348-7011	Tuscaloosa

| | (205) 348-7621 | Tuscaloosa International |
| | (205) 727-6307 | Tuskegee University |

State Offices

Consumer Complaints	(800) 392-5658	Montgomery
Department of Revenue	(205) 261-3257	
Loan Information	(205) 264-5441	
Minority Business	(205) 261-2825	
Procurement	(205) 934-7260	
State Development Office	(205) 263-0048	
State Export	(205) 284-8722	
Enterprise Zones	(205) 284-8777	William Wallace

Other U.S. Government Offices

IRS	(800) 424-1040	Birmingham
Farmers' Home Administration	(205) 832-7077	Montgomery
Department of Commerce	(205) 731-1331	Birmingham
Department of Labor, Wage/Hour Division	(205) 731-1305	Birmingham
Occupational Safety and Health Administration	(205) 822-7100	
	(205) 690-2131	Mobile
International Trade Administration	322-8591*	
Federal Information Centers	438-1421*	Mobile

Alaska Region X

Small Business Administration
District Office
701 C St., Box 67
Anchorage, AK 99513

Business Development	(907) 271-4022	
Financial Assistance	(907) 271-4022	
Veterans' Affairs Officer	(907) 271-4022	Mike Siemion
Women's Business Ownership	(907) 271-4022	Jean Sawyer

State Offices

Small Business Program Loan Information:	(907) 465-2018	
Alaska Industrial Development	(907) 274-1651	Anchorage
Department of Revenue	(907) 276-2678	Anchorage

*Number may be used only within this city.

Alaska Region X

| State Export | (907) 465-2200 | Juneau |
| Insurance | (907) 465-2515 | John George |

Other U.S. Government Offices

IRS	561-7484 *	Anchorage
Farmers' Home Administration	(907) 745-2176	Palmer
Department of Commerce	(907) 271-5041	Anchorage
Department of Energy	(907) 271-5954	Anchorage
Department of Labor, Wage/Hour Division	(206) 442-4482	Seattle, WA
Occupational Safety and Health Administration	(907) 271-5152	Anchorage
International Trade Administration	(907) 271-5041	Anchorage
Federal Information Center	(907) 271-3650/3542	Anchorage
National Marine Fisheries Service	(907) 271-5006	Anchorage

Arizona Region IX

Small Business Administration
District Office
2005 N. Central Ave. 5th Floor
Phoenix, AZ 85004

Post of Duty Office
300 W. Congress St., Rm.
3V, Tucson, AZ 85701

Business Development		
Phoenix	(602) 261-3732	
Tucson	(602) 629-6715	
Financial Assistance		
Phoenix	(602) 261-3732	
Tucson	(602) 629-6715	
Veterans' Affairs Officer	(602) 261-3732	Vince Tammelleo

State Offices

Consumer Complaints	(800) 352-8431	
Department of Revenue	(602) 255-3381	Phoenix
Small Business Program	(602) 255-5705	
Insurance	(602) 255-1986	S. David Childers

Other U.S. Government Offices

| IRS | (800) 424-1040 | Phoenix |
| Farmers' Home Administration | (602) 261-6701 | |

*Number may be used only within this city.

Department of Commerce	(602) 261-3285	
Department of Labor, Wage/Hour Division	(602) 241-2990	
Occupational Safety and Health Administration	(602) 241-2007	
International Trade Administration	(602) 261-3285	
Federal Information Centers	(602) 261-3313	

Arkansas Region VI

Small Business Administration
District Office
320 W. Capitol Ave., Rm. 601
Little Rock, AR 72201

Business Development	(501) 378-5813	
Financial Assistance	(501) 378-5871	
Veterans' Affairs Officer	(501) 378-5871	Walter Thayer
Women's Business Ownership	(501) 378-5871	Charlotte Vitro
Small Business Development Centers		
	(501) 246-5511, ext. 327	Arkadelphia
	(501) 450-3190	Conway
	(501) 575-5148	Fayetteville
	(800) 482-5850, ext. 5381	Little Rock
	(501) 268-6161, ext. 497	Searcy
	(501) 972-3517	State University
	(501) 371-5381	Little Rock

State Office

Consumer Complaints	(800) 482-8982	Little Rock
Department of Revenue	(501) 371-1476	
Loan Information	(501) 374-9247	
Minority Business	(501) 371-1121	
Small Business Program	(501) 371-1121	
State Development Office	(501) 371-2052	
Insurance	(501) 371-1325	Robert M. Eubanks
Enterprise Zones	(501) 371-5123	Oscar Rodriguez
State Export	(501) 371-7781	

Other U.S. Government Offices

IRS	(800) 424-1040	Little Rock
Farmers' Home Administration	(501) 378-6281	

Arkansas Region VI

Department of Commerce	(501) 378-5794
Department of Energy	(501) 371-1370
Department of Labor, Wage/Hour Division	(501) 378-5292
Occupational Safety and Health Administration	(501) 378-6291
International Trade Administration	(501) 378-5794
Federal Information Center	378-6177*
Veterans' Administration	(800) 482-5434

California Region IX

Small Business Administration
District Offices
211 Main St., 4th Floor
San Francisco, CA 94105
2202 Monterey St., Rm. 108
Fresno, CA 93721
350 S. Figueroa St., 6th Floor
Los Angeles, CA 90071
880 Front St., Rm. 4-S-29
San Diego, CA 85701

Branch Offices
660 J St., Room 215
Sacramento, CA 95814
2700 N. Main St., Rm. 400
Santa Ana, CA 92701

Business Development		
Fresno	(209) 487-5605	
Los Angeles	(213) 894-7172/3016	Joseph F. Sachs
Sacramento	(916) 551-1440	
San Diego	(619) 293-7250	
San Francisco	(415) 974-0590	
Santa Ana	(714) 836-2494	

Financial Assistance	
Fresno	(209) 487-5189
Los Angeles	(213) 894-4005
Sacramento	(916) 551-1426
San Diego	(619) 293-7273
San Francisco	(415) 974-0617 (recording)
Santa Ana	(714) 836-2494

*Number may be used only within this city.

Veterans' Affairs
Officers

Fresno	(209) 487-5790	Warren Kightlinger
Los Angeles	(213) 894-7900	Geo Symons
Sacramento	(916) 551-1436	Paul Rudolph
San Diego	(619) 293-7254	Roger Dalagon
San Francisco	(415) 974-0590	Don McMahon

Women's Business
Ownership

Fresno	(209) 487-5798	Margaret Gonzalez
Los Angeles	(213) 894-4086	Marie D. Teeple
Sacramento	(916) 551-1440	Jim Lortz
San Diego	(619) 293-7250	Darlene McKinnon
San Francisco	(415) 974-0634	Nell Klas

Disaster Home Loan Service Center	(714) 836-2327	Karen Aubry

State Offices

Department of Commerce	(916) 322-1394	
Small Business Program Loan Information:	(916) 322-5060	Sacramento
California Office of Small Business Development	(916) 322-5060	
Alternative Energy Source Financing	(916) 324-3000	Sacramento
Office of Small and Minority Business	(916) 322-5060	
Department of State	(916) 369-0500	
Franchise Tax Board		
State Banking	(415) 557-0963	San Francisco
State Export	(916) 324-5511	
Export Financing	(213) 620-2433	Los Angeles, Fargo Wells
Consumer Complaints	(916) 445-0660	
Enterprise Zones	(916) 324-8211	Kurt Shilcott
Insurance	(213) 736-2551	Raxani Gillespie

Other U.S. Government Offices

IRS	See White Pages	Los Angeles
	(415) 839-1040	San Francisco
Farmers' Home Administration	(916) 666-3382	Woodland
Department of Commerce	(213) 736-3680	Los Angeles
	(619) 293-5395	San Diego
Department of Energy	(916) 273-4428	Sacramento
Department of Labor, Wage/Hour Division	(818) 240-5274	Glendale
	(916) 978-4233	Sacramento
	(714) 836-2156	Santa Ana

California Region IX

	(415) 974-0535	San Francisco
	(213) 252-7566	Los Angeles
Occupational Safety and	(213) 514-6387	Long Beach
Health Administration		
International Trade	(213) 209-6707	Los Angeles
Administration	(714) 836-2332	Orange County
Federal Information	(213) 894-3800	Los Angeles
Centers	(619) 293-6030	San Diego
	275-7422*	San Jose
	836-2386*	Santa Ana
Small Business Service	(213) 894-5307	
Center		
Bureau of the Census	(213) 209-6612	Los Angeles

Colorado Region VIII

Small Business Administration
District Office
721 19th St., Rm. 454
Denver, CO 80202

Business Development	(303) 844-3984	SCORE
	(303) 534-7518	
Financial Assistance	(303) 844-3568	
Veterans' Affairs Officer	(303) 844-6514	Al Lopez
Women's Business	(303) 844-4446	Dianne Gray
Ownership		

State Offices

Department of Revenue	(303) 534-1209	Denver
Minority Business	(303) 866-2077	
Procurement	(303) 757-9011	
Information		
State Export	(303) 866-2205	
Insurance	(303) 866-3201	J. Richard Barnes

Other U.S. Government Offices

IRS	(800) 424-1040	
Farmers' Home	(303) 964-0150	
Administration		
Department of	(303) 844-3888	Denver
Commerce		
Department of Energy	(303) 236-2000	
Department of Labor,	(303) 844-4405	
Wage/Hour Division		

*Number may be used only within this city.

Occupational Safety and Health Administration	(303) 844-5285	
International Trade Administration	(303) 844-2900	
Federal Information Centers	471-9491*	Colorado Springs
	544-9523*	Pueblo
Enterprise Zones-HUD	(303) 844-5121	

Connecticut Region I

Small Business Administration
District Office
One Hartford Sq., West
Hartford, CT 06106

Business Development	(203) 722-2544	
Financial Assistance	(203) 722-3600	
Veterans' Affairs Officer	(203) 722-2544	Kitty Duncan
Women's Business Ownership	(203) 722-2544	Maria Cirurgiao
Small Business Development Centers		
	(203) 335-3800	Bridgeport
	(203) 774-1130	Danielson
	(203) 241-4983	Hartford
	(203) 787-6735	New Haven
	(203) 442-9192	New London
	(203) 359-3220	Stamford
	(203) 486-4135	Storrs
	(203) 486-4135	Storrs Export
	(203) 486-2770	Storrs Law
	(203) 757-0701	Waterbury
	(203) 241-4982	West Hartford

State Offices

Small Business Program	(203) 566-4051	Hartford
State Development Office	(203) 566-3787	
Loan Information:		
Connecticut Product Development Corporation (risk capital to established manufacturing firms with a primary focus on job creation)	(203) 566-2920	

*Number may be used only within this city.

Connecticut Region I

Department of Economic Development (enterprise-zone business start-ups)	(203) 566-4051	
Procurement Information	(203) 566-4051	
Department of Revenue	(203) 566-8520	Hartford
State Export	(203) 566-3842	
Consumer Complaints	(800) 842-2649	
Ombudsman	(203) 566-7035	
Department of Energy	(203) 566-5803	
Product Development Corporation	(203) 566-2920	
Enterprise Zones	(203) 566-3322	
Insurance	(203) 566-5275	Peter W. Gilles
Venture Capital	(203) 566-2920	Burt Jonap

Other U.S. Government Offices

IRS	(800) 424-1040	Hartford
Farmers' Home Administration	(413) 253-3471	Amherst, MA
Federal Information	527-2617*	Hartford
Centers	624-4720*	New Haven
Department of Commerce	(203) 722-3530	Hartford
Department of Energy	(800) 424-0256	Hartford
Department of Labor, Wage/Hour Division	(203) 722-2660	Hartford
Occupational Safety and Health Administration	(203) 722-2294	Hartford
International Trade Administration	(203) 722-3530	Hartford

Delaware Region III

Small Business Administration
Branch Office
844 King St., Rm. 5207
Wilmington, DE 19801

Business Development	(302) 573-6295	
Financial Assistance	(302) 573-6295	
Veterans' Affairs Officer	(302) 573-6295	John J. Giannini
Small Business Development Center University of Delaware	(302) 451-2747	

*Number may be used only within this city.

State Offices

Small Business Program	(302) 736-4271	Dover
Loan Information	(302) 736-4271	
Department of Revenue	(302) 571-3300	Wilmington
State Export	(302) 736-4271	
Insurance	(302) 736-4251	David N. Levinson
Enterprise Zones	(302) 736-4271	Dorothy Sbriglin
	(800) 441-8846	

Other U.S. Government Offices

IRS	(800) 424-1040	Wilmington
Department of Commerce	(215) 597-2866	Philadelphia, PA
Department of Energy	(302) 736-5644	Dover
Department of Labor, Wage/Hour Division	(302) 573-6112	Wilmington
Occupational Safety and Health Administration	(302) 573-6115	Wilmington
International Trade Administration	(215) 597-2866	Philadelphia, PA

District of Columbia Region III

Small Business Administration
District Office
1111 18th St., N.W., Sixth Floor
Washington, DC 20036

Business Development	(202) 634-6200	
Financial Assistance	(202) 634-6200	
Veterans' Affairs Officer	(202) 634-4975	Michael Dowd
Women's Business Ownership	(202) 634-1805	Janice Wolfe
Small Business Development Centers		
Howard University, DC	(202) 636-5150	
Georgetown University, DC	(202) 676-7463	
George Mason University, VA	(703) 323-2568	
Montgomery College, MD	(301) 656-7482	
University of Maryland, MD	(301) 454-5072	

State Offices

Loan Information	(202) 727-6600
Procurement Information	(202) 727-0171
IRS	(202) 566-5000

District of Columbia Region III

Department of Revenue	(202) 629-4665	
Consumer Complaints	(202) 727-7000	
Telephone Consumer Hotline, Inc.	(202) 483-4100	
Licensing	(202) 727-7089	
Insurance	(202) 727-1273	Marguerite C. Stokes

Other U.S. Government Offices

IRS	(202) 566-5000	
Farmers' Home Administration	(202) 447-4323	
Department of Commerce	(202) 377-2000	
Department of Energy	(202) 252-5000	
Department of Labor, Wage/Hour Division	(301) 436-6776	Hyattsville, MD
Occupational Safety and Health Administration	(202) 523-8151	
International Trade Administration	(202) 377-3181	
Federal Information Center	(202) 472-1082	

Florida Region IV

Small Business Administration
District Office
400 W. Bay St., Rm. 261
Jacksonville, FL 32202-4487
1320 S. Dixie Hwy., Ste. 501
Coral Gables, FL 33146

Post of Duty Offices
700 Twiggs St., Rm. 607
Tampa, FL 33602
3550 45th St., Ste. 6
West Palm Beach, FL 33407

Business Development	
Jacksonville	(904) 791-3105
Miami	(305) 536-5521
Tampa	(813) 228-2594
West Palm Beach	(305) 689-2223
Financial Assistance	
Jacksonville	(904) 791-3782
Miami	(305) 536-5521
Tampa	(813) 228-2594
West Palm Beach	(305) 689-2223

Veterans' Affairs
Officers
Jacksonville	(904) 791-3107	Fred W. Bethea
Miami	(305) 536-5521	Jack Geis

Women's Business
Ownership
Jacksonville	(904) 791-3782	Lucille Trotter
Miami	(305) 536-5521	Patricia McCartney

Small Business
Development Centers
(305) 467-4238	Boca Raton
(904) 734-1066	Deland
(904) 244-1036	Eglin AFB
(305) 467-4238	Fort Lauderdale
(904) 377-5621	Gainesville
(904) 646-2476	Jacksonville
(305) 294-8481	Key West
(904) 752-1822	Lake City
(305) 554-2272	Miami
(305) 940-5790	North Miami
	International
(305) 275-2796	Orlando
(305) 627-4278	Palm Beach
(904) 763-0378	Panama City
(305) 987-0100	Pembrook
(904) 474-3016	Pensacola
(813) 893-9529	St. Petersburg
(904) 644-6524	Tallahassee
(904) 599-3407	Tallahassee A&M
(904) 644-2053/4091	Tallahassee SU
(813) 974-4274	Tampa

State Offices
Small Business Program	(800) 342-0771	
	(904) 488-9357	
State Economic	(904) 488-6300	Tallahassee
Development Office		
Department of Revenue	(904) 488-2574	
Consumer Complaints	(800) 342-2176	
International Trade	(904) 488-5280	
	(904) 488-6124	
High-Tech	(904) 487-1314	
Enterprise Zones	(904) 488-7956	Priscilla Howard
Insurance	(904) 488-3440	William Gunter

Other U.S. Government Offices
IRS	(800) 424-1040	
	(904) 354-1760	Jacksonville
Farmers' Home	(904) 376-3218	Gainesville
Administration		

Florida Region IV

Department of	(305) 536-5267	Miami
Commerce	(813) 461-0011	Clearwater
	(305) 425-1234	Orlando
Governor's Energy	(904) 488-2475	Tallahassee
Office		
Department of Labor,	(904) 791-2489	Jacksonville
Wage/Hour Division	(305) 527-7262	Fort Lauderdale
	(305) 536-5767	Miami
	(813) 228-2154	Tampa
Occupational Safety and	(305) 527-7292	Fort Lauderdale
Health Administration	(813) 228-2821	Tampa
	(904) 791-2895	Jacksonville
International Trade	(305) 350-5267	Miami
Administration		
Federal Information	522-8531*	Fort Lauderdale
Centers	354-4756*	Jacksonville
	(305) 536-4155	Miami
	422-1800*	Orlando
	(813) 893-3495	St. Petersburg
	229-7911*	Tampa
	833-7566*	West Palm Beach
	(800) 282-8556	North Florida
	(800) 432-6668	South Florida
National Marine Fisheries	(813) 893-3141	St. Petersburg
Service		

Georgia Region IV

Small Business Administration
District Office
1720 Peachtree Rd., N.W., 6th Floor
Atlanta, GA 30309

Post of Duty Office
52 N. Main St., Rm. 225
Statesboro, GA 30458

Business Development		
Atlanta	(404) 347-2441	
Statesboro	(912) 489-8719	
Financial Assistance		
Atlanta	(404) 347-3583	
Statesboro	(912) 489-8719	
Veterans' Affairs Officer		
Atlanta	(404) 347-2441	Hartsel Brady

*Number may be used only within this city.

Women's Business
Ownership
Atlanta   (404) 347-2441   Paula Hill

Small Business
Development Centers
                                (912) 439-7232   Albany
                                (404) 542-7436   Athens
                                (404) 658-3550   Atlanta
                                (404) 737-1790   Augusta
                                (912) 264-7343   Brunswick
                                (404) 571-7433   Columbus
                                (912) 741-8023   Macon
                                (404) 429-2800   Marietta
                                (404) 961-3414   Morrow
                                (404) 295-6327   Rome
                                (912) 681-5194   Statesboro

State Offices
State Development   (404) 656-3556   Atlanta
Office
Procurement   (404) 656-5514
Information
Minority Business   (404) 656-6315
Department of Revenue   (404) 656-4015
State Export   (404) 656-3571
Consumer Complaints   (800) 282-4900
High-Tech   (404) 894-3575
Enterprise Zones   (404) 656-3568   Alton Moultrie
Insurance   (404) 656-2056   Warren Evans

Other U.S. Government Offices
IRS   (800) 424-1040
Farmers' Home   (404) 546-2162   Athens
Administration
Department of   (912) 944-4205   Savannah
Commerce   (404) 347-7000   Atlanta
Department of Labor,   (404) 347-4801   Atlanta
Wage/Hour Division   (912) 944-4222   Savannah
Occupational Safety and   (404) 331-4767   Tucker
Health Administration   (912) 233-3923   Savannah
International Trade   (404) 347-7000   Atlanta
Administration   (912) 944-4204   Savannah
Federal Information   (404) 331-6891   Atlanta
Center
Enterprise Zones-HUD   (404) 331-5139   William Melvin

Hawaii Region IX

Small Business Administration
District Office
300 Ala Moana, Rm. 2213
Honolulu, HI 96850

Business Development	(808) 546-3119	
Financial Assistance	(808) 546-3151	
Veterans' Affairs Officer	(808) 546-7336	Richard Waidzunas
Women's Business Ownership	(808) 546-3119	

State Offices

Small Business Program	(808) 548-4608	Honolulu
State Development Office	(808) 548-3033	
Loan Information	(800) 367-5218	
	(808) 548-4616	
Department of Taxation	(808) 548-7650	
Insurance	(808) 548-6522	Mario R. Ramil

Other U.S. Government Offices

IRS	(800) 424-1040	
Farmers' Home Administration	(808) 961-4781	Hilo
Department of Commerce	(808) 546-8694	Honolulu
Department of Energy	(808) 548-2306	
Department of Labor, Wage/Hour Division	(808) 546-8363	
Occupational Safety and Health Administration	(808) 546-3157	
International Trade Administration	(808) 546-8694	
State Office	(808) 548-3048	
Federal Information Centers	(808) 546-8620	

Idaho Region X

Small Business Administration
District Office
1020 Main St., Ste. 290
Boise, ID 83702

Business Development	(208) 334-1780	
Financial Assistance	(208) 334-1696	
Veterans' Affairs Officer	(208) 334-1156	Michael G. Morfitt

Women's Business Ownership	(208) 334-1780	Sharon Barber
Small Business Development Center Boise	(208) 385-1640	

State Offices (all under new State Department of Commerce [Boise])

Small Business Program	(208) 334-3416	Boise
Permits and Licensing	(call county/city court house)	
Department of Revenue	(208) 334-3560	
Insurance	(208) 334-2250	Wayne Soward

Other U.S. Government Offices

IRS	(800) 424-1040	
	(208) 336-1040	Boise
Farmers' Home Administration	(208) 334-1301	Boise
Department of Commerce	(208) 334-2470/9254	Boise
Department of Energy	(208) 334-3800	Boise
Department of Labor, Wage/Hour Division	(208) 334-1029	Boise
Occupational Safety and Health Administration	(208) 334-1867	Boise
International Trade Administration	(208) 334-3416	

Illinois Region V

Small Business Administration
District Office
219 S. Dearborn St., Rm. 437
Chicago, IL 60604

Branch Office
Four North
Old State Capital Plaza,
Springfield, IL 62701

Business Development Chicago	(312) 353-7723	
Springfield	(217) 492-4416	
Financial Assistance Chicago	(312) 353-4486	
Springfield	(217) 492-4416	
Veterans' Affairs Officers Chicago	(312) 353-5125	Stan Magiera
Springfield	(217) 492-4768	Jim Ryan

Illinois Region V

Women's Business Ownership		
Chicago	(312) 353-4578	Delores La Valle
Springfield	(217) 492-4416	Valerie Ross
Small Business Development Centers		
	(618) 536-2424	Carbondale
	(312) 670-0432	Chicago
	(217) 875-7215	Decatur
	(815) 753-1403	DeKalb
	(618) 692-2929	Edwardsville
	(309) 298-1128	Macomb
	(309) 762-3661	Moline
	(309) 677-2309	Peoria
	(217) 492-4772	Springfield
	(312) 534-5000	University Park

State Offices

Small Business Program	(800) 252-2923	
	(312) 917-6596	Chicago
State Development Office	(217) 782-7500	Springfield
Illinois Department of Commerce and Community Affairs: Small Business Development Center Network (counseling)	(800) 252-2923	
Loan Information		
Illinois Industrial Development Authority	(618) 997-4371	Marion
Central	(309) 677-2309	
Quad Cities, Chamber of Commerce	(309) 762-3661	
Sangamon/Menard	(217) 786-2209	
Western University (SBDC)	(309) 298-1555	
Investment Pool	(800) 252-1774	
Cooperative Extension	(800) 847-6883	
Secretary of State	(800) 252-8980	
Management Info Systems	(800) 252-2923	
OHSA	(800) 972-4216	
Disaster (State Info)	(800) 782-7860	
Energy Info	(800) 252-8955	
Procurement Information	(217) 782-4705	

Minority Business	(312) 917-4194	
Department of Revenue	(800) 252-8972	
	(217) 782-3336	
State Export	(312) 917-2086	
Consumer Affairs	(800) 642-3112	
Enterprise Zones	(217) 785-6128	
Insurance	(312) 917-2420	Harry E. Eakin

Other U.S. Government Offices

IRS	(800) 424-1040	
	(312) 435-1040	Chicago
Farmers' Home Administration	(217) 398-5235	Champaign
U.S. Foreign and Commercial Service	(312) 353-4450	Chicago
Department of Energy	(217) 785-2009	Springfield
Department of Labor, Wage/Hour Division	(312) 353-8145	
	(217) 492-4060	Springfield
Occupational Safety and Health Administration	(312) 891-3800	Calumet City
	(312) 896-8700	North Aurora
	(309) 671-7033	Peoria
	(312) 631-8200	Niles
International Trade Administration	(312) 353-4450	
Federal Information Center	(312) 353-4242	
Enterprise Zones-HUD	(312) 353-1680	

Indiana Region V

Small Business Administration
District Office
575 N. Pennsylvania St., Rm. 578
Indianapolis, IN 46204-1584

Business Development	(317) 269-7264	
Financial Assistance	(317) 269-7272	
Veterans' Affairs Officer	(317) 269-5566	Robert Gastineau
Women's Business Ownership	(317) 269-7269	Robert Gastineau

State Offices

Small Business Program	(317) 634-8418	Indianapolis
State Development Office	(317) 232-8800	
Loan Information		
Corporation for Innovation Development	(317) 635-7325	Indianapolis
Department of Commerce	(800) 622-4464	Indianapolis

Indiana Region V

Department of Revenue	(317) 232-2330	Indianapolis
International Trade	(317) 232-8845	
Consumer Complaints	(800) 382-5516	
Secretary of State	(317) 232-6534	
Enterprise Zones	(317) 232-8783	Diane Lupke
Insurance	(317) 232-2386	Harry E. Eakins
Venture Capital	(317) 635-7325	Mr. Marion Dietrich
Economic Development-White/ Monticello City	(219) 583-6557	John Fuller

Other U.S. Government Offices

IRS	(800) 424-1040	
	(317) 269-5477	Indianapolis
Farmers' Home Administration	(317) 248-4440	Indianapolis
Department of Commerce	(317) 269-6214	
Department of Energy	(317) 232-8940	
Department of Labor, Wage/Hour Division	(317) 232-2680 (219) 236-8331	South Bend
Occupational Safety and Health Administration	(317) 269-7290	Indianapolis
International Trade Administration	(317) 269-6214	
Federal Information Centers	883-4110* (317) 269-7373	Gary/Hammond (Indianapolis)

Iowa Region VII

Small Business Administration
District Office
373 Collins Rd., N.E.
Cedar Rapids, IA 52402
210 Walnut St., Rm. 749
Des Moines, IA 50309

Business Development		
Cedar Rapids	(319) 399-2571	
Des Moines	(515) 284-4760	
Financial Assistance		
Cedar Rapids	(319) 399-2571	
Des Moines	(515) 284-4422	
Veterans' Affairs Officers		
Cedar Rapids	(319) 399-2571	Roger Hoffman
Des Moines	(515) 284-4562	Vern Sample

*Number may be used only within this city.

Iowa Region VII

Women's Business
Ownership
Cedar Rapids | (319) 399-2571 | Carolyn Puntenney
Des Moines | (515) 284-4762 | Cheryl Eftink
Small Business
Development Centers
| (515) 292-6355 | Ames
| (712) 563-3165 | Audubon
| (319) 273-2696 | Cedar Falls
| (712) 325-3260 | Council Bluffs
| (319) 322-4499 | Davenport
| (515) 271-2655 | Des Moines
| (319) 588-3350 | Dubuque
| (319) 353-5340 | Iowa City
| (515) 421-4342 | Mason City
| (712) 279-6286 | Sioux City

State Offices
Small Business Program | (515) 281-8310
| (800) 532-1216 | Des Moines
State Development | (515) 281-3251
Office
Loan Information | (515) 281-4058
  Iowa Product | (515) 281-5459
  Development
  Corporation
Procurement | (515) 281-3089
Information
Department of Revenue | (515) 281-3114
Department of Energy | (515) 281-4420
State Export | (515) 281-3581
Ombudsman | (515) 281-3592
Insurance | (515) 281-5705 | William Hager

Other U.S. Government Offices
IRS | (800) 424-1040
| (515) 283-0523 | Des Moines
Farmers' Home | (515) 284-4663
Administration
Department of | (515) 284-4222
Commerce
Department of Labor, | (515) 284-4625
Wage/Hour Division
Occupational Safety and | (515) 284-4794
Health Administration
International Trade | (515) 284-4222
Administration
Federal Information | (515) 284-4448
Centers | (800) 532-1556

Kansas Region VII

Small Business Administration
District Offices
110 E. Waterman St.,
Wichita, KS 67202
1103 Grande Ave., Rm. 512
Kansas City, MO 64106

Business Development		
Kansas City	(816) 374-5868	
Wichita	(316) 269-6273	
Financial Assistance		
Kansas City	(816) 374-3416	
Wichita	(316) 269-6571	
Veterans' Affairs Officers		
Kansas City	(816) 374-5868	Gene Anderson
Wichita	(316) 269-6273	Ted Little
Women's Business Ownership		
Kansas City	(816) 374-3416	Linda Rusche
Wichita	(316) 269-6273	
Small Business Development Centers		
	(316) 343-1200, ext. 308	Emporia
	(913) 628-5340	Hays
	(913) 864-3536	Lawrence
	(913) 469-8500, ext. 3623	Overland Park
	(316) 231-8267	Pittsburg
	(913) 295-6305	Topeka
	(316) 689-3193	Wichita

State Offices		
Small Business Program	(913) 296-3480	Topeka
State Development Office	(913) 296-3481	
Procurement Information	(913) 296-2376	
Minority Business	(913) 296-3480	
Department of Revenue	(913) 296-3909	
State Export	(913) 296-3483	
Consumer Complaints	(800) 432-2310	
High-Tech	(913) 296-3480	
Enterprise Zones	(913) 296-3485	Nancy McCabe
Insurance	(913) 296-3071	W. Fletcher Bell

Other U.S. Government Offices		
IRS	(800) 424-1040	
	(316) 263-2161	Wichita

Farmers' Home Administration	(913) 295-2870	Topeka
Department of Commerce	(816) 374-3142	Kansas City, MO
Department of Labor, Wage/Hour Division	(816) 374-5721	Kansas City, MO
Occupational Safety and Health Administration	(316) 269-6644, ext. 644	Wichita
International Trade Administration	(816) 374-3142	Kansas City, MO
Federal Information Center	(800) 432-2934	Other Kansas locations

Kentucky Region IV

Small Business Administration
District Office
600 Federal Pl., Rm. 188
Louisville, KY 40201

Business Development	(502) 582-5976	
Financial Assistance	(502) 582-5973	
Veterans' Affairs Officer	(502) 582-5976	Forest Haynes
Women's Business Ownership	(502) 582-5971	Rita Thilo
Small Business Development Centers		
	(606) 329-8011	Ashland
	(502) 745-2901	Bowling Green
	(606) 589-4514	Cumberland
	(502) 765-6737	Elizabethtown
	(502) 564-4252	Frankfort
	(606) 572-6558	Highland Heights
	(606) 572-6559	
	(606) 257-1751	Lexington
	(502) 452-8282, ext. 111	Louisville
	(606) 783-2077	Morehead
	(502) 762-2856	Murray
	(502) 926-8085	Owensboro
	(606) 432-5848	Pikeville
	(606) 679-8501	Somerset

State Offices		
Minority Small Business Program	(502) 564-2064	Frankfort
State Development Office	(502) 564-7670	
Loan Information	(502) 564-4554	
Procurement Information	(502) 564-2064	

Kentucky Region IV

Department of Revenue	(502) 564-8054	
State Export	(502) 564-2170	
Consumer Complaints	(800) 432-9257	
Insurance	(502) 564-3630	Gil McCarty
Enterprise Zones	(502) 564-7140	Sara Bell

Other U.S. Government Offices

IRS	(800) 424-1040	
	(502) 582-6259	Louisville
Farmers' Home Administration	(606) 233-2733	Lexington
Department of Commerce	(502) 582-5066	
Department of Labor, Wage/Hour Division	(502) 582-5226	Louisville
Occupational Safety and Health Administration	(502) 227-7024	Frankfort
International Trade Administration	(502) 582-5066	
Federal Information Center	(502) 582-6261	

Louisiana Region VI

Small Business Administration
District Office
1661 Canal St., Ste. 2000
New Orleans, LA 70112

Business Development	(504) 589-2354	
Financial Assistance	(504) 589-2705	
Veterans' Affairs Officer	(504) 589-2705	Pierre Charles
Women's Business Ownership	(504) 589-2354	Ella Materne
Small Business Development Centers		
	(504) 922-0998	Economic Development
	(504) 549-3831	Hammond
	(318) 231-5751	Lafayette
	(318) 437-5529	Lake Charles
	(504) 865-2775	Loyola
	(318) 342-2129	Monroe
	(318) 357-5611	Natchitoches
	(504) 286-6978	New Orleans University
	(318) 257-3537	Ruston
	(318) 797-5144	Shreveport
	(504) 282-4401, ext. 308	Southern University
	(504) 446-8111, ext. 429	Thibodaux

State Offices

Small Business Program	(504) 342-5366	Baton Rouge
Loan Information	(504) 342-5367	
	(504) 342-5382	
Procurement Information	(504) 922-0074	
Minority Business	(504) 342-6491	
Department of Revenue	(504) 568-5233	
State Export	(504) 342-9232	
Consumer Complaints	(800) 272-9868	
High-Tech	(504) 342-5361	
Insurance	(504) 342-5328	Sherman A. Bernard
Enterprise Zones	(504) 342-5399	Diane Barksdale
Venture Capital	(504) 342-9213	Jean B. Armstrong

Other U.S. Government Offices

IRS	(800) 424-1040	New Orleans
Farmers' Home Administration	(318) 473-7920	Alexandria
Department of Commerce	(504) 589-6546	
Department of Energy	(504) 342-4500	Baton Rouge
Department of Labor, Wage/Hour Division	(504) 589-6171	
Occupational Safety and Health Administration	(504) 389-0474	Baton Rouge
International Trade Administration	(504) 589-6546	
Federal Information Center	(504) 589-6696	

Maine Region I

Small Business Administration
District Office
40 Western Ave., Rm. 512
Augusta, ME 04330

Business Development	(207) 622-8242	
Financial Assistance	(207) 622-8227	
Veterans' Affairs Officer	(207) 622-8265	Victor Reinfelds
Women's Business Ownership	(207) 622-8265	Victor Reinfelds
Small Business Development Centers		
	(207) 783-9186	Auburn
	(207) 622-0733	Augusta
	(207) 942-6389	Bangor
	(207) 498-8736	Caribou

Maine Region I

	(207) 255-3313	Machias, University of Maine
	(207) 780-4420	Portland
	(207) 882-7552	Wiscasset

State Offices

Small Business Program	(207) 289-5700	Augusta
Loan Information	(207) 289-5700	
Procurement Information	(207) 942-6389	
State Income Tax Department	(207) 289-3695	
State Export	(207) 622-0234	
Department of Energy Resources	(207) 289-3811	
Insurance	(207) 289-3101	Theodore T. Briggs

Other U.S. Government Offices

IRS	(800) 424-1040	
Farmers' Home Administration	(207) 866-4929	Orono
Department of Commerce	(207) 622-8249	Augusta
Department of Labor, Wage/Hour Division	(207) 780-3344	Portland
Occupational Safety and Health Administration	(207) 622-8417	
International Trade Administration	(207) 622-8249	Boston

Maryland Region III

*Small Business Administration
District Office*
10 N. Calvert St.,
Equitable Bldg., 3d Floor
Baltimore, MD 21202

Business Development	(301) 962-2235; (301) 962-2233	SCORE
Financial Assistance	(301) 962-2150	
Veterans' Affairs Officer	(301) 962-2235	O. J. Phillips
Women's Business Ownership	(301) 962-2235	Mindie Hankin
Small Business Development Centers		
	(301) 454-5072	College Park
	(301) 656-7482	Montgomery College

State Offices

Small Business Program	(800) 654-7336	
State Development Office	(301) 269-3174	Annapolis
Loan Information		
Enterprise Zones	(301) 269-3381	Edward Wise
Short-Term Working Capital for Companies with Procurement Contracts	(301) 659-4270	Baltimore
Industrial Development Financing Authority (not for retail or service businesses)	(301) 659-4262	
Established Businesses	(301) 828-4711	
Procurement Information	(301) 269-2945	
Minority Business	(301) 383-5555	
Montgomery County	(301) 984-0999	Steve Ames
Department of Revenue	(800) 424-1040	
Consumer Complaints: Telephone Consumer Hotline, Inc.	(800) 332-1124	
Small Business Assistance	(800) OK-GREEN	
Anne Arundel County	(301) 224-1122	Samuel F. Minnitte
Insurance	(301) 659-4029 (800) 492-6116	
Venture Capital	(301) 659-4270	Stanley Tucker

Other U.S. Government Offices

IRS	(800) 424-1040	
Farmers' Home Administration	(301) 228-3250	Dorchester County
Department of Commerce	(301) 962-3560	Baltimore
Department of Energy	(301) 225-1810	
Department of Labor, Wage/Hour Division	(301) 962-2265	
Occupational Safety and Health Administration	(301) 962-2840	
International Trade Administration	(301) 962-3560	
Federal Information Center	(301) 962-4980	

Massachusetts Region I

Small Business Administration
District Office
150 Causeway St., 10th Floor
Boston, MA 02114

Branch Office
1550 Main St.
Springfield, MA 01103

Business Development		
Boston	(617) 223-7991	
Springfield	(413) 785-0268	
Financial Assistance		
Boston	(617) 223-3125	
Springfield	(413) 785-0369	
Veterans' Affairs Officer		
Boston	(617) 223-7991	Goulhurne Busby
Springfield	(413) 785-0484	
Women's Business Ownership		
Boston	(617) 223-3212	Ethel Fredericks
Springfield	(413) 785-0080	
Small Business Development Centers		
	(413) 549-4930	Amherst
	(617) 734-1960	Boston
	(617) 552-4091	Chestnut Hill
	(617) 673-9783	Fall River
	(617) 458-7261	Lowell
	(413) 737-6712	Springfield
	(617) 793-7615	Worcester

State Offices

Small Business Program	(800) 632-8181	
	(617) 727-4005	Boston
State Development Office	(617) 727-8380	
Loan Information		
High-Tech Businesses with High Employment and Growth Potential	(617) 723-4920	
Community Development Corporation Programs	(617) 742-0366	
Business Expansions	(617) 536-3900	
Industrial Finance	(617) 451-2477	
Procurement Information	(617) 727-4005	

Minority Business	(617) 727-8692	
Department of Revenue	(617) 727-4393	
Insurance	(617) 727-3333	Peter Hiam
Venture Capital	(617) 536-3900	William J. Torpey, Jr.

Other U.S. Government Offices

IRS	(800) 424-1040	
Farmers' Home Administration	(413) 253-3471	Amherst
Department of Commerce	(617) 223-2312	Boston
Department of Energy	(617) 727-4732	
Department of Labor, Wage/Hour Division	(617) 223-6751	Boston
Occupational Safety and Health Administration	(617) 647-8681	Waltham
	(413) 785-0123	Springfield
International Trade Administration	(617) 223-2312	
Federal Information Center	(617) 223-7121	
National Marine Fisheries Service	(617) 281-3600	Gloucester

Michigan Region V

Small Business Administration
District Office
477 Michigan Ave., Rm. 515
Detroit, MI 48226

Branch Office
300 S. Frank St.
Marquette, MI 49855

Business Development		
Detroit	(313) 226-6075	
	(313) 226-7947	SCORE
Marquette	(906) 225-1108	
Financial Assistance		
Detroit	(313) 226-6075	
Marquette	(906) 225-1108	
Veterans' Affairs Officer		
Detroit	(313) 226-6075	Allen Cook
Women's Business Ownership		
Detroit	(313) 226-6075	Jackie Booker
Small Business Development Centers		
	(313) 662-0550	Ann Arbor
	(517) 893-4567	Bay City
	(313) 577-4850	Detroit

Michigan Region V

	(313) 964-5030	Research
	(906) 786-9234	Escanaba
	(313) 232-7101	Flint
	(616) 242-6613	Grand Rapids
	(517) 539-2173	Harrison
	(616) 873-7141	Hart
	(906) 487-1245	Houghton
	(616) 343-1137	Kalamazoo
	(517) 635-3561	Marlette
	(906) 227-1629	Marquette
	(517) 839-9901	Midland
	(517) 774-3736	Mount Pleasant
	(616) 777-0201	Muskegon
	(616) 726-4848	
	(517) 754-8222	Saginaw
	(313) 281-0700, ext. 171	Southgate
	(313) 482-4920	Ypsilanti

State Offices

Small Business Program	(517) 373-0638	Lansing
State Development	(517) 373-1820	
Office	(517) 373-3530	
Loan Information:		
Emphasis on High-Tech and Growth Industries	(517) 373-4330	
Procurement Information	(517) 373-8430	
Department of Revenue	(517) 373-9626	
State Export	(517) 373-6390	
Consumer Complaints	(800) 292-4204	
Ombudsman and	(800) 232-2727	
Licensing Information	(517) 373-6241	
High-Tech	(517) 373-7550	
Insurance	(517) 373-9273	
Venture Capital	(517) 373-4330	Michael Finn

Other U.S. Government Offices

IRS	(800) 424-1040	Other cities
Farmers' Home Administration	(517) 337-6631	East Lansing
Department of Labor, Wage/Hour Division	(616) 456-2333	Grand Rapids
International Trade Administration	(313) 226-3650	
Federal Information Centers	(313) 226-7016	

Minnesota Region V

Small Business Administration
District Office
100 N. Sixth St., Ste. 610
Minneapolis, MN 55403

Business Development	(612) 349-3574	
Financial Assistance	(612) 349-3549	
Veterans' Affairs Officer	(612) 349-3523	George Saumweber
Women's Business Ownership	(612) 349-3544	Cynthia Wright

Small Business
Development Centers

(218) 827-2373	Babbitt
(218) 755-2750	Bemidji
(612) 830-9395	Bloomington
(218) 828-5302	Brainerd
(612) 448-8810	Chaska
(218) 726-8761	Duluth
(218) 773-3441	East Grand Forks
(218) 365-3256	Ely
(507) 332-7444	Fairbault
(218) 327-2241	Grand Rapids
(218) 285-7722, ext. 259	International Falls
(507) 389-1648	Mankato
(507) 537-7386	Marshall
(800) 642-1073	Minneapolis
(218) 236-2289	Moorehead
(612) 629-6764	Pine City
(507) 285-7157	Rochester
(612) 423-8471	Rosemont
(612) 255-4842	St. Cloud
(612) 376-3433	St. Paul
(612) 647-5840	
(218) 681-5424	Thief River Falls
(218) 631-3530, ext. 371	Wadena
(612) 770-2351	White Bear Lake
(612) 235-5114	Willmar
(507) 457-5089	Winona

State Offices

Small Business Program	(800) 652-9747*	
	(612) 296-5023	St. Paul

*The toll-free (800) numbers are for Minnesota residents outside the Twin Cities' metropolitan area only.

Minnesota Region V

State Department of Energy and Economic Development	(612) 296-6424	
Loan Information	(612) 296-5021	
Procurement Information	(612) 296-6949	
Department of Revenue	(612) 642-0372	
Department of Energy	(800) 652-9747	
	(612) 296-5175	
State Export	(612) 297-1317	
Consumer Complaints	(612) 296-3353	
Ombudsman	(612) 296-3871	
Licenses	(612) 296-5023	
High-Tech	(612) 297-4368	
Enterprise Zones	(612) 297-1304	Patrick Connoy
Insurance	(612) 296-4026	Michael A. Hatch

Other U.S. Government Offices

IRS	(800) 424-1040	
Farmers' Home Administration	(612) 725-5842	
Department of Commerce	(612) 349-3338	Minneapolis
Department of Labor, Wage/Hour Division	(612) 349-3701	Minneapolis
Occupational Safety and Health Administration	(612) 349-5994	
International Trade Administration	(612) 349-3338	
Federal Information Center	(612) 349-5333	

Mississippi Region IV

Small Business Administration
District Office
100 W. Capitol St., Ste. 322
Jackson, MS 39269

Branch Office
One Hancock Plaza, Ste. 1001
Gulfport, MS 39501

Business Development
Gulfport   (601) 863-4449
Jackson   (601) 965-5332

Financial Assistance
Gulfport   (601) 863-4449
Jackson   (601) 965-4378

Veterans' Affairs
Officers
Gulfport   (601) 863-4449   Jerry Haley
Jackson   (601) 965-5334   Tommy Traxler

Women's Business
Ownership
Jackson   (601) 965-5338   Reatha Chapman

Small Business
Development Centers
                                (601) 329-4750   Columbus
                                (601) 865-0011   Gulfport
                                (601) 982-6760   Jackson
                                (601) 865-4578   Long Beach
                                (601) 483-8241   Meridian
                                (601) 325-3817   Starkville
                                (601) 844-5413   Tupelo
                                (601) 234-2120   University

State Offices
Small Business Program   (601) 359-3437   Jackson
State Development   (601) 359-3449
Office
Department of Revenue   (601) 359-1141
State Export   (601) 359-3444
Industrial Division   (800) 343-1112
Consumer Complaints   (800) 223-5615
Insurance   (601) 359-3569   George Dale
Enterprise Zones   (601) 359-3029   Jim Craig

Other U.S. Government Offices
IRS   (800) 424-1040   Jackson
Farmers' Home   (601) 965-4316
Administration
Department of   (601) 965-4388
Commerce
Department of Labor,   (601) 965-4347
Wage/Hour Division
Occupational Safety and   (601) 965-4606
Health Administration
International Trade   (601) 965-4388
Administration

Missouri Region VII

Small Business Administration
District Offices
1103 Grande Ave., Rm. 512
Kansas City, MO 64106
815 Olive St., Rm. 242
St. Louis, MO 63101

Missouri Region VII

Branch Office
309 N. Jefferson, Rm. 150
Springfield, MO 65803

Business Development		
Kansas City	(816) 374-5868	
Springfield	(417) 864-7670	
St. Louis	(314) 425-6600	
Financial Assistance		
Kansas City	(816) 374-3416	
Springfield	(417) 864-7670	
St. Louis	(314) 425-6600	
Veterans' Affairs Officers		
Kansas City	(816) 374-5868	Gene Anderson
		Harold Kruse
St. Louis	(314) 425-6600	Jim Gravitt
Springfield	(417) 864-7670	Jim Laas
Womens' Business Ownership		
Kansas City	(816) 374-3416	Linda Rusche
St. Louis	(314) 425-6600	Kathy Frazier
Small Business Development Centers		
	(314) 651-4462	Cape Girardeau
	(314) 882-2691	Columbia
	(314) 751-3906	Jefferson City High-Tech
	(816) 926-4572	Kansas City
	(816) 785-4307	Kirksville
	(816) 562-1701	Maryville
	(314) 431-4593	Mineral Area, College Flat River
	(314) 341-4559	Rolla
	(417) 836-5685	Springfield
	(314) 534-7232	St. Louis
	(314) 882-7096	University

State Offices		
Small Business Program	(314) 751-4982	Jefferson City
State Development Office	(314) 751-3946	
Loan Information	(314) 751-2686	
Department of Revenue	(314) 751-2151	
State Export/ Department of Economic Development	(314) 751-4855	
Consumer Complaints	(800) 392-8222	

High-Tech	(314) 751-3906	
Enterprise Zones	(314) 751-4572	Robert C. Simonds
Insurance	(314) 751-4126	Mary Hall

Other U.S. Government Offices

IRS	(800) 424-1040	
	(314) 342-1040	St. Louis
Farmers' Home Administration	(314) 425-4400	Columbia
Department of Commerce	(314) 425-3302	St. Louis
	(816) 374-3142	Kansas City
Department of Energy	(314) 751-4000	Jefferson City
Department of Labor, Wage/Hour Division	(314) 425-4706	St. Louis
	(816) 374-5721	Kansas City
Occupational Safety and Health Administration	(816) 374-2756	Kansas City
	(314) 263-2749	St. Louis
International Trade Administration	(816) 374-3142	Kansas City
Federal Information Centers	(800) 982-5808 (area codes 816, 417)	
	(800) 392-7711 (in state only)	
	(816) 374-2466	Kansas City
	(314) 425-4106	St. Louis
Enterprise Zones-HUD	(816) 374-2661	Gary Uttican

Montana Region VIII

Small Business Administration
District Office
301 S. Park, Rm. 528
Helena, MT 59626

Post of Duty Office
2601 First Ave., North
Rm. 216, Billings, MT 59101

Business Development		
Billings	(406) 657-6047	
Helena	(406) 449-5381	
Financial Assistance		
Billings	(406) 657-6047	
Helena	(406) 449-5381	
Veterans' Affairs Officer		
Helena	(406) 449-5381	Jerry Christison
Women's Business Ownership		
Helena	(406) 449-5381	Mary Bryson

State Offices

Small Business Program	(800) 444-3923	Helena

Montana Region VIII

State Development Office	(406) 444-3494	
Loan Information/ High-Tech	(406) 444-3707	
Procurement Information	(406) 444-3707	
Minority Business	(406) 444-4723	
Department of Revenue	(406) 444-2460	
State Export	(406) 444-4280	
Consumer Complaints	(800) 332-2272	
Licensing/Ombudsman	(406) 444-3923	
High-Tech	(406) 444-3707	
Venture Capital	(406) 444-2090	
Insurance	(406) 444-2040	Andrea Hemstad

Other U.S. Government Offices

IRS	(800) 424-1040	Helena
Farmers' Home Administration	(406) 587-5271, ext. 4211	Bozeman
Department of Commerce	(307) 778-2220	Cheyenne, WY
Department of Energy	(406) 449-3780	
Department of Labor, Wage/Hour Division	(801) 524-5706	Salt Lake City, UT
Occupational Safety and Health Administration	(406) 657-6649	Billings
International Trade Administration	(303) 837-3246	Denver, CO

Nebraska Region VII

Small Business Administration
District Office
11145 Mill Valley Rd.
Omaha, NE 68154

Business Development	(402) 221-3604	
Financial Assistance	(402) 221-3622	
Veterans' Affairs Officer	(402) 221-3626	Stephen Lewis
Women's Business Ownership	(402) 221-3626	Betty Raygor
Small Business Development Centers		
	(308) 432-4451	Chadron
	(308) 234-8344	Kearney
	(402) 472-3276	Lincoln
	(402) 554-8381	Omaha
	(402) 375-2004	Wayne

State Offices

Small Business Program	(402) 471-3111	Lincoln
Loan Information	(402) 477-4406	
Procurement Information	(402) 471-3769	
Department of Revenue	(402) 471-2971	
State Export	(402) 471-4668	
Consumer Complaints	(402) 471-2035	
Ombudsman	(402) 471-2035	
Patent Development Program	(402) 472-5604	
Insurance	(402) 471-2201	Mike Dugan

Other U.S. Government Offices

IRS	(800) 642-9960	
	(402) 422-1500	Omaha
Farmers' Home Administration	(402) 471-5551	Lincoln
Department of Commerce	(402) 221-3664	Omaha
Department of Energy	(402) 471-2867	
Department of Labor, Wage/Hour Division	(402) 221-4682	
Occupational Safety and Health Administration	(402) 221-3182	
International Trade Administration	(402) 221-3664	
Federal Information Centers	(402) 221-3353	
	(800) 642-8383	Other Nebraska locations

Nevada Region IX

Small Business Administration
District Office
301 E. Stewart St.
Las Vegas, NV 89125

Post of Duty Office
50 S. Virginia St., Rm. 238
Reno, NV 89505

Business Development		
Las Vegas	(702) 388-6611	
Reno	(702) 784-5268	
Financial Assistance		
Las Vegas	(702) 388-6611	
Reno	(702) 784-5268	
Veterans' Affairs Officer		
Las Vegas	(702) 388-6611	Robert Garrett

Nevada Region IX

Women's Business
Ownership
Las Vegas   (702) 388-6611   Marie Papile

Small Business
Development Centers
                                (702) 738-8493   Elko
                                (702) 739-0852   Las Vegas
                                (702) 784-1717   Reno

State Offices
Small Business Program   (702) 885-4420   Audrey Allen
State Development   (702) 885-4325   Jeanne Douglas
Office
Loan Information   (702) 323-3033   Nancy Riley
Consumer Complaints   (800) 992-0900
Insurance   (702) 885-4270   David Gates
Enterprise Zones   (702) 885-4325   George Ormiston

Other U.S. Government Offices
IRS   (800) 424-1040
                                (702) 784-5521   Reno
                                (702) 388-6291   Las Vegas (recording)
Farmers' Home   (801) 524-5027   Salt Lake City, UT
Administration
Department of   (702) 784-5203
Commerce
Department of Energy   (702) 886-5157   Carson City
Department of Labor,   (602) 241-2990   Phoenix, AZ
Wage/Hour Division
Occupational Safety and   (702) 388-6163   Las Vegas
Health Administration
International Trade   (702) 784-5203   Reno
Administration

New Hampshire Region I

Small Business Administration
District Office
55 Pleasant St., Rm. 211
Concord, NH 03301

Business Development   (603) 225-1400

Financial Assistance   (603) 225-1400

Veterans' Affairs Officer   (603) 225-1400   Robert C. Kelly

Women's Business   (603) 225-1400   Bonnie F. Johnson
Ownership

Small Business
Development Centers

	(603) 868-6367	Durham
	(603) 352-1909, ext. 238	Keene
	(603) 668-0700	Manchester
	(603) 536-1550	Plymouth

State Offices

Industrial Development	(603) 271-2391	Concord
Department of Revenue	(603) 271-2191	
State Export	(603) 271-2591	
Insurance	(603) 271-2261	Louis E. Bergeron

Other U.S. Government Offices

IRS	(800) 424-1040	
Farmers' Home Administration	(802) 223-2371	Montpelier, VT
Department of Commerce	(617) 223-2312	Boston, MA
Governor's Energy Office	(603) 271-2711	Concord
Department of Labor, Wage/Hour Division	(207) 780-3344, ext. 344	Portland, ME
Occupational Safety and Health Administration	(603) 225-1629	Concord
International Trade Administration	(617) 223-2314	Boston, MA

New Jersey Region II

Small Business Administration
District Office
60 Park Pl., 4th Floor
Newark, NJ 07102

Post of Duty Office
1800 E. Davis St., Rm. 110
Camden, NJ 08104

Business Development

Camden	(609) 757-5183	
Newark	(201) 645-2434	

Financial Assistance

Camden	(609) 757-5183	
Newark	(201) 645-2434	
Newark SCORE Loan Information	(201) 645-3982	(10:00 A.M. to 3:00 P.M.)

Veterans' Affairs Officer

Newark	(201) 645-3251	Ted Luszcz

New Jersey Region II

Women's Business Ownership		
Newark	(201) 645-6491	Janis Sullivan
Small Business Development Centers		
	(609) 343-4810	Atlantic City
	(609) 757-6221	Camden
	(201) 842-1900, ext. 551	Lincroft
	(201) 648-5950	Newark
	(609) 586-4800, ext. 469	Trenton

State Offices

Small Business Program	(609) 984-4442	Trenton
Loan Information		
High-Tech	(609) 984-1671	
Economic Develop-	(609) 292-1800	
ment Authority	(609) 984-4442	
Procurement	(609) 984-4442	
Information		
Minority-Business	(609) 292-0500	
Enterprise		
Department of Revenue	(609) 292-7592	
State Export	(201) 648-3518	Newark
Consumer Complaints	(800) 792-8600	
Ombudsman	(609) 292-0700	
High-Tech	(609) 984-2444	
Enterprise Zones	(609) 292-2765	Stephen C. Brame
Insurance	(609) 292-5363	Hazel F. Gluck

Other U.S. Government Offices

IRS	(800) 424-1040	
	(201) 622-0600	Newark
Farmers' Home	(609) 259-9886	Robinsville
Administration		
Department of	(609) 292-2444	Newark
Commerce		
Department of Energy	(201) 648-3904	Newark
Department of Labor,	(201) 645-2279	Newark
Wage/Hour Division	(609) 989-2247	Trenton
Occupational Safety and	(201) 750-3270	Avenel
Health Administration	(201) 288-1700	Hasbrouck Heights
	(609) 757-5181	Camden
	(201) 361-4050	Dover
International Trade	(609) 989-2100	Trenton
Administration		

Federal Information	(201) 645-3600	Newark
Centers	523-0717*	Patterson/Passaic
	396-4400*	Trenton

New Mexico Region VI

Small Business Administration
District Office
5000 Marble Ave., N.E., Rm. 320
Albuquerque, NM 87100

Business Development	(505) 766-3588	
Financial Assistance	(505) 766-3430	
Veterans' Affairs Officer	(505) 766-1145	Deward Stegall
Women's Business Ownership	(505) 766-1159	Carolyn Rigirozzi

State Offices

Small Business Program	(505) 827-0300	Santa Fe
Business Development Corporation	(505) 827-6207	
Minority Business	(505) 827-0425	
Department of Revenue	(505) 988-2290	Santa Fe
State Export	(505) 827-0300	
Consumer Complaints	(505) 827-6060	
Licensing	(505) 827-6318	
Insurance	(505) 827-4535	Vincent B. Jasso
Venture Capital/Energy Resource Development	(505) 827-5900	Larry Icerman

Other U.S. Government Offices

IRS	(800) 424-1040	Albuquerque
Farmers' Home Administration	(505) 766-2462	
Department of Commerce	(505) 766-2386	
Department of Energy	(505) 827-5950	Santa Fe
Department of Labor, Wage/Hour Division	(505) 766-2477	Albuquerque
Occupational Safety and Health Administration	(505) 766-3411	
International Trade Administration	(505) 766-2386	
Federal Information Center	(505) 766-3091	

*Number may be used only within this city.

New York Region II

Small Business Administration
District Offices
26 Federal Plaza, Rm. 3100
New York, NY 10278
100 S. Clinton St., Rm. 1071
Syracuse, NY 13260

Branch Offices
35 Pinelawn Rd., Rm. 102E
Melville, NY 11747
111 W. Huron St., Rm. 1311
Buffalo, NY 14202
333 E. Water St.
Elmira, NY 14901

Post of Duty Offices
445 Broadway, Rm. 236B
Albany, NY 12207
100 State St., Rm. 601
Rochester, NY 14614

Business Development		
Albany	(518) 472-6300	
Buffalo	(716) 846-4517	
Elmira	(607) 734-8130	
Melville	(516) 454-0750	
New York City	(212) 264-4314	
Rochester	(716) 263-6700	
Stone Ridge	(914) 687-7621, ext. 345	SCORE
Syracuse	(315) 423-5376	
Financial Assistance		
Albany	(518) 472-6300	
Buffalo	(716) 846-4301	
Elmira	(607) 734-8130	
Melville	(516) 454-0750	
New York City	(212) 264-1480	
Rochester	(716) 263-6700	
Syracuse	(315) 423-5364	
Veterans' Affairs Officers		
Buffalo	(716) 846-5664	Richard Keffer
Elmira	(607) 734-8143	Howard Garrity
Melville	(516) 454-0750	Robert V. Miller
New York City	(212) 264-3437	Ernest D'Addario
Syracuse	(315) 423-5364	David Laveck
Women's Business Ownership		
Buffalo	(716) 846-4517	Carol Kruszona
Elmira	(607) 734-3358	Yvonne Koury

Melville	(516) 454-0750	Walter Leavitt
New York City	(212) 264-4349	Susan Fleming
Syracuse	(315) 423-5386	Shirley Wild

Disaster Home Servicing
Center

New York City Area Only	(212) 620-3734	Dave Crown

Small Business
Development Centers

(518) 473-5398	Albany
(607) 777-4024	Binghamton
(716) 878-4030	Buffalo
(516) 420-2765	Farmingdale
(718) 403-1070	New York City
(518) 564-2214	Plattsburgh
(716) 693-1910, ext. 102	Sanborn
(914) 687-0768	Stone Ridge
(914) 285-6656	Valhalla
(315) 782-5250, ext. 252	Watertown

State Offices

Department of Commerce Small Business Program	(212) 309-0400	New York City
	(518) 474-7756	Albany
Commerce State Development Office	(518) 474-4100	Albany
Loan Information	(212) 818-1700	
	(212) 309-0400	
Procurement	(212) 309-0400	Ray Gillen, Fort Drum
Information	(518) 474-7756	
Minority/Women in Business	(518) 473-0137	
Department of Revenue	(800) 342-3536	tax kit
	(518) 457-7177	Albany
State Export	(212) 309-0500	
Consumer Complaints	(212) 488-7530	
	(212) 577-0111	
Ombudsman	(212) 309-0400	
Licensing	(800) 342-3464	
	(518) 474-8275	
High-Tech	(518) 474-4349	
Insurance	(212) 602-0203	James Corcoran
	(800) 342-3736	

Other U.S. Government Offices

IRS	(516) 724-5000	Suffolk County
	(718) 732-0100	Staten Island
	(518) 997-1510	Rockland County
	(718) 596-3770	Queens

New York Region II

	(516) 222-1131	Nassau
	(518) 997-1510	Westchester County
	(212) 732-0100	Bronx
	(800) 424-1040	Albany
	(716) 855-3955	Buffalo
	(212) 732-0100	New York City
	(718) 596-3770	Brooklyn
Farmers' Home	(315) 423-5290	Syracuse
Administration		
Department of	(716) 846-4191	Buffalo
Commerce	(212) 264-0634	New York City
Department of Energy	(518) 473-4375	Albany
Department of Labor,		
Wage/Hour Division	(716) 846-4891	Buffalo
	(516) 227-3100	Long Island
	(212) 264-8185	New York City
	(212) 824-2158	Bronx
	(518) 472-3596	Albany
Occupational Safety and		
Health Administration	(212) 264-9840	New York City
	(518) 472-6085	Albany
	(315) 423-5188	Syracuse
	(716) 684-5347	Buffalo
	(516) 334-3344	Westbury
International Trade	(716) 846-4191	Buffalo
Administration	(212) 264-0634	New York
Federal Information		
Centers	463-4421*	Albany
	(716) 846-4010	Buffalo
	(212) 264-4464	New York City
	546-5075*	Rochester
	476-8545*	Syracuse
Enterprise Zones-HUD	(212) 264-0765	Tony Gamble

North Carolina Region IV

Small Business Administration
District Office
230 S. Tryon St., Rm. 700
Charlotte, NC 28202

Business Development		
Charlotte	(704) 371-6563	
Financial Assistance		
Charlotte	(704) 371-6563	
Veterans' Affairs Officer		
Charlotte	(704) 371-6588	Joyce Starnes

*Number may be used only within this city.

Women's Business
Ownership
Charlotte   (704) 371-6587   Gerilyn McDonald

Small Business
Development Centers

	(704) 227-7494	Cullowhee
	(919) 335-3247	Elizabeth City
	(919) 334-7744	Greensboro
	(919) 733-4643	Raleigh
	(919) 761-2141	Winston-Salem

State Offices

Small Business Program	(919) 733-6254	Raleigh
State Development Office	(919) 733-4151	
Procurement Information	(919) 733-7232	
Minority Business	(919) 733-2712	
Department of Revenue	(919) 829-4682	
State Export	(919) 733-7193	
	(919) 737-3793	
High-Tech	(919) 549-0671	
Insurance	(919) 733-7343	James E. Long

Other U.S. Government Offices

IRS	(800) 424-1040	
	(919) 333-5620	Greensboro
Farmers' Home Administration	(919) 856-4196	Raleigh
Department of Commerce	(919) 333-5345	Greensboro
Department of Energy	(919) 733-2230	Raleigh
Department of Labor, Wage/Hour Division	(704) 371-6120	Charlotte
	(919) 856-4190	
Occupational Safety and Health Administration	(919) 733-7166	

North Dakota Region VIII

Small Business Administration
District Office
657 Second Ave., North Rm. 218
Fargo, ND 58108

Business Development	(701) 237-5771, ext. 131	
Financial Assistance	(701) 237-5771, ext. 131	
Veterans' Affairs Officer	(701) 237-5771	James Floyd
Women's Business Ownership	(701) 237-5771	Carla L. Veitenheimer

North Dakota Region VIII

Small Business Development Centers

	(701) 237-8870	Fargo
	(701) 227-2096	Dickinson
	(701) 780-3403	Grand Forks
	(701) 857-3843	Minot

State Offices

Small Business Program	(701) 224-2810	Bismarck
Loan Information	(701) 224-5600	Bismarck
Department of Revenue	(701) 224-2770	Bismarck
State Export	(701) 224-2810	Bismarck
Consumer Complaints	(800) 472-2600	Bismarck
Rural Development	(701) 237-7375	Fargo
Insurance	(701) 224-2444	Earl Pomeroy

Other U.S. Government Offices

IRS	(800) 424-1040	Fargo
Farmers' Home Administration	(701) 255-4011, ext. 4781	Bismarck
Department of Commerce	(402) 221-3664	Omaha, NE
Department of Energy	(701) 255-4011, ext. 240	Bismarck
Department of Labor, Wage/Hour Division	(303) 844-4405	Denver, CO
Occupational Safety and Health Administration	(701) 255-4011, ext. 521	Bismarck
International Trade Administration	(402) 221-3664	Omaha, NE

Ohio Region V

Small Business Administration
District Offices
1240 E. Ninth St., Rm. 317
Cleveland, OH 44199
85 Marconi Blvd.
Columbus, OH 43215

Branch Office
550 Main St., Rm. 5028
Cincinnati, OH 45202

Business Development

Cincinnati	(513) 684-2817
Cleveland	(216) 522-4195
Columbus	(614) 469-5548

Financial Assistance

Cincinnati	(513) 684-2814

Cleveland	(216) 522-4191	
Columbus	(614) 469-6860/2359	

Veterans' Affairs Officers

Cincinnati	(513) 684-2817	Morris B. Moore
Cleveland	(216) 522-4194	Larry Pier
Columbus	(614) 469-2351	Gerry Garman

Women's Business Ownership

Cincinnati	(513) 684-2817	Gene C. O'Connell
Cleveland	(216) 522-4195	Corliss Newsome
Columbus	(614) 469-5548	Lisa Perrin, Brenda Young

Small Business Development Centers

(614) 594-5791	Athens
(216) 376-5550	Akron
(216) 621-3300	Cleveland
(614) 221-1321	Columbus
(513) 226-8230	Dayton
(419) 243-8191	Toledo

State Offices

Small Business Program	(800) 282-1085	
	(614) 466-4945	Columbus
State Development	(614) 466-3379	
Office	(614) 446-5111	
Loan Information:	(800) 282-1085	
	(614) 466-4945	
Loans Funded by	(614) 466-5420	
Public Employees'	(614) 466-2085	Robert McLaughlin
Retirement System		
Procurement	(800) 282-1085	
Information	(614) 466-5700	
Department of Revenue	(614) 466-7910	
State Export	(216) 522-4750	Cleveland
	(614) 466-5017	
Consumer Complaints	(800) 282-0515	
Licensing/Permits	(800) 248-4040	
High-Tech	(614) 466-3887	
Women's Resource	(614) 466-4945	
Center		
Technology Transfer	(614) 466-4286	
Minority Contractors	(614) 466-5700	
Training	(614) 466-4155	
Enterprise Zones	(614) 466-4551	Howard Wise
Insurance	(614) 466-2691	Robert Lee Ratchford
Venture Capital/	(614) 466-5420	Dennis V. Yacobozzi
Economic Development		

Ohio Region V

Other U.S. Government Offices

IRS	(800) 424-1040	
	(216) 522-3000	Cleveland
	(800) 424-1040	
	(513) 621-6281	Cincinnati
Farmers' Home Administration	(614) 469-5606	Columbus
Department of Commerce	(513) 684-2944	Cincinnati
	(216) 522-4750	Cleveland
Department of Energy	(614) 466-1805	Columbus
Department of Labor, Wage/Hour Division	(513) 684-2942	
	(614) 469-5677	
	(216) 522-3892	
Occupational Safety and Health Administration	(216) 522-3818	
	(513) 684-3784	
	(614) 469-5582	
	(419) 259-7542	Toledo
International Trade Administration	(513) 684-2944	
Federal Information Centers		
	375-5628*	Akron
	(513) 684-2801	
	(216) 522-4040	
	221-1014*	Columbus
	223-7377*	Dayton
	241-3223*	Toledo

Oklahoma Region VI

Small Business Administration
District Office
200 N.W. Fifth St., Ste. 670
Oklahoma City, OK 73102

Business Development	(405) 231-4491	
Financial Assistance	(405) 231-5605	
Veterans' Affairs Officer	(405) 231-4438	Jim Martin
Women's Business Ownership	(405) 231-4514	Pearlie Miles
Small Business Development Centers		
	(405) 436-3190	Ada
	(405) 327-5883	Alva
	(405) 924-0277	Durant
	(405) 341-2980	Edmond

*Number may be used only within this city.

	(800) 522-6154	Statewide
	(918) 458-0802	Tahlequah
	(918) 592-2700	Tulsa
	(405) 772-6611, ext. 3050	Weatherford

State Offices

Small Business Program	(405) 521-2401	Oklahoma City
Oklahoma Tax Commission	(405) 521-4321	
State Export	(405) 521-3501	
Insurance	(405) 521-2828	Gerald Grimes
Enterprise Zones	(405) 521-2401	Grover Phillips

Other U.S. Government Offices

IRS	(800) 424-1040	
Farmers' Home Administration	(405) 624-4250	Stillwater
Department of Commerce	(405) 231-5302	Oklahoma City
Department of Labor, Wage/Hour Division	(918) 581-7695	Tulsa
Occupational Safety and Health Administration	(405) 231-5351	
International Trade Administration	(405) 231-5302	
Federal Information Centers	(405) 231-4868	
	584-4193*	Tulsa

Oregon Region X

Small Business Administration
District Office
1220 S.W. Third Ave., Rm. 676
Portland, OR 97204

Business Development	(503) 221-2682	
Financial Assistance	(503) 294-5220	
Veterans' Affairs Officer	(503) 294-5214	Joe A. Martinez
Women's Business Ownership	(503) 294-5218	Toni Mc Kissen

Small Business
Development Centers

	(503) 967-6112	Albany
	(503) 482-5838	Ashland
	(503) 325-0910, ext. 270	Astoria
	(503) 842-2551	Bay City
	(503) 382-6112, ext. 224	Bend
	(503) 888-2525, ext. 259	Coos Bay
	(503) 296-2231	The Dalles

*Number may be used only within this city.

Oregon Region X

	(503) 484-2126, ext. 530	Eugene
	(503) 479-5541, ext. 216	Grants Pass
	(503) 667-7225	Gresham
	(503) 883-7556	Klamath Falls
	(503) 963-1551	La Grande
	(503) 772-3478	Medford
	(503) 889-6493, ext. 50	Ontario
	(503) 657-8400, ext. 414	Oregon City
	(503) 276-1260, ext. 293	Pendleton
	(503) 842-2551	Pillamock
	(503) 283-2541	Portland
	(503) 440-4600, ext. 651	Roseburg
	(503) 399-5181	Salem
	(503) 738-3347	Seaside

State Offices

Small Business Program	(503) 373-1200	Salem
Loan Information	(503) 378-4111	
	(503) 373-1215	
Minority/Women-Owned Business	(503) 378-1250	
Department of Revenue	(503) 378-3184	
State Export	(503) 229-5625	
Consumer Complaints	(800) 452-7813	
High-Tech	(503) 373-1200	
Insurance	(503) 378-4271	
Enterprise Zones	(503) 378-5773	Norman Solomon
	(800) 547-7842	
	(800) 233-3306	In-state

Other U.S. Government Offices

IRS	(800) 424-1040	
	(503) 221-3960	Portland
	(503) 485-8286	Eugene
	(503) 581-8721	Salem
Farmers' Home Administration	(503) 221-2731	
Department of Commerce	(503) 221-3001	
Department of Energy	(503) 754-3004	Corvallis
Department of Labor, Wage/Hour Division	(503) 221-3057	Portland
Occupational Safety and Health Administration	(503) 221-2251	
International Trade Administration	(503) 221-3001	
Federal Information Center	(503) 221-2222	

Pennsylvania Region III

Small Business Administration
District Offices
231 St. Asaphs Rd.
One Bala Cynwyd Plaza, Ste. 400
E. Lobby, Bala
Cynwyd, PA 19004
960 Penn Ave., 5th Floor
Pittsburgh, PA 15222

Branch Offices
100 Chestnut St., Ste. 309
Harrisburg, PA 17101
20 N. Pennsylvania Ave.
Wilkes-Barre, PA 18701

Business Development
Harrisburg	(717) 782-4405	
Philadelphia	(215) 596-5834	
Pittsburgh	(412) 644-5441	
Wilkes-Barre	(717) 826-6495	

Financial Assistance
Harrisburg	(717) 782-3846	
Philadelphia	(215) 596-5889	
Pittsburgh	(412) 644-5442	
Wilkes-Barre	(717) 826-6498	

Veterans' Affairs
Officers
Harrisburg	(717) 782-3846	Kenneth J. Olson
Philadelphia	(215) 596-5828	Robert E. Light
Pittsburgh	(412) 644-5431	Michael J. Loftis
Wilkes-Barre	(717) 826-6697	John F. Gallagher

Women's Business
Ownership
Philadelphia	(215) 596-5828	Doris Young
Pittsburgh	(412) 644-5441	Ray Becki

Small Business
Development Centers
(215) 861-3980	Bethlehem
(814) 226-2626	Clarion
(814) 871-7370	Erie
(215) 951-1416	LaSalle-Philadelphia
(215) 861-3980	Lehigh
(717) 524-1249	Lewisburg
(814) 472-7000, ext. 401	Loretto
(717) 948-6031	Middletown
(412) 434-6231	Pittsburgh
(412) 624-6435	

Pennsylvania Region III

	(717) 961-7588	Scranton
	(215) 787-7282, ext. 881	Temple-Philadelphia
	(215) 898-4861	University of Pennsylvania, Philadelphia
	(215) 898-4861	Wharton
	(717) 824-4651, ext. 222	Wilkes-Barre

State Offices

Small Business Action Center	(717) 783-5700	Harrisburg
Economic Development Office	(717) 787-3003	
Loan Information		
State Department of Commerce	(717) 787-4147	
Pennsylvania Milrite Council	(717) 783-7408	
Pennsylvania Capital Loan Fund	(717) 783-1768	
Procurement Information	(717) 783-5700	
Minority Business	(717) 783-1127	
Department of Revenue	(717) 787-8201	
State Export	(717) 787-7190/6500	
High-Tech	(717) 783-4147	
Insurance	(717) 782-3840	
Enterprise Zones	(717) 787-7402	James Brandon

Other U.S. Government Offices

IRS	(800) 242-0250	Western
	(800) 462-4000	Eastern
	(412) 281-0112	Pittsburgh
	(215) 574-9900	Philadelphia
Farmers' Home Administration	(717) 782-4476	Harrisburg
Department of Commerce	(412) 644-2850	
	(215) 597-2866	Philadelphia
Governor's Energy Council	(717) 783-8610	
	(800) 822-8400	Harrisburg
Department of Labor, Wage/Hour Division	(412) 644-2996	
	(215) 597-4950	
Occupational Safety and Health Administration	(215) 597-4955	
	(412) 644-2905	
	(717) 826-6538	Wilkes-Barre
	(717) 782-3902	
	(814) 453-4531	Erie
International Trade Administration	(215) 597-2866	
	(412) 644-2850	

Federal Information	(215) 597-7042	
Centers	(412) 644-3456	
Enterprise Zones-HUD	(215) 597-1917	Pat Mulligan

Puerto Rico Region II

Small Business Administration
District Office
Carlos Chardon Ave., Rm. 691
Hato Rey, PR 00919

Business Development	(809) 753-4572	
Financial Assistance	(809) 753-4572	
Veterans' Affairs Officer	(809) 753-4519	Raul Garcia
Women's Business Ownership	(809) 753-4519	Eldaa Conde
Disaster Home Loan Servicing Center	(809) 753-4012	
Small Business Development Centers		
	(809) 834-3790	Mayaguez
	(809) 763-5880	Rio Piedras
	(809) 778-5380	St. Croix
	(809) 776-3206	St. Thomas

State Offices

Small Business Program	(809) 724-0542	
State Development Office	(212) 245-1200	
Loan Information	(809) 726-2525 726-4675*	
Department of Revenue	(809) 724-9000	
State Export	(809) 725-7254	
Consumer Complaints	(809) 725-7555	
Ombudsman	(809) 724-7373	
Insurance	(809) 724-6565	Rolando Cruz

Other U.S. Government Offices

IRS	(809) 753-4040	San Juan
Farmers' Home Administration	(809) 753-4549	
Department of Commerce	(809) 753-4555, ext. 555	San Juan
Department of Energy	(809) 727-0154	Santurce
Department of Labor, Wage/Hour Division	(809) 753-4463	Hato Rey
Occupational Safety and Health Administration	(809) 753-4457	Hato Rey

*Number may be used only within this city.

Puerto Rico Region II

International Trade Administration	(809) 753-4555, ext. 555

Rhode Island Region I

Small Business Administration
District Office
380 Westminster Mall
Providence, RI 02903

Business Development	(401) 528-4583	
Financial Assistance	(401) 528-4586	
Veterans' Affairs Officer	(401) 528-7500	Anthony Ricci
Women's Business Ownership	(401) 528-7500, ext. 4583	Linda Smith
Small Business Development Centers		
	(401) 792-2451	Kingston
	(401) 846-5533	Newport
	(401) 831-1330	Providence
	(401) 232-6111	Smithfield
	(401) 272-4400	South Providence

State Offices

Small Business Development Program	(401) 277-2601, ext. 21	
Loan Information	(401) 277-2601, ext. 13	
Procurement Information	(401) 277-2601, ext. 42	
Minority Business	(401) 277-2601, ext. 26	
Department of Revenue	(401) 277-2934	Providence
State Export	(401) 277-2601	
Ombudsman	(401) 277-2080	
Enterprise Zones	(401) 277-3134	Jerome Lessuck
Insurance	(401) 277-2223	Thomas J. Caldarone

Other U.S. Government Offices

IRS	(800) 424-1040	
	(401) 521-6440	Providence
Farmers' Home Administration	(413) 253-3471	Amherst, MA
Department of Commerce	(401) 277-2605	Providence
Governor's Office of Energy Assistance	(401) 277-3370	
Department of Labor, Wage/Hour Division	(401) 528-5141	

Occupational Safety and Health Administration	(401) 528-4669	
International Trade Administration	(617) 223-2312	Boston, MA
Federal Information Center	331-5565*	Providence

South Carolina Region IV

Small Business Administration
District Office
1835 Assembly, Third Floor
Columbia, SC 29202

Business Development	(803) 765-5132	
Financial Assistance	(803) 765-5376	
Veterans' Affairs Officer	(803) 765-5913	Philip H. Black
Women's Business Ownership	(803) 765-5132	Lois Johnson

Small Business
Development Centers

(803) 524-3380, ext. 258	Beaufort
(803) 792-4065	Charleston
(803) 656-3227	Clemson
(803) 777-5118	Columbia
(803) 347-3161	Conway
(803) 662-8151, ext. 249	Florence
(803) 271-4259	Greenville
(803) 227-6110	Greenwood
(803) 534-6894	Orangeburg
(803) 323-2283	Rockhill
(803) 578-6233	Spartanburg

State Offices

Small Minority Business	(803) 734-0455	Columbia
State Development Office	(803) 734-1400	
Loan Information	(803) 734-1470	
Procurement Information	(803) 737-8910	
Department of Revenue	(803) 734-0374	
Consumer Complaints	(800) 922-1594	
High-Tech	(803) 734-9818	
Insurance	(803) 737-6117	John G. Richards

Other U.S. Government Offices

IRS	(800) 424-1040

*Number may be used only within this city.

South Carolina Region IV

Farmers' Home Administration	(803) 765-5163	Columbia
Department of Commerce	(803) 765-5345	
	(803) 724-4361	Charleston
	(803) 235-5919	Greenville
Department of Labor, Wage/Hour Division	(803) 765-5981	
Occupational Safety and Health Administration	(803) 765-5904	
International Trade Administration	(803) 765-5345	

South Dakota Region VIII

*Small Business Administration
District Office
101 S. Main Ave., Ste. 101
Sioux Falls, SD 57102*

Business Development	(605) 336-2980, ext. 231	
Financial Assistance	(605) 336-2980, ext. 231	
Veterans' Affairs Officer	(605) 336-2980, ext. 231	Richard Bruflat
Women's Business Ownership	(605) 336-2980, ext. 231	Darlene Michael
Small Business Development Centers		
	(605) 225-2860	Aberdeen
	(605) 394-5725	Rapid City
	(605) 677-5272	Vermillion
	(605) 886-7224	Watertown

State Offices

Small Business Program	(605) 773-5032	Pierre
Loan Information	(605) 773-5032	
Procurement Information	(605) 773-3405	
Minority Business	(605) 773-4906	
Consumer Complaints	(800) 592-1865	
Rural Assistance Program	(605) 688-4147	
Insurance	(605) 773-3563	

Other U.S. Government Offices

IRS	(800) 424-1040	
	(605) 225-9112	Aberdeen
Farmers' Home Administration	(605) 353-1430	

Department of Commerce	(402) 221-3664	Omaha, NE
Department of Energy	(605) 773-3603	Pierre
Department of Labor, Wage/Hour Division	(303) 844-4405	Denver, CO

Tennessee Region IV

Small Business Administration
District Office
404 James Robertson Pkwy., Ste. 1012
Nashville, TN 37219

Business Development	(615) 736-5881	
Financial Assistance	(615) 736-5881	
Veterans' Affairs Officer	(615) 736-7176	Bob Card
Women's Business Ownership	(615) 736-7932	Paul Middlebrooks

Small Business
Development Centers

	(615) 372-3649	Cookeville
	(901) 285-6910	Dyersburg
	(615) 929-5630	Johnson City
	(615) 584-6103	Knoxville
	(901) 587-7236	Martin
	(901) 454-2500	Memphis
	(901) 377-4111	
	(615) 581-2121	Morristown
	(615) 898-2700	Murfreesboro
	(615) 251-1505	Nashville
	(615) 455-8511	Tullahoma

State Offices

Small Business Program	(615) 741-2626	Nashville
State Development Office	(615) 741-1888	
Procurement Information	(615) 741-1035	
Minority Business (in state)	(800) 342-8470	
Minority Business (interstate)	(800) 251-8594	
Department of Revenue	(615) 741-2801	
State Export	(615) 741-5870	
Consumer Complaints	(800) 342-8385	
High-Tech	(615) 741-5070	
Insurance	(615) 741-2241	John C. Neff
Enterprise Zones	(615) 741-2373	Michael McGuire

Tennessee Region IV

Other U.S. Government Offices

IRS	(800) 424-1040	
	(615) 259-4601	Nashville
Farmers' Home Administration	(615) 736-7341	
Department of Commerce	(901) 521-4826	Memphis
	(615) 736-5161	Nashville
Department of Labor, Wage/Hour Division	(615) 736-5452	
Occupational Safety and Health Administration	(615) 736-5313	
International Trade Administration	(901) 521-4826	Memphis
	(615) 736-5161	Nashville
Federal Information Centers	265-8231*	Chattanooga
	(901) 521-3285	Memphis
	242-5056*	Nashville

Texas Region VI

Small Business Administration
District Offices
1100 Commerce St., Rm. 3C36
Dallas, TX 75242
10737 Gateway West, Ste. 320
El Paso, TX 79902
222 E. Van Buren St., Rm. 500
Harlingen, TX 78550
2525 Murworth, Rm. 112
Houston, TX 77054
1611 Tenth St., Ste. 200
Lubbock, TX 79401
727 E. Durango St., Rm. A-513
San Antonio, TX 78206

Branch Offices
221 W. Lancaster Ave., Rm. 1007
Fort Worth, TX 76102
400 Mann St., Ste. 403
Corpus Christi, TX 78408

Post of Duty Offices
100 S. Washington St., Rm. G-12
Marshall, TX 75670
300 E. Eighth St., Rm. 780
Austin, TX 78701

Business Development		
Austin	(512) 482-5288	
Corpus Christi	(512) 888-3306	

*Number may be used only within this city.

Dallas	(214) 767-0495
El Paso	(915) 541-7560
Fort Worth	(817) 334-3613
Harlingen	(512) 423-8934
Houston	(713) 660-4420
Lubbock	(806) 743-7481
Marshall	(214) 935-5257
San Antonio	(512) 229-6270

Financial Assistance

Austin	(512) 482-5288
Corpus Christi	(512) 888-3331
Dallas	(214) 767-0484
El Paso	(915) 541-7591
Fort Worth	(817) 334-3613
Harlingen	(512) 423-8934
Houston	(713) 660-4453
Lubbock	(806) 743-7466
Marshall	(214) 935-5257
San Antonio	(512) 229-6250

Veterans' Affairs Officers

Corpus Christi	(512) 888-3331	Jesse Sendejo
Dallas	(214) 767-0605	David Long
El Paso	(915) 541-7164	Conrad Ramirez
Harlingen	(512) 423-8934	Phillip Nelson
Houston	(713) 660-4409	Eugene Black, Jr.
Lubbock	(806) 743-7466	Clyde Green
San Antonio	(512) 229-6280	Anthony Reyna

Women's Business Ownership

Corpus Christi	(512) 888-3332	Diane Fuertes
Dallas	(214) 767-0382	Diane Cheshier
El Paso	(915) 541-7560	Abby H. Carter
Harlingen	(512) 423-8934	Graciela Guillen
Houston	(713) 660-4460	Laura Sanders
Lubbock	(806) 743-7471	Barbara Swanner
San Antonio	(512) 229-6250	Geraldine Cook

Disaster Home Loan Service Center	(915) 541-7590	Conrad Ramirez

Small Business Development Centers

(713) 488-7676	Clearlake
(713) 223-5800	Houston
(713) 578-1500	West Institute
(713) 359-1624	Kingwood

Texas Region VI

State Offices

Small Business Program	(512) 472-5059	Austin
Loan Information	(512) 472-5059	
Procurement Information	(512) 472-5059, ext. 654	
Minority Business Department of Revenue	(512) 472-5059	
State Export	(512) 472-5059	
	(713) 229-2578	Houston
	(512) 472-5559	
Ombudsman	(512) 472-5059	
High-Tech	(409) 845-0538	
Insurance	(512) 472-5059	
Enterprise Zones	(512) 472-5059	Harry L. Lucero
	(512) 630-5257	Karin Richmond

Other U.S. Government Offices

IRS	(800) 424-1040	
	(512) 472-1974	Austin
	(512) 888-9431	Corpus Christi
	(214) 742-2440	Dallas
	(512) 534-6460	El Paso
	(713) 965-0440	Houston
	(512) 229-1700	San Antonio
	(713) 226-5142	Houston
	(214) 767-1428	Dallas
Farmers' Home Administration	(817) 774-1301	Temple
	(214) 767-0542	Dallas
Department of Labor, Wage/Hour Division	(214) 767-6294	Dallas
	(817) 334-2678	Fort Worth
	(512) 888-3156	Corpus Christi
	(512) 229-6125	San Antonio
Occupational Safety and Health Administration	(713) 750-1727	Houston
	(806) 743-7681	Lubbock
	(512) 482-5783	Austin
	(214) 767-5347	Irving
International Trade Administration	(214) 767-0542	Dallas
Federal Information Centers	472-5494*	Austin
	767-8585*	Dallas
	(817) 334-3624	Fort Worth

*Number may be used only within this city.

Utah Region VIII

Small Business Administration
District Office
125 S. State St., Rm. 2237
Salt Lake City, UT 84138

Business Development	(801) 524-3212	
Financial Assistance	(801) 524-3215	
Veterans' Affairs Officer	(801) 524-5800	Lyman Kano
Women's Business Ownership	(801) 524-5800	Josie Valdez
Small Business Development Centers		
	(801) 586-5405	Cedar City
	(801) 750-2358	Logan
	(801) 626-7232	Ogden
	(801) 637-1995	Price
	(801) 378-2664	Provo
	(801) 581-7905	Salt Lake City

State Offices

Small Business Program	(801) 533-5325	Salt Lake City
State Development Office	(801) 533-5325	
Loan Information		
High-Tech, R&D, Emerging Businesses	(801) 533-5325	
New Product	(801) 533-5325	
Development Funding Through State Employees' Pension Fund	(801) 355-3884	
Procurement Information	(801) 533-5325	
Minority Business	(801) 533-4060	
Department of Revenue	(801) 328-5111	
State Export	(801) 533-5325	
Consumer Complaints	(801) 530-6601	
Venture Capital	(801) 533-5325	Grant Cannon
Insurance	(801) 530-6400	Roger C. Day

Other U.S. Government Offices

IRS	(800) 424-1040	
	(801) 524-5767	Salt Lake City
Farmers' Home Administration	(801) 524-5027	
Department of Commerce	(801) 524-5116	
Department of Energy	(801) 538-5428	

Utah Region VIII

Department of Labor, Wage/Hour Division	(801) 524-5706	
Occupational Safety and Health Administration	(801) 524-5080	
International Trade Administration	(801) 524-5116	
Federal Information Centers	399-1347* (801) 524-5353	Ogden

Vermont Region I

Small Business Administration
District Office
87 State St., Rm. 204
Montpelier, VT 05602

Business Development	(802) 229-9801	
Financial Assistance	(802) 229-0538	
Veterans' Affairs Officer	(802) 229-0538	Ora H. Paul
Women's Business Ownership	(802) 229-0538	Joan Innes
Small Business Development Centers		
	(802) 257-7967	Brattleboro
	(802) 656-4479	Burlington
	(802) 223-2389	Montpelier
	(802) 773-3349	Rutland
	(802) 748-8177	St. Johnsbury
	(802) 655-4452	Winooski

State Offices

Small Business Program	(802) 828-3221	Montpelier
State Development Office	(802) 828-3211	
Loan Information	(802) 223-7226	
Procurement Information	(802) 223-7226	
Department of Revenue	(802) 828-2509	
State Export	(802) 828-3221	
Consumer Complaints	(800) 642-5149	
Insurance	(802) 828-3301	David T. Bard

Other U.S. Government Offices

IRS	(800) 424-1040	Burlington
Farmers' Home Administration	(802) 223-2371	Montpelier

*Number may be used only within this city.

Department of Commerce	(617) 223-2312	Boston, MA
Department of Labor, Wage/Hour Division	(617) 223-6751	Boston, MA
Occupational Safety and Health Administration	(603) 225-1629	Concord
International Trade Administration	(617) 223-2312	Boston, MA

Virginia Region III

Small Business Administration
District Office
400 N. Eighth St., Rm. 3015
Richmond, VA 23240

Business Development	(804) 771-2410	
Financial Assistance	(804) 771-2765	
Veterans' Affairs Officer	(804) 771-2618	Guy R. Cooter
Women's Business Ownership	(804) 771-2765	Carol Brown
Small Business Development Center George Mason University	(703) 323-2568	

State Offices

Small Business Program	(804) 786-3791	
Minority Business	(804) 786-5560	
Department of Revenue	(804) 257-8031	
State Export	(804) 786-3791	
Consumer Hotline	(800) 332-1124	
Insurance	(800) 652-7945	James M. Thomson
	(804) 786-3741	Richmond
Enterprise Zone	(804) 786-4966	Stan Kidwell

Other U.S. Government Offices

IRS	(800) 424-1040	
	(804) 649-2361	Richmond
	(703) 557-9230	North Virginia
Farmers' Home Administration	(804) 771-2451	
Department of Commerce	(804) 771-2246	
	(703) 560-6460	Fairfax
Department of Energy	(804) 743-7000	Richmond
Department of Labor, Wage/Hour Division	(804) 771-2995	
Occupational Safety and Health Administration	(804) 771-2864	

Virginia Region III

International Trade Administration	(804) 771-2246	
Federal Information Centers	(804) 441-3101	Norfolk
	643-4928*	Richmond
	982-8591*	Roanoke
Enterprise Zones-HUD	(804) 786-4966	John Marelles

Washington Region X

Small Business Administration
District Offices
915 Second Ave., Rm. 1792
Seattle, WA 98174
920 W. Riverside Ave., Rm. 651
Spokane, WA 99210

Business Development		
Seattle	(206) 442-5534	
Spokane	(509) 456-3786	
Financial Assistance		
Seattle	(206) 442-4518	
Spokane	(509) 456-5346	
Veterans' Affairs Officers		
Seattle	(206) 442-5645	David Morado
Spokane	(509) 456-5348	Dan Mitchell
Women's Business Ownership		
Seattle	(206) 442-8404	Bonnie Galloway
Spokane	(509) 456-5365	Art Oquist
Small Business Development Centers		
	(206) 676-3899	Bellingham
	(206) 745-0430	Everett
	(206) 753-5616	Olympia
	(509) 335-7869	Pullman
	(206) 464-5450	Seattle
	(509) 456-2781	Spokane
	(206) 272-7232	Tacoma
	(206) 693-2555	Vancouver
	(509) 575-2284	Yakima
State Offices		
Small Business Program	(206) 753-5614	Seattle
State Development Office	(206) 753-5630	

*Number may be used only within this city.

Loan Information	(206) 586-1667	
Minority Business	(206) 753-9693	
State Export	(206) 753-5632	
Consumer Complaints	(800) 552-0700	
Licensing	(800) 562-8203	
High-Tech	(206) 753-5632	
Insurance	(206) 753-7301	Richard Marquardt

Other U.S. Government Offices

IRS	(800) 424-1040	
	(206) 442-1040	Seattle
Farmers' Home Administration	(509) 662-4353	Wenatchee
Department of Commerce	(206) 442-5615	Seattle
Department of Labor, Wage/Hour Division	(206) 442-4482	Seattle
Occupational Safety and Health Administration	(206) 442-7520	Bellevue
International Trade Administration	(206) 442-5616	Seattle
Federal Information Centers	(206) 442-0570	Seattle
	383-5230*	Tacoma
National Marine Fisheries Service	(206) 526-6150	Seattle
Enterprise Zones-HUD	(206) 442-4521	Robert Gilliland

West Virginia Region III

Small Business Administration
District Office
186 W. Maine St., 6th Floor
Clarksburg, WV 26301

Branch Office
550 Eagan St., Ste. 309
Charleston, WV 25301

Business Development		
Charleston	(304) 347-5220	
Clarksburg	(304) 623-5631	

Financial Assistance		
Charleston	(304) 347-5220	
Clarksburg	(304) 623-5631	

Veterans' Affairs Officers		
Charleston	(304) 347-5220	William Durham
Clarksburg	(304) 623-5631	Victor Benoit

*Number may be used only within this city.

West Virginia Region III

Women's Business
Ownership
Clarksburg   (304) 623-5631   Debbie Flanagan

Small Business
Development Centers
                                  (304) 384-9811   Athens
                                  (304) 348-2960   Charleston
                                  (800) 225-5982
                                  (304) 624-9896   Clarksburg
                                  (304) 367-4125   Fairmont
                                  (304) 788-3011   Keyser
                                  (304) 752-5900   Logan
                                  (800) 642-3089
                                  (304) 696-6797   Marshall
                                  (304) 442-5501   Montgomery
                                  (304) 293-5837   Morgantown
                                  (304) 424-8277   Parkersburg
                                  (800) 344-5231, ext. 261   Shepherdstown

State Offices
  Small Business Program   (800) 225-5982
  State Development   (800) 225-5982
  Office
  Loan Information   (800) 225-5982
  Procurement   (800) 225-5982
  Information
  Department of Revenue   (800) 225-5982
  State Export   (800) 225-5982
  Consumer Complaints   (800) 332-1124
  Telephone Consumer
  Hotline, Inc.
  Insurance   (304) 348-3386   Fred E. Wright

Other U.S. Government Offices
  IRS   (800) 424-1040
                                  (304) 422-8551, ext. 1255   Parkersburg
  Farmers' Home   (304) 291-4791   Morgantown
  Administration
  Department of   (304) 343-6181, ext. 375   Charleston
  Commerce
  Department of Energy   (304) 348-8860   Charleston
  Department of Labor,   (304) 347-5207
  Wage/Hour Division
  Occupational Safety and   (304) 347-5937
  Health Administration
  International Trade   (304) 347-5123
  Administration

Wisconsin Region V

Small Business Administration
District Office
212 E. Washington Ave., Rm. 213
Madison, WI 53703

Branch Office
310 W. Wisconsin Ave., Rm. 400
Milwaukee, WI 53203

Post of Duty Office
500 S. Barstow St., Rm. 17
Eau Claire, WI 54701

Business Development		
Eau Claire	(715) 834-9012	
Madison	(608) 264-5117	SCORE
Milwaukee	(414) 291-1095	

Financial Assistance		
Eau Claire	(715) 834-9012	
Madison	(608) 264-5261	
Milwaukee	(414) 291-3941	

Veterans' Affairs Officers		
Madison	(608) 264-5261	Robert Johnson
Milwaukee	(414) 291-3941	Arthur Greve

Women's Business Ownership		
Madison	(608) 264-5261	Thomas Guppy
Milwaukee	(414) 291-3941	Karen I. Sakihama

Small Business Development Centers		
	(715) 836-5811	Eau Claire
	(414) 465-2167	Green Bay
	(414) 553-2047	Kenosha
	(608) 785-8782	La Crosse
	(608) 263-2221	Madison
	(715) 232-1252	Menomonie
	(414) 224-4758	Milwaukee
	(414) 424-1541	Oshkosh
	(715) 346-2004	Stevens Point
	(715) 394-8351	Superior
	(414) 472-3217	Whitewater

State Offices		
Small Business Program	(608) 266-0562	Madison
State Development Office	(608) 266-1018	

Wisconsin Region V

Loan Information:

High-Tech, New Product	(608) 266-7968	
MESBIC	(608) 266-8380	
Development Fund/General Purposes	(414) 271-5900	Milwaukee
Energy-related Employing Unemployed Youth	(608) 256-1620	
Community Development Projects	(608) 266-0590*	
Procurement Information	(608) 266-2605	
Minority Business	(608) 267-9550	
Department of Revenue	(608) 266-1961	
State Export	(608) 266-1767	
Consumer Complaints	(800) 362-3020	
Ombudsman	(608) 266-0562	
Permit Information	(800) HELP-BUSINESS	
Legislative Hotline	(800) 362-9696	
High-Tech	(608) 266-1018	
Insurance	(608) 266-3585	

Other U.S. Government Offices

IRS	(800) 424-1040	
	(414) 271-3780	Milwaukee
Farmers' Home Administration	(715) 341-5900	Stevens Point
Department of Commerce	(414) 291-3473	Milwaukee
Department of Energy	(608) 263-1662	Madison
Department of Labor, Wage/Hour Division	(414) 291-3585	
	(608) 264-5221	
Occupational Safety and Health Administration	(414) 291-3315	
	(414) 734-4521	Appleton
International Trade Administration	(414) 291-3473	Milwaukee
Federal Information Center	(608) 271-2273	
Insurance	(307) 777-7401	Robert W. Schrader

*503-Certified Development Corp. Wisconsin Business Development Finance Corp. 217 S. Hamilton, Ste. 405 Madison, WI 53707

Wyoming Region VIII

Small Business Administration
District Office
100 E. B St., Rm. 4001
Casper, WY 82602

Business Development	(307) 261-5761	Joe Barber
Financial Assistance	(307) 261-5761	Henry Ise
Veterans' Affairs Officer	(307) 261-5761	Philo Macdonald
Women's Business Ownership	(307) 261-5761	R. Jean Micek
Small Business Development Centers		
	(307) 235-4827	Casper
	(307) 634-5853	Cheyenne
	(307) 358-4090	Douglass
	(307) 686-0297	Gillette
	(307) 766-2363	Laramie
	(307) 754-3746	Powell
	(307) 362-8107	Rocksprings
	(307) 235-4825	Wyoming (state office)

State Offices

Small Business Program	(307) 777-7287	
State Development Office	(307) 777-7284	Bill Budd
Loan Information Industrial Development Corporation	(307) 234-5351	Scott Weaver
Department of Revenue	(307) 777-5287	Jim Petry

Other U.S. Government Offices

IRS	(800) 424-1040	
Department of Energy	(307) 721-2247	Laramie
Department of Labor, Wage/Hour Division	(303) 844-4405 (801) 524-5706	Denver, CO Salt Lake City, UT
Occupational Safety and Health Administration	(303) 884-5285	Denver, CO
International Trade Administration	(303) 837-3246	Denver, CO

SBA REGIONAL OFFICES

Boston Regional Office (Region I)
60 Batterymarch, 10th Floor
Boston, MA 02210-3298

FTS Number: -8-223 + ext.
(617) 223 + ext.

Regional Administrator, John Moffitt, Tel.: 6660
Deputy Regional Administrator, John Barbas, Tel.: 4495
Regional Advocate (Concord, NH), Ward Brown, Tel.: (603) 225-1400
Export Development Specialist, Arnold Rosenthal, Tel.: 7661
Regional Counsel, Tel.: 7742

Assistant Regional Administrator for:
　　Administration, Tel.: 3204
　　Business Development, Tel.: 1005
　　Finance and Investment, Tel.: 3891
　　Minority Small Business/COD, Tel.: 7761
　　Procurement and Technology, Tel.: 4485
　　Public Affairs and Communications, Tel.: 0408

New York Regional Office (Region II)
26 Federal Plaza, Rm. 29-118
New York, NY 10278

FTS Number: -8-264 + ext.
(212) 264 + ext.

Regional Administrator, Charles Freeman, Tel.: 1450
Regional Advocate (Syracuse), Harry Bellardini, Tel.: (315) 423-5350
Export Development Specialist, John Miller, Tel.: 7759
Regional Counsel, Tel.: 2845

Assistant Regional Administrator for:
　　Administration, Tel.: 2455
　　Business Development, Tel.: 7755
　　Finance and Investment, Tel.: 2451
　　Minority Small Business/COD, Tel.: 1046
　　Procurement and Technology Assistance, Tel.: 1452
　　Public Affairs and Communications, Tel.: 4480

Philadelphia Regional Office (Region III)
W. Lobby, Ste. 640
One Bala Cynwyd Plaza
231 St. Asaphs Rd.
Bala Cynwyd, PA 19004

FTS Number: -8-596 + ext.
(215) 596 + ext.

Regional Administrator, Robert H. Miller, Tel.: 5901
Deputy Regional Administrator, Michael Wilkin, Tel.: 5908
Regional Advocate, Richard Johnson, Tel.: 5913
Export Development Specialist, Ed Wilford, Tel.: 5911
Regional Counsel, Tel.: 5966

Assistant Regional Administrator for:
  Administration, Tel.: 5952
  Business Development, Tel.: 5972
  Finance and Investment, Tel.: 5979
  Minority Small Business/COD, Tel.: 5965
  Procurement and Technology, Tel.: 5962
  Public Affairs and Communications, Tel.: 5955

Atlanta Regional Office (Region IV)
1375 Peachtree St., N.E.
Atlanta, GA 30367

FTS Number: -8-257 + ext.
(404) 881 + ext.

Regional Administrator, June Nichols, Tel.: 4999
Deputy Regional Administrator, Wiley S. Messick, Tel.: 4281
Regional Advocate, Sue McConnell, Tel.: 3081
Export Development Specialist, Charles E. Boyanton, Tel.: 4948
Regional Counsel, Tel.: 4950

Assistant Regional Administrator for:
  Administration, Tel.: 4735
  Business Development, Tel.: 4948
  Finance and Investment, Tel.: 2009
  Minority Small Business/COD, Tel.: 3683
  Procurement and Technology Assistance, Tel.: 4483
  Public Affairs and Communications, Tel.: 2797

Chicago Regional Office (Region V)
230 S. Dearborn St., Rm. 510
Chicago, IL 60604-1593

FTS Number: -8-353 + ext.
(312) 353 + ext.

Regional Administrator, James Thompson, Tel.: 0357
Deputy Regional Administrator, James L. Charney, Tel.: 4493
Regional Advocate, Juanita Pierman, Tel.: 2957
Export Development Specialist, Nagi Kheir, Tel.: 0848
Regional Counsel, Tel.: 0355

Assistant Regional Administrator for:
  Administration, Tel.: 6614
  Business Development, Tel.: 4252
  Financial Investment, Tel.: 4507
  Minority Small Business/COD, Tel.: 6847

Procurement Assistance, Tel.: 1395
Public Affairs and Communications, Tel.: 0359

Dallas Regional Office (Region VI)
8625 King George Dr., Bldg. C
Dallas, TX 75235-3391

FTS Number: -8-729 + ext.
(214) 767 + ext.

Regional Administrator, Joseph Pena, Tel.: 7611
Deputy Regional Administrator, Tel.: 7654
Regional Advocate, Mary Faye Kamm, Tel.: 7635
Export Development Specialist, Carlos de la Vega, Tel.: 7643
Regional Counsel, Tel.: 7626

Assistant Regional Administrator for:
    Administration, Tel.: 7651
    Business Development, Tel.: 7678
    Financial Assistance, Tel.: 7652
    Minority Small Business/COD, Tel.: 7631
    Procurement and Technology Assistance, Tel.: 7654
    Public Affairs and Communications, Tel.: 7614

Kansas City Regional Office (Region VII)
911 Walnut St., 13th Floor
Kansas City, MO 64106

FTS Number: -8-758 + ext.
(816) 374 + ext.

Regional Administrator, William A. Powell, Tel.: 3316
Deputy Regional Administrator, Harold W. Nossaman, Tel.: 3210
Regional Advocate, Judy Krueger, Tel.: 2803
Export Development Specialist, Ken Bonar, Tel.: 3927
Regional Counsel, Tel.: 2658

Assistant Regional Administrator for:
    Administration, Tel.: 2989
    Business Development, Tel.: 3210
    Finance and Investment, Tel.: 3210
    Minority Small Business/COD, Tel.: 3516
    Procurement Assistance, Tel.: 5201
    Public Affairs and Communications, Tel.: 3607

Denver Regional Office (Region VIII)
Executive Tower Bldg., 22d Floor
1405 Curtis St.
Denver, CO 80202-2395

FTS Number: -8-564 + ext.
(303) 844 + ext.

Regional Administrator, Gil Cisneros, Tel.: 5441
Deputy Regional Administrator, Jerry Carroll, Tel.: 5441

Regional Advocate, James Henderson, Tel.: 5441
Export Development Specialist, Don Davis, Tel.: 5441
Regional Counsel, Tel.: 5441

Assistant Regional Administrator for:
Administration, Tel.: 5441
Business Development, Tel.: 5441
Finance and Investment, Tel.: 5441
Minority Small Business/COD, Tel.: 5441
Procurement and Technology Assistance, Tel.: 5441
Public Affairs and Communications, Tel.: 5441

San Francisco Regional Office (Region IX)
450 Golden Gate Ave.
P.O. Box 36044
San Francisco, CA 94102

FTS Number: -8-556 + ext.
(415) 556 + ext.

Regional Administrator, Thomas Topuzes, Tel.: (415) 556-7487
Deputy Regional Administrator, James P. Guyer, Tel.: 3565
Regional Advocate, Kim Getto, Tel.: FTS-556-7697
Export Development Specialist, James Lucas, Tel.: 9902
Regional Counsel, Tel.: 7780

Assistant Regional Administrator for:
Administration, Tel.: 5935
Business Development, Tel.: 4724
Finance and Investment, Tel.: 7782
Minority Small Business/COD, Tel.: 9614
Procurement Assistance, Tel.: 7784
Public Affairs and Communications, Tel.: 2820

Seattle Regional Office (Region X)
2615 Fourth Ave., Rm. 440
Seattle, WA. 98121

FTS Number: -8-399 + ext.
(206) 442 + ext.

Regional Administrator, Stephen J. Hall, Tel.: 5676
Deputy Regional Administrator, Robert F. Caldwell, Tel.: 5676
Regional Advocate, David Dougherty, Tel.: 5231
Export Development Specialist, Pru Balatero, Tel.: 8333
Regional Counsel, Tel.: 7276

Assistant Regional Administrator for:
Administration, Tel.: 8532
Business Development, Tel.: 1456
Finance and Investment, Tel.: 2928
Minority Small Business/COD, Tel.: 2872
Procurement Assistance, Tel.: 0309
Public Affairs and Communications, Tel.: 8403

REGIONAL ADVOCATES

The Office of Advocacy is supported by the efforts of regional advocates. These advocates are the Chief Counsel's direct link to the U.S. small business community. They maintain contact with local businesses, regional business groups, SBA district offices, and state and local government officials. Regional advocates are in an excellent position to determine the specific needs of local small businesses and to assess their regions' unique small business problems, thereby establishing a two-way communication network between the Chief Counsel and the small business community.

REGION I
Ward Brown
P.O. Box 1257
Concord, NH 03301
(603) 225-1400
FTS-834-4410

REGION II
Harry Bellardini
100 S. Clinton
Federal Bldg., Rm. 1071
Syracuse, NY 13260
(315) 423-5350
FTS-950-5350

REGION III
Richard Johnson
One Bala Cynwyd Plaza, Ste. 640
Bala Cynwyd, PA 19004
(215) 596-5913
FTS-596-5913

REGION IV
Sue McConnell
1375 Peachtree St., N.E.
Atlanta, GA 30367
(404) 881-3081
FTS-257-3081

REGION V
Regional Advocate
230 S. Dearborn St., Rm. 510
Chicago, IL 60604
(312) 353-2957/4492
FTS-353-2957

REGION VI
Mary Faye Kamm
8625 King George Dr., Bldg. C
Dallas, TX 75235-3391
(214) 767-7635
FTS-729-7635

REGION VII
Judy Krueger
911 Walnut St., 13th Floor
Kansas City, MO 64106
(816) 374-2803
FTS-758-2803

REGION VIII
James Henderson
Executive Tower Bldg., 22d Floor
1405 Curtis St.
Denver, CO 80202-2395
(303) 844-5441, ext. 33
FTS-564-5441, ext. 33

REGION IX
Kim Getto
450 Golden Gate Ave.
San Francisco, CA 94102
(415) 556-7697
FTS-556-7697

REGION X
David Dougherty
2615 Fourth Ave., Rm. 440
Seattle, WA 98121
(206) 442-5231
FTS-399-5231

SBA CENTRAL OFFICE PROGRAM TELEPHONE NUMBERS

Administrator, (202) 653-6605
Advisory Councils, (202) 653-6892
Business Development, (202) 653-6881

Congressional Relations, (202) 653-7581
Disaster Assistance, (202) 653-6879
Economic Development (503), (202) 653-6416
Employee Locator, (202) 653-6600
Equal Opportunity, (202) 653-6050
Financial Assistance, (202) 653-6574
Financial Institutions, (202) 653-2585
Freedom of Information, (202) 653-6460
General Counsel, (202) 653-6642
Hearing and Appeals, (202) 653-6805
Inspector General, (202) 653-6597
International Trade, (202) 653-7794
Law Library, (202) 653-6556
Loan Processing, (202) 653-6470
Minority, (202) 653-6407
PASS, (202) 653-6442
Pollution Control Loans, (202) 653-2548
Private Sector Initiatives (incubators), (202) 653-7880
Procurement, (202) 653-6938
Procurement (8a), (202) 653-6813
Public Communications, (202) 653-6832
Reference Library, (202) 653-6914
SCORE/ACE, (202) 653-6279
Secondary Market Activity, (212) 264-5877
Size Standards, (202) 653-6373
Small Business Development Center, (202) 653-6768
Small Business Innovation Research (SBIR), (202) 653-6458
Small Business Institute (SBI), (202) 653-6628
Surety Bond (Ballston), (703) 235-2900
Veterans' Affairs, (202) 653-8220
Women's Business, (202) 653-8000

SBA OFFICE OF ADVOCACY

Office of the Chief Counsel

Frank Swain, Chief Counsel; Tel.: (202) 653-6533
Charles Cadwell, Deputy Chief Counsel; Tel.: (202) 634-4968
Jackie Woodard, Director, State and Local Affairs; Tel.: (202) 634-7235

Interagency Affairs

Doris Freedman, Director, Regulatory Affairs; Tel.: (202) 634-6115

Economic Research

Thomas Gray, Director; Tel.: (202) 634-7550
William Whiston, Branch Chief, Research Contracts; Tel.: (202) 634-7584
Jules Lichtenstein, Branch Chief, Applied Policy; Tel.: (202) 634-7550
Bruce Phillips, Branch Chief, Data Base; Tel.: (202) 634-7550

G. A. Chiaruttini, Acting Director, Tel.: (202) 634-7600
Robert Clairmont, Coordinator, Answer Desk; Tel.: (202) 634-7509 or (800) 368-5855

SBA DISASTER LOAN PROGRAM

Types of Disaster Loans

Business Physical Disaster Loans: Loans to businesses to repair or replace disaster-related damaged property owned by the business, including inventory and supplies.

Economic Injury Disaster Loans (EIDL): Working capital loans (referred to as EIDL) to small businesses and to small agricultural cooperatives to assist them through the disaster recovery period. These loans are available only if the business or its owners cannot obtain this type of assistance from nongovernment sources. This determination is made by SBA.

Credit Requirements

These are loans, and applicants must show that they have the ability to repay them. Loans in excess of $5,000 must be secured with collateral. Generally, for individuals, collateral will include a lien on the applicant's real estate. However, loans will not be declined for lack of a fixed amount of collateral.

There are different interest rates and terms for these loans, depending on whether or not the applicant could recover from disaster damage using personal funds or funds from nongovernment sources. The determination of whether there is "credit available elsewhere" or "credit not available elsewhere" is made by SBA.

Interest Rates

BUSINESS DISASTER LOANS

Credit Available Elsewhere	8 percent
Credit Not Available Elsewhere	4 percent
(applies to EIDL also)	
Nonprofit, Eleemosynary Institutions	10.5 percent

Loan Amount

For business physical damage loans, the loan amount is up to 100 percent of the uninsured SBA-verified loss, not to exceed $500,000. For economic injury, the loan amount is up to $500,000.

The *total* loan amount to any one business entity (including affiliates) for *combined* economic injury and business disaster loans cannot exceed $500,000.

Loan Term

For businesses with "credit available elsewhere," the maximum loan term is up to three years.

Loan Limitations

No loans are made for damages to secondary homes, or for damage to personal pleasure boats, planes, recreational vehicles, antiques, collections, and so on. There are limitations on loan amounts for landscaping, family swimming pools, and so on.

Flood Insurance Requirements

Applicants who have SBA loans that require them to maintain flood insurance are not eligible for loans if they have not maintained their insurance. If your property is located in a special flood hazard area, you must purchase and maintain flood insurance *for the insurable value* of your property, *regardless of the amount of your loan.*

SBA DISASTER AREA OFFICES

Regions I and II		
Carl J. Jordan, Acting Dir.	FTS:	8-348-0011
Disaster Area 1 Office	Commercial:	(201) 794-8195
Small Business Administration	Interstate:	(800) 221-2093
15-01 Broadway		(800) 221-2091
In NJ:		
Fair Lawn, NJ 07410		

Regions III, IV, and V		
Richard J. Nash, Dir.	FTS:	8-257-3771
Disaster Area 2 Office	Commercial:	(404) 347-3771
Small Business Administration	In GA:	(800) 241-5625
120 Ralph McGill Blvd., N.E., 14th Floor		
Atlanta, GA 30308		

Regions VI and VII		
George L. Darby, Dir.	FTS:	8-729-7571
Disaster Area 3 Office	Commercial:	(214) 767-7571
Small Business Administration	Interstate:	(800) 527-7735
2306 Oak La., Ste. 110	In TX:	(800) 442-7206
Grand Prairie, TX 75051		

Regions VIII, IX, and X		
Robert L. Belloni, Dir.	FTS:	8-460-4571
Disaster Area 4 Office		
Small Business Administration	Commercial:	(916) 978-4578

Regions VIII, IX, and X		
77 Cadillac Dr., Ste. 158 P.O. Box 13795 Sacramento, CA 95853-4795	Interstate: In CA:	(800) 468-1710 (800) 468-1713

SBA SMALL BUSINESS INVESTMENT CORPORATIONS (SBICS)

Area I

Region I (Connecticut, Maine, Massachusetts, New Hampshire, Rhode Island, Vermont)
Region III (Delaware, District of Columbia, Maryland, Virginia, West Virginia)
Region V (Illinois, Indiana, Michigan, Minnesota, Ohio, Wisconsin)
Lawrence F. Friess, Chief; Tel.: (202) 653-6427

Area II

Region II (New York, New Jersey, Puerto Rico, Virgin Islands)
Region III (Pennsylvania)
Joseph L. Newell, Chief; Tel.: (202) 653-6690

Area III

Region IV (Alabama, Florida, Georgia, Kentucky, Mississippi, North Carolina, South Carolina, Tennessee)
Region VI (Arkansas, Louisiana, Texas)
Patricia W. DiMuzio, Chief; Tel.: (202) 653-6926

Area IV

Region VI (New Mexico, Oklahoma)
Region VII (Iowa, Kansas, Missouri, Nebraska)
Region VIII (Colorado, Montana, North Dakota, South Dakota, Utah, Wyoming)
Region IX (Arizona, California, Guam, Hawaii, Nevada)
Region X (Alaska, Idaho, Oregon, Washington)
Marvin D. Klapp, Chief; Tel.: (202) 653-6473

SBA PROCUREMENT CENTER REPRESENTATIVES

Name	City	State	Phone
Dick Cates	Huntsville	AL	(205) 876-7373
John Vickers	Huntsville	AL	(205) 876-9613
David Wilson	Huntsville	AL	(205) 876-4513
Ian Snyder	Little Rock	AR	(501) 378-5871

Name	City	State	Phone
Arlene S. Pinkney	Long Beach	CA	(213) 547-7427
Amanda M. Gallegos	Los Angeles	CA	(213) 643-0086
Klaude Swinney	Sacramento	CA	(916) 643-2829
Thomas Warner	Sacramento	CA	(916) 643-4131
Robert S. Burnside	San Diego	CA	(714) 294-5438
Anthony R. Marcinek	San Francisco	CA	(415) 556-7784
Don Foster	Denver	CO	(303) 236-7353
Susan Monge	Washington-DOT	DC	(202) 366-1930
Robert S. Coates	Washington-GSA	DC	(703) 557-7994
Susan Monge	Washington-USDA	DC	(202) 447-7117
Verl Zanders	Washington	DC	(202) 475-0330
Dewey White	Washington-HHS	DC	(202) 692-6465
Sara (Sally) Long	Eglin AFB	FL	(904) 882-9159
James Rollins	Eglin AFB	FL	(904) 882-2605
Lawrence Feldman	Orlando	FL	(305) 646-5515
Dianne Sisson	Atlanta	GA	(404) 347-7587
T. C. Hollingsworth	Warner Robins	GA	(912) 926-5874
Louise G. Guerrerd	Honolulu	HI	(808) 546-8634
Frank Villacci, Jr.	Hines	IL	(312) 681-6008
D. Veer Khurana	Indianapolis	IN	(317) 353-3024
Richard Doyle	Cambridge	MA	(617) 494-2025
J. Mazzone	Hanscom	MA	(617) 377-2737
Ron Schille	Hanscom	MA	(617) 377-2737
Joseph Peck	Warren	MI	(313) 574-7387
Nicholas E. Lind	Warren	MI	(313) 574-8124
Herschel Merchant	Kansas City	MO	(816) 926-5307
Lyle C. Evans	St. Louis	MO	(314) 263-3951
Cecil Shaffer	St. Louis	MO	(314) 263-3057
Richard Plaster	St. Louis	MO	(314) 263-3057
Sylvester Jackson	St. Louis	MO	(314) 263-3951
Larry Mallory	Dover	NJ	(201) 724-6960
John Kusciuch	Fort Monmouth	NJ	(201) 532-3419
John Tracy	Fort Monmouth	NJ	(201) 532-3419
Alexander Munro	Fort Monmouth	NJ	(201) 532-3419
Robert F. Schleicher	Kirkland AFB	NM	(505) 844-3985
Andy Zuber	Fort Drum	NY	(212) 264-1452
Marie Holford	New York	NY	(212) 264-5576
Joseph Musil	New York	NY	(212) 264-5576
Jean Trombetta	Columbus	OH	(614) 469-2279
Francis G. Skrobot	Columbus	OH	(614) 469-2410
Kenneth Myron	Dayton-DLA	OH	(513) 296-5233
John Evans	Dayton-DLA	OH	(513) 296-5233
John R. Schneider	Wright-Pat.	OH	(513) 255-3333
Frank G. Miller	Tinker AFB	OK	(405) 739-7821

Name	City	State	Phone
Harry Turk	Tinker AFB	OK	(405) 231-4784
Emile D. Vangoidtsnoven	Mechanicsburg	PA	(717) 790-3629
Ronald Tyler	Mechanicsburg	PA	(717) 790-7525
B. J. Koehler	Philadelphia	PA	(215) 897-5406
Francis Seymour	Philadelphia	PA	(215) 697-6340
Joseph D. Holston	Philadelphia-DISC	PA	(215) 697-3817
Wayne Lawley	Philadelphia-DISC	PA	(215) 697-6696
Joseph Giordano	Philadelphia-ASL	PA	(215) 697-6161
Thomas W. McGrath	Philadelphia-DPSC	PA	(215) 952-5912
Vacant	Newport	RI	(401) 841-3692
Donna Barber	Charleston	SC	(803) 554-2558
Lyle Ferguson	Fort Worth	TX	(814) 334-2997
Joseph Best	Kelly AFB	TX	(512) 229-5608
Robert Curiel	Kelly AFB	TX	(512) 229-5608
Kenneth Williams	Ogden	UT	(801) 625-5586
Patrick Verfurth	Ogden	UT	(801) 625-5586
Sherman Hinkley	Alexandria-DFSC	VA	(202) 274-6326
Joseph Foglia	Hampton	VA	(804) 865-3396
J. Blackwood	Richmond-DGSC	VA	(804) 275-3154
Robert S. Coates	Richmond-DGSC	VA	(804) 275-3940

SBA SURETY BOND GUARANTEE OFFICERS

REGION I
Dorothy Kleeschulte, Surety Bond Officer
Small Business Administration
60 Batterymarch St., 10th Floor
Boston, MA 02110
(617) 223-5726

REGION II
Edward J. Ryan, Surety Bond Guarantee
  Officer
26 Federal Plaza, Rm. 29-118
Small Business Administration
New York, NY 10278
(212) 264-4395/2451

REGION III
James L. Higgins, Surety Bond Guarantee
  Officer
Al Moony, Surety Bond Specialist
Small Business Administration
231 St. Asaphs Rd.
One Bala Cynwyd Plaza
W. Lobby, Ste. 640
Bala Cynwyd, PA 19004
(215) 596-5969

REGION IV
Eugene Merriday, Chief
Surety Bond Division
Walter Hank, Surety Bond Specialist
Small Business Administration
1375 Peachtree St., N.E., Ste. 560
Atlanta, GA 30367
(404) 347-2386

REGION V
Anthony J. Zanetello, Surety Bond Officer
Elizabeth Gutierrez, Surety Bond Specialist
Small Business Administration
230 S. Dearborn St., Fifth Floor
Chicago, IL 60604
(312) 353-3835

REGION VI
Cliff Justice, Surety Bond Officer
June Trickett, Surety Bond Assistant
Tina Ray, Surety Bond Assistant
Small Business Administration
8625 King George Dr., Bldg. C
Dallas, TX 75235-3391
(214) 767-7664

REGION VII
Florence Kelley, Chief Surety Bond Specialist
Small Business Administration
911 Walnut St., 13th Floor
Kansas City, MO 64106
(816) 374-3927

REGION VIII
Helen Edwards, Surety Bond Officer
Harry Hastings, Surety Bond Assistant
Small Business Administration
Executive Tower Bldg., 22d Floor
1405 Curtis St.
Denver, CO 80202-2395
(303) 844-5441

REGION IX
Richard R. Burns, Surety Bond Officer
Jeffrey Johnston, Surety Bond Specialist
Small Business Administration
450 Golden Gate Ave.
P.O. Box 36044
San Francisco, CA 94102
(415) 556-7236

REGION X
Thomas B. Sault, Surety Bond Officer
Thomas Ewbank, Surety Bond Assistant
Small Business Administration
Fourth and Vine Bldg.
2615 Fourth Ave., Rm. 440
Seattle, WA 98121
(206) 442-0960

GENERAL SERVICES ADMINISTRATION SMALL BUSINESS SERVICE CENTERS

National Capital Region
7th & D Sts., N.W.
Washington, DC 20407
(202) 472-1804

1. John W. McCormack Federal Bldg.
Boston, MA 02109
(617) 223-2868

2. 26 Federal Plaza
New York, NY 10278
(212) 264-1234

3. 9th and Market Sts.
Philadelphia, PA 19107
(215) 597-9613

4. 75 Spring St., S.W.
Atlanta, GA 30303
(404) 331-5103

5. 230 S. Dearborn St.
Chicago, IL 60604
(312) 353-5383

6. 1500 E. Bannister Rd.
Kansas City, MO 64131
(816) 926-7203

7. 819 Taylor St.
Fort Worth, TX 76102
(817) 334-3284

8. Bldg. No. 41
Denver Federal Center
Denver, CO 80225
(303) 236-7407

9. 525 Market St.
San Francisco, CA 94105
(415) 974-9000

300 N. Los Angeles
Los Angeles, CA 90012
(213) 894-3210

10. 915 Second Ave.
Seattle, WA 96174
(206) 442-5556

GOVERNMENT PRINTING OFFICE BOOKSTORES SPONSORED BY SBA*

9220-B Pkwy. East
Birmingham, AL
(205) 731-1056

ARCO Plaza
505 S. Flower St.
Los Angeles, CA
(213) 894-5841

*Publications may be ordered by phone and charged to a major credit card.

450 Golden Gate Ave.
San Francisco, CA
(415) 556-0642

1961 Stout St.
Denver, CO
(303) 844-3964

720 N. Main
Majestic Bldg.
Pueblo, CO
(303) 554-3142

400 W. Bay St.
Jacksonville, FL
(904) 791-3801

275 Peachtree St., N.E.
Atlanta, GA
(404) 331-6947

219 S. Dearborn St.
Chicago, IL
(312) 353-5133

John F. Kennedy Federal Bldg.
Sudbury St.
Boston, MA
(617) 565-2488

477 Michigan Ave.
Detroit, MI
(313) 226-7816

601 E. 12th St.
Kansas City, MO
(816) 765-2256

1240 E. Ninth St.
Cleveland, OH
(216) 522-4922

200 N. High St.
Columbus, OH
(614) 469-6956

600 Arch St.
Philadelphia, PA
(215) 597-0677

1000 Liberty Ave.
Pittsburgh, PA
(412) 644-2721

1100 Commerce St.
Dallas, TX
(214) 767-0076

College Center
9319 Gulf Freeway
Houston, TX
(713) 229-3515

915 Second Ave.
Seattle, WA
(206) 442-4270

Main Bookstore
710 N. Capitol St.
Washington, DC
(202) 275-2091

Commerce Department
Pennsylvania Ave., N.W.
Washington, DC
(202) 377-3527

Retail Sales Branch
8660 Cherry La.
Laurel, MD
(301) 953-7974

1717 H St., N.W.
Washington, DC
(202) 653-5075

519 E. Wisconsin Ave.
Milwaukee, WI
(414) 291-1304

OFFICES OF SMALL AND DISADVANTAGED BUSINESS UTILIZATION (OSDBU)

Agency for International Development
Joe Bennett
Dir., Business Relations
Rm. 1400A, State Annex TT-2
Washington, DC 20523
(202) 875-1551

U.S. Air Force
Don Rellins

Dir., OSDBU
Rm. 4C255, The Pentagon
Washington, DC 20330
(202) 697-4126

Army
Office of Assistant Secretary
Juanita Watts
Dir., OSDBU

Rm. 2A712, The Pentagon
Washington, DC 20310
(202) 697-7753

Defense Department
Office of the Secretary
Norma B. Leftwich
Dir., OSDBU
Rm. 2A330, The Pentagon
Washington, DC 20301
(202) 694-1151

Defense Logistics Agency
Ray Dellas
Dir., OSDBU
Cameron Station
Alexandria, VA 22314
(202) 274-6471

Department of Agriculture
Casey Mann
Associate Dir., OSDBU
Administration Bldg., 127W
Washington, DC 20250
(202) 447-7117

Department of Commerce
James P. Maruca
Dir., OSDBU
14th & Constitution Ave., N.W., Rm. 6411
Washington, DC 20230
(202) 377-1472

Department of Health and Human Services
Richard Clinkscales
Dir., OSDBU
200 Independence Ave., S.W.
Rm. 513D
Washington, DC 20201
(202) 245-7300

Education Department
Daniel Levin
Dir., OSDBU
400 Maryland Ave., S.W., Rm. 4329
Switzer Bldg.
Washington, DC 20202-2410
(202) 732-4500

Energy Department
John W. Shepard
Dir., OSDBU
Rm. 1E061
Washington, DC 20585
(202) 252-8201

Environmental Protection Agency
John M. Ropes
Dir., OSDBU
401 M St., S.W., A-149-C
Washington, DC 20460
(202) 557-7777

Executive Office of the President
Strat Valakis, Dir.
Office of Procurement and Contracts
Rm. 424, OEOB
Washington, DC 20500
(202) 395-3314

Export-Import Bank
Helene H. Wall
Dir., OSDBU
811 Vermont Ave., N.W.
Rm. 1031
Washington, DC 20571
(202) 566-8951

Federal Home Loan Bank Board
Chris Jude
Dir., OSDBU
1700 G St., N.W., 4th Floor 3G
Washington, DC 20552
(202) 377-6245

Federal Trade Commission
Robert S. Walton III
Dir., OSDBU
Sixth St. & Pennsylvania Ave., N.W., Ste. 700
Washington, DC 20580
(202) 523-5552

General Services Administration
John F. Wynn, Jr.
Dir., OSDBU
Rm. 6013
Washington, DC 20405
(202) 566-1021

Housing and Urban Development
Bernice Williams
Dir., OSDBU
Rm. 10226
Washington, DC 20410
(202) 755-1428

Interior Department
Charlotte B. Spann
Dir., OSDBU
Rm. 2527

Washington, DC 20240
(202) 343-8493

Interstate Commerce Commission
Dan King
Small-Business Assistance Office
12th St. & Constitution Ave., N.W.
Washington, DC 20423
(202) 275-7597

Justice Department
Enos E. Roberts
Dir., OSDBU
Rm. 1022 Todd
Washington, DC 20530
(202) 724-6271

Labor Department
Walter C. Terry
Dir., OSDBU
Rm. S-1004
Washington, DC 20210
(202) 523-9148

National Aeronautics and Space Administration
Eugene D. Rosen
Dir., OSDBU
NASA Headquarters, Code K
Washington, DC 20546
(202) 453-2088

National Credit Union Administration
Benny Henson
Dir., OSDBU
1776 G St., N.W., Rm. 7261
Washington, DC 20456
(202) 357-1025

National Science Foundation
Donald Senich
Dir., OSDBU
1800 G St., N.W., Rm. 511A
Washington, DC 20550
(202) 357-9666

Navy
Office of the Secretary
H. Robert Saldivar
Dir., OSDBU
Rm. 120, Crystal Plaza Five
Washington, DC 20360-5000
(202) 692-7122

Nuclear Regulatory Commission
William B. Kerr

Dir., OSDBU
Maryland National Bank Bldg.
Washington, DC 20555
(202) 492-4665

Personnel Management Office
Tom Simon
Dir., OSDBU
Office of Management
1900 E St., N.W., Rm. 5542
Washington, DC 20415
(202) 632-6161 (Mr. Wisoff)

Postal Service
Peter Evanko
Dir., OSDBU
475 L'Enfant Plaza West, S.W., Rm. 2012
Washington, DC 20260
(202) 245-5663

State Department
Robert Cooper
Dir., OSDBU
M/SDBU, Rm. 513 SA-6
Washington, DC 20520
(202) 235-9579

Tennessee Valley Authority
Franklin E. Alfred
Dir., OSDBU
940 Chestnut St. Tower
Chattanooga, TN 37403
(615) 751-6264
FTS-858-6272

Transportation Department
Amparo B. Bouchey
Dir., OSDBU
Rm. 9414
Washington, DC 20590
(202) 366-1930

Treasury Department
Debra Sonderman
Small-Business Program Mgr.
15th & Pennsylvania Ave., N.W., Rm. 1450
Washington, DC 20220
(202) 566-9616

U.S. Information Agency
Susan Schnell
Dir., OSDBU
400 Seventh St., S.W.
Nassif Bldg. Rm. PL 1200
Washington, DC 20547
(202) 366-0145

Veterans Administration
Susan Livingstone
Dir., OSDBU

810 Vermont Ave., N.W.
Washington, DC 20420
(202) 389-2192

PARTICIPATING SMALL BUSINESS INNOVATION RESEARCH AGENCIES (SBIRS)

Department of Agriculture
Dr. Joseph E. Varner
Office of Grants and Program Systems
West Auditors Bldg., Rm. 112
15th St. & Independence Ave., S.W.
Washington, DC 20251
(202) 475-5022

Department of Commerce
James P. Maruca
Dir., OSDBU
14th St. & Constitution Ave., N.W., Rm.
  6411
Washington, DC 20230
(202) 377-1472

Department of Defense
Horace Crouch
Dir., Small Business and Economic Utiliza-
  tion
Office of Secretary of Defense
Rm. 2A340, The Pentagon
Washington, DC 20301-3061
(202) 697-9383

Department of Education
John Christensen
SBIR Program Coordinator
Office of Educational Research and Improve-
  ment-1612
Washington, DC 20208
(202) 357-6065

Department of Energy
Gerry Washington
SBIR Program Spokesperson
ER-16
Washington, DC 20545
(301) 353-5867

Department of the Interior
Dr. Thomas Henrie

Chief Scientist
Bureau of Mines
2401 E St., N.W.
Washington, DC 20241
(202) 634-1305

Department of Transportation
George Kovatch
SBIR Program Mgr.
Transportation Systems Center
Kendall Sq.
Cambridge, MA 02142
(617) 494-2051

Environmental Protection Agency
Walter H. Preston
Office of Research and Development
401 M St., S.W.
Washington, DC 20460
(202) 382-5744

National Aeronautics and Space Administration
Carl Schwenk
SBIR Office-Code RB
600 Independence Ave., S.W.
Washington, DC 20546
(202) 453-2848

National Science Foundation
Roland Tibbetts
SBIR Program Mgr.
1800 G St., N.W.
Washington, DC 20550
(202) 357-7527

Nuclear Regulatory Commission
Ray Gustave
Office of Nuclear Regulatory Research
Washington, DC 20460
(301) 443-7770

U.S. GOVERNMENT TOLL-FREE NUMBERS

Agency	Number
Agriculture Fraud Hotline	(800) 424-9121
Agriculture Information Hotline	(800) 433-0703

Agency	Number
Commerce Department Fraud Hotline	(800) 424-5197
Consumer Product Safety Commission	(800) 638-2772
Defense Fraud Hotline	(800) 424-9098
Energy Inquiry and Referral (Energy Department)	(800) 523-2929
EPA Asbestos Hotline	(800) 334-8571
EPA Hazardous Waste Hotline	(800) 424-9346
EPA Industry Assistance Hotline	(800) 424-9065
EPA Radon Hotline	(800) 334-8571
EPA Small Business Hotline	(800) 368-5888
Export-Import Bank	(800) 424-5201
Fair Housing and Equal Opportunity (HUD)	(800) 424-8590
Federal Crime Insurance	(800) 638-8780
Federal Deposit Insurance Corporation	(800) 424-5488
Federal Election Commission	(800) 424-9530
Federal Home Loan Bank Board	(800) 424-5405
Flood Insurance	(800) 638-6620
General Accounting Office Fraud Hotline	(800) 424-5454
Health Info Clearinghouse (HHS)	(800) 336-4797
Highway Traffic Safety Administration	(800) 424-9393
Housing Discrimination Hotline (HUD)	(800) 424-8590
Interior Department Fraud Hotline	(800) 424-5081
Internal Revenue Service	(800) 424-1040
Labor Fraud Hotline	(800) 424-5409
National Consumer Co-op Bank	(800) 424-2481
National Technical Information Service	(800) 336-4700
Overseas Private Investment Corporation	(800) 424-6742
Small Business Answer Desk	(800) 368-5855
SBA-PASS users and large corporations	(800) 231-PASS
Talking Books Program (Library of Congress)	(800) 424-9100
Veterans Administration Fraud Hotline	(800) 368-5899
Women's Economic Development Corps	(800) 222-2933

NATIONAL TRADE ASSOCIATIONS

Training or business-education services may be provided by trade groups or associations. There are several hundred trade associations in addition to those listed below that may provide useful business information. Trade association directories may be found in local libraries. Items below are listed alphabetically by trade.

American Association for Hispanic
  CPAs
308 E. Capitol St., N.E.
Washington, DC 20002
(202) 546-3424

American Institute of CPAs
1211 Avenue of the Americas
New York, NY 10036-8775
(212) 575-6200

National Association of Accountants
10 Paragon Dr.
P.O. Box 433
Montvale, NJ 01645
(201) 573-9000

National Society of Public Accountants
1010 N. Fairfax St.
Alexandria, VA 22314
(703) 549-6400

American Advertising Federation
1400 K St., N.W., Ste. 1000
Washington, DC 20005
(202) 659-1800

Business Advertising Council
3450 Michigan Ave.
Cincinnati, OH 45208
(513) 321-7990

Specialty Advertising Association International
1404 Walnut Hill La.
Irving, TX 75062
(214) 258-0404

National Association of Aircraft and Communication Suppliers
2828 Pennsylvania Ave., N.W., Ste. 203
Washington, DC 20007
(202) 965-7000

Amusement and Music Operations Association
2000 Spring Rd., Ste. 200
Oak Brook, IL 60521
(312) 654-2662

American Institute of Architects
1735 New York Ave., N.W.
Washington, DC 20006
(202) 626-7300

Architectural Precast Association
825 E. 64th St.
Indianapolis, IN 46220
(317) 253-0486

American Society of Artists
P.O. Box 1326
Palatine, IL 60078
(312) 751-2500

National Automobile Dealers Association
8400 Westpark Dr.
McLean, VA 22102
(703) 821-7000

Automotive Services Councils, Inc.
188 Industrial Dr., Ste. 112
Elmhurst, IL 60126
(312) 530-2330

Automotive Warehouse Distributors Association
9140 Ward Pkwy.

Kansas City, MO 64114
(816) 444-3500

Independent Bakers Association
1701 K St., N.W.
Washington, DC 20006
(202) 223-2325

American Bankers Association
1120 Connecticut Ave., N.W.
Washington, DC 20036
(202) 467-4000

Independent Association of American Bankers
One Thomas Circle, Ste. 950
Washington, DC 20005
(202) 659-8111

National Association of Bank Women, Inc.
500 N. Michigan Ave., Ste. 1020N
Washington, DC 20036
(202) 452-8100

National Bankers Association
122 C St., N.W., Ste. 240
Washington, DC 20001
(202) 783-3200

Outboard Boating Club of America
401 N. Michigan Ave.
Chicago, IL 60611
(312) 836-4760

Christian Booksellers Association
P.O. Box 200
Colorado Springs, CO 80901
(303) 576-7880

National Association of Brick Distributors
1000 Duke St.
Alexandria, VA 22314
(703) 549-2555

National Broiler Council
1155 15th St., N.W.
Washington, DC 20005
(202) 296-2622

Associated Builders and Contractors
729 15th St., N.W.
Washington, DC 20005
(202) 637-8800

International Association of Building Service Contractors
8315 Lee Hwy., Ste. 30

Fairfax, VA 22031
(703) 698-8810

Institute of Certified Business Counselors
3301 Vincent Rd.
Pleasant Hill, CA 94523
(415) 945-8440

United Business Owners of America
1275 K St., N.W., Ste. 800
Washington, DC 20005
(202) 484-5623

National Cable Television Association
1724 Massachusetts Ave., N.W.
Washington, DC 20036
(202) 775-3550

American Camping Association
Bradford Woods
Martinsville, IN 46151
(317) 342-8456

National Campground Owners Association
804 D St., N.E.
Washington, DC 20002
(202) 543-6260

National Candy Wholesalers Association
1120 Vermont Ave., N.W., Ste. 1120
Washington, DC 20005
(202) 463-2124

National Association of Catalog Showroom
  Merchandisers
230 Park Ave.
New York, NY 10017
(212) 687-8930

U.S. Chamber of Commerce
Center for Small Business
1615 H St., N.W.
Washington, DC 20006
(202) 659-6000

National Association of Chemical Distributors
1110 Vermont Ave., N.W.
Washington, DC 20005
(202) 296-9200

National Association for Child Care Management
1800 M St., N.W., Ste. 1030N
Washington, DC 20036
(202) 452-8100

International Communication Industries Association
3150 Spring St.
Fairfax, VA 22030
(703) 273-7200

Computer and Business Equipment Manufacturers Association
311 First St., N.W., Ste. 500
Washington, DC 20001
(202) 737-8888

National Computer Graphics Association
8401 Arlington Blvd., Ste. 601
Fairfax, VA 22031
(703) 698-9600

National Concrete Masonry Association
P.O. Box 781
Herndon, VA 22070
(703) 435-4900

National Precast Concrete Association
825 E. 64th St.
Indianapolis, IN 46220
(317) 253-0486

Associated General Contractors of America
1957 E St., N.W.
Washington, DC 20006
(202) 393-2040

Association of Independent Corrugated Con-
  verters
801 N. Fairfax St.
Alexandria, VA 22314
(703) 836-2422

National Association for the Cottage Industry
P.O. Box 14460
Chicago, IL 60614
(312) 472-8116

American Dairy Association
6300 N. River Rd.
Rosemont, IL 60018
(312) 696-1880

National Industry Dairy Foods Association
321 D St., S.E.
Washington, DC 20002
(202) 543-3838

United Dairy Industry Association
6300 N. River Rd.

Rosemont, IL 60018
(312) 696-1860

Association of Data Processing Service Organizations
1300 N. 17th St.
Arlington, VA 22209
(703) 522-5055

American Dental Trade Association
4222 King St.
Alexandria, VA 22302
(703) 379-7755

National Association of Development Companies
1612 K St., N.W., Ste. 706
Washington, DC 20006
(202) 785-8484

Direct Selling Association
1776 K St., N.W.
Washington, DC 20006
(202) 293-5760

Door and Hardware Institute
7711 Old Springhouse Rd.
McLean, VA 22102-3474
(703) 556-3990

National Association of Retail Druggists
205 Dangerfield Rd.
Alexandria, VA 22314
(703) 683-8200

American Consulting Engineers Council
1015 15th St., N.W., Ste. 802
Washington, DC 20005
(202) 347-7474

National Electrical Contractors Association, Inc.
7315 Wisconsin Ave.
Bethesda, MD 20814
(301) 657-3110

Electronic Representatives Association
P.O. Box 569
Jefferson City, MO 65102
(314) 355-9300

Equipment Distributors Association
1612 K St., N.W., Ste. 1400
Washington, DC 20006
(202) 785-5585

National Family Business Council
P.O. Box 67
Westville, NJ 08093
(609) 456-0933

National Fastener Distributors Association
3094 Cressing Pl.
Columbus, OH 43227
(614) 237-0252

National Institute of Fisheries
2000 M St., N.W., Ste. 580
Washington, DC 20036
(202) 296-5090

National Floor Covering Association
13-186 Merchandise Mart
Chicago, IL 60654
(312) 527-4141

Retail Floor Covering Institute
1725 DeSales St., N.W., Ste. 401
Washington, DC 20036
(202) 833-3875

Society of American Florists
1601 Duke St.
Alexandria, VA 22314
(703) 836-8700

Society of American Florists and Ornamental Horticulturists
901 N. Washington St.
Alexandria, VA 22314
(703) 836-8700

Florists Transworld Delivery Association
29200 Northwestern Hwy.
Southfield, MI 48037
(313) 355-9300

Urethane Foam Contractors Association
4302 Airport Blvd.
Austin, TX 78722-1099
(512) 454-0041

International Foodservice Distributors Association
201 Park Washington Court
Falls Church, VA 22046
(703) 532-9400

American Forestry Association
1319 18th St., N.W.
Washington, DC 20036
(202) 467-5810

International Franchise Association
1350 New York Ave., N.W., Ste. 900
Washington, DC 20005
(202) 628-8000

United Fresh Fruit and Vegetable Association
N. Washington at Madison
Alexandria, VA 22314
(703) 836-3410

National Association of Frozen Food
604 W. Derry Rd.
P.O. Box 398
Hershey, PA 17033
(717) 534-1601

American Furniture Manufacturers Association
P.O. Box HP7
High Point, NC 27261
(919) 884-5000

Furniture Rental Association of America
1828 L St., N.W., Ste. 660
Washington, DC 20036
(202) 785-2050

Garden Centers of America
1250 Eye St., N.W., Ste. 500
Washington, DC 20005
(202) 779-2900

Associated Gas Distributors
1100 Connecticut Ave., N.W.
Washington, DC 20036
(202) 466-5329

Chicago Gift Show Inc.
Two Park Ave., Ste. 1100
New York, NY 10016
(212) 986-8000

National Grocers Association
1825 Samuel Morse Dr.
Reston, VA 22090
(703) 955-8400

National Retail Hardware Association
770 N. High School Rd.
Indianapolis, IN 46224
(317) 248-1261

North American Heating and Air Conditioning Wholesalers Association

P.O. Box 16790
1389 Dublin Rd.
Columbus, OH 43215
(614) 488-1835

International Helicopter Association
1616 Duke St.
Alexandria, VA 22314
(703) 683-4646

National Alliance of Homebased Businesses
P.O. Box 95
Norwood, NJ 07648
(201) 423-1026

National Association of Home Builders of the United States
15th & M Sts., N.W.
Washington, DC 20005
(202) 822-0200

National Association of Home Care
519 C St., N.E.
Washington, DC 20002
(202) 547-7424

American Federation of Home Health Agencies, Inc.
1320 Fenwick La., Ste. 500
Silver Spring, MD 20910
(301) 588-1454

Independent Business Association of Wisconsin
415 E. Washington Ave.
Madison, WI 53703
(608) 251-5546

National Federation of Independent Business
150 W. 20th Ave.
San Mateo, CA 94403
(415) 341-7441

National Council for Industrial Innovation
1725 K St., N.W., Ste. 308
Washington, DC 20006
(202) 775-1135

United Infants' and Children's Wear Association
520 Eighth Ave.
New York, NY 10018
(212) 244-2953

Independent Insurance Agents of America
600 Pennsylvania Ave., S.E., Ste. 200
Washington, DC 20003
(202) 544-5833

American Association of Minority Small
  Business Investment Companies
915 15th St., N.W., Ste. 700
Washington, DC 20005
(202) 347-8600

Association of Investment Companies
44 Beaver St.
New York, NY 10004
(212) 608-5656

National Association of Small Business Investment Companies
1156 15th St., N.W., Ste. 1101
Washington, DC 20005
(202) 833-8230

Jewelers of America
1271 Avenue of the Americas
New York, NY 10020
(212) 489-0023

Society of Professional Journalists
840 N. Lake Shore Dr., Ste. 801 W
Chicago, IL 60611
(312) 649-0060

Professional Lawn Care Association of
  America
1225 Johnson Ferry Rd., N.E., Ste. B220
Marietta, GA 30067
(404) 977-5222

Small Business Legislative Council
15th St., N.W.
Washington, DC 20005
(202) 639-8500

Livestock Marketing Association
301 E. Armour Blvd., Ste. 500
Kansas City, MO 64111
(816) 531-2235

Log Homes Council
15th & M Sts., N.W.
Washington, DC 20005
(202) 822-0576

National Machinery Dealers Association
1110 Spring St.

Silver Spring, MD 20910
(301) 585-9494

Association of Management Consultants
500 N. Michigan Ave., Ste. 1400
Chicago, IL 60611
(312) 661-1700

Manufactured Housing Institute
1745 Jefferson Davis Hwy., Ste. 511
Arlington, VA 22202
(703) 979-6620

Manufacturers Agents National Association
P.O. Box 3467
Laglina Hills, CA 92654
(714) 859-4040

Latin American Manufacturers Association
419 New Jersey Ave., S.E.
Washington, DC 20003
(202) 546-3803

National Association of Manufacturers
1776 F St., N.W.
Washington, DC 20006
(202) 626-3700

Smaller Manufacturers Council
339 Boulevard of the Allies
Pittsburgh, PA 15222
(412) 391-1622

Marketing Device Association
708 Church St.
Evanston, IL 60201
(312) 328-3540

Marketing Livestock Association
301 E. Armour Blvd., Ste. 500
Kansas City, MO 64111
(816) 531-2235

Menswear Retailers of America
2011 Eye St., N.W., Ste. 600
Washington, DC 20008
(202) 347-1932

National Milk Producers Federation
1850 Wilson Blvd.
Arlington, VA 22201
(703) 243-6111

National Association of Minority Contractors
806 15th St., Ste. 340

Washington, DC 20005
(202) 347-8259

American Movers Conference
P.O. Box 2303
Arlington, VA 22202
(703) 521-1111

National Moving and Storage Association
124 S. Royal St.
Alexandria, VA 22314
(703) 549-9263

Newsletter Association of America, Inc.
1341 G St., N.W. Ste. 603
Washington, DC 20005
(202) 347-5220

American Association of Nursery Men
1250 Eye St., N.W., Ste. 500
Washington, DC 20005
(202) 789-2900

National Association of Ocean Industries
1050 17th St., N.W., Ste. 700
Washington, DC 20036
(202) 785-5116

National Association of Office Machine
    Dealers
810 Lively Blvd., Box 707
Wood Dale, IL 60191
(312) 860-9400

National Office Products Association
301 N. Fairfax St.
Alexandria, VA 22314
(703) 549-9040

National Association of Manufacturing Op-
    ticians
13140 Coit Rd., LB 144
Dallas, TX 75240
(214) 231-6266

Opticians Association of America
10341 Democracy La.
Fairfax, VA 22030
(703) 691-8355

Optical Society of America
1816 Jefferson Pl., N.W.
Washington, D.C. 20036
(202) 223-8130

Packaging Institute, U.S.A.
20 E. 46th St.

New York, NY 10017
(212) 687-8874

National Paint Distributors, Inc.
Two Talcott Rd.
Park Ridge, IL 60068
(312) 696-1590

Painting and Decorating Contractors
7223 Lee Hwy.
Falls Church, VA 22046
(703) 534-1201

American Paper Institute, Inc.
260 Madison Ave.
New York, NY 10016
(212) 340-0600

National Parking Association
1112 16th St., N.W., Ste. 2000
Washington, DC 20036
(202) 296-4336

Petroleum Marketers Association of
    America
1120 Vermont Ave., N.W., Ste. 1130
Washington, DC 20005
(202) 331-1198

Association of Physical Fitness Centers
600 Jefferson St., Ste. 202
Rockville, MD 20852
(301) 424-7744

National Association of Plumbing-Heating
    Cooling Contractors
180 S. Washington St.
Falls Church, VA 22046
(703) 237-8100

Power and Communications Contractors
    Association
6301 Stevenson Ave., Ste. One
Alexandria, VA 22304
(703) 823-1555

Power Tool Institute, Inc.
5105 Tollview Dr.
Rolling Meadows, IL 60008
(312) 577-8350

Printing Industries of America
1730 N. Lynn St.
Arlington, VA 22209
(703) 841-8100

Public Relations Society of America
845 Third Ave.
New York, NY 10022
(212) 826-1750

American Association of Publishers
One Park Ave.
New York, NY 10016
(212) 689-8920

American Industrial Real Estate Association
350 S. Figueroa St., Ste. 275
Los Angeles, CA 90071
(213) 687-8777

National Association of Realtors
777 14th St., N.W.
Washington, DC 20005
(202) 383-1074

International Reciprocal Trade Association
4012 Moss Pl.
Alexandria, VA 22304
(703) 823-8707

National Recreation and Park Association
3101 Park Center Dr.
Alexandria, VA 22302
(703) 820-4940

Recreation Vehicle Dealers Association of
   North America
3251 Old Lee Hwy., Ste. 500
Fairfax, VA 22030
(703) 591-7130

Recreation Vehicle Industry Association
P.O. Box 2999
1896 Preston White Dr.
Reston, VA 22021
(703) 620-6003

National Association of the Remodeling Industry
1901 N. Moore St., Ste. 808
Arlington, VA 22209
(703) 276-7600

American Rental Association
1900 19th St.
Moline, IL 61265
(309) 764-2475

Association of Research, Engineering and
   Technical Service Companies
P.O. Box 9411

McLean, VA 22102
(703) 468-9346

National Restaurant Association
311 First St., N.W.
Washington, DC 20001
(202) 638-6100

American Retail Federation
1616 H St., N.W.
Washington, DC 20006
(202) 783-7971

National Retail Merchants Association
100 W. 31st St.
New York, NY 10001
(212) 244-8780

Pacific Seafood Processors Association
1620 S. Jackson St.
Seattle, WA 98144
(206) 328-1205

National Association of Securities Dealers
1735 K St., N.W., 10th Floor
Washington, DC 20006
(202) 728-8000

National Association for the Self-Employed
2121 Precinct Line Rd., Ste. 204
Hurst, TX 76054
(817) 656-6395

Independent Sewing Machine Dealers
P.O. Box 338
Hillard, OH 43026
(614) 870-7211

National Shoe Retailers Association
1414 Avenue of the Americas, 7th Floor
New York, NY 10019
(212) 752-2555

National Small Business Association
1155 15th St., N.W., Ste. 710
Washington, DC 20005
(202) 293-8830
(800) THE-NSBA

Small Business Council of America, Inc.
P.O. Box 1558
Columbus, GA 31902
(404) 324-0251

Association of Small Business Development
   Centers
1050 17th St., N.W., Ste. 810

Washington, DC 20036
(202) 887-5599

National Small Business Government Contractors Association
405 Northfield Ave., Ste. LL3
West Orange, NJ 07052
(201) 736-1055

Mid Continent Small Business United
1608 Holmes St.
Kansas City, MO 64108
(816) 252-6256

United Federation of Small Business
4307 Euclid Ave.
San Diego, CA 92115
(619) 287-9671

Smaller Business Association of New
England
69 Hickory Dr.
Waltham, MA 02154
(617) 890-9070

Council of Smaller Enterprises
690 Huntington Bldg.
Cleveland, OH 44115
(216) 621-3300

Association of Sporting Goods Manufacturers
200 Castlewood Dr.
North Palm Beach, FL 33408
(305) 842-4100

Stationery and Office Equipment Board of
Trade
341 Madison Ave.
New York, NY 10017
(212) 687-8790

Self-Service Storage Association
P.O. Box 110
Eureka Springs, AR 72632
(501) 253-7701

Alliance of Independent Store Owners and
Professionals
4150 Multifoods Tower
Minneapolis, MN 55402
(612) 333-5411

American Subcontractors Association
1004 Duke St.

Alexandria, VA 22314
(703) 684-3450

U.S. Telephone Association
1801 K St., N.W., Ste. 1201
Washington, DC 20006
(202) 872-1200

National Association of Temporary Services
119 S. Asaphs St.
Alexandria VA 22314
(703) 549-6287

National Association of Textile and Apparel
Wholesalers
734 E. Boston Post Rd.
Mamaroneck, NY 10543
(914) 381-5660

American Textile Machinery Association
7297 N. Lee Hwy.
Falls Church, VA 22042
(703) 533-9251

American Textile Manufacturers Institute,
Inc.
1101 Connecticut Ave., N.W., Ste. 300
Washington, DC 20036
(202) 862-0500

American Institute of Timber Construction
333 W. Hampden Ave.
Englewood, CO 80110
(303) 761-3212

National Association of Tire Dealers and
Retreaders
1250 Eye St., N.W., Ste. 400
Washington, DC 20005
(202) 789-2300

Retail Tobacco Dealers of America Inc.
55 Maple Ave.
Rockville Center, NY 11570
(516) 766-4100

National Tooling and Machining Association
9300 Livingston Rd.
Fort Washington, MD 20744
(301) 248-6200

National Tour Association
120 Kentucky Ave., Ste. A-1
Tudor Sq.

Lexington, KY 40502
(606) 253-1036

Toy Manufacturers of America, Inc.
200 Fifth Ave., Ste. 740
New York, NY 10010
(212) 675-1141

Association of Retail Travel Agents
25 S. Riverside
Croton-on-Hudson, NY 10520
(914) 271-9000

Travel Industry Association of America
1899 L St., N.W., Ste. 600
Washington, DC 20036
(202) 293-1433

American Trucking Association, Inc.
2200 Mill Rd.
Alexandria, VA 22314
(703) 838-1798

National Association of Truck Stop Owners
1199 N. Fairfax St., Ste. 801
Alexandria, VA 22314
(703) 549-2100

National Turkey Federation
11319 Sunset Hill Rd.
Reston, VA 22090
(703) 435-7206

Web Sling Association
P.O. Box Drawer F
Jamesburg, NJ 08831
(201) 521-4441

National Wine Distributors Association
101 E. Ontario St., Ste. 580
Chicago, IL 60611
(312) 951-8878

National Association of Woman Business
  Owners
918 16th St., N.W., Ste. 406
Washington, DC 20006
(202) 296-2030

American Wood Council
1619 Massachusetts Ave., N.W., Ste. 500
Washington, DC 20036
(202) 265-7766

International Woodworkers of America
1622 N. Lombard St.
Portland, OR 97212
(503) 285-5281

National Association of Wool
  Growers
8 E. Broadway, Ste. 415
Salt Lake City, UT 84111
(801) 363-4484

STATE AND REGIONAL SMALL BUSINESS ORGANIZATIONS

Many of the previously listed organizations have state and local affiliates. This list
does not imply any endorsement of the organizations included.

Alabama

Alabama Retail Association
P.O. Box 1909
Montgomery, AL 36103
(205) 263-5757

The Business Council of Alabama
P.O. Box 76
Montgomery, AL 36195
(205) 834-6000

Chamber of Commerce Executives Association of Alabama
P.O. Box 972
Jasper, AL 35501
(205) 384-4571

National Federation of Independent Business
P.O. Box 248
Montgomery, AL 36192
(205) 264-2261

Alaska

Alaska State Chamber of Commerce
310 Second St.
Juneau, AK 99801
(907) 586-2323

National Federation of Independent Business
P.O. Box 210194

Auke Bay, AK 99821
(907) 586-4100

Arizona

National Federation of Independent Business
112 N. Central Ave., Ste. 717
Phoenix, AZ 85004
(602) 254-1541

Phoenix Metropolitan Chamber of Commerce
34 W. Monroe, Ste. 900
Phoenix, AZ 85003
(602) 254-5521

Small Business Council of Arizona
Arizona Chamber of Commerce
1366 East Thomas Rd., Ste. 202
Phoenix, AZ 85014
(602) 248-9172

Tempe Chamber of Commerce
504 E. Southern Ave.
Tempe, AZ 85282
(602) 967-7891

Tucson Chamber of Commerce
P.O. Box 991
Tucson, AZ 85702
(602) 792-1212

Arkansas

Arkansas State Chamber of Commerce
P.O. Box 3645
Little Rock, AR 72203-3645
(501) 374-9225

National Federation of Independent Business
P.O. Box 1513
Little Rock, AR 72203
(501) 372-7593

California

California Alliance of Small Business
4152 Crondall Way
Sacramento, CA 95125
(916) 485-7670

California Business Alliance
4982 Stevens Creek Blvd., Ste. C
San Jose, CA 95129
(408) 248-6222

The California Association of Independent Business
600 N. Mountain Ave., Ste. A-202
Upland, CA 91786
(714) 981-5912

California Chamber of Commerce
P.O. Box 1736
Sacramento, CA 95808
(916) 444-6670

California Manufacturers Association
P.O. Box 1138
Sacramento, CA 95805
(916) 441-5420

Golden State Business League
333 Hegenberger Rd., #315
Wells Fargo Bank Bldg.
Oakland, CA 94621
(415) 635-5900

National Association of Women Business Owners
505 S. Flower St., Level C
Los Angeles, CA 90071
(213) 489-3472

National Federation of Independent Business
1121 L St., Ste. 1000
Sacramento, CA 95814
(916) 448-9904
(619) 273-4060

Southern California Women Business Owners
P.O. Box 20099X-186
San Diego, CA 92120

Women in Business
815 Moraga Dr.
Los Angeles, CA 90049
(213) 461-2936

Colorado

Colorado Association of Commerce and Industry
1860 Lincoln, Ste. 550
Denver, CO 80295-0501
(303) 831-7411

National Federation of Independent Business
1391 N. Speer Blvd., Ste. 470

Denver, CO 80204
(303) 534-1631

Connecticut

Connecticut Business and Industry Association
370 Asylum St.
Hartford, CT 06103
(203) 547-1661

National Federation of Independent Business
60 Washington St., Ste. 207
Hartford, CT 06106
(203) 522-9623

Delaware

Delaware State Chamber of Commerce
One Commerce Center, Ste. 200
Wilmington, DE 29801
(302) 655-7221

District of Columbia

District of Columbia Chamber of Commerce
2100 M St., N.W., Ste. 607
Washington, DC 20037
(202) 296-0335

Florida

Associated Industries of Florida, Inc.
P.O. Box 784
Tallahassee, FL 32302-0784
(904) 222-8831

Central Florida Small Business Association
P.O. Box 30533
Orlando, FL 32862-0533
(305) 859-5013

Florida Federation of Independent Business
P.O. Box 8871
Jacksonville, FL 32239
(904) 725-3980

Florida Retail Federation
100 E. Jefferson St.
Tallahassee, FL 32301
or
P.O. Box 10024
Tallahassee, FL 32302
(904) 222-4082

National Federation of Independent Business
#1 129 W. College
Tallahassee, FL 32302
(904) 681-0416

Georgia

Business Council of Georgia
1280 S. Omni International
Atlanta, GA 30335
(404) 223-2264

National Federation of Independent Business
1447 Peachtree St., N.E., #804
Atlanta, GA 30309
(404) 876-8516

Small Business Association of the Southeast
c/o Hyatt and Rhoads
245 Peachtree Center Ave., N.E.
2400 Marquis One Tower
Atlanta, GA 30303
(404) 659-6600

Hawaii

Hawaii Business League
1177 Kapiolani Blvd., Ste. 201
Honolulu, HI 96814
(808) 533-6819

Hawaii Chamber of Commerce
Dillingham Bldg.
735 Bishop St.
Honolulu, HI 96813
(808) 531-4111

National Federation of Independent Business
1588 Piikea
Honolulu, HI 96818
(808) 422-2163 (recording)

The Small Business Council represents all of the above groups; it can be contacted through the Small Business Center, Hawaii Chamber of Commerce.

Small Business Hawaii
811A Cooke St.
Honolulu, HI 96813
(808) 533-2183

Small Business Information Service, Department of Planning and Economic Development
P.O. Box 2359
Honolulu, HI 96804
(808) 548-7645/7887

Idaho

Idaho Association of Commerce and Industry
P.O. Box 389
Boise, ID 83701
(208) 343-1849

National Federation of Independent Business
277 N. Sixth St., Ste. 200
Boise, ID 83701
(208) 343-3289

Illinois

Chicago Association of Commerce and Industry
200 N. LaSalle St.
Chicago, IL 60601
(312) 580-6971

Illinois Manufacturers Association
175 W. Jackson Blvd., Ste. 1321
Chicago, IL 60604
(312) 922-6575

The Illinois Retail Merchants Association
36 S. Wabash, Rm. 1226
Chicago, IL 60603
(312) 726-4600

Illinois Small Businessmen's Association
407 S. Dearborn
Chicago, IL 60605
(312) 427-0207

Illinois Society of Association Executives
P.O. Box 281
Springfield, IL 62701
(217) 522-0993

Illinois State Chamber of Commerce
215 E. Adams St.
Springfield, IL 62701
(217) 522-5512

Independent Business Association of Illinois
8565 W. Dempster St., Ste. 200

Niles, IL 60648
(312) 692-7306

National Association of Women Business Owners, Illinois Chapter
c/o Peggy Leonard and Associates
28 S. Sixth St.
Geneva, IL 60134
(312) 232-1421

National Federation of Independent Business
516 E. Monroe St., Ste. 601
Springfield, IL 62701
(217) 523-5471

Indiana

Indiana Society of Association Executives
310 N. Alabama, Ste. A
Indianapolis, IN 46204
(317) 638-4402

Indiana State Chamber of Commerce
One N. Capitol, Ste. 200
Indianapolis, IN 46204
(317) 634-6407

National Federation of Independent Business
7 N. Meridian, Ste. 700
Indianapolis, IN 46204
(317) 638-4447

Women's Bureau
203 W. Wayne St.
Fort Wayne, IN 46802
(219) 424-7977

Iowa

Call One
Iowa Development Commission
600 E. Court Ave.
Des Moines, IA 50309
(515) 281-8310
(800) 532-1216

Iowa Association of Business and Industry
Employers Mutual Bldg., Ste. 706
717 Mulberry
Des Moines, IA 50309
(515) 244-6149

Iowa Small Business Employers
P.O. Box 437

Mason City, IA 50401
(515) 424-3187

National Federation of Independent Business
319 E. Fifth St., Ste. 1
West Des Moines, IA 50309
(515) 243-4723

Kansas

Kansas Association of Certified Development Companies
P.O. Box 8776
Pratt, KS 67124
(316) 672-9421

Kansas Chamber of Commerce and Industry
500 Bank IV Tower
Topeka, KS 66603
(913) 357-6321

Kansas Department of Economic Development
400 W. Eighth, 5th Floor
Topeka, KS 66603-3957
(913) 296-3480

Kansas Small-Business Development Center
Clinton Hall, Rm. 021
P.O. Box 148
Wichita State University
Wichita, KS 67208
(316) 689-3193

National Federation of Independent Business
10039 Mastin Dr.
Shawnee Mission, KS 66212
(913) 888-2235

Kentucky

Associated Industries of Kentucky
200 W. Chestnut St.
Louisville, KY 40202
(502) 587-0769

Entrepreneur Society
2001 Neburg Rd.
Louisville, KY 40605
(502) 637-5666

Kentucky Chamber of Commerce
P.O. Box 817
Frankfort, KY 40602
(502) 695-4700

Kentucky Retail Federation
P.O. Box 237
Georgetown, KY 40324
(502) 863-1628

National Federation of Independent Business
417 W. Second St.
Frankfort, KY 40601
(502) 223-5819

Louisiana

Louisiana Association of Business and Industry
P.O. Box 80258
Baton Rouge, LA 70898-0258
(504) 928-5388

National Federation of Independent Business
13454 Jefferson Hwy.
Baton Rouge, LA 70817
(504) 291-4996
(504) 383-9165

Maine

Maine Chamber of Commerce and Industry
126 Sewall St.
Augusta, ME 04330
(207) 623-4568

National Federation of Independent Business
146 State St.
Augusta, ME 04330
(207) 623-4000

Maryland

Maryland Chamber of Commerce
60 West St.
Annapolis, MD 21401
(301) 261-2858

National Federation of Independent Business
7401 Wisconsin Ave., Ste. 514
Bethesda, MD 20014
(301) 652-0721 (recording)

Massachusetts

Massachusetts Businessmen's Association
135 Wood Rd.

Braintree, MA 02184
(617) 848-4950

National Federation of Independent Business
101 Tremont St., Ste. 609
Boston, MA 02108
(617) 482-1327

Smaller Business Association of New England
69 Hickory Dr.
Waltham, MA 02154
(617) 890-9070

Michigan

Grand Rapids Area Chamber of Commerce
17 Fountain St., N.W.
Grand Rapids, MI 59503
(616) 459-7221

Greater Ann Arbor Council
211 E. Huron St., Ste. 1
Ann Arbor, MI 48104
(313) 665-4433

Michigan Manufacturers Association
124 E. Kalamazoo St.
Lansing, MI 48933
(517) 372-5900

Michigan Retailers Association
221 N. Pine St.
Lansing, MI 48933
(517) 372-5656

Michigan Society of Association Executives
Oakland County Bar Association
1200 N. Telegraph, Ste. 532
Pontiac, MI 48053
(313) 398-3937

Michigan State Chamber of Commerce
Business and Trade Center, Ste. 400
200 N. Washington Sq.
Lansing, MI 48933
(517) 371-2100

National Federation of Independent Business
109 W. Michigan #819
Lansing, MI 48933-2121
(517) 485-3409

Small Business Association of Michigan
Administrative Office

490 W. South St.
P.O. Box 1105
Kalamazoo, MI 49007
(616) 342-2400

Small Business Association of Michigan
Legislative Office
530 W. Ionia St.
Lansing, MI 48933
(517) 484-2277

Minnesota

Greater Minneapolis Chamber of Commerce
15 S. Fifth St.
Minneapolis, MN 55402
(612) 370-9132

Independent Business Association of Minnesota
7800 Dupont Ave., South,
Minneapolis, MN 55420
(612) 881-1331

Minnesota Association of Commerce and Industry
300 Hanover Bldg.
480 Cedar St.
St. Paul, MN 55101
(612) 292-4650

National Association of Women Business Owners—Minnesota
1450 Energy Park Dr.
P.O. Box 60
St. Paul, MN 55108
(612) 644-2511

National Federation of Independent Business
480 Cedar St., Ste. 235
St. Paul, MN 55101
(612) 293-1283

St. Paul Area Chamber of Commerce
600 N. Central Tower
445 Minnesota St.
St. Paul, MN 55101
(612) 222-5561

Mississippi

Department of Economic Development
P.O. Box 849
Jackson, MS 39205
(601) 359-3437

Mississippi Economic Council
P.O. Box 1849
Jackson, MS 39215-1849
(601) 969-0022

Mississippi Manufacturers Association
P.O. Box 22607
Jackson, MS 39225-2607
(601) 948-1222

Mississippi Research and Development
Center
P.O. Box 203
Tupelo, MS 38802
(601) 844-5413

Mississippi Research and Development–Gulf
Coast Manufacturing Assistance Center
P.O. Box 1268
1106 31st Ave.
Gulfport, MS 39502-1268
(601) 865-0011

Mississippi SBDC and USM/Research and
Development Management Assistance
Center
USM/Gulf Park Campus
Long Beach, MS 39560
(601) 865-4579

National Federation of Independent Business
528 N. State St., Ste. A
Jackson, MS 39201
(601) 969-3217

Missouri

Mid-Continent Small Business United
3501 Sterling, Lower Level Ste. H
Independence, MO 64052
(816) 252-6256

Missouri Chamber of Commerce
Missouri Center for Free Enterprise
P.O. Box 149
428 E. Capitol Ave.
Jefferson City, MO 65102
(314) 634-3616

Missouri Merchants and Manufacturers Association
910 Clayton Rd., Ste. 322
Baldwin, MO 63011
(314) 458-2051

National Federation of Independent Business
111 Madison
P.O. Box 1543
Jefferson City, MO 65102
(314) 636-2822

St. Louis Regional Commerce and Growth
Association
Ten Broadway
St. Louis, MO 63102
(314) 231-5555

Montana

Montana Chamber of Commerce
P.O. Box 1730
Helena, MT 59624
(406) 442-2405

National Federation of Independent Business
9 N. Last Chance Gulch
Helena, MT 59601
(406) 443-3797

Nebraska

National Federation of Independent Business
525 S. 13th St.
Lincoln, NE 68508
(402) 474-3570

Nebraska Association of Commerce and Industry
P.O. Box 95128
1320 Lincoln Mall
Lincoln, NE 68509
(402) 474-4422

Retail Merchants Association of Nebraska,
Inc.
P.O. Box 94606
Lincoln, NE 68509
(402) 474-5255

Nevada

Chamber of Commerce
P.O. Box 3499
Reno, NV 89505
(702) 786-3030

Commission on Economic Development
Capital Complex

Carson City, NV 89710
(702) 885-4325

Greater Las Vegas Chamber of Commerce
2301 E. Sahara Ave.
Las Vegas, NV 89104
(702) 457-4664

Latin Chamber of Commerce
P.O. Box 7534
Las Vegas, NV 89125
(702) 329-6006
(702) 385-7367

National Federation of Independent Business
P.O. Box 2184
Carson City, NV 89702
(702) 883-3072

New Hampshire

Business and Industry Association of New
Hampshire
23 School St.
Concord, NH 03301
(603) 224-5388

National Federation of Independent Business
4 Park St.
P.O. Box 218
Concord, NH 03301
(603) 783-4232
(603) 228-3477 (recording)

New England Business Association
P.O. Box 535
Plaistow, NH 03856
(603) 382-4711

New Jersey

National Federation of Independent Business
407 W. State St.
Trenton, NJ 08608
(609) 989-8777

New Jersey Coalition of Small Business Organizations
c/o Concorde Chemical Company
17th & Federal Sts.
Camden, NJ 08105
(609) 966-1526

New Jersey State Chamber of Commerce
5 Commerce St.
Newark, NJ 07102
(201) 622-7690
(201) 623-7070
(201) 624-6888

Women Entrepreneurs of New Jersey
Quality Inn
50 Park Pl.
Newark, NJ 07102
(201) 622-7690

New Mexico

Association of Commerce and Industry of
New Mexico
117 Quincy, N.E.
Albuquerque, NM 87108

National Federation of Independent Business
P.O. Box 2488
Santa Fe, NM 87502
(505) 988-2728
(505) 982-8184

New York

Business Council of New York State
152 Washington Ave.
Albany, NY 12210
(518) 465-7511

National Federation of Independent Business
8 Elk St.
Albany, NY 12207
(518) 434-1262

North Carolina

Department of Community Colleges
Small Business and Business Occupations
20 Education Bldg.,
Raleigh, NC 27603-1712
(919) 733-6385

International Trade Center
North Carolina State University
P.O. Box 7401
Raleigh, NC 27695
(919) 737-3793

North Carolina Citizens for Business Industry
P.O. Box 2508
Raleigh, NC 27602
(919) 828-0758

North Carolina Department of Commerce
Small Business Assistance Division
430 N. Salisbury St.
Raleigh, NC 27611
(919) 733-4962

North Carolina Department of Commerce
Technological Development Authority
430 N. Salisbury St., Rm. 4216
Raleigh, NC 27611
(919) 733-7022

North Dakota

Greater North Dakota Association/State
   Chamber of Commerce
P.O. Box 2467
Fargo, ND 58108
(701) 237-9461

National Federation of Independent Business
400 E. Broadway, Ste. 414
Bismarck, ND 58501
(701) 224-8333

Ohio

Columbus Area Chamber of Commerce
37 N. High St.
Columbus, OH 43215
(614) 221-1321

Council of Smaller Enterprises
690 Huntington Bldg.
Cleveland, OH 44115
(216) 621-3307

Greater Cincinnati Chamber of Commerce
120 W. Fifth St.
Cincinnati, OH 45202
(513) 579-3149

National Federation of Independent Business
50 W. Broad St., Ste. 1705
Columbus, OH 43215
(614) 221-4107

Ohio Chamber of Commerce
35 E. Gay St., 2d Floor
Columbus, OH 43215-3181
(614) 228-4201

Ohio Manufacturers Association
100 E. Broad St.
Columbus, OH 43215
(614) 224-5111

Ohio Small Business Council
35 E. Gay St.
Columbus, OH 43215
(614) 228-4201

Ohio Society of Association Executives
21 E. State St., Ste. 730
Columbus, OH 43215
(614) 221-1900

Small Business Council
The Ohio Manufacturers Association
100 E. Broad St.
Columbus, OH 43215
(614) 224-5111

Small-Business Development Center
1980 Kettering Tower
Dayton, OH 45423
(513) 226-1444

Toledo Area Small Business Association
218 Huron St.
Toledo, OH 43604
(419) 259-7598

Oklahoma

National Federation of Independent Business
515 Central Park Dr., Ste. 409
Oklahoma City, OK 73105
(405) 521-8967

Oklahoma State Chamber of Commerce
4020 N. Lincoln Blvd.
Oklahoma City, OK 73105
(405) 424-4003

Oregon

Associated Oregon Industries, Inc.
P.O. Box 12519
Salem, OR 97309
(503) 588-0050

National Federation of Independent Business
707 13th St., S.E.
Salem, OR 97301
(503) 364-4450

Oregon's Small Business Council
P.O. Box 455
Salem, OR 97308
(503) 585-5846

Small Business Advocates, Inc.
1270 Chemeketa St., N.E.
Salem, OR 97301
(503) 370-7019

Pennsylvania

Pennsylvania Chamber of Commerce
222 N. Third St.
Harrisburg, PA 17101
(717) 255-3252

Smaller Manufacturers Council
339 Boulevard of the Allies
Pittsburgh, PA 15222
(421) 391-1622

Puerto Rico

Puerto Rico Chamber of Commerce
100 Tetuan St.
P.O. Box 3789
San Juan, PR 00904
(809) 721-6060

Rhode Island

National Federation of Independent Business
159 Elmgrove Ave.
Providence, RI 02906
(401) 421-0483

South Carolina

Governor's Office/OSMBA
1205 Pendleton St.
Edgar A. Brown Bldg., Ste. 303
Columbia, SC 29201-3786
(803) 758-7804

National Federation of Independent Business
P.O. Box 244
Lexington, SC 29072
(803) 359-6300

Small Business Development Center
Nurses Bldg., Rm. 134
USCS
Spartanburg, SC 29303
(803) 271-4259

South Carolina Chamber of Commerce
P.O. Box 11278
Columbia, SC 29211
(803) 799-4601

South Dakota

National Federation of Independent Business
319 Coteau St.
P.O. Box 280
Pierre, SD 57501
(605) 224-7102

South Dakota Industry and Association of Commerce
P.O. Box 190
Pierre, SD 57501
(605) 224-6161

Tennessee

Chamber of Commerce
161 Fourth Ave., North
Nashville, TN 37219
(615) 259-3900

Memphis Regional Minority Purchasing Council
P.O. Box 224
Memphis, TN 38101
(901) 523-2322

Middle Tennessee Regional Minority Purchasing Council
1719 W. End Executive Bldg., Ste. 817
Nashville, TN 37203
(615) 329-4705

Mid-South Hardware Association, Inc.
2500 Hillsboro Rd.
Nashville, TN 37215

National Federation of Independent Business
2100 W. End Ave., #900
Nashville, TN 37207
(615) 297-9955

Tennessee Manufacturers and Taxpayers Association
226 Capitol Blvd., Ste. 800
Nashville, TN 37219
(615) 256-5141

Tennessee Retail Grocers Association
Music Park Office Bldg.
107 Music City Circle
Nashville, TN 37214

Tennessee Small Business Roundtable
c/o Brookmeade Hardware
208 Russell St.
Nashville, TN 37213
(615) 256-0450

Tennessee Utility Contractors Association
P.O. Box 428
Henderson, TN 38340
(615) 244-1851

Texas

National Federation of Independent Business
815 Brazos Bldg., Ste. 400-L
Austin, TX 78701
(512) 476-9847

Texas Association of Business
6900 Fannin, Ste. 240
Houston, TX 77030-3880
(713) 790-1010

Texas State Chamber of Commerce
206 W. 13th, Ste. A
Austin, TX 78701
(512) 472-1594

Utah

National Federation of Independent Business
136 E. South Temple, Ste. 1840
Salt Lake City, UT 84111
(801) 531-4986

Utah Council of Small Business
10 S. Main, Ste. 210
Salt Lake City, UT 84101
(801) 322-1338

Vermont

National Federation of Independent Business

P.O. Box 123
Colchester, VT 05446
(802) 879-6323

Vermont State Chamber of Commerce
P.O. Box 37
Montpelier, VT 05602
(802) 229-4619
(802) 223-3443

Virginia

National Federation of Independent Business
1001 E. Main St.
Richmond, VA 23219
(804) 780-1258

The Virginia Chamber of Commerce
9 S. Fifth St.
Richmond, VA 23219
(804) 644-1607

Virgin Islands

St. Thomas, St. John Chamber of Commerce
P.O. Box 324
St. Thomas, VI 00801

Washington

Association of Washington Business
P.O. Box 658
Olympia, WA 98507-0658
(206) 943-1600

Independent Business Association of Washington
920 108th N.E., Ste. 3
Bellevue, WA 98004
(206) 453-8621

National Federation of Independent Business
711 S. Capital Way, Ste. 201-9
Olympia, WA 98501
(206) 786-8675

Seattle Chamber of Commerce
1200 One Union Sq.
Seattle, WA 98101
(206) 447-7285

West Virginia

National Federation of Independent Business

2253 Miller Rd.
Huntington, WV 25701
(304) 529-3471

West Virginia Chamber of Commerce
P.O. Box 2789
Charleston, WV 25330
(304) 342-1115

Wisconsin

Independent Business Association of Wisconsin
415 E. Washington Ave.
Madison, WI 53703
(608) 251-5546

Metro Milwaukee Association of Commerce
756 N. Milwaukee St.
Milwaukee, WI 53202
(414) 273-3000

National Federation of Independent Business
P.O. Box 1072
217 S. Hamilton St.
Madison, WI 53701
(608) 255-6083

Wisconsin Association of Manufacturers and Commerce
111 E. Wisconsin Ave., Ste. 1600
Milwaukee, WI 53202
(608) 255-2312

Wisconsin Society of Association Executives
34615 Rd. E
Oconomowoc, WI 53066

Wisconsin Women Entrepreneurs
P.O. Box 132
Racine, WI 53401
(414) 554-8301

Wyoming

National Federation of Independent Business
1805 Capital Ave., Ste. 201
Cheyenne, WY 82001
(307) 778-4045

The Greater Cheyenne Chamber of Commerce
P.O. Box 1147
Cheyenne, WY 82003
(307) 638-3388

Small Business Development Centers

The Small Business Development Center (SBDC) Program, sponsored by SBA, is a cooperative effort among the educational community, state and local governments, the federal government, and the diverse areas of the private sector. The program has one unifying purpose: to further economic development by providing management and technical assistance to existing and prospective small businesses. The SBDC program represents a partnership, in the truest sense of the word, of the federal government, the state governments, and the private sector. It serves as the focal point for bringing together various available resources to help small businesses and works to strengthen the economic growth of the communities served.

The SBDC program began as a pilot program at the business college of a single university in 1977; there are now 49 SBDCs in 42 states, the District of Columbia, Puerto Rico, and the Virgin Islands. In each state, a "lead" organization, endorsed by the governor, sponsors the SBDC; the statewide director manages the program through this lead organization. The lead SBDC coordinates activities by enlisting the participation of other organizations which, in turn, establish SBDC subcenters and satellite service locations. These subcenters are located at colleges, universities, vocational schools, chambers of commerce, economic development corporations, and other local state agencies.

The total SBDC network presently consists of nearly 500 different satellite locations; each provides assistance specifically tailored to the local area and the needs of individual clients. A list of locations and contact persons for each SBDC follows.

SMALL BUSINESS DEVELOPMENT CENTERS AND SUBCENTERS

Alabama

University of Alabama at Birmingham
Sherry Dilbeck, Acting State Dir.
Small Business Development Center of Alabama
1717 11th Ave. South, Ste. 419
Birmingham, AL 35294
(205) 934-7260

University of Alabama at Birmingham*
Vernon Nabors, Dir.
Small Business Development Center
901 15th St.
Bldg. 4, Rm. 150
Birmingham, AL 35294
(205) 934-6760

Alabama A&M University
Dr. Edwin D. Marsh, Dir.
Small Business Development Center
School of Business
Normal, AL 35762
(205) 859-7481

University of Alabama at Huntsville
Edward F. Stafford Jr., Dir.
Alabama High-Technology Assistance Center

*Denotes recipient organization (lead SBDC).

School of Administrative Science
327 Morton Hall
Huntsville, AL 35899
(205) 895-6409

College of Commerce and Business Administration
Nisa Bacon, Dir.
Alabama International Trade Center
P.O. Box 1996
University, AL 35486
(205) 348-7621

Alabama State University
Jacqueline Gholston, Acting Dir.
Small Business Development Center
915 S. Jackson St.
Montgomery, AL 36195
(205) 269-1102

Auburn University
Dr. Ed Kern, Dir.
Small Business Development Center
School of Business
Auburn, AL 36830
(205) 826-4030

Jacksonville State University
Pat W. Shaddix, Dir.
Small Business Development Center
College of Commerce and Business Administration
Jacksonville, AL 36265
(205) 231-5271

Livingstone University
Ann Lowery, Dir.
Small Business Development Center
College of Business and Commerce
Station 35
Livingstone, AL 35470
(205) 652-9661, ext. 439

Troy State University
Joseph W. Creek, Dir.
Small Business Development Center
School of Business and Commerce
Troy, AL 36081
(205) 566-7665

Tuskegee Institute
Marius Jones, Dir.
Small Business Development Center
Department of Business

Tuskegee, AL 36088
(205) 727-8710

University of Alabama
Paavo Hanninen, Dir.
Small Business Development Center
Box J
Tuscaloosa, AL 35486
(205) 348-7011

Arkansas

University of Arkansas at Little Rock*
Paul McGinnis, State Dir.
Small Business Development Center
College of Business
New Business Bldg., Rm. 512
33d St. & University Ave.
Little Rock, AR 72204
(501) 371-5381
(800) 482-5850, ext. 5381

Arkansas State University
Jeffrey Pittman, Dir.
Small Business Development Center
P.O. Drawer 2650
State University, AR 72467
(501) 972-3517

Harding University
Dr. Bob Reely, Dir.
Small Business Development Center
Department of Business and Economics
Searcy, AR 72143
(501) 268-6161, ext. 497

Henderson State University
Bill Akin, Dir.
Small Business Development Center
Box 2231
Arkadelphia, AR 71923
(501) 246-5511, ext. 327

University of Arkansas at Fayetteville
Dr. Don Cook, Dir.
Small Business Development Center
College of Business-BA 117
Fayetteville, AR 72701
(501) 575-5148

University of Arkansas at Monticello
Mr. G. E. Triplett, Dir.
Small Business Development Center
Department of Business Administration

Monticello, AR 71655
(501) 367-7926, ext. 37

University of Central Arkansas
Dr. Homer Saunders, Dir.
Small Business Development Center
College of Business Administration
Conway, AR 72032
(501) 450-3190

Connecticut

University of Connecticut*
John O'Connor, State Dir.
Neal Wehr, Jr., Assistant Dir.
Small Business Development Center
School of Business Administration
Box U-41, Rm. 422
368 Fairfield Rd.
Storrs, CT 06226
(203) 486-4135

Center for Minority Business Development†
Ronald V. Williams, Dir.
Small Business Development Center
c/o Hartford Enterprise Zone
P.O. Box 6574
Hartford, CT 06106
(203) 722-8008

Community Accounting Aid and Services†
Richard Rogers, Dir.
Small Business Development Center
c/o UCONN MBA
39 Woodland St.
Hartford, CT. 06105
(203) 241-4984

Quinebaug Valley Community College
Richard Fontaine, Dir.
Small Business Development Center
P.O. Box 59
Maple St.
Danielson, CT 06239
(203) 774-1160

UCONN MBA
Lester Killen, Dir.
Small Business Development Center
1800 Asylum Ave.

West Hartford, CT 06117
(203) 241-4982

Business/Industry Council
Ronald Adinolfi, Dir.
Small Business Development Center
180 Fairfield Ave.
Bridgeport, CT. 06601
(203) 335-3800

The Greater New Haven Chamber of Commerce
Neal Wehr, Jr., Dir.
Small Business Development Center
195 Church St.
New Haven, CT 06506
(203) 787-6735

Chamber of Commerce of Southeastern Connecticut
William Lockwood, Dir.
Small Business Development Center
One Whale Oil Row
New London, CT 06320
(203) 442-9192

SACIA
George Ahl, Dir.
Small Business Development Center
One Landmark Sq.
Stamford, CT 06901
(203) 359-3220

Greater Waterbury Chamber of Commerce
Robert Suchy, Dir.
Small Business Development Center
32 N. Main St.
Waterbury, CT 06702
(203) 757-0701

University of Connecticut†
Dr. Subhash Jain, Dir.
Small Business Development Center
Export Marketing Center
School of Business Administration
Marketing Department, Rm. 418
Storrs, CT 06268
(203) 486-4133

University of Connecticut†
Dr. Madelyn Huffmire, Dir.

†Denotes specialized center.

Small Business Development Center
Business Law Center
School of Business Administration
Business Environment and Policy, Rm.
  319
Storrs, CT 06268
(203) 486-2770

Delaware

University of Delaware*
David Park, Acting State Dir.
Small Business Development Center
Purnell Hall, Ste. 005
Newark, DE 19716
(302) 451-2747

District of Columbia

Howard University*
Nancy Flake, Dir.
Small Business Development Center of
  Washington, D.C.
6th & Fairmount Sts., N.W., Rm. 128
Washington, DC 20059
(202) 636-5150

George Mason University
Dr. Jon English, Dir.
Small Business Development Center
School of Business Administration
4400 University Blvd.
Fairfax, VA 22030
(703) 323-2568

George Washington University
Peter Aron, Dir.
Small Business Development Center
National Law Center
Stockton Hall
720 20th St., N.W.
Washington, DC 20052
(202) 676-7463

George Washington University
Dr. Cynthia Jones, Dir.
Small Business Development Center
Division of Continuing Education and
  Summer Sessions
2121 I St., N.W., 6th Floor
Washington, DC 20052
(202) 676-7463

Georgetown University
Dr. Phyllis O'Callaghan, Dir.
Small Business Development Center
School of Summer and Continuing Educa-
  tion Programs
The Intercultural Center
802 22d St., N.W.
Washington, DC 20052
(202) 625-3014

Montgomery College
Janice B. Carmichael, Dir.
Small Business Development Center
Bethesda Center
7815 Woodmont Ave.
Bethesda, MD 20814
(301) 656-7482

University of the District of Columbia
Dr. Patrick Hughes, Dir.
Small Business Development Center
Institute for Management and Entre-
  preneurial Development
Riggs Bank Bldg., Ste. 1003
900 F St., N.W.
Washington, DC 20004
(202) 727-1051

University of Maryland (UMCP)
Michael Anikeeff, Dir.
Small Business Development Center
College of Business and Management
Tydings Hall
College Park, MD 20742
(301) 454-5072

Florida

**Small Business Development Center of
Florida**
Gregory L. Higgins, State Dir.
Jerry Widman, Associate State Dir.
University of West Florida
Bldg. 38, Rm. 107
Pensacola, FL 32514
(904) 474-3016

University of West Florida*
Donald M. Clause, Dir.
Small Business Development Center
College of Business, Bldg. 8
Pensacola, FL 32514
(904) 474-2908

University of West Florida
Walter Craft, Coordinator
Small Business Development Center
P.O. Box 1527
Bldg. 251, Rm. 122
Eglin AFBase, FL 32542
(904) 678-1143

Florida A&M University
Patricia McGowan, Dir.
Small Business Development Center
Commons Bldg., Rm. 7
P.O. Box 708
Tallahassee, FL 32307
(904) 599-3407

Florida Atlantic University
William Marina, Dir.
Small Business Development Center
School of Public Administration
College of Business and Public Administration
Boca Raton, FL 33431
(305) 393-3662

Fort Lauderdale Small Business Development Center
William Levi, Regional Dir.
One River Plaza Bldg.
303 S. Andrews Ave.
Fort Lauderdale, FL 33301
(305) 467-4238

Palm Beach Junior College
Teresa Geist, Regional Dir.
Small Business Development Center
North Campus
3160 PGA Blvd.
Palm Beach Gardens, FL 33410
(305) 627-4278

Florida International University
Marvin Nesbit, Dir.
Small Business Development Center
Division of Continuing Education
Trailer MO1, Tamiami Campus
Miami, FL 33199
(305) 554-2272

Broward Community College
William Healy, Branch Mgr.
Small Business Development Center
7200 Hollywood Blvd.

Pembrook Pines, FL 33024-9990
(305) 987-0100

Florida International University
Royland Jarrett, Regional Mgr.
Small Business Development Center
Bay Vista Campus (N. Miami Campus)
Academic Bldg. #1, Rm. 384
Miami, FL 33181
(305) 940-5790

Florida Keys Community College
Dr. William M. Smith, Jr., Dir.
Small Business Development Center
602 Duval St.
Key West, FL 33040
(305) 294-8481

Florida State University
Dr. John Kerr, Dir.
Small Business Development Center
Business Bldg., Rm. 426
College of Business
Tallahassee, FL 32306
(904) 644-2053

Lake City Community College
Martha Yopp, Mgr.
Small Business Development Center
102 N. Marion
Lake City, FL 32055
(904) 752-1822

Florida State University
Marilyn Thompson, Mgr.
Small Business Development Center
Eastwood Office Plaza, Ste. 1
Tallahassee, FL 32308
(904) 644-6524

Florida State University
Ron Barber, Mgr.
Small Business Development Center
4917 N. Bay Dr.
Panama City, FL 32405
(904) 763-0378

University of Central Florida
Al Polfer, Dir.
Small Business Development Center
College of Business Administration, Bldg. 52
P.O. Box 25000
Orlando, FL 32816
(305) 275-2796

Stetson University
Robert J. Heckel, Regional Dir.
Small Business Development Center
School of Business Administration
P.O. Box 1429
Deland, FL 32720
(904) 734-1066

University of North Florida
Ted Alden, Dir.
Small Business Development Center
College of Business
4567 St. John's Bluff Rd., South
Bldg. 11, Rm. 2197
Jacksonville, FL 32216
(904) 646-2476

Small Business Development Center
William Stensgaard, Mgr.
TREEO Center
3900 S.W. 63d Blvd.
Gainesville, FL 32608
(904) 377-5621

University of South Florida
William Manck, Dir.
Small Business Development Center
College of Business, Rm. 3331
Tampa, FL 33620
(813) 974-4274

University of South Florida
William Manck, Acting Mgr.
Small Business Development Center
St. Petersburg Campus
College of Business
830 First St., South, Rm. 119
St. Petersburg, FL 33701
(813) 893-9529

Georgia

Small Business Development Center of Georgia
Dr. Frank Hoy, State Dir.
Chicopee Complex
Athens, GA 30602
(404) 542-5760

University of Georgia*
Gerald Rucker, Dir.
Northeast Georgia Small Business Development Center

Chicopee Complex
Athens, GA 30602
(404) 542-7436

Albany Junior College
Sabrina Smith, Dir.
Southwest Georgia Small Business Development Center
P.O. Box 348
Albany, GA 31702
(912) 439-7232

Augusta College/Central Savannah River Area Small Business Development Center
Ray Chestnut, Dir.
School of Business
2500 Walton Way
Augusta, GA 30910
(404) 737-1790

Brunswick Junior College/Savannah State College
George Eckerd, Dir.
Coastal Area Small Business Development Center
Altama at Fourth
Brunswick, GA 31523
(912) 264-7343

Clayton Junior College
George L. St. Germain, Dir.
Small Business Development Center
P.O. Box 285
Morrow, GA 30260
(404) 961-3414

Columbus College
Benno Rothschild, Dir.
West Central Georgia Small Business Development Center
P.O. Box 2441
Columbus, GA 31902
(404) 571-7433

Floyd Junior College
Betty Nolen, Dir.
Northwest Georgia Small Business Development Center
P.O. Box 1864
Rome, GA 30163
(404) 295-6327

Georgia College/Macon Jr. College
Clyde Conine, Dir.

Central Georgia Small Business Development Center
P.O. Box 169
Macon, GA 31061
(912) 741-8023

Georgia Southern College
Jeff Jones, Dir.
Southwest Georgia Small Business Development Center
L.B. 8156, GSC
Statesboro, GA 30460
(912) 681-5194

Georgia State University
Mr. Lee Quarterman, Dir.
Small Business Development Center
P.O. Box 874
University Plaza
Atlanta, GA 30303
(404) 658-3550

Kennesaw College
Mr. Wray Buchanan, Dir.
Kennesaw Area Small Business Development Center
P.O. Box 444
Marietta, GA 30061
(404) 429-2800

Valdosta State College
John Oliver, Dir.
South Georgia Small Business Development Center
Pound Hall
Valdosta, GA 31698
(912) 333-5963

Idaho

Boise State University*
Ronald R. Hall, State Dir.
Small Business Development Center of Idaho
Control Center
College of Business
1910 University Dr.
Boise, ID 83725
(208) 385-1640

Downtown Boise Small Business Development Center
Ronald R. Hall, Dir.
7270 Potomac Dr.

Boise, ID 83704
(208) 385-1640

Illinois

Department of Commerce and Community Affairs*
Jeff Mitchell, State Dir.
Illinois Small Business Development Center
620 E. Adams St., 5th Floor
Springfield, IL 62701
(217) 785-6267

Blackhawk Community College
Bill Barrett, Dir.
Small Business Development Center
c/o Quad-Cities Chamber of Commerce
622 19th St.
Moline, IL 61265
(309) 762-3661

Bradley University
Fred L. Fry, Dir.
Small Business Development Center
Baker Hall, Rm. 421
Peoria, IL 61625
(309) 672-4316

City Colleges of Chicago
Roy G. Filson, Dir.
Small Business Development Center
30 E. Lake St.
Chicago, IL 60601
(312) 670-0432

Governors State University
Dr. Richard Schreve, Dir.
Small Business Development Center
College of Business and Public Administration
University Park, IL 60466
(312) 534-5000, ext. 2241

Lincoln/Land Community College
Dr. Michael Paulisin, Dir.
Capital Area Small Business Development Center
Four North
Old State Capitol Plaza
Springfield, IL 62701
(217) 492-4772

Northern Illinois University
Diane Robertson, Dir.

Small Business Development Center
Department of Management
Wirtz Hall, Rm. 122
Dekalb, IL 60115
(815) 753-1403

Richland Community College
Nancy Cooper, Dir.
Small Business Development Center
Continuing Education Department
2425 Federal Dr.
Decatur, IL 62526
(217) 875-7215

Southern Illinois University at Carbondale
Irene Carlton, Dir.
Small Business Development Center
College of Business Administration
Carbondale, IL 62901
(618) 536-2424

Southern Illinois University at Edwards-
ville
Dr. Arnold Franke, Dir.
Small Business Development Center
P.O. Box 51, Bldg. II, Rm. 3315
Edwardsville, IL 62026
(618) 692-2929

Western Illinois University
Steven C. Roberts, Dir.
Small Business Development Center
515 Stipes Hall
MaComb, IL 61455
(309) 298-1128

Indiana

Indiana Economic Development Council*
Randy Meadows, State Dir.
Small Business Development Center
One N. Capitol, Ste. 200
Indianapolis, IN 46204
(317) 634-6407

Metropolitan Evansville Chamber of
Commerce
Connell Jones, Dir.
Small Business Development Center
329 Main St.
Evansville, IN 47708
(812) 424-7709

Fort Wayne Chamber of Commerce
Connie Bullard, Dir.

Small Business Development Center
825 Ewing St.
Fort Wayne, IN 46802
(219) 424-SBDC

Muncie-Delaware County Chamber of
Commerce
Mary Kaye Ruth, Dir.
Small Business Development Center
500 N. Walnut
Muncie, IN 47305
(317) 288-6681

South Bend Chamber of Commerce
Carolyn Anderson, Dir.
Small Business Development Center
300 N. Michigan
South Bend, IN 46601
(219) 282-4350

Iowa

Small Business Development Center of Iowa
Louise H. Brinkman, State Dir.
Iowa State University
Engineering Annex, Rm. 205
Ames, IA 50011
(515) 294-3420

Iowa State University*
Mr. Jan DeYoung, Dir.
Small Business Development Center
80 Heady Hall
Ames, IA 50011
(515) 294-8069

Audubon Pilot Project†
Ann Nielson, Dir.
Audubon Chamber of Commerce
Small Business Development Center
Audubon, IA 50025
(712) 563-3780

Drake University
Louis Wood, Dir.
Small Business Development Center
210 Aliber Hall
25th & University
Des Moines, IA 50311
(515) 271-2655

Dubuque Area Chamber of Commerce
Mark Hemming, Dir.
Northwest Iowa Small Business Develop-
ment Center

880 Locust St.
Dubuque, IA 52001
(319) 588-3350

Eastern Community College
Jon Ryan, Dir.
East Central Iowa Small Business Development Center
20804 Eastern Ave.
Davenport, IA 52803
(319) 322-5015

Indian Hills Community College
Bryan Ziegler, Dir.
Southeast Iowa Small Business Development Center
Grandview & Elm
Ottumwa, IA 52501
(515) 683-5127

Iowa State University
Ms. Carmi Spicer, Dir.
Inventor's Program†
University Extension-CIRAS
Engineering Annex, Rm. 205
Ames, IA 50011
(515) 294-3420

Iowa Western Community College
Ron Helms, Dir.
Southwest Iowa Small Business Development Center
2700 College Rd., Box 4C
Council Bluffs, IA 51502
(712) 325-3260

North Iowa Area Community College
Richard Petersen, Dir.
North Central Iowa Small Business Development Center
500 College Dr.
Mason City, IA 50401
(515) 421-4342

Siouxland Interstate Metropolitan Planning Council
Sharolyn Craft, Dir.
West Central Iowa Small Business Development Center
400 Orpheum Electric Bldg.
520 Pierce St.
Sioux City, IA 51102
(712) 279-6572

University of Iowa
Paul Heath, Dir.
Small Business Development Center
College of Business
Iowa City, IA 52242
(319) 353-5340

University of Northern Iowa
Al Pelham, Dir.
Small Business Development Center
School of Business
121 Seerley Hall
Cedar Falls, IA 50613
(319) 273-2696

Kansas

Wichita State University
Susan Osborne-Howes, State Dir.
Small Business Development Center of Kansas
College of Business Administration
Campus Box 48
021 Clinton Hall
Wichita, KS 67208
(316) 689-3193

Wichita State University*
Mary Jenkins, Dir.
Small Business Development Center
College of Business Administration
Campus Box 48
021 Clinton Hall
Wichita, KS 67208
(316) 689-3193

Emporia State University
Dr. Bart Finney, Dir.
Small Business Development Center
1200 Commercial
Cremer Hall, Rm. 207
Emporia, KS 66801
(316) 343-1200, ext. 308

Fort Hays State University
Dr. Robert C. Camp, Dir.
Small Business Development Center
600 Park St.
McCartney Hall, Rm. 203
Hays, KS 67601
(913) 628-5340

Johnson County Community College
David Smith, Dir.

Small Business Development Center
Business and Economic Division
12345 College at Quivira
OCB 257
Overland Park, KS 66210
(913) 469-8500, ext. 3623

Kansas State University
Dr. J. Barton-Dobenin, Dir.
Small Business Development Center
College of Business Administration
Calvin Hall, Rm. 114
Manhattan, KS 66506
(913) 532-5827

Pittsburg State University
Dr. Terry L. Mendenhall, Dir.
Small Business Development Center
Kelce School of Business and Economics
Pittsburg, KS 66762
(316) 231-8267

University of Kansas
Dr. Marilyn L. Taylor, Dir.
Small Business Development Center
313E Summerfield Hall
Lawrence, KS 66045
(913) 864-3117

Washburn University of Topeka
Dr. Frank A. Sotrines, Dir.
Small Business Development Center
School of Business
Henderson Learning Center, Rm. 110
Topeka, KS 66621
(913) 295-6305

Kentucky

Small Business Development Center of Kentucky
Jerry Owen, State Dir.
University of Kentucky
18 Porter Bldg.
Lexington, KY 40506-0205
(606) 257-1751

University of Kentucky*
Bill Morley, Dir.
Central Kentucky Small Business Development Center
18 Porter Bldg.

Lexington, KY 40506-0205
(606) 257-1751

Ashland Small Business Development
Center
Linda Akers, Dir.
Ashland Chamber of Commerce Bldg.
P.O. Box 830
Ashland, KY 41101
(606) 329-8011

Bellarmine College
Georgeann Musson, Dir.
Small Business Development Center
School of Business
Newburg Rd.
Louisville, KY 40205
(502) 452-8282

Kentucky Department of Commerce
Joe Brown, Dir.
Small Business Development Center
Small Business Branch
Capitol Plaza Tower, 22d Floor
Frankfort, KY 40601
(502) 564-4252

Morehead State University
Wilson Grier, Dir.
Small Business Development Center
East Kentucky District Office
Morehead, KY 40351
(606) 783-2077

Murray State University
Otis H. Erwin, Dir.
Small Business Development Center
West Kentucky District Office
College of Business
Murray, KY 42071
(502) 762-2856

Murray State University at Owensboro
Mickey Johnson, Dir.
Small Business Development Center
3860 U.S. Hwy. 60 West
Owensboro, KY 42301
(502) 926-8085

Northern Kentucky University
Roger Marshall, Dir.
Small Business Development Center
BEP Center 437

Highland Heights, KY 41076
(606) 572-6558

Pikeville Chamber of Commerce
Carolyn Price, Dir.
Pikeville Small Business Development
  Center
101 Hussman Ave.
Pikeville, KY 41501
(606) 432-5848

Somerset Community College
David Elam, Dir.
Small Business Development Center
Monticello Rd.
Somerset, KY 42501
(606) 678-8174

Southeast Community College
Mr. Cortez Davis, Dir.
Small Business Development Center
119 Christman Hall
Cumberland, KY 40823
(606) 589-4514

University of Kentucky
Denver Woodring, Dir.
Small Business Development Center
240 W. Dixie Hwy.
Elizabethtown, KY 42701
(502) 765-6737

Western Kentucky University
Richard S. Horn, Dir.
Small Business Development Center
519 Grise Hall
Bowling Green, KY 42101
(502) 745-2901

Louisiana

Northeast Louisiana University
John Baker, State Dir.
Small Business Development Center of Loui-
  siana
College of Business Administration
Adm. 2-123
Monroe, LA 71209
(318) 342-2464

Northeast Louisiana University*
Dr. Paul Dunn, Dir.
Small Business Development Center
College of Business Administration

Adm. 2-104
Monroe, LA 71209
(318) 342-2129

Louisiana Department of Commerce
Nadia Goodman, Dir.
Small Business Development Center
P.O. Box 44185
Baton Rouge, LA 70804
(504) 342-5404

Louisiana State University
Charles C. Holbrook, Dir.
Small Business Development Center
Economic Development Center
Baton Rouge, LA 70803
(504) 922-0998

Louisiana State University at Shreveport
Charlotta Nordyke, Dir.
Small Business Development Center
College of Business Administration
8515 Youree Dr.
Shreveport, LA 71105
(318) 797-5144

Louisiana Technical University
Rick Hebert, Dir.
Small Business Development Center
P.O. Box 10318, Tech Station
Ruston, LA 71272-0046
(318) 257-3537

Loyola University
Dr. John L. Folkenroth, Dir.
Small Business Development Center
College of Business Administration
P.O. Box 78
New Orleans, LA 70125
(504) 865-2775

McNeese State University
Paul Arnold, Dir.
Small Business Development Center
College of Business Administration
Lake Charles, LA 70601
(318) 437-5529

Nicholls State University
Dr. Aubry Fowler, Dir.
Small Business Development Center
College of Business Administration
Thibodaux, LA 70310
(504) 446-8111, ext. 429

Northwestern State University
Dr. John Hix, Dir.
Small Business Development Center
College of Business Administration
Natchitoches, LA 71497
(318) 357-5611

Southeastern Louisiana University
Dr. Tom Griffin, Dir.
Small Business Development Center
College of Business Administration
P.O. Box 522, University Station
Hammond, LA 70402
(504) 549-3831

Southern University
Jon Johnson, Dir.
Small Business Development Center
Division of Business Administration
6400 Press Dr.
New Orleans, LA 70126
(504) 282-4401, ext. 308

University of New Orleans
Ivan J. Miestchovich, Jr., Dir.
Small Business Development Center
Center for Economic Development
College of Business Administration
Lakefront Campus
New Orleans, LA 70122
(504) 286-6978

University of Southwestern Louisiana
Hal P. Langford, Dir.
Small Business Development Center
College of Business Administration
P.O. Box 43732
Lafayette, LA 70504
(318) 231-5751

Maine

University of Southern Maine*
Warren Purdy, Dir.
Small Business Development Center
246 Deering Ave.
Portland, ME 04102
(207) 780-4420

  Androscoggin Valley Council of Governments
  John Jaworski, Dir.
  Small Business Development Center

70 Court St.
Auburn, ME 04210
(207) 783-9186

Coastal Enterprises Inc.
Jim Burbank, Dir.
Small Business Development Center
Middle St.
P.O. Box 268
Wiscasset, ME 04578
(207) 882-7552

Eastern Maine Development Corp.
Michael Aube, Dir.
Small Business Development Center
10 Franklin St.
Bangor, ME 04401
(207) 942-6389

International Trade State Development
  Office
Michael Davis, Dir.
Small Business Development Center
193 State St.
State House Station 59
Augusta, ME 04333
(207) 289-2656

Maine Development Foundation
Henry Bourgeois, Dir.
Small Business Development Center
One Memorial Circle
Augusta, ME 04330
(207) 622-6345

Northern Maine Regional Planning Commission
James Baressi, Dir.
Small Business Development Center
McElwain House
P.O. Box 779
2 Main St.
Caribou, ME 04736
(207) 498-8736

University of Maine at Machias
Dr. William Little, Dir.
Small Business Development Center
Math and Science Bldg.
Machias, ME 04654
(207) 255-3313

Massachusetts

University of Massachusetts*
John Ciccarelli, State Dir.
Small Business Development Center
203 School of Management
Amherst, MA 01003
(413) 549-4930, ext. 303

Boston College
Dr. Jack McKiernan, Dir.
Metropolitan Boston Regional Small Business Development Center
96 College Rd., Rahner House
Chestnut Hill, MA 02167
(617) 552-4091

Capital Formation Service
Laurence Jutras, Dir.
Small Business Development Center
University of Massachusetts
203 School of Management
Amherst, MA 01003
(413) 549-4930

Clark University
William Naumes, Dir.
Central Regional Small Business Development Center
950 Main St.
Worcester, MA 01610
(617) 793-7615

Roxbury Community College
Dr. Kenneth Edison, Dir.
Minority Business Training and Resource Center
625 Huntington Ave.
Boston, MA 02115
(617) 734-1960

Southeastern Massachusetts University
Clyde Mitchell, Dir.
Southeastern Regional Small Business Development Center
200 Pocasset St.
Fall River, MA 02722
(617) 673-9783

University of Lowell
Rudolph Winston, Dir.
Northeast Regional Small Business Development Center

450 Aiken St.
Lowell, MA 01854
(617) 458-7261

University of Massachusetts
Merwin Tober, Dir.
Western Regional Small Business Development Center
101 State St., Rm. 216
Springfield, MA 01103
(413) 737-6712

Michigan

Wayne State University
Norman J. Schlafmann, State Dir.
Small Business Development Center of Michigan
2727 Second Ave.
Detroit, MI 48201
(313) 577-4848

Wayne State University*
Raymond M. Genick, Dir.
Small Business Development Center
2727 Second Ave.
Detroit, MI 48201
(313) 577-4850

Ann Arbor Area Chamber of Commerce
Carol M. Benson, Dir.
Small Business Development Center
912 N. Main St.
Ann Arbor, MI 48104
(313) 662-0550

Bay Area Chamber of Commerce
Teresa J. Wilbur, Dir.
Small Business Development Center
205 Fourth St.
P.O. Box 838
Bay City, MI 48707
(517) 893-4567

Central Michigan University
Dr. Norman Deunk, Dir.
Small Business Development Center
School of Business Administration
Mount Pleasant, MI 48858
(517) 774-3736

Central Upper Peninsula Business Development Center
Peter Cambier, Dir.

2415 14th Ave., South
Escanaba, MI 49829
(906) 786-9234

Downriver Small Business Development
    Center
William E. Cheff, Dir.
15100 Northline Rd.
Southgate, MI 48195
(313) 281-0700

Ferris State College
Linda Kolodsick, Dir.
Small Business Development Center
Alumni 203
Big Rapids, MI 49307
(616) 796-0461, ext. 3545

Flint Area Chamber of Commerce
Patrick J. Martin, Dir.
Small Business Development Center
708 Root St.
Flint, MI 48503
(313) 232-7101

Grand Rapids Area Small Business Assis-
    tance Network
Mary Ann McDonald, Dir.
2 Fountain St., Ste. 100
Grand Rapids, MI 49503
(616) 242-6613

Jackson Community College
M. Richard Shaink, Dir.
Center for Small Business and Entre-
    preneurial Development
2111 Emmons Rd.
Jackson, MI 49201-8399
(517) 787-0800, ext. 315

Kalamazoo College
Thomas Breznau, Dir.
Small Business Development Center
L. Lee Stryker Center
1327 Academy
Kalamazoo, MI 49007
(616) 383-8594

Kalamazoo Small Business Development
    Center
James E. DeHaan, Dir.
130 N. Kalamazoo Mall
Kalamazoo, MI 49007
(616) 343-1137

Macomb County Business Assistance Cen-
    ter
Donald L. Morandini, Dir.
Small Business Development Center
115 S. Groesbeck
Mount Clemens, MI 48043
(313) 469-5118

Michigan Energy and Resource Research
    Association†
M. Todd Anuskiewicz, Dir.
Small Business Development Center
1200 Sixth St., Ste. 328
Detroit, MI 48226
(313) 964-5030

Michigan Technological University
Richard Tieder, Dir.
Small Business Development Center
Bureau of Industrial Development
Houghton, MI 49930
(906) 487-2470

Midland County Growth Council
Robert C. Stein, Acting Dir.
Small Business Development Center
300 Rodd St.
Midland, MI 48640
(517) 839-9901

Monroe Community College
John A. Joy, Dir.
Small Business Development Center
1555 S. Rainsinville Rd.
Monroe, MI 48161
(313) 242-7300, ext. 344

Muskegon Community College
Dennis A. Wilson, Dir.
Small Business Development Center
221 S. Quarterline Rd.
Muskegon, MI 49442
(616) 777-0201

Muskegon County Small Business Devel-
    opment Center
John J. Lindale, Dir.
One Lumberman's Sq.
Muskegon, MI 49440
(616) 726-4848

Northeast Michigan Consortium
Gordon H. Campbell, Dir.
Small Business Development Center

P.O. Box 711
Onaway, MI 49765
(517) 733-8548

Northern Michigan University
Allen Raymond, Dir.
Small Business Development Center
206 Cohodas Administrative Center
Marquette, MI 49855
(906) 227-2568

Oceana Economic Development
  Corp.
Lora E. Swenson, Dir.
Small Business Development Center
P.O. Box 168
Hart, MI 49420
(616) 873-7141

Region 7B Small Business Development
  Center
Thad C. Aaron, Dir.
P.O. Box 408
402 N. First St.
Harrison, MI 48625
(517) 539-2173

Saginaw Area Growth Alliance
JoAnn T. Crary, Dir.
Small Business Development Center
124 S. Jefferson Ave., 6th Floor
Saginaw, MI 48607
(517) 754-8222

Saginaw Valley State College
Leonard F. Herk, Dir.
Small Business Development Center
Business and Industrial Development In-
  stitute
2250 Pierce Rd.
University Center, MI 48710
(517) 790-4048

Thumb Area Small Business Development
  Center
Marvin Pichla, Dir.
3078 S. Main St.
Marlette, MI 48453
(517) 635-3561

Ypsilanti Area Chamber of Commerce
Mr. G. Merritt Martin, Dir.
Small Business Development Center
11 N. Adams

Ypsilanti, MI 48197
(313) 482-4920

Minnesota

College of St. Thomas
Jerry Cartwright, State Dir.
Small Business Development Center of Minnesota
1107 Hazeltine Gates Blvd., Ste. 452
Chaska, MN 55318
(612) 448-8810

College of St. Thomas*
Tom Trautna, Dir.
Small Business Development Center
2115 Summit Ave.
St. Paul, MN 55105
(612) 647-5840

Bemidji State University
Arthur R. Gullette, Dir.
Small Business Development Center
Business Administrative Office
Bemidji, MN 56601
(218) 755-2750

Brainerd Area Vocational Technical Institute
Ron Johnson, Dir.
Small Business Development Center
300 Quince St.
Brainerd, MN 56401
(218) 828-5302

Mankato State University
Dr. Chloe Elmgren, Dir.
Small Business Development Center
Mankato, MN 56001
(507) 389-1648

Moorhead State University
Len Sliwoski, Dir.
Small Business Development Center
Moorhead, MN 56560
(218) 236-2289

Southwest State University
Albert Hattis, Dir.
Small Business Development Center, Rm.
  AS 214
Marshall, MN 56258
(507) 537-7386

St. Cloud State University
Dr. Dwaine Tallent, Dir.
Small Business Development Center
College of Business
St. Cloud, MN 56301
(612) 255-4842

University of Minnesota
Bud Crewdson, Dir.
Small Business Development Center
College of Business, Rm. 248
1994 Buford Ave.
St. Paul, MN 55108
(612) 376-3433

University of Minnesota at Duluth
Chandra Subramaniam, Dir.
Small Business Development Center
Business Administration Department
Duluth, MN 55812
(218) 726-8761

Winona State University
Amy Caucutt, Dir.
Small Business Development Center
Eighth & Johnson
Winona, MN 55987
(507) 457-5089

Red Wing Area Vocational Technical Institute
Marv Bollom, Dir.
Small Business Development Center
Hwy. 58 at Pioneer Rd.
Red Wing, MN 55066
(800) 642-3344, ext. 12

Faribault Area Vocational Technical Institute
Ken Henrickson, Dir.
Small Business Development Center
1225 S.W. Third St.
Faribault, MN 55021
(507) 332-7444

Wadena Small Business Development Center
Paul Kinn, Dir.
317 S. Jefferson
Wadena, MN 56482
(218) 631-3530, ext. 371

Minnesota Project Innovation
Jim Swiderski, Dir.

Small Business Development Center
511 11th Ave., South, P.O. Box 210
Minneapolis, MN 55415
(612) 375-8084
(800) 642-1073

Normandale Community College
Scott Harding, Dir.
Small Business Development Center
9700 France Ave., South
Bloomington, MN 55431
(612) 830-9395

Dakota County Area Vocational Technical Institute
Dorothy Dodds, Dir.
Small Business Development Center
County Rd. 42 at Akren Ave.
Rosemount, MN 55068
(612) 423-8471

District #916 Area Vocational Technical Institute
Charles DeVore, Dir.
Small Business Development Center
330 Century Ave., North
White Bear Lake, MN 55110
(612) 770-2351

Small Business Development Center
Amy Caucutt, Dir.
716 28th St., N.W.
Rochester, MN 55901
(507) 285-7157

East Grand Forks Area Vocational Technical Institute
Galen Carivou, Dir.
Small Business Development Center
East Grand Forks, MN 56721
(218) 773-3441

Pine City Technical Institute
John Sparling, Dir.
Small Business Development Center
Pine City, MN 55063
(612) 629-6764

Small Business Development Center
Ms. Cali Beals, Dir.
25 Locust Dr.
Babbitt, MN 55706
(218) 827-2373
(218) 365-3256

Grand Rapids Business and Technical Institute
Diane Weber, Dir.
Small Business Development Center
Grand Rapids, MN 55744
(218) 327-2241

Area Vocational Technical Institute
Orley Gunderson, Dir.
Small Business Development Center
Hwy. One East
Thief River Falls, MN 56701
(218) 681-5424

Rainy River Community College
Ralph Anderson, Acting Provost
Small Business Development Center
International Falls, MN 56649
(218) 285-7722, ext. 259

Willmar Area Vocational Technical Institute
Dennie Wild, Dir.
Small Business Development Center
Willmar, MN 56201
(612) 235-5114

Mississippi

University of Mississippi*
Dr. Robert D. Smith, State Dir.
Small Business Development Center
School of Business Administration
3825 Ridgewood Rd.
Jackson, MS 39211
(601) 982-6760

Millsaps College International Trade Center†
Dr. Richard B. Baltz, Dir.
Small Business Development Center
P.O. Box 15395
Jackson, MS 39210
(601) 354-5201, ext. 407

Mississippi Research and Development Center
Van Evans, Dir.
3825 Ridgewood Rd.
Jackson, MS 39211-6453
(601) 982-6714

Mississippi State University
Dr. Garry Smith, Dir.

Small Business Development Center
104 McCool Hall
College of Business and Industry
Starkville, MS 39762
(601) 325-3817

Mississippi University for Women
Morgan Miles, Dir.
Small Business Development Center
Box W-239
Columbus, MS 39701
(601) 329-4750

Northeast Mississippi Manufacturing Assistance Center
Bob Gray, Mgr.
Small Business Development Center
P.O. Box 203
Tupelo, MS 38802
(601) 844-5413

University of Mississippi at Oxford
Raleigh Byars, Dir.
Small Business Development Center
Old Chemistry, Rm. 220
University, MS 38677
(601) 232-5001

University of Southern Mississippi
Marie Dean, Acting Dir.
Gulf Park Campus
Long Beach, MS 39560
(601) 865-4581

Missouri

St. Louis University
Fred O. Hale, State Dir.
Small Business Development Center of Missouri
O'Neil Hall, 100
3642 Lindell Blvd.
St. Louis, MO 63108
(314) 534-7232

St. Louis University*
Joan J. Weber, Dir.
Small Business Development Center
O'Neil Hall, 100
3642 Lindell Blvd.
St. Louis, MO 63108
(314) 534-7232

Northeast Missouri State University
William Ruble, Dir.

Small Business Development Center
207 E. Patterson
Kirksville, MO 63501
(816) 785-4307

Northwest Missouri State University
Dale Maudlin, Dir.
Small Business Development Center
Maryville, MO 64468
(816) 562-1701

Rockhurst College
Judy Burngen, Dir.
Small Business Development Center
Massman Hall
5225 Troost Ave.
Kansas City, MO 64116
(816) 926-4572

SBIR/Hi-Tech Program†
State of Missouri
Dr. Don Myers, Dir.
Community and Economic Development
P.O. Box 118
Jefferson City, MO 65102
(314) 751-3906

Southeast Missouri State University
Small Business Development Center
Cape Girardeau, MO 63701
(Contact St. Louis University for the director's name and telephone number.)

Southwest Missouri State University
Linda Timmerman, Dir.
Small Business Development Center
Cheek Hall, Rm. 124
901 S. National
Springfield, MO 65804
(417) 836-5685

University of Missouri at Columbia†
Dr. Owen Miller, Dir.
Small Business Development Center
111 Electrical Engineering Bldg.
Columbia, MO 65211
(314) 882-2691

University of Missouri at Rolla
Dr. John Amos, Dir.
Small Business Development Center
206 Harris Hall
Rolla, MO 55401
(314) 341-4561/4559

Nebraska

University of Nebraska at Omaha
Robert Bernier, State Dir.
Sterling Kent, Assistant Dir., Training
Leon Milobar, Assistant Dir., Counseling
Small Business Development Center of Nebraska
Peter Kiewit Center
1313 Farnam-on-the-Mall
Omaha, NE 68182
(402) 554-2521/3291

University of Nebraska at Omaha*
Fred Layberger, Dir.
Small Business Development Center
Peter Kiewit Center
1313 Farnam-on-the-Mall
Omaha, NE 68182
(402) 554-3291

Chadron State College
Cliff Hanson, Dir.
Small Business Development Center
Chadron, NE 69337
(308) 432-4451

Kearney State College
Kay Payne, Dir.
Small Business Development Center
West Center Bldg., Rm. E-107
Kearney, NE 68847
(308) 234-8344

University of Nebraska at Lincoln
Dr. Robert Justis, Dir.
Small Business Development Center
College of Business Administration
Lincoln, NE 68508
(402) 472-3276

Wayne State College
Tim Garvin, Dir.
Small Business Development Center
Connell Hall
Wayne, NE 68787
(402) 375-2004

Nevada

University of Nevada Reno*
Sam Males, State Dir.
Small Business Development Center

College of Business Administration
Reno, NV 89557-0016
(702) 784-1717

Northern Nevada Community College
John Pryor, Dir.
Small Business Development Center
901 Elm St.
Elko, NV 89801
(702) 738-8493

University of Nevada at Las Vegas
Richard Whitney, Dir.
Small Business Development Center
College of Business and Economics
4505 Maryland Pkwy.
Las Vegas, NV 89154
(702) 739-0852

New Hampshire

University of New Hampshire*
Craig Seymour, State Dir.
Small Business Development Center
McConnell Hall
Durham, NH 03824
(603) 862-3558

University of New Hampshire at Manchester
Jeffrey Donohoe, Dir.
Small Business Development Center
Hackett Hill Rd.
Manchester, NH 03102
(603) 668-0700

Seacoast Regional Small Business Development Center
Michele Sweet, Dir.
58 Main St., Ste. 4
Durham, NH 03824
(603) 868-6367

Keene State College
David LaMar, Dir.
Small Business Development Center
Keene, NH 03431
(603) 352-1909

Plymouth State College
Tom Fitzpatrick, Dir.
Small Business Development Center
Hyde Hall

Plymouth, NH 03264
(603) 536-1550

New Jersey

Rutgers University
Adele Kaplan, State Dir.
Russell Mass, Associate Dir.
Small Business Development Center of New Jersey
Third Floor, Ackerson Hall
180 University St.
Newark, NJ 07102
(201) 648-5950

Rutgers University at Newark*
Mr. Lee Merrel, Dir.
Small Business Development Center
Third Floor, Ackerson Hall
180 University St.
Newark, NJ 07102
(201) 648-5950

Atlantic Community College
Barry Kramer, Dir.
Small Business Development Center
1535 Bacharach Blvd.
Atlantic City, NJ 08401
(609) 347-3707

Brookdale Community College
Business/Management Team
Larry Novick, Dir.
Small Business Development Center
Newman Springs Rd.
Lincroft, NJ 07738
(201) 842-1900, ext. 551

Mercer County Community College
Richard Walsh, Dir.
Small Business Development and Management Training Center
1200 Old Trenton Rd.
Trenton, NJ 08690
(609) 586-4800, ext. 278

Rutgers University at Camden
J. Fredrick Ekstrom, Dir.
Small Business Development Center
311 N. Fifth St.
Camden, NJ 08102
(609) 757-6221

New York

State University of New York (SUNY)*
James L. King, State Dir.
Karl E. Lampson, Assistant Dir.
Small Business Development Center of New
 York (Upstate)
SUNY Central Administration S-523
SUNY Plaza
Albany, NY 12246
(518) 473-5398
(800) 732-SBDC

State University of New York
Peter George, Dir.
Small Business Development Center, Al-
 bany Region
Draper Hall, 107
135 Western Ave.
Albany, NY 12222
(518) 442-5577

State University of New York
David Patterson, Dir.
Small Business Development Center
Binghamton Region
Vestal Pkwy. East
Binghamton, NY 13901
(607) 777-4024

State University of New York
Dr. Jack C. Brueckman, Jr., Dir.
Small Business Development Center
Buffalo Region
HB 228
1300 Elmwood Ave.
Buffalo, NY 14222
(716) 878-4030

State University of New York
Stephen Hyde, Dir.
Small Business Development Center
Plattsburgh Region
Technical Assistance Center
Plattsburgh, NY 12901
(518) 564-2214

State University of New York
Wilfred Bordeau, Dir.
Small Business Development Center
Technical Assistance Center
Niagra County Community College

3111 Saunders Settlement Rd.
Sanborn, NY 14132
(716) 693-1910

State University of New York (SUNY)*
James L. King, Dir.
Karl E. Lampson, Assistant Dir.
Small Business Development Center of New
 York (Downstate)
SUNY Central Administration S-523
SUNY Plaza
Albany, NY 12246
(518) 473-5398
(800) 732-SBDC

Fashion Institute of Technology
Elaine Stone, Dir.
Small Business Development Center
227 W. 27th St.
New York, NY 10001
(212) 760-7250

Jefferson Community College
John W. Deans, Dir.
Small Business Development Center
Watertown, NY 13601
(315) 782-5250, ext. 235

State University Agricultural and Techni-
 cal College
Cleveland Johnson, Jr., Dir.
Small Business Development Center
Farmingdale, NY 11735
(516) 420-2144

Ulster County Community College
John Decker, Dir.
Small Business Development Center
Stone Ridge, NY 12484
(914) 687-0768

Westchester Community College
Elaine Sall, Dir.
Small Business Development Center
75 Grasslands Rd.
Valhalla, NY 10595
(914) 285-6659

North Carolina

University of North Carolina
Scott R. Daugherty, State Dir.
Small Business Development Center of
 North Carolina

820 Clay St.
Raleigh, NC 27605
(919) 733-4643

University of North Carolina*
Mr. Hague C. Bowman, Dir.
Small Business Development Center
Research Triangle Park Area
820 Clay St.
Raleigh, NC 27605
(919) 733-4643

Elizabeth City State University
Ulysses Bell, Dir.
Small Business Development Center
ECSU, Box 5
Elizabeth City, NC 27909
(919) 335-3247

North Carolina Agricultural and Technical University
Mr. C. B. Claiborne, Dir.
Small Business Development Center
Greensboro, NC 27411
(919) 379-7744

University of North Carolina at Greensboro
Thomas Petit, Dir.
Small Business Development Center
School of Business and Economics
Greensboro, NC 27412
(919) 379-5482

Western Carolina University
Thomas E. McClure, Dir.
Small Business Development Center
Center for Improving Mountain Living
Cullowhee, NC 28723
(704) 227-7492

Winston-Salem State University
David Carroll, Dir.
Small Business Development Center
P.O. Box 13025
Winston-Salem, NC 27110
(919) 761-2164

North Dakota

University of North Dakota*
Tom Rausch, State Dir.
Small Business Development Center

College of Business and Public Administration
Grand Forks, ND 58202
(701) 777-2224

Ohio

Ohio Department of Development*
Holly I. Schick, State Dir.
Small Business Development Center
30 E. Broad St.
P.O. Box 1001
Columbus, OH 43215
(614) 466-4945

Akron Regional Development Board
Charles Smith, Dir.
Small Business Development Center
One Cascade Plaza, 8th Floor
Akron, OH 44308
(216) 379-3167

Columbus Area Chamber of Commerce
Burton Schildhouse, Co Dir.
Karl E. Case, Co-Dir.
Small Business Development Center
37 N. High St.
Columbus, OH 43216
(614) 221-1321

Dayton Area Chamber of Commerce
Deborah S. Cahill, Dir.
Small Business Development Center
1980 Kettering Tower
Dayton, OH 45423
(513) 226-8230

Greater Cleveland Growth Association
Carol Rivchun, Dir.
Small Business Development Center
690 Huntington Bldg.
Cleveland, OH 44115
(216) 621-3300

Innovation Center
John Schanzenbach, Dir.
Southeastern Ohio Small Business Development Center
One President St.
Athens, OH 45701
(614) 594-5791

Toledo Area Chamber of Commerce
Joseph D. Kelly, Dir.

Small Business Development Center
218 N. Huron St.
Toledo, OH 43604
(419) 243-8191

Oklahoma

Southeastern Oklahoma State University*
Lloyd Miller, State Dir.
Small Business Development Center
Station A, P.O. Box 4194
Durant, OK 74701
(405) 924-0277

Central State University
Dr. Herbert O. Giles, Dir.
Small Business Development Center
100 N. University Dr.
Edmond, OK 73034
(405) 341-2980, ext. 2836, 2423

East Central University
Tom Beebe, Dir.
Small Business Development Center
1036 E. Tenth
Ada, OK 74820
(405) 436-3190

Northeastern State University
Edward Polivka, Dir.
Small Business Development Center
Tahlequah, OK 74464
(918) 456-5511, ext. 3086

Northwestern Oklahoma State University
Dr. J. Randall Kilbourne, Dir.
Small Business Development Center
Alva, OK 73717
(405) 327-1700, ext. 318

Southwestern Oklahoma State University
Dr. Clint Roush, Dir.
Small Business Development Center
100 Campus Dr.
Weatherford, OK 73096
(405) 772-6611, ext. 3050

Oregon

Lane Community College
Mr. Sandy Cutler, State Dir.
Small Business Development Center of Oregon
Downtown Center
1059 Willamette St.

Eugene, OR 97401
(503) 726-2250

Lane Community College*
Charles Reich, Dir.
Small Business Development Center
1059 Willamette St.
Eugene, OR 97401
(503) 726-2255

Blue Mountain Community College
Tom Hampson, Dir.
Small Business Development Center
37 S.E. Dorian
Pendleton, OR 97801
(503) 276-6233

Central Oregon Community College
Reese Shepard, Dir.
Small Business Development Center
2600 N.W. College Way
Bend, OR 97701
(503) 382-6112, ext. 237

Chemeketa Community College
Ken Atwell, Dir.
Small Business Development Center
4000 Lancaster Dr., N.E.
P.O. Box 14007
Salem, OR 97309
(503) 399-5181

Clackamas Community College
Bruce Borquist, Dir.
Small Business Development Center
108 Eighth St.
Oregon City, OR 97045
(503) 656-4447

Clatstop Community College
Dianne Jackson, Dir.
Small Business Development Center
1240 S. Holladay
Seaside, OR 97108
(503) 738-3347

Eastern Oregon State College
Sally Snyder, Dir.
Small Business Development Center
Regional Services Institute
LaGrande, OR 97850
(503) 963-1551
(800) 452-8639, ext. 1551

Innovation Institute†
Gerald Udell, Dir.
Small Business Development Center
2265 Shields Ave.
Eugene, OR 97405
(503) 484-0260

Linn-Benton Community College
Mary Spilde, Dir.
Small Business Development Center
6500 S.W. Pacific Blvd.
Albany, OR 97321
(503) 967-6112

Mount Hood Community College
Mike Dillon, Dir.
Small Business Development Center
26000 S.E. Stark St.
Gresham, OR 97030
(503) 667-7658

Oregon Institute of Technology
John Ward, Dir.
Small Business Development Center
Klamath Falls, OR 97601
(503) 883-7556
(503) 883-7562

Portland Community College
Bill MacDonald, Dir.
Small Business Development Center
705 N. Killingsworth
Portland, OR 97217
(503) 283-2541, ext. 428

Portland Metro International Trade Center†
John Dier, Dir.
Small Business Development Center
26000 S.E. Stark St.
Gresham, OR 97030
(503) 667-7658

Rouge Community College
Mr. Lee Merritt, Dir.
Small Business Development Center
350 S.W. H St.
Grants Pass, OR 97526
(503) 772-3478

Southern Oregon State College/Ashland
Cynthia Ford, Dir.
Small Business Development Center
Regional Service Institute

Ashland, OR 97520
(503) 482-5838

Southern Oregon State College/Medford
Jon Trivers, Dir.
Small Business Development Center
Regional Service Institute
229 N. Bartlett
Medford, OR 97501
(503) 772-3478

Southwestern Oregon Community College
John Qualley, Dir.
Small Business Development Center
1988 New Market St.
Coos Bay, OR 97420
(503) 888-2525, ext. 259

Tillamook Bay Community College
Jim O'Donnell, Dir.
Small Business Development Center
401 B Main St.
Bay City, OR 97141
(503) 842-2551

Treasure Valley Community College
Christine Krygier, Dir.
Small Business Development Center
173 S.W. First St.
Ontario, OR 97914
(503) 889-2617

Treaty Oaks Community College
Bob Cole, Dir.
Small Business Development Center
404 W. Second St.
The Dalles, OR 97058
(503) 296-2231

Umpqua Community College
Mr. Terry Swagerty, Dir.
Small Business Development Center
744 S.E. Rose
Roseburg, OR 97470
(503) 672-3679

Willamette Valley World Trade Center†
Shary Sahr, Dir.
Small Business Development Center
Eugene Area Chamber of Commerce
1401 Willamette St.
Eugene, OR 97401
(503) 484-1314

Pennsylvania

University of Pennsylvania*
Susan Garber, State Dir.
Small Business Development Center of Pennsylvania
The Wharton School
3201 Steinberg Hall-Dietrich Hall/CC
Philadelphia, PA 19104
(215) 898-1219

Bucknell University
Charles Coder, Dir.
Small Business Development Center
109 Dana Engineering Bldg.
Lewisburg, PA 17837
(717) 524-1249

Clarion University of Pennsylvania
Dr. Woodrow Yeaney, Dir.
Small Business Development Center
Dana Still Bldg.
Clarion, PA 16214
(814) 226-2626

Duquesne University
Small Business Development Center
Rockwell Hall, Rm. 10 Concourse
600 Forbes Ave.
Pittsburgh, PA 15282
(412) 434-6231

Gannon University
Dr. Norris H. Barbre, Dir.
Small Business Development Center
Carlisle Bldg., 3d Floor
Erie, PA 16541
(814) 871-7370

LaSalle University
Dr. Bernard Goldner, Dir.
Small Business Development Center
Benilde Hall 111
20th & Olney Sts.
Philadelphia, PA 19141
(215) 951-1416

Lehigh University
Edith Ritter, Dir.
Small Business Development Center
412 S. New St. #203
Bethlehem, PA 18015
(215) 861-3980

Pennsylvania State University
Dr. David Watkin, Dir.
Small Business Development Center
Capitol Campus
Crags Bldg., Rte. 230
Middletown, PA 17057
(717) 948-6031

St. Francis College
David D'Arcangelo, Dir.
Small Business Development Center
Loretto, PA 15940
(814) 472-7000, ext. 401

University of Scranton
Jerome F. McCormack, Dir.
Small Business Development Center
O'Hara Hall
Scranton, PA 18510
(717) 961-7588

Temple University
Dr. George J. Titus, Dir.
Small Business Development Center
Ritter Hall Annex-004-00, Rm. 481
Philadelphia, PA 19122
(215) 787-7282

University of Pennsylvania
William M. Madway, Dir.
Small Business Development Center
The Wharton School
University City Science Center
3440 Market St., Ste. 202/TD
Philadelphia, PA 19104
(215) 898-4861

University of Pittsburgh
Clarence K. Curry, Dir.
Small Business Development Center
Rm. 372 Mervis
Pittsburgh, PA 15260
(412) 624-6435

Wilkes College
Frederick A. Lohman, Dir.
Small Business Development Center
Ross Hall
251 S. River St.
Wilkes-Barre, PA 18766
(717) 824-4651, ext. 222

Puerto Rico

University of Puerto Rico*
Jose M. Romaguera, Commonwealth Dir.
Juan Cubeles, Dir.
Small Business Development Center
College Station, Bldg. B
Mayaguez, PR 00708
(809) 834-3590/3790

    University of Puerto Rico
    Otto Riollano, Dir.
    Small Business Development Center
    College Station
    Rio Piedras, PR 00936
    (809) 763-5880/5933

Rhode Island

Bryant College*
Douglas Jobling, State Dir.
Small Business Development Center
Douglas Pike, Rte. 7
Smithfield, RI 02917
(401) 232-6111

Opportunities Industrialization Center
Ms. Jackie Johnson, Acting Dir.
Small Business Development Center
One Hilton St.
South Providence, RI 02905
(401) 272-4400

    Providence Downtown Small Business Development Center
    Margie Edwards, Dir.
    270 Weybosset St.
    Providence, RI 02903
    (401) 831-1330

    University of Rhode Island
    Sue Barker, Dir.
    Small Business Development Center
    Ballantine Hall
    Kingston, RI 02881
    (401) 792-2451

South Carolina

University of South Carolina
Mr. W. F. Littlejohn, State Dir.
Small Business Development Center of South
    Carolina
College of Business Administration

Columbia, SC 29208
(803) 777-4907

University of South Carolina*
Mr. Casey Blonaisz, Dir.
Small Business Development Center
College of Business Administration
Columbia, SC 29208
(803) 777-5118

    College of Charleston
    Joseph Ksenzak, Mgr.
    Small Business Development Center
    Department of Business and Economics
    4 Green Way
    Charleston, SC 29424
    (803) 792-3167

Beaufort Technical Institute
W. Russell Studenmund, Mgr.
Small Business Development Center
Ribaut Rd.
P.O. Box 1288
Beaufort, SC 29902
(803) 524-3380, ext. 258

Clemson University
Mr. Pat Cunningham, Dir.
Small Business Development Center
College of Commerce and Industry
Sirrine Hall
Clemson, SC 29631
(803) 656-3227

    Greenville City Hall
    John Bickley, Mgr.
    Small Business Development Center
    P.O. Box 2207
    Greenville, SC 29602
    (803) 271-4259

    Lander College
    David Taylor, Mgr.
    Small Business Development Center
    P.O. Box 6143
    Greenwood, SC 29646
    (803) 227-6110

    University of South Carolina at Spartanburg
    DeDe Cargill, Mgr.
    Small Business Development Center
    Media Bldg., Rm. 157

Spartanburg, SC 29303
(803) 578-6233

South Carolina State College
Jerry Govan, Dir.
Small Business Development Center
School of Business Administration
Orangeburg, SC 29117
(803) 534-6894

Winthrop College
Larry Durham, Dir.
Small Business Development Center
School of Business Administration
119 Thurman Bldg.
Rock Hill, SC 29733
(803) 323-2283

    Coastal Carolina College
    Jack Shutters, Mgr.
    Small Business Development Center
    School of Business Administration
    Conway, SC 29526
    (803) 347-3161

    Florence Darlington Technical College
    Daniel Dubose, Mgr.
    Small Business Development Center
    Box F-8000
    Florence, SC 29501
    (803) 662-8151, ext. 249

South Dakota

University of South Dakota
Donald Greenfield, State Dir.
Small Business Development Center of South
    Dakota
Business Research Bureau
School of Business
Vermillion, SD 57069
(605) 677-5272

University of South Dakota*
Anne Shank-Bolk, Dir.
Small Business Development Center
Business Research Bureau
School of Business
Vermillion, SD 57069
(605) 677-5279

    Aberdeen Community College
    Small Business Development Center
    516 S. Main

Aberdeen, SD 57401
(605) 225-2860

Rapid City Small Business Development
    Center
Ann Wainwright, Dir.
444 Mount Rushmore Rd., North
Rapid City, SD 57709
(605) 343-1744

University of South Dakota
Small Business Development Center
124 First Ave., N.W.
Watertown, SD 57201
(605) 352-4753

Tennessee

Memphis State University
Dr. Leonard Rosser, State Dir.
Small Business Development Center of
    Tennessee
Fogelman College of Business and Econom-
    ics
Memphis, TN 38152
(901) 454-2500

Memphis State University*
Edgar R. Cole, Regional Dir.
Small Business Development Center
Fogelman College of Business and Econom-
    ics
Memphis, TN 38152
(901) 454-2500

    Dyersburg State Community College
    Dr. Janet Smith, Dir.
    Small Business Development Center
    P.O. Box 648
    Dyersburg, TN 38024
    (901) 285-6910

    East Tennessee State University
    Dr. Don Wilkinson, Dir.
    Small Business Development Center
    College of Business
    P.O. Box 23470A
    Johnson City, TN 37614-0002
    (615) 929-5630

    Middle Tennessee State University
    Dr. Ron Moser, Dir.
    Small Business Development Center
    School of Business

P.O. Box 487
Murfreesboro, TN 37132
(615) 898-2745, ext. 2745

Motlow State Community College
Dr. Carr McCalla, Dir.
Small Business Development Center
Tullahoma, TN 37388
(615) 455-8511

State Technical Institute at Knoxville
Dr. Michael L. Hudson, Dir.
Small Business Development Center
P.O. Box 19802
Knoxville, TN 37919
(615) 584-6103

State Technical Institute at Memphis
Dr. James E. Golden, Dir.
Small Business Development Center
5983 Macon Cove
Memphis, TN 38134
(901) 377-4177

Tennessee State University
Dr. Millicent Lownes, Dir.
Small Business Development Center
School of Business
10th & Charlotte Ave.
Nashville, TN 37203
(615) 251-1505

Tennessee Technological University
Dr. Robert R. Bell, Dir.
Small Business Development Center
College of Business Administration
P.O. Box 5023
Cookeville, TN 38505
(615) 528-3371

University of Tennessee at Martin
Dr. Carl Savage, Dir.
Small Business Development Center
School of Business Administration
Martin, TN 38238
(901) 587-7236

Walters State Community College
Dr. James M. Coburn, Dir.
Small Business Development Center
500 S. Davy Crockett Pkwy.
Morristown, TN 38713-6899
(615) 581-2121

Texas

University of Houston*
Dr. Jon P. Goodman, State Dir.
Small Business Development Center
University Park
127 Heyne
4800 Calhoun
Houston, TX 77004
(713) 749-4236

North Harris County College
John Stefeck, Dir.
Small Business Development Center
East Campus
20000 Kingwood Dr.
Kingwood, TX 77339
(713) 359-1624

Utah

Small Business Development Center of Utah
Mr. Kumen Davis, State Dir.
University of Utah
420 Chipeta Way, Ste. 110
Salt Lake City, UT 84108
(801) 581-4869

University of Utah*
James E. Bean, Dir.
Small Business Development Center
Rm. 410 BUC
Graduate School of Business
Salt Lake City, UT 84108
(801) 581-7905

Brigham Young University
Dr. Warner Woodworth, Dir.
Small Business Development Center
784 Tanner Bldg.
Provo, UT 84602
(801) 378-6832

College of Eastern Utah
Ms. Boni Nichols, Dir.
Small Business Development Center
Applied Sciences
451 East, 400 North
Price, UT 84501
(801) 637-1995

Southern Utah State College
Dr. Harold Hiskey, Dir.

Small Business Development Center
Department of Business
Cedar City, UT 84720
(801) 586-5401

Utah State University
Frank Prante, Dir.
Small Business Development Center
Department of Business Administration
UMC 35
Logan, UT 84322
(801) 750-2283

Weber State College
Dr. Gordon Jaycox, Dir.
Small Business Development Center
3750 S. Harrison
Ogden, UT 84403
(801) 626-6070

Vermont

University of Vermont*
Extension Service
Mr. Norris Elliott, State Dir.
Small Business Development
Morrill Hall
Burlington, VT 05405
(802) 656-4479

Chittenden County
Frederick Rice, Specialist
Northwestern Small Business Develop-
ment Center
University of Vermont Extension Office
Winooski, VT 05404
(802) 656-4420

Rutland County
Linda Aines, Specialist
Southwestern Small Business Develop-
ment Center
University of Vermont Extension Office
Rutland, VT 05701
(802) 773-3349

Calendonia County
Stephen Brown, Specialist
Northeastern Small Business Develop-
ment Center
University of Vermont Extension Office
St. Johnsbury, VT 05819
(802) 748-8177

Washington County
Barry Stryker, Specialist
Central Small Business Development Cen-
ter
University of Vermont Extension Office
Montpelier, VT 05602
(802) 223-2389

Windham County
Robert Townsend, Specialist
Southeastern Small Business Development
Center
University of Vermont Extension Office
Brattleboro, VT 05301
(802) 257-7967

Virgin Islands

College of the Virgin Islands*
Dr. Solomon S. Kabuka, Dir.
Small Business Development Center
P.O. Box 1087
Charlotte Amalie, St. Thomas, VI 00802
(809) 776-3206

St. Croix Chamber of Commerce
Waldemar Hill, Dir.
Small Business Development Center
Christianstad, St. Croix, VI 00820
(809) 773-1435

Washington

Washington State University*
Lyle M. Anderson, Acting State Dir.
Small Business Development Center
441 Todd Hall
Pullman, WA 99164-4740
(509) 335-1576

Community Colleges of Spokane
Mr. Leigh Hales, Dir.
Small Business Development Center
W. 1500 Fourth Ave., Ste. 150
Spokane, WA 99204
(509) 456-2781

Columbia River Economic Development
Council
Jacquie Collier, Dir.
Small Business Development Center
404 E. 15th St.
Vancouver, WA 98663
(206) 694-2190

Edmonds Community College
Jack Wicks, Dir.
Small Business Development Center
917 134th St., S.W.
Everett, WA 98204
(206) 745-0430

Small Business Development Center
Neal Miller, Dir.
Olympia Branch Office
1000 Plum St.
P.O. Box 1427
Olympia, WA 98507
(206) 753-5616

Small Business Development Center
William Jacobs, Dir.
Seattle Branch Office
180 Nickerson, Ste. 310
Seattle, WA 98109
(206) 464-5450

Small Business Development Center
Marvin Carlson, Dir.
Tacoma Branch Office
735 St. Helens Ave.
Tacoma, WA 98402
(206) 272-7232

Small Business Development Center
Earl True, Dir.
Yakima Branch Office
303 E. D St., Ste. 2
Yakima, WA 98901
(509) 575-2284

Western Washington University
Max King, Dir.
Small Business Development Center
College of Business
Bellingham, WA 98226
(206) 676-3899

Wisconsin

University of Wisconsin
Dr. Robert Pricer, State Dir.
Dr. William Bernhagen, Assistant Dir.
Dr. Wesley Mott, Information Specialist
Small Business Development Center of Wisconsin
602 State St., 2d Floor
Madison, WI 53703
(608) 263-7766/1662/7830

University of Wisconsin*
Bill Pinkovitz, Dir.
Small Business Development Center
602 State St., 2d Floor
Madison, WI 53703
(608) 263-2221

University of Wisconsin at Eau Claire
Jim Webb, Dir.
Small Business Development Center
Schneider Hall, #113
Eau Claire, WI 54701
(715) 836-5811

University of Wisconsin at Green Bay
Larry Kostroski, Dir.
Small Business Development Center
Library Learning Center, Rm. 710
Green Bay, WI 54302
(414) 465-2167

University of Wisconsin at La Crosse
Dr. A. William Pollman, Dir.
Small Business Development Center
School of Business Administration
La Crosse, WI 54601
(608) 785-8782

University of Wisconsin at Milwaukee
Jerry White, Dir.
Small Business Development Center
929 N. Sixth St.
Milwaukee, WI 53226
(414) 224-4758

University of Wisconsin at Oshkosh
John Mozingo, Dir.
Small Business Development Center
Clow Faculty Bldg., Rm. 107
Oshkosh, WI 54901
(414) 424-1541

University of Wisconsin at Parkside
Bill Hughes, Dir.
Small Business Development Center
Molinaro Bldg., Rm. 344
Kenosha, WI 53141
(414) 553-2047

University of Wisconsin at Stevens Point
George Seyfarth, Dir.
Small Business Development Center
Rm. 452

Stevens Point, WI 54481
(715) 346-2004

University of Wisconsin/Stout†
John Entorf, Dir.
Small Business Development Center
Center for Innovation and Development
Menomonie, WI 54751
(715) 232-1252

University of Wisconsin at Superior
Ms. Tuula Harris, Dir.
Small Business Development Center
1800 Grand Ave.
Superior, WI 54880
(715) 394-8351

University of Wisconsin at Whitewater
Dr. John Farah, Dir.
Small Business Development Center
4133 Carlson
Whitewater, WI 53190
(414) 472-3217

Wyoming

Casper Community College*
Mac C. Bryant, State Dir.

Small Business Development Center of Wyoming
125 College Dr.
Casper, WY 82601
(307) 235-4825

Casper Community College
Steve Elledge, Dir.
Small Business Development Center
944 E. Second St.
Casper, WY 82601
(307) 235-4827

Northwest Community College
Lloyd Snyder, Dir.
Small Business Development Center
146 S. Bent #103
Powell, WY 82435
(307) 754-3746

Sheridan College
Robert Palmer, Dir.
Small Business Development Center
720 W. Eighth
Gillette, WY 82716
(307) 686-0297

Small Business Innovation Research Program

President Reagan has signed a bill that will extend the life of the Small Business Innovation Research (SBIR) program (originally scheduled to expire in October 1988) through FY 1993. The SBIR program was created by the Small Business Innovation Development Act of 1982, which requires federal agencies with R&D budgets of $100 million or more to set aside 1.25 percent of those funds for small businesses through the SBIR program. The purpose of the program is to stimulate technological innovation by encouraging small science- and technology-based firms to participate in government-funded research. In addition, the SBIR program provides incentives for converting research results into commercial applications.

The program provides funding and technical assistance for research and product-development stages, as well as assistance in obtaining private-sector financing in the commercialization stage. Businesses of 500 or fewer employees that are organized for profit are eligible to compete for SBIR funding.

The following agencies participate in the SBIR program:

Department of Agriculture, Tel.: (202) 475-5022
Department of Commerce, Tel.: (202) 477-1472
Department of Defense, Tel.: (202) 697-9838
Department of Education, Tel.: (202) 254-8247
Department of Energy, Tel.: (202) 353-5867
Department of Interior, Tel.: (202) 634-4704
Department of Health and Human Services, Tel.: (202) 245-7300
Department of Transportation, Tel.: (617) 494-2051
Environmental Protection Agency, Tel.: (202) 382-7445
NASA, Tel.: (202) 357-7527
National Science Foundation, Tel.: (202) 257-7527
Nuclear Regulatory Commission, Tel.: (301) 427-4250

SBA can provide comprehensive information on the SBIR program.
Office of Innovation Research and Technology
Small Business Administration
1441 L St., N.W., Rm. 500-A
Washington, DC 20416
(202) 653-6458

Especially active in the Small Business Innovation Research Act, the Small Business High-Technology Institute is a political group founded by Milton Stewart, an old friend of small business, to promote high-technology among entrepreneurs.

Milton Stewart
Small Business High-Technology Institute
3300 N. Central Ave., Ste. 1740
Phoenix, AZ 85012
(602) 277-6603

The Innovation Development Institute publishes a useful newsletter on the SBIR program.

Ann Eskarean
Innovation Development Institute
45 Beach Bluff, Ste. 300
Swampscott, MA 01907
(617) 595-2920

LEADER OF THE PACK

I'm going to tell a story. It's a personal story, and it might help explain why entrepreneurs think and act the way they do.

It all begins with my poor eyesight, which had been 20/500 in each eye since I was a boy. I had gone through life wearing cumbersome glasses until recently, when I heard about a new, experimental surgery that corrects myopia. The technique is called radial keratotomy, and it was developed accidentally ten years ago. A nearsighted Russian suffered a superficial cut on the cornea of his eye. When the cut healed, he found that his myopia had disappeared. The cut had flattened the cornea, the outer layer of the eye, enough to correct the imperfection that caused his nearsightedness.

The Soviets have since developed a technique for making incisions in the cornea to surgically correct those imperfections. The operation has no long-term side effects, but it leaves the patient's eyes tender for a few days. In the Soviet Union, this technique is quite common, but in the United States, surgeons consider such surgery far from routine.

As soon as I heard about radial keratotomy, it appealed to me. I actually enjoyed the fact that few people in this country had tried it. So I decided to sign up for the surgery and rid myself of my thick glasses once and for all. After the operation, my vision improved immediately to 20/60, and after only a quick "touch-up" session a month later, my vision was at last perfect.

It was only then that I thought about how quickly and eagerly I had signed up for the surgery, and I realized I had just gained a valuable insight into the mind-set of an entrepreneur. It's my entrepreneurial nature to *seek out* what's new and different. Entrepreneurs, I realized, have a passionate and inexplicable need to be first in everything we do—in both our professional and our personal lives. That's why we forge ahead into new business ventures against unbelievable odds. And that's why entrepreneurs are more than willing to undergo risky medical procedures.

A Penchant for the Bizarre

A publisher I met through my CEO club recently heard of a bizarre new method for reducing weight. He was more than a little pudgy, so the news piqued his interest. In this procedure, a doctor inserts a balloon into a person's stomach and inflates it. The balloon, of course, takes up a great deal of space and fools the stomach into thinking that it's full. Consequently, the person eats less and loses weight quickly. After four months, the balloon is deflated and removed from the person's stomach. The publisher flew to California to have the balloon inserted. His bill for the entire procedure was $3,000.

This drive to be first often turns entrepreneurs into gadget freaks as well as guinea pigs: We want to be ahead of everyone else when it comes to owning the latest high-tech device. For example, entrepreneurs were among the first to buy microwave ovens and color television sets. We want that new gadget, it seems, just for the sake of having it. The publisher who opted for the balloon procedure owns cellular telephones, satellite dishes, and hosts of video peripherals. He has also fallen in love with the new laser printers that are used with personal computers.

This love of gadgetry sometimes leads to new businesses. Portia Isaacson, founder of Future Computing in Dallas, Tex., recently wired her whole house to her computer just for fun. She regulates the water temperature in her pool, operates her audio system, and turns her lights on and off via computer. In fact, she is about to market the system to a small number of very wealthy people who, she says, would pay almost anything to have their houses automated.

My own story has an entrepreneurial twist to it too, although it certainly won't lead to any new businesses. Because radial keratotomy is considered "experimental" in the United States, Blue Cross, my health insurance company, would not cover the cost of the operation. That seemed unfair, so I sued the company in small claims court, on the grounds that the surgery wasn't as experimental as Blue Cross maintained. In fact, I took Blue Cross to court twice—once for each eye—and won the full price of the operation: $3,000. That's what I call a good return on my investment.

PARTICIPATING AGENCY SBIR REPRESENTATIVES

A list of SBA's Office of Innovations, Research, and Technology agencies follows.

Department of Energy
Gerry Washington
c/o SBIR Program Mgr.
Washington, DC 20545
(301) 353-5867

Department of Health and Human
  Services
Richard Clinkscales
Director, OSDBU
Office of the Secretary

Washington, DC 20201
(202) 245-7300

Department of Transportation
Dr. George Kovatch
Chief, University Research and Technology
  Innovation Office (DTS-23)
Transportation Systems Center
Kendall Sq.
Cambridge, MA 02142
(617) 494-2051

Environmental Protection
  Agency
Walter H. Preston
SBIR Program Mgr.
Research Grants Staff (RD-675)
Office of Research and Development
401 M St., S.W.
Washington, DC 20460
(202) 382-7445

National Aeronautics and Space Administration
Harry Johnson
Director, SBIR Office, Code IR
600 Independence Ave., S.W.

Washington, DC 20546
(202) 453-1502

National Science Foundation
Roland Tibbetts
Ritchie Coryell
SBIR Program Mgrs.
1800 G St., N.W.
Washington, DC 20550
(202) 357-7527

Nuclear Regulatory Commission
William Forehand
SBIR Program Mgr.
Washington, DC 20555
(301) 443-7679

HOW TO OBTAIN THE SBIR PROPOSAL PREPARATION PAMPHLET

To assist small business concerns planning to participate in the SBIR program with
their selection of projects and preparation of proposals, SBA has published a pamphlet titled *Proposal Preparation for Small Business Innovation Research (SBIR)* (SBIR
T1). Copies of this pamphlet may be obtained from the following SBA regional
offices.

Boston Regional Office
60 Batterymarch, 10th Floor
Boston, MA 02110

New York Regional Office
26 Federal Plaza, Rm. 29-118
New York, NY 10278

Philadelphia Regional Office
231 St. Asaphs Rd., Ste. 640-W
Bala Cynwyd, PA 19004

Atlanta Regional Office
1375 Peachtree St., N.E., 5th Floor
Atlanta, GA 30367-8102

Chicago Regional Office
230 S. Dearborn St., Rms. 510, 440
Chicago, IL 60604

Dallas Regional Office
8625 King George Dr., Bldg. C
Dallas, TX 75235-3391

Kansas City Regional Office
911 Walnut St., 13th Floor
Kansas City, MO 64106

Denver Regional Office
1405 Curtis St., 22d Floor
Denver, CO 80202-2395

San Francisco Regional Office
450 Golden Gate Ave.
San Francisco, CA 94102

Seattle Regional Office
2615 Fourth Ave.
Seattle, WA 98121

Small Business Investment Companies

This chapter contains a directory of Small Business Investment Companies (SBICs) that have received licenses from SBA; their licenses remain outstanding. Currently licensed SBICs in the process of surrendering their licenses or subject to legal proceedings that may terminate their licenses are not listed. Appearance on this list should not be interpreted as an approval of a company's operations, as a recommendation by SBA, or as an endorsement of the relative merits, as investment companies or otherwise, of the listed licensees.

The directory is composed of two parts: Part I lists SBICs; part II lists 301(d) SBICs, which assist small businesses owned by socially or economically disadvantaged persons. SBICs are listed alphabetically by state.

PART I: SBIC LICENSEES

Licensee	License No.	Private Capital	SBA Leverage	Investment Policy	Owner Code*
Alabama					
First SBIC of Alabama David Delaney, Pres. 16 Midtown Park, East Mobile, AL 36606 (205) 476-0700	04/04-0143	2,166,700	6,500,000	Diversified	5
Date Lic.:	07/20/78				
Hickory Venture Capital Corp. J. Thomas Noojin, Pres. 699 Gallatin St., Ste. A-2 Huntsville, AL 35801 (205) 539-1931	04/04-0235	8,000,000	0	Diversified	1
Date Lic.:	03/28/85				
The Remington Fund, Inc. Lana Sellers, Pres. 1927 First Ave. North	04/04-0238	1,500,100	0	Diversified	5

*Owner Code: 1, bank dominated (50 percent or more owned by bank or bank holding company); 2, bank associated (10 percent to 49 percent owned by bank or bank holding company); 3, financial organization other than bank or bank holding company (public or nonpublic); 4, nonfinancial organization (public or nonpublic); 5, individually owned (privately held); 6, 40′ act company. An owner code followed by "P" signifies partnership.

Licensee	License No.	Private Capital	SBA Leverage	Investment Policy	Owner Code*
Birmingham, AL 35202 (205) 324-7709 Date Lic.:	05/16/86				
Alaska Alaska Business Investment Corp. James Cloud, V.P. 301 W. Northern Lights Blvd. Anchorage, AK 99510 (907) 278-2071 Date Lic.:	10/10-0180 12/10/82	2,500,000	0	Diversified	1
Arizona FBS SBIC, Ltd. Partnership William B. McKee, Pres. 6900 E. Camelback Rd. Scottsdale, AZ 85251 (602) 941-2638 Date Lic.:	09/09-0345 09/27/84	3,000,000	0	Diversified	1-P
Rocky Mountain Equity Corp. Anthony J. Nicoli, Pres. 4530 Central Ave. Phoenix, AZ 85012 (602) 274-7534 Date Lic.:	09/09-0289 09/22/81	600,000	500,000	Diversified	5
VNB Capital Corp. Nathan C. Collins, Pres. 241 N. Central Ave. Phoenix, AZ 85073 (602) 261-1577 Date Lic.:	09/09-0337 04/04/84	15,000,000	0	Diversified	1
Arkansas First SBIC of Arkansas, Inc. Fred Burns, Pres. Worthen Bank Bldg., Fifth Floor	06/06-0182	587,759	0	Diversified	1

Licensee	License No.	Private Capital	SBA Leverage	Investment Policy	Owner Code*
Little Rock, AR 72201 (501) 378-1508 Date Lic.:	09/07/76				
Independence Financial Services, Inc. Jeffrey Hance, Gen. Mgr. Town Plaza Office Park P.O. Box 3878 Batesville, AR 72501 (501) 793-4533 Date Lic.:	06/06-0257 10/26/82	500,100	500,000	Diversified	5
Small Business Investment Capital, Inc. Charles E. Toland, Pres. 10003 New Benton Hwy. P.O. Box 3627 Little Rock, AR 72203 (501) 455-3590 Date Lic.:	06/06-0175 03/06/75	1,150,000	3,250,000	Grocery Stores	4
California AMF Financial, Inc. William Temple, V.P. 9910-D Mira Mesa Blvd. San Diego, CA 92123 (619) 695-0233 Date Lic.:	09/09-0302 10/26/82	500,000	0	Diversified	5
Atlanta Investment Co., Inc. 141 El Camino Dr. Beverly Hills, CA 90212 (213) 273-1730 (See listing under New York for full information.)					
BNP Venture Capital Corp.	09/09-0348	1,550,000	0	Diversified	1

Licensee	License No.	Private Capital	SBA Leverage	Investment Policy	Owner Code*
Edgerton Scott II, Pres. 3000 Sand Hill Rd. Bldg. 1, Ste. 125 Menlo Park, CA 94025 (414) 854-1084 Date Lic.:	10/12/84				
Bancorp Venture Capital, Inc. Paul R. Blair, Pres. 2082 Michelson Dr., Ste. 302 Irvine, CA 92715 (714) 752-7220 Date Lic.:	09/09-0335 05/04/84	2,250,000	2,250,000	Diversified	1
BankAmerica Ventures, Inc. Patrick Topolski, Pres. 555 California St. San Francisco, CA 94104 (415) 953-3001 Date Lic.:	09/12-0007 11/12/59	22,500,000	0		1
Bay Venture Group William R. Chandler, G.P. 1 Embarcadero Center, Ste. 3303 San Francisco, CA 94111 (415) 989-7680 Date Lic.:	09/09-0287 04/30/81	1,463,382	2,500,000	Diversified	5-P
Brentwood Capital Corp. T. M. Pennington, Chairman 11661 San Vincente Blvd. Los Angeles, CA 90049 (213) 826-6581 Date Lic.:	09/09-0239 03/19/79	4,661,010	11,500,000	Diversified	3
CFB Venture Capital Corp.	09/09-0319	1,000,000	0	Diversified	1

Licensee	License No.	Private Capital	SBA Leverage	Investment Policy	Owner Code*
Pieter Westerbeek III, Chief Financial Officer 530 B. St., Third Floor San Diego, CA 92101 (619) 230-3304 Date Lic.: or 350 California St., Mezzanine San Francisco, CA 94104 (415) 445-0594	08/03/83				
California Capital Investors, Ltd. Arthur H. Bernstein, Managing G.P. 11812 San Vincente Blvd. Los Angeles, CA 90049 (213) 820-7222 Date Lic.:	09/09-0292 09/25/81	2,505,895	4,000,000	Diversified	5-P
California Partners Draper Assoc. Corporate General Partner Bill Edwards, Pres. c/o Timothy C. Draper 3000 Sand Hill Rd., Bldg. 4, #210 Menlo Park, CA 94025 (415) 493-5600 Date Lic.:	09/09-0242 09/12/79	2,015,000	2,000,000	Diversified	5-P
Camden Investments, Inc. Edward G. Victor, Pres. 9560 Wilshire Blvd., Ste. 310 Los Angeles, CA 90212 (213) 281-3995 Date Lic.:	09/09-0349 11/08/84	1,264,000	0	Diversified	5

Licensee	License No.	Private Capital	SBA Leverage	Investment Policy	Owner Code*
Citicorp Venture Capital, Ltd. 2 Embarcadero Pl. 2200 Geny Rd., Ste. 203 Palo Alto, CA 94303 (415) 424-8000 (See listing under New York for full information.)					
City Capital Corp. Howard Engleman, Chairman 9080 Santa Monica Blvd., Ste. 201 Los Angeles, CA 90069 (213) 273-4080 Date Lic.:	09/14-0060 06/05/62	1,000,000	0	Diversified	5
City Ventures, Inc. Warner Heineman, Vice Chairman 1880 Century Park East, Ste. 413 Los Angeles, CA 90067 (213) 550-0416 Date Lic.:	09/09-0308 06/04/82	2,000,000	0	Diversified	1
Crosspoint Investment Corp. Max Simpson, Pres. 1951 Landings Dr. Mountain View, CA 94043 (415) 968-0930 Date Lic.:	09/09-0245 09/26/79	592,000	960,000	Diversified	3
Developers Equity Capital Corp. Larry Sade, Chairman 1880 Century Park East, Ste. 311 Los Angeles, CA 90067 (213) 277-0330 Date Lic.:	09/14-0079 06/12/74	677,000	1,500,000	100% Real Estate	5

Licensee	License No.	Private Capital	SBA Leverage	Investment Policy	Owner Code*
Equis Investment Robert G. Perring, Pres. Three Embarcadero, Ste. 2560 San Francisco, CA 94111 (415) 362-4181 Date Lic.:	09/09-0353 02/12/85	1,575,000	0	Diversified	5-P
First Interstate Capital, Inc. William Sudmann, Chairman 445 S. Figueroa St., Ste. 2940 Los Angeles, CA 90071 (213) 622-1922 Date Lic.:	09/09-0224 07/05/78	9,000,000	0	Diversified	1

First SBIC of
California
Tim Hay, Pres.
650 Town Center Dr.,
17th Floor
Costa Mesa, CA 92626
(714) 556-1964
Date Lic.:
  or
155 N. Lake Ave., Ste.
1010
Pasadena, CA 91109
(818) 304-3451
  or
5 Palo Alto Sq., Ste.
938
Palo Alto, CA 94306
(415) 424-8011
	09/14-0009
	
	01/29/60
		25,000,000	0	Diversified	1

G C & H Partners James C. Gaither, G.P. One Maritime Plaza, 20th Floor San Francisco, CA 94110 (415) 981-5252 Date Lic.:	09/09-0342 04/30/84	1,216,489	300,000	Diversified	5-P

Licensee	License No.	Private Capital	SBA Leverage	Investment Policy	Owner Code*
H & R Investment Capital Co. Herman Christensen, Pres. 801 American St. San Carlos, CA 94070 (415) 365-4691 Date Lic.:	09/12-0083 12/14/62	483,000	0	66⅔% Real Estate	5
HMS Capital, Ltd. Michael Hone, Pres. 555 California St., Rm. 5070 San Francisco, CA 94109 (415) 221-1225 Date Lic.:	09/09-0301 12/06/83	1,657,000	0	Diversified	5
Hamco Capital Corp. William R. Hambrecht, Pres. 235 Montgomery St. San Francisco, CA 94104 (415) 986-6567 Date Lic.:	09/09-0300 03/01/82	3,070,000	7,000,000	Diversified	5
I.K. Capital Loans, Ltd. Iraj Kermanshahchi, Pres. 9460 Wilshire Blvd., Ste. 608 Beverly Hills, CA 90212 (213) 278-2478 Date Lic.:	09/09-0326 10/20/83	530,000	0	Diversified	5
Imperial Ventures, Inc. Donald B. Prell, Pres. 9920 S. Lacienega Blvd. (Mail: P.O. Box 92991; Los Angeles 90009) Inglewood, CA 90301 (213) 417-5888 Date Lic.:	09/09-0203 08/31/78	2,000,000	0	Diversified	1

Licensee	License No.	Private Capital	SBA Leverage	Investment Policy	Owner Code*
Ivanhoe Venture Capital, Ltd. Alan Toffler, G.P. 737 Pearl St., Ste. 201 LaJolla, CA 92037 (619) 454-8882 Date Lic.: 12/29/82	09/09-0314	624,061	500,000	Diversified	5
Jupiter Partners John M. Bryan, Pres. 600 Montgomery St., 35th Floor San Francisco, CA 94111 (415) 421-9990 Date Lic.: 10/26/62	09/12-0079	3,253,720	3,700,000		5-P
Latigo Capital Partners Donald Peterson, G.P. 1015 Gayley Ave., Ste. 202 Los Angeles, CA 90024 (218) 208-3892 Date Lic.: 08/30/83	09/09-0324	1,000,000	2,000,000	Diversified	5-P
Latigo Capital Partners, II Robert A. Peterson, G.P. 1015 Gayley Ave., Ste. 202 Los Angeles, CA 90024 (218) 208-3892 Date Lic.: 09/20/85	09/09-0357	1,000,000	0	Diversified	5
Marwit Capital Corp. Martin W. Witte, Pres. 180 Newport Center Drive, Ste. 200 Newport Beach, CA 92660 (714) 640-6234 Date Lic.: 05/03/62	09/02-0175	1,117,253	1,250,000	Diversified	5
Merrill Pickard Anderson & Eyre I	09/09-0271	29,730,806	0	Diversified	1-P

Licensee	License No.	Private Capital	SBA Leverage	Investment Policy	Owner Code*
Steven L. Merrill, Pres. Two Palo Alto Sq., Ste. 425 Palo Alto, CA 94306 (415) 856-8880 Date Lic.:	11/26/80				
Metropolitan Venture Co., Inc. Rudolph J. Lowy, Chairman 5757 Wilshire Blvd., Ste. 670 Los Angeles, CA 90036 (213) 938-3488 Date Lic.:	09/09-0293 09/30/81	1,000,000	0	Diversified	5
Nelson Capital Corp. 10000 Santa Monica Blvd., Ste. 300 Los Angeles, CA 90067 (213) 556-1944 (See listing under New York for full information.)					
New West Partners Timothy P. Haidinger, G.P. 4600 Campus Dr., Ste. 103 Newport Beach, CA 92660 (714) 756-8940 Date Lic.: or 4350 Executive Dr., Ste. 206 San Diego, CA 92121 (619) 457-0722	09/09-0288 04/22/82	2,000,000	3,409,000	Diversified	5-P
PBC Venture Capital Inc. Henry L. Wheeler, Mgr. 1408-18th St. (Mail: P.O. Box 6008;	09/09-0266	540,000	0	Diversified	1

Licensee	License No.	Private Capital	SBA Leverage	Investment Policy	Owner Code*
Bakersfield 93386) Bakersfield, CA 93301 (805) 395-3555 Date Lic.:	09/28/80				
PCF Venture Capital Corp. Eduardo B. Cu Unjieng, Pres. 675 Mariners' Island Blvd., Ste. 103 San Mateo, CA 94404 (415) 574-4747 Date Lic.:	09/09-0313 05/04/83	1,580,000	1,500,000	Diversified	2
Peerless Capital Co., Inc. Robert W. Lautz, Jr., Pres. 2450 Mission St., Ste. 6 San Marino, CA 91108 (818) 799-4136 Date Lic.:	09/09-0368 07/11/86	1,000,000	0	Diversified	5
Ritter Partners William C. Edwards, Pres. 150 Isabella Ave. Atherton, CA 94025 (415) 854-1555 Date Lic.:	09/12-0075 10/18/62	3,228,802	3,795,000		5-P
Round Table Capital Corp. Richard Dumke, Pres. 601 Montgomery St. San Francisco, CA 94111 (415) 392-7500 Date Lic.:	09/09-0262 04/28/80	900,000	2,700,000	Diversified	5
San Joaquin Capital Corp. Chester Troudy, Pres. 1675 Chester Ave., Third Floor P.O. Box 2538 Bakersfield, CA 93303	09/14-0037	1,086,971	3,000,000	Diversified	5

Licensee	License No.	Private Capital	SBA Leverage	Investment Policy	Owner Code*
(805) 323-7581					
Date Lic.:	05/11/62				
San Jose SBIC Robert T. Murphy, Pres. 100 Park Center, Ste. 427 San Jose, CA 95113 (408) 293-7708	09/09-0195	1,350,000	2,800,000	Diversified	5
Date Lic.:	09/02/77				
Seaport Ventures, Inc. Michael Stopler, Pres. 525 B St., Ste. 630 San Diego, CA 92101 (619) 232-4069	09/09-0311	1,255,000	1,000,000	Diversified	5
Date Lic.:	11/22/82				
Union Venture Corp. John Ulrich, Pres. 225 S. Lake Ave., Ste. 601 Pasadena, CA 91101 (818) 304-1980	09/12-0145	10,000,000	0	Diversified	1
Date Lic.: or 445 S. Figueroa St. Los Angeles, CA 90071 (213) 236-6292	09/30/67				
VK Capital Co. Franklin Van Kasper, G.P. 50 California St., Ste. 2350 San Francisco, CA 94111 (415) 391-5600	09/09-0365	1,000,000	500,000	Diversified	5-P
Date Lic.:	02/07/86				
Vista Capital Corp. Frederick J. Howden, Jr., Chairman 701 B St., Ste. 760 San Diego, CA 92101 (619) 236-1900	09/09-0310	574,029	0	Diversified	5
Date Lic.:	02/02/83				

Licensee	License No.	Private Capital	SBA Leverage	Investment Policy	Owner Code*
Walden Capital Partners Arthur S. Berliner, Pres. 303 Sacramento St. San Francisco, CA 94109 (415) 391-7225 Date Lic.:	09/09-0175 12/17/74	1,294,227	3,350,000	Diversified	2-P
Westamco Investment Co. Leonard G. Muskin, Pres. 8929 Wilshire Blvd., Ste. 400 Beverly Hills, CA 90211 (213) 652-8288 Date Lic.:	09/14-0024 07/24/61	800,000	0	66⅔% Real Estate	4

Colorado

Licensee	License No.	Private Capital	SBA Leverage	Investment Policy	Owner Code*
Associated Capital Corp. Rodney J. Love, Pres. 1983 Tower Rd. Mail: (P.O. Box 5528 Terminal Anx. Denver 80011) Aurora, CO 80011 (303) 367-7000 Date Lic.:	08/08-0039 11/16/76	2,125,000	2,500,000	Grocery Stores	4
Intermountain Ventures, Ltd. Norman L. Dean, Pres. 1110 Tenth St. P.O. Box 1406 Greely, CO 80632 (303) 356-1200 Date Lic.:	08/08-0061 03/20/84	1,025,000	3,000,000	Diversified	5
UBD Capital, Inc. Richard B. Wigton, Pres. 1700 Broadway Denver, CO 80274	08/08-0146	1,000,000	0	Diversified	1

Licensee	License No.	Private Capital	SBA Leverage	Investment Policy	Owner Code*
(303) 863-6329 Date Lic.:	10/23/85				
Connecticut AB SBIC, Inc. Adam J. Bozzuto, Pres. 275 School House Rd. Cheshire, CT 06410 (203) 272-0203 Date Lic.:	01/01-0280 11/17/76	500,000	1,000,000	Grocery Stores	4
All State Venture Capital Corp. Thomas H. Brown, Jr., Pres. 830 Post Rd., East P.O. Box 442 Westport, CT 06880 (203) 226-9376 Date Lic.:	01/02-0215 11/02/62	338,230	0	Diversified	6
Capital Impact Corp. Kevin S. Tierney, Pres. 961 Main St. Bridgeport, CT 06601 (203) 384-5670 Date Lic.:	01/01-0335 03/01/85	3,000,000	4,000,000	Diversified	1
Capital Resource Co. of Connecticut I. Martin Fierberg, Managing Partner 699 Bloomfield Ave. Bloomfield, CT 06002 (203) 243-1114 Date Lic.:	01/01-0285 03/23/77	976,365	2,945,000	Diversified	5-P
Dewey Investment Corp. George E. Mrosek, Pres. 101 Middle Turnpike West Manchester, CT 06040 (203) 649-0654 Date Lic.:	01/02-0145 04/09/62	510,650	910,000	Diversified	5
First Connecticut SBIC David Engelson, Pres.	01/02-0013	7,402,968	24,350,000	50% Real Estate	6

Licensee	License No.	Private Capital	SBA Leverage	Investment Policy	Owner Code*
177 State St. Bridgeport, CT 06604 (203) 366-4726 Date Lic.:	05/06/60				
Marcon Capital Corp. Martin A. Cohen, Pres. 49 Riverside Ave. Westport, CT 06880 (203) 226-6893 Date Lic.:	01/01-0277 10/23/75	617,000	2,250,000	Diversified	4
Northeastern Capital Corp. Louis W. Mingione, Pres. 61 High St. East Haven, CT 06512 (203) 469-7901 Date Lic.:	01/02-0062 03/08/61	412,076	700,000	Diversified	6
Regional Financial Enterprises, Ltd. Partnership Robert M. Williams, Chairman 36 Grove St. New Canaan, CT 06840 (203) 966-2800 Date Lic.:	01/01-0307 07/01/80	10,107,679	10,000,000	Diversified	1-P
The SBIC of Connecticut, Inc. Kenneth F. Zarrilli, Pres. 1115 Main St. Bridgeport, CT 06603 (203) 367-3282 Date Lic.:	01/02-0052 01/31/61	617,160	750,000	Diversified	6
District of Columbia Allied Investment Corp. David J. Gladstone, Pres. 1666 K St., N.W., Ste. 901	03/04-0003	3,784,708	10,500,000	100% In Any One Industry	6

Licensee	License No.	Private Capital	SBA Leverage	Investment Policy	Owner Code*
Washington, DC 20006 (202) 331-1112 Date Lic.:	12/23/59				
American Security Capital Corp., Inc. William G. Tull, Pres. 730 Fifteenth St., N.W. Washington, DC 20013 (202) 624-4843 Date Lic.:	03/03-0174 08/13/84	2,500,000	0	Diversified	1
DC Bancorp Venture Capital Co. Allan A. Weissburg, Pres. 1801 K St., N.W. Washington, DC 20006 (202) 955-6970 Date Lic.:	03/03-0178 07/18/85	1,500,000	0	Diversified	2
Washington Ventures, Inc. Kenneth A. Swain, Pres. 1320 18th St., N.W., Ste. 100 Washington, DC 20036 (202) 895-2560 Date Lic.:	03/03-0180 12/03/86	1,000,000	0	Diversified	1

Florida

Allied Investment Corp. 111 E. Las Olas Blvd. Fort Lauderdale, FL 33301 (305) 763-8484 (See listing under District of Columbia for full information.)					
Caribank Capital Corp. Michael E. Chaney, Pres. 255 E. Dania Beach Blvd. Dania, FL 33004 (305) 925-2211 Date Lic.:	04/04-0213 07/07/82	1,500,000	4,000,000	Diversified	1

Licensee	License No.	Private Capital	SBA Leverage	Investment Policy	Owner Code*
College Venture Equity Corp. 1617 Second Ave. Tampa, FL 33605 (813) 875-1251 (See listing under New York for full information.)					
First North Florida SBIC J. B. Higdon, Pres. 1400 Gadsden St. P.O. Box 1021 Quincy, FL 32351 (904) 875-2600 Date Lic.:	04/05-0022 12/17/60	1,500,108	2,500,000	Grocery Stores	5
First Tampa Capital Corp. Thomas L. duPont, Pres 6200 Courtney Campbell Causeway, Ste. 340 Tampa, FL 33607 (813) 874-3112 Date Lic.:	04/04-0226 01/18/84	1,975,000	0	Diversified	5
Gold Coast Capital Corp. William I. Gold, Pres. 3550 Biscayne Blvd., Rm. 601 Miami, FL 33137 (305) 576-2012 Date Lic.:	04/05-0010 12/22/59	680,000	1,930,092	Diversified	5
J & D Capital Corp. Jack Carmel, Pres. 12747 Biscayne Blvd. North Miami, FL 33181 (305) 893-0303 Date Lic.:	04/04-0188 07/09/80	594,106	1,750,000	Diversified	5
Market Capital Corp. E. E. Eads, Pres. 1102 N. 28th St. P.O. Box 22667	04/05-0086	786,000	1,800,000	Grocery Stores	4

Licensee	License No.	Private Capital	SBA Leverage	Investment Policy	Owner Code*
Tampa, FL 33622 (813) 247-1357 Date Lic.:	03/24/64				
SBIC of Panama City, Florida Charles Smith, Pres. 2612 W. 15th St. Panama City, FL 32401 (904) 785-9577 Date Lic.:	04/05-0082 12/06/63	3,600,000	11,588,712	80% In Lodging Places & Amusements	1
Southeast Venture Capital Limited I James R. Fitzsimons, Jr., Pres. One S.E. Financial Center Miami, FL 33131 (305) 375-6470 Date Lic.:	04/05-0095 01/08/68	5,970,420	6,500,000	Diversified	1-P
Western Financial Capital Corp. Dr. F. M. Rosemore, Pres. 1380 N.E. Miami Gardens Dr., Ste. 225 North Miami Beach, FL 33179 (305) 949-5900 Date Lic.:	04/04-0183 02/22/80	3,546,744	9,140,000	Medical	6
Georgia Investor's Equity, Inc. I. Walter Fisher, Pres. 2940 First National Bank Tower Atlanta, GA 30383 (404) 523-3999 Date Lic.:	04/05-0018 08/10/61	2,183,700	0	Diversified	5
Mighty Capital Corp. Gary Korynoski, Gen. Mgr. 50 Technology Park/Atlanta, Ste. 100	04/04-0221	505,000	1,500,000	Diversified	5

Licensee	License No.	Private Capital	SBA Leverage	Investment Policy	Owner Code*
Norcross, GA 30092 (404) 448-2232 Date Lic.:	05/03/83				
North Riverside Capital Corp. Tom Barry, Pres. 5775 D Peachtree Dunwoody Rd., Ste. 650 Atlanta, GA 30342 (404) 252-1076 Date Lic.:	04/04-0230 08/24/84	3,010,500	3,000,000	Diversified	5
Hawaii Bancorp Hawaii SBIC James D. Evans, Jr., Pres. 111 S. King St., Ste. 1060 Honolulu, III 96813 (808) 521-6411 Date Lic.:	09/09-0340 02/17/84	1,000,000	500,000	Diversified	1
Illinois Abbott Capital Corp. Richard E. Lassar, Pres. 9933 Lawler Ave. Skokie, IL 60077 (312) 982-0404 Date Lic.:	05/07-0082 01/11/71	727,840	0	Diversified	5
Alpha Capital Venture Partners, Ltd. Partnership Andrew H. Kalnow, G.P. Three First National Plaza, 14th Floor Chicago, IL 60602 (312) 372-1556 Date Lic.:	05/05-0191 04/23/84	1,290,000	0	Diversified	2-P
Business Ventures, Inc. Milton Lefton, Pres. 20 N. Wacker Dr., Ste. 550 Chicago, IL 60606 (312) 346-1580	05/05-0172	531,000	0	Diversified	5

Licensee	License No.	Private Capital	SBA Leverage	Investment Policy	Owner Code*
Date Lic.:	10/31/83				
Continental Illinois Venture Corp. John L. Hines, Pres. 209 S. LaSalle St. (Mail: 231 S. LaSalle St.) Chicago, IL 60693 (312) 828-8023	05/07-0078	25,011,800	1,500,000	Diversified	1
Date Lic.:	04/02/70				
First Capital Corp. of Chicago John A. Canning, Jr., Pres. Three First National Plaza, Ste. 1330 Chicago, IL 60670 (312) 732-5400	05/07-0042	44,000,000	3,600,000	Diversified	1
Date Lic.:	06/08/61				
Frontenac Capital Corp. David A. R. Dullum, Pres. 208 S. LaSalle St., Rm. 1900 Chicago, IL 60604 (312) 368-0047	05/05-0114	6,400,000	4,600,000	Diversified	2
Date Lic.:	12/29/76				
Mesirow Capital Partners SBIC, Ltd. Lester A. Morris, G.P. 350 N. Clark St., Third Floor Chicago, IL 60610 (312) 670-6098	05/05-0168	1,250,000	3,000,000	Diversified	5-P
Date Lic.:	07/07/82				
Northern Capital Corp. Robert L. Underwood, Pres. 50 S. LaSalle St. Chicago, IL 60604 (312) 444-5399	05/05-0199	1,902,941	0	Diversified	1
Date Lic.:	01/17/85				

Licensee	License No.	Private Capital	SBA Leverage	Investment Policy	Owner Code*
Walnut Capital Corp. Burton W. Kanter, Chairman 208 S. LaSalle St. Chicago, IL 60604 (312) 346-2033 Date Lic.:	05/02-0430 11/07/83	2,220,000	4,000,000	Diversified	5
Indiana 1st Source Capital Corp. Eugene L. Cavanaugh, Jr., V.P. 100 N. Michigan St. (Mail: P.O. Box 1602; South Bend 46634) South Bend, IN 46601 (219) 236-2180 Date Lic.:	05/05-0194 12/23/83	1,800,000	0	Diversified	1
Circle Ventures, Inc. Robert Salyers, Pres. 20 N. Meridian St., Rm. 312 Indianapolis, IN 46204 (317) 633-7303 Date Lic.:	05/05-0171 08/18/83	1,000,000	0	Diversified	5
Equity Resource Co., Inc. Michael J. Hammes, V.P. One Plaza Pl. 202 S. Michigan St. South Bend, IN 46601 (219) 237-5255 Date Lic.:	05/05-0193 12/27/83	2,000,000	0	Diversified	1
Heritage Venture Group, Inc. Arthur A. Angotti, Pres. 2400 One Indiana Sq. Indianapolis, IN 46204 (317) 635-5696 Date Lic.:	05/05-0154 08/12/81	3,061,540	500,000	Diversified	5
Mount Vernon Venture Capital Co. Thomas J. Grande,	05/05-0174	2,090,500	0	Diversified	5-P

Licensee	License No.	Private Capital	SBA Leverage	Investment Policy	Owner Code*
Gen. Mgr. 8330 Woodfield Crossing Blvd., Ste. 200 Indianapolis, IN 46240 (317) 846-5106 Date Lic.:	09/29/83				
White River Capital Corp. John H. Cragoe, Pres. 500 Washington St. P.O. Box 929 Columbus, IN 47201 (812) 372-0111 Date Lic.:	05/05-0165 03/31/82	1,048,000	900,000	Diversified	1
Iowa MorAmerica Capital Corp. Donald E. Flynn, Pres. American Bldg., Ste. 200 Cedar Rapids, IA 52401 (319) 363-0263 Date Lic.:	07/07-0006 09/30/59	5,000,000	12,150,440	Diversified	3
Kansas Kansas Venture Capital, Inc. Larry J. High, Pres. 1030 First National Bank Tower One Townsite Plaza Topeka, KS 66603 (913) 235-3437 Date Lic.:	07/07-0077 06/17/77	1,075,240	0	Diversified	3
Kentucky Financial Opportunities, Inc. Gary Duerr, Mgr. 833 Starks Bldg. Louisville, KY 40202 (502) 584-8259 Date Lic.:	04/04-0113 10/17/74	900,000	3,600,000	Diversified	4
Mountain Ventures, Inc.	04/04-0146	1,640,000	0	Diversified	5

Licensee	License No.	Private Capital	SBA Leverage	Investment Policy	Owner Code*
Lloyd R. Moncrief, Pres. 911 N. Main St. P.O. Box 628 London, KY 40741 (606) 864-5175 Date Lic.:	12/19/78				
Louisiana					
Capital Equity Corp. · Arthur J. Mitchell, Gen. Mgr. 1885 Wooddale Blvd. Baton Rouge, LA 70806 (504) 924-9206 Date Lic.:	06/06-0263 03/11/83	1,164,974	0	Diversified	1
Capital for Terrebonne, Inc. Hartwell A. Lewis, Pres. 27 Austin Dr. Houma, LA 70360 (504) 868-3930 Date Lic.:	06/06-0195 01/24/78	750,000	480,000	Diversified	5
Commercial Capital, Inc. Milton Coxe, Pres. Holiday Sq. Office Plaza (Mail: P.O. Box 1776; Covington, LA 70434) Covington, LA 70433 (504) 626-1171 Date Lic.: or 1809 W. Thomas St. Hammond, LA 70404 (504) 892-4921	06/10-0124 09/06/62	890,000	2,035,000	Diversified	3
Dixie Business Investment Co. L. W. Baker, Pres. 401½ Lake St. P.O. Box 588 Lake Providence, LA 71254	06/06-0173	501,118	1,500,000	Diversified	2

Licensee	License No.	Private Capital	SBA Leverage	Investment Policy	Owner Code*
(318) 559-1558 Date Lic.:	08/21/74				
First Southern Capital Corp. Charest Thibaut, Pres. 6161 Perkins Rd., Ste. 2C P.O. Box 14418 Baton Rouge, LA 70898 (504) 769-3004 Date Lic.:	06/12-0023 05/11/61	1,500,000	2,650,000	Diversified	6
Louisiana Equity Capital Corp. G. Lee Griffin, Pres. 451 Florida St. Baton Rouge, LA 70821 (504) 389-4421 Date Lic.:	06/06-0169 02/21/74	4,260,639	0	Diversified	1
Walnut Street Capital Co. William D. Humphries, Managing G.P. 231 Carondelet St., Ste. 702 New Orleans, LA 70130 (504) 525-2112 Date Lic.:	06/10-0096 08/06/82	1,476,000	2,350,000	Diversified	5-P
Maine Maine Capital Corp. David M. Coit, Pres. Seventy Center St. Portland, ME 04101 (207) 772-1001 Date Lic.:	01/01-0306 08/07/80	1,000,000	1,000,000	Diversified	1
Maryland First Maryland Capital, Inc. Joseph A. Kenary, Pres. 107 W. Jefferson St. Rockville, MD 20850	03/03-0169	616,600	0	Diversified	5

Licensee	License No.	Private Capital	SBA Leverage	Investment Policy	Owner Code*
(301) 251-6630 Date Lic.:	07/12/84				
Greater Washington Investors, Inc. Don A. Christensen, Pres. 5454 Wisconsin Ave. Chevy Chase, MD 20815 (301) 656-0626 Date Lic.:	03/04-0011 02/09/60	14,811,617	2,513,720	Diversified	6
Suburban Capital Corp. Henry Linsert, Jr., Pres. 6610 Rockledge Dr. Bethesda, MD 20817 (301) 493-7025 Date Lic.:	03/03-0154 05/31/83	5,000,000	3,000,000	Diversified	1
Massachusetts Advent Atlantic Capital Co., Ltd. Partnership David D. Croll, Managing Partner 45 Milk St. Boston, MA 02109 (617) 338-0800 Date Lic.:	01/01-0327 11/28/83	7,326,890	10,500,000	Diversified	5-P
Advent III Capital Co. David D. Croll, Managing Partner 45 Milk St. Boston, MA 02109 (617) 338-0800 Date Lic.:	01/01-0291 08/14/78	4,003,000	5,000,000	Diversified	5-P
Advent IV Capital Co. David D. Croll, Managing Partner 45 Milk St. Boston, MA 02109 (617) 338-0800 Date Lic.:	01/01-0316 07/27/82	12,050,000	12,000,000	Diversified	5-P

Licensee	License No.	Private Capital	SBA Leverage	Investment Policy	Owner Code*
Advent V Capital Co., Ltd. Partnership David D. Croll, Managing Partner 45 Milk St. Boston, MA 02109 (617) 338-0800 Date Lic.:	01/01-0331 09/05/84	20,935,000	35,000,000	Diversified	5-P
Advent Industrial Capital Co., Ltd. Partnership David D. Croll, Managing Partner 45 Milk St. Boston, MA 02109 (617) 338-0800 Date Lic.:	01/01-0332 11/09/84	3,326,400	7,000,000	Diversified	3-P
Atlantic Energy Capital Corp. Joost S. Tjaden, Pres. 260 Franklin St., 15th Floor Boston, MA 02109 (617) 451-6220 Date Lic.:	01/01-0319 07/27/82	1,000,000	0	Diversified	5
BancBoston Ventures, Inc. Paul F. Hogan, Pres. 100 Federal St. Boston, MA 02110 (617) 434-2441 Date Lic.:	01/01-0001 05/08/59	10,000,000	0	Diversified	1
Bever Capital Corp. Richard Tadler, Pres. 260 Franklin St., 15th Floor Boston, MA 02109 (617) 451-9192 Date Lic.:	01/01-0325 10/31/83	2,000,000	0	Diversified	5
Boston Hambro Capital Co. Edwin Goodman, Pres.	01/01-0299	4,746,924	2,000,000	Diversified	5-P

Licensee	License No.	Private Capital	SBA Leverage	Investment Policy	Owner Code*
One Boston Pl. Boston, MA 02106 (617) 722-7055 Date Lic.:	01/04/80				
Business Achievement Corp. Julian H. Katzeff, Pres. 1280 Centre St. Newton Centre, MA 02159 (617) 965-0550 Date Lic.:	01/01-0055 08/08/63	450,000	1,120,000	Diversified	5
Chestnut Capital International II, Ltd. Partnership David D. Croll, Managing Partner 45 Milk St. Boston, MA 02109 (617) 338-0800 Date Lic.:	01/01-0336 07/10/85	6,754,236	12,500,000	Diversified	5-P
Chestnut Capital Corp. David D. Croll, Chairman 45 Milk St. Boston, MA 02109 (617) 338-0800 Date Lic.:	01/01-0305 08/20/80	2,000,000	1,500,000	Diversified	5
Chestnut Street Partners, Inc. David D. Croll, Pres. 45 Milk St. Boston, MA 02109 (617) 574-6763 Date Lic.:	01/01-0339 12/03/86	2,500,000	0	Diversified	5-P
First Capital Corp. of Chicago 133 Federal St., Sixth Floor Boston, MA 02110 (617) 542-9185 (See listing under Illinois for full information.)					

Licensee	License No.	Private Capital	SBA Leverage	Investment Policy	Owner Code*
First United SBIC, Inc. Alfred W. Ferrara, V.P. 135 Will Dr. Canton, MA 02021 (617) 828-6150 Date Lic.:	01/01-0284 10/29/76	300,000	0	Diversified	4
Fleet Venture Resources, Inc. Carlton V. Klein, V.P. 60 State St. Boston, MA 02109 (617) 367-6700 (See listing under Rhode Island for full information.)					
Monarch-Narragansett Ventures, Inc. George W. Siguler, Pres. One Financial Plaza Springfield, MA 01102 (413) 781-3000 Date Lic.:	01/01-0340 12/08/86	10,000,000	28,970,000	Diversified	3
New England Capital Corp. Z. David Patterson, V.P. One Washington Mall, Seventh Floor Boston, MA 02108 (617) 722-6400 Date Lic.:	01/01-0023 08/21/61	5,000,000	0	Diversified	1
Northeast SBI Corp. Joseph Mindick, Treasurer 16 Cumberland St. Boston, MA 02115 (617) 267-3983 Date Lic.:	01/01-0275 05/07/74	412,076	730,000	Diversified	5
Orange Nassau Capital Corp. Richard D. Tadler, Pres.	01/01-0313	2,000,000	1,000,000	Diversified	5

Licensee	License No.	Private Capital	SBA Leverage	Investment Policy	Owner Code*
260 Franklin St., 15th Floor Boston, MA 02109 (617) 451-6220 Date Lic.:	07/08/81				
Pioneer Ventures Ltd. Partnership Christopher W. Lynch, Managing Partner 60 State St. Boston, MA 02109 (617) 742-7825 Date Lic.:	01/01-0337 11/20/86	3,000,080	0	Diversified	3-P
Stevens Capital Corp. Edward Capuano, Pres. 168 Stevens St. Fall River, MA 02721 (617) 679-0044 Date Lic.:	01/01-0323 06/21/84	506,000	0	Diversified	5
UST Capital Corp. Stephen R. Lewinstein, Pres. 40 Court St. Boston, MA 02108 (617) 542-6300 Date Lic.:	01/01-0027 10/06/61	1,182,800	2,755,000	Diversified	1
Vadus Capital Corp. Joost S. Tjaden, Pres. 260 Franklin St., 15th Floor Boston, MA 02109 (617) 451-6220 Date Lic.:	01/01-0314 11/03/81	2,000,000	1,000,000	Diversified	5
Worcester Capital Corp. John M. Lydon, Clerk 446 Main St. Worcester, MA 01608 (617) 793-4269 Date Lic.:	01/01-0068 12/27/67	1,000,000	0	Diversified	1
Michigan Comerica Capital Corp.	05/05-0150	5,000,000	0	Diversified	1

Licensee	License No.	Private Capital	SBA Leverage	Investment Policy	Owner Code*
John D. Berkaw, Pres. 30150 Telegraph Rd., Ste. 245 Birmingham, MI 48010 (313) 258-5800 Date Lic.:	06/23/81				
Doan Resources Ltd. Partnership Herbert D. Doan, Partner 2000 Hogback Rd., Ste. 2 Ann Arbor, MI 48105 (313) 971-3100 Date Lic.:	05/05-0098 02/25/74	3,300,000	0	Diversified	3-P
Michigan Capital & Service, Inc. Joseph Conway, Pres. 500 First National Bldg. 201 S. Main St. Ann Arbor, MI 48104 (313) 663-0702 Date Lic.:	05/15-0021 08/30/66	29,544,765	0	Diversified	1
Michigan Tech Capital Corp. Clark L. Pellegrini, Pres. Technology Park 601 W. Sharon Ave. P.O. Box 364 Houghton, MI 49931 (906) 487-2970 Date Lic.:	05/05-0169 08/20/82	642,500	0	Diversified	5
Minnesota Control Data Capital Corp. D. C. Curtis, Jr., Pres. 3601 W. 77th St. France Place-MNBO7V Minneapolis, MN 55435 (612) 921-4391 Date Lic.:	05/05-0117 10/19/77	5,000,000	11,000,000	Diversified	4

Licensee	License No.	Private Capital	SBA Leverage	Investment Policy	Owner Code*
DGC Capital Co. Robert F. Poirier, Pres. 525 Lake Ave., South, Ste. 216 Duluth, MN 55802 (218) 722-0058 Date Lic.:	05/05-0189 10/29/84	500,000	0	Diversified	5
FBS SBIC, Ltd. Partnership Brademar Office Park 8000 W. 78th St., Ste. 300 Edina, MN 55435 (612) 829-1122 (See listing under Arizona for full information.)					
First Midwest Capital Corp. William Franta, Pres. 914 Plymouth Bldg. 12 S. Sixth St. Minneapolis, MN 55402 (612) 339-9391 Date Lic.:	05/08-0002 03/19/59	2,500,000	2,700,000	Diversified	3
Itasca Growth Fund, Inc. Carroll Bergerson, Gen. Mgr. One N.W. Third St. Grand Rapids, MN 55744 (218) 327-6200 Date Lic.:	05/05-0200 05/06/85	1,056,000	0	Diversified	4
North Star Ventures II, Inc. Terrence W. Glarner, Pres. 100 S. Fifth St., Ste. 2200 Minneapolis, MN 55402	05/05-0190	3,001,085	3,000,000	Diversified	5

Licensee	License No.	Private Capital	SBA Leverage	Investment Policy	Owner Code*
(612) 333-1133 Date Lic.:	05/17/84				
Northland Capital Corp. George G. Barnum, Jr., Pres. 613 Missabe Bldg. Duluth, MN 55802 (218) 722-0545 Date Lic.:	05/08-0018 06/30/67	862,750	800,000	Diversified	5
Northwest Venture Partners Robert F. Zicarelli, Managing G.P. 2800 Piper Jaffray Tower 222 S. Ninth St. Minneapolis, MN 55402 (612) 372-8770 Date Lic.:	05/05-0182 10/13/83	42,000,000	0	Diversified	2-P
Norwest Growth Fund, Inc. Daniel J. Haggerty, Pres. 2800 Piper Jaffray Tower 222 S. Ninth St. Minneapolis, MN 55402 (612) 372-8770 Date Lic.:	05/08-0006 02/25/60	15,000,000	20,670,000	Diversified	1
Retailers Growth Fund, Inc. Cornell L. Moore, Pres. 2318 Park Ave. Minneapolis, MN 55404 (612) 872-4929 Date Lic.:	05/08-0015 10/04/62	699,151	1,700,000	Franchised Retailers	4
Shared Ventures, Inc. Howard W. Weiner, Pres.	05/05-0157	752,000	1,200,000	Diversified	5

Licensee	License No.	Private Capital	SBA Leverage	Investment Policy	Owner Code*
6550 York Ave., South, Ste. 419 Edina, MN 55435 (612) 925-3411 Date Lic.:	09/18/81				
Threshold Ventures, Inc. T. D. Sanford, Pres. 430 Oak Grove St., Ste. 202 Minneapolis, MN 55403 (612) 874-7199 Date Lic.:	05/05-0183 03/20/84	1,351,500	1,500,000	Diversified	5

Mississippi

| North Riverside Capital Corp. 317 E. Capitol St., Ste. 101 Jackson, MS 39201 (601) 949-3145 (See listing under Georgia for full information.) | | | | | |
| Vicksburg SBIC David L. May, Pres. 302 First National Bank Bldg. Vicksburg, MS 39180 (601) 636-4762 Date Lic.: | 04/05-0011 06/09/60 | 800,000 | 509,000 | Diversified | 5 |

Missouri

| Bankers Capital Corp. Raymond E. Glasnapp, Pres. 3100 Gillham Rd. Kansas City, MO 64109 (816) 531-1600 Date Lic.: | 07/07-0075 02/12/76 | 632,000 | 900,000 | Diversified | 5 |
| Capital for Business, Inc. James B. Hebenstreit, Pres. | 07/09-0002 | 3,500,000 | 0 | Diversified | 1 |

Licensee	License No.	Private Capital	SBA Leverage	Investment Policy	Owner Code*
1000 Walnut, 18th Floor Kansas City, MO 64106 (816) 234-2357 Date Lic.: or 11 S. Meramec, Ste. 804 St. Louis, MO 63105 (314) 854-7427	10/15/59				
Intercapco West, Inc. Thomas E. Phelps, Pres. 7800 Bonhomme Ave. St. Louis, MO 63105 (314) 863-0600 Date Lic.:	07/07-0076 02/02/77	525,000	2,000,000	Diversified	4
MBI Venture Capital Investors, Inc. Anthony Sommers, Pres. 850 Main St. Kansas City, MO 64105 (816) 471-1700 Date Lic.:	07/07-0092 12/11/84	3,000,000	0	Diversified	1
MorAmerica Capital Corp. 911 Main St., Ste. 2724A Commerce Tower Bldg. Kansas City, MO 64105 (816) 842-0114 (See listing under Iowa for full information.)					
United Missouri Capital Corp. Joe Kessinger, Mgr. 928 Grand Ave., First Floor Kansas City, MO	07/07-0091	2,510,000	0	Diversified	1

Licensee	License No.	Private Capital	SBA Leverage	Investment Policy	Owner Code*
64106 (816) 556-7333 Date Lic.:	09/21/84				
Nebraska United Financial Resources Corp. Dennis L. Schulte, Mgr. 6211 L St. P.O. Box 1131 Omaha, NE 68101 (402) 734-1250 Date Lic.:	07/07-0087 07/07/83	500,000	0	Grocery Stores	5
Nevada Enterprise Finance Cap Development Corp. Robert N. Hampton, Pres. First Interstate Bank of Nevada Bldg. One E. First St., Ste. 1100 Reno, NV 89501 (702) 329-7797 Date Lic.:	08/08-0059 12/29/83	1,000,000	800,000	Diversified	5
New Hampshire Granite State Capital, Inc. Stuart D. Pompian, Mgr. 10 Fort Eddy Rd. Concord, NH 03301 (603) 228-9090 Date Lic.:	01/01-0326 12/29/83	1,000,000	0	Diversified	1
Lotus Capital Corp. Richard J. Ash, Pres. 875 Elm St. Manchester, NH 03101 (603) 668-8802 Date Lic.:	01/01-0330 01/10/85	1,142,500	0	Diversified	5
New Jersey Capital SBIC, Inc. Isadore Cohen, Pres. 691 State Hwy. #33	02/03-0051	739,000	0	85% Real Estate	5

Licensee	License No.	Private Capital	SBA Leverage	Investment Policy	Owner Code*
Trenton, NJ 08619 (609) 394-5221 Date Lic.:	02/27/63				
ESLO Capital Corp. Leo Katz, Pres. 2401 Morris Ave. East Wing, Ste. 220 Union, NJ 07083 (201) 687-4920 Date Lic.:	01/01-0300 05/31/79	639,323	1,500,000	Diversified	5
First Princeton Capital Corp. S. Lawrence Goldstein, Pres. 227 Hamburg Turnpike Pompton Lakes, NJ 07442 (201) 831-0330 Date Lic.:	02/02-0449 03/08/83	1,125,000	500,000	Diversified	5
Monmouth Capital Corp. Eugene W. Landy, Pres. 125 Wycoff Rd. Midland National Bank Bldg. P.O. Box 335 Eatontown, NJ 07724 (201) 542-4927 Date Lic.:	02/02-0088 05/28/61	2,453,931	6,072,000	Diversified	6
Tappan Zee Capital Corp. Karl Kirschner, Pres. 201 Lower Notch Rd. Little Falls, NJ 07424 (201) 256-8280 Date Lic.:	02/02-0209 11/16/63	750,000	2,250,000	66% Real Estate	5
Unicorn Ventures II, Ltd. Partnership Frank P. Diassi, G.P. 6 Commerce Dr. Cranford, NJ 07016 (201) 276-7880 Date Lic.:	02/02-0477 10/09/84	4,553,000	2,000,000	Diversified	5-P

Licensee	License No.	Private Capital	SBA Leverage	Investment Policy	Owner Code*
Unicorn Ventures, Ltd. Frank P. Diassi, Pres. 6 Commerce Dr. Cranford, NJ 07016 (201) 276-7880 Date Lic.:	02/02-0405 11/10/81	2,508,513	6,000,000	Diversified	5-P
New Mexico Albuquerque SBIC Albert T. Ussery, Pres. 501 Tijeras Ave., N.W. P.O. Box 487 Albuquerque, NM 87103 (505) 247-0145 Date Lic.:	06/06-0191 11/16/77	502,000	1,000,000	Diversified	5
Equity Capital Corp. Jerry A. Henson, Pres. 231 Washington Ave., Ste. 2 Sante Fe, NM 87501 (505) 988-4273 Date Lic.:	06/06-0274 01/24/84	787,724	1,250,000	Diversified	5
The Franklin Corp. 4209 San Mateo, N.E. Albuquerque, NM 87110 (505) 243-9680 (See listing under New York for full information.)					
Southwest Capital Investments, Inc. Martin J. Roe, Pres. The Southwest Bldg. 3500-E Comanche Rd., N.E. Albuquerque, NM 87107 (505) 884-7161 Date Lic.:	06/06-0229 04/30/76	830,552	2,180,000	Diversified	3
New York 767 Ltd. Partnership H. Wertheim, General Partner H. Mallement, G.P.	02/02-0464	1,375,333	1,500,000	Diversified	5-P

Licensee	License No.	Private Capital	SBA Leverage	Investment Policy	Owner Code*
767 Third Ave. New York, NY 10017 (212) 838-7776 Date Lic.:	06/18/84				
ASEA-Harvest Partners II Harvey Wertheim, G.P. 767 Third Ave. New York, NY 10017 (212) 838-7776 Date Lic.:	02/02-0478 10/09/84	1,000,000	0	Diversified	5-P
American Commercial Capital Corp. Gerald J. Grossman, Pres. 310 Madison Ave., Ste. 1304 New York, NY 10017 (212) 986-3305 Date Lic.:	02/02-0443 12/30/82	1,000,000	3,000,000	Diversified	5
American Energy Investment Corp. John J. Hoey, Chairman 645 Fifth Ave., Ste. 1900 New York, NY 10022 (212) 688-7307 Date Lic.:	02/06-0236 02/20/81	2,500,000	500,000	Energy Industries	5
Amev Capital Corp. Martin Orland, Pres. One World Trade Center, 50th Floor New York, NY 10048 (212) 775-9100 Date Lic.:	02/02-0370 08/14/79	5,500,000	7,500,000	Diversified	5
Atalanta Investment Company, Inc. L. Mark Newman, Chairman 450 Park Ave. New York, NY 10022 (212) 832-1104 Date Lic.:	02/02-0357 06/22/79	6,572,196	12,800,000	Diversified	4

Licensee	License No.	Private Capital	SBA Leverage	Investment Policy	Owner Code*
BT Capital Corp. James G. Hellmuth, Pres. 280 Park Ave., 10 West New York, NY 10017 (212) 850-1916 Date Lic.:	02/02-0295 11/10/72	41,702,390	21,300,000	Diversified	1
Beneficial Capital Corp. John Hoey, Pres. 645 Fifth Ave., Ste. 1900 New York, NY 10022 (212) 688-7307 Date Lic.:	02/02-0076 05/15/61	500,000	600,000	Diversified	5
Bohlen Capital Corp. Harvey J. Wertheim, Pres. 767 Third Ave. New York, NY 10017 (212) 838-7776 Date Lic.:	02/02-0317 09/24/76	1,590,000	4,500,000	Diversified	5
Boston Hambro Capital Co. 17 E. 71st St. New York, NY 10021 (212) 288-9106 (See listing under Massachusetts for full information.)					
CMNY Capital Co., Inc. Robert Davidoff, V.P. 77 Water St. New York, NY 10005 (212) 437-7078 Date Lic.:	02/02-0180 03/14/62	1,776,480	6,700,000	Diversified	3
The Central New York SBIC Robert E. Romig, Pres. 351 S. Warren St. Syracuse, NY 13202 (315) 478-5026 Date Lic.:	02/02-0044 04/28/61	150,000	50,000	Vending Machine	4

Licensee	License No.	Private Capital	SBA Leverage	Investment Policy	Owner Code*
Chase Manhattan Capital Corp. Gustav H. Koven, Pres. 1 Chase Manhattan Plaza, 23d Floor New York, NY 10081 (212) 552-6275 Date Lic.:	02/02-0228 08/02/62	24,785,000	0	Diversified	1
Chemical Venture Capital Associates Steven J. Gilbert, Pres. 277 Park Ave., 10th Floor New York, NY 10172 (212) 310-7578 Date Lic.:	02/02-0479 10/22/84	20,000,000	0	Diversified	1-P
Citicorp Venture Capital, Ltd. William Comfort, Chairman 153 E. 53d St. New York, NY 10043 (212) 559-1127 Date Lic.:	02/02-0266 12/18/67	126,933,484	10,000,000	Diversified	1
Clinton Capital Corp. Mark Scharfman, Pres. 419 Park Ave., South New York, NY 10016 (212) 696-4688 Date Lic.:	02/02-0410 10/22/80	12,000,000	35,000,000	Diversified	5
College Venture Equity Corp. Francis M. Williams, Pres. 256 Third St. P.O. Box 135 Niagara Falls, NY 14303 (716) 285-8455 Date Lic.:	02/02-0409 12/01/80	620,000	620,000	Diversified	5
County Capital Corp. Myron Joffe, Pres. 215 Hilton Ave. Hempstead, NY 11530	02/02-0463	500,000	0	Diversified	5

Licensee	License No.	Private Capital	SBA Leverage	Investment Policy	Owner Code*
(516) 538-2400					
Date Lic.:	12/08/83				
Croyden Capital Corp. Victor L. Hecht, Pres. 45 Rockefeller Plaza, Ste. 2165 New York, NY 10111 (212) 974-0184	02/02-0472	1,457,963	0	Diversified	5
Date Lic.:	05/23/84				
EAB Venture Corp. Richard C. Burcaw, Pres. 10 Hanover Sq. New York, NY 10015 (212) 437-4182	02/02-0403	5,000,000	9,000,000	Diversified	1
Date Lic.:	08/18/80				
Edwards Capital Co. Edward H. Teitlebaum, Pres. 215 Lexington Ave., Ste. 805 New York, NY 10016 (212) 686-2568	02/02-0366	4,200,000	12,450,000	Transportation	5-P
Date Lic.:	06/22/79				
European Development Corp. Ltd. Partnership Harvey J. Wertheim, Pres. 767 Third Ave. New York, NY 10017 (212) 867-9709	02/02-0355	2,757,774	9,750,000	Diversified	5-P
Date Lic.:	05/03/79				
Fairfield Equity Corp. Matthew A. Berdon, Pres. 200 E. 42d St. New York, NY 10017 (212) 867-0150	02/02-0151	997,109	2,400,000	Diversified	5
Date Lic.:	11/16/61				
Ferranti High Technology, Inc. Sandford R. Simon, Pres. 515 Madison Ave.	02/02-0457	3,000,000	1,000,000	Diversified	5

Licensee	License No.	Private Capital	SBA Leverage	Investment Policy	Owner Code*
New York, NY 10022 (212) 688-9828 Date Lic.:	05/31/83				
Fifty-Third Street Ventures, Ltd. Partnership Particia Cloherty, G.P. Dan Tessler, G.P. 420 Madison Ave. New York, NY 10017 (212) 752-8010 Date Lic.:	02/02-0315 07/29/76	5,759,584	5,460,000	Diversified	5
First New York SBIC Israel Mindick, G.P. 20 Squadron Blvd., Ste. 480 New City, NY 10956 (914) 638-1550 Date Lic.:	02/02-0400 12/30/85	1,000,000	0	Diversified	5-P
The Franklin Corp. Alan L. Farkas, Pres. 1185 Avenue of the Americas, 27th Floor New York, NY 10036 (212) 719-4844 Date Lic.:	02/02-0005 09/17/59	10,003,114	8,640,000	Diversified	6
Fundex Capital Corp. Howard Sommer, Pres. 525 Northern Blvd. Great Neck, NY 11021 (516) 466-8551 Date Lic.:	02/02-0340 05/18/78	1,101,000	2,820,000	Diversified	5
GHW Capital Corp. Nesta Stewart, V.P. 489 Fifth Ave. New York, NY 10017 (212) 687-1708 Date Lic.:	02/02-0491 11/13/85	1,000,000	0	Diversified	1
Genesee Funding, Inc. A. Keene Bolton, Pres. 183 E. Main St., Ste. 1450 Rochester, NY 14604 (716) 262-4716 Date Lic.:	02/02-0499 11/26/86	1,000,000	0	Diversified	5

Licensee	License No.	Private Capital	SBA Leverage	Investment Policy	Owner Code*
The Hanover Capital Corp. Daniel J. Sullivan, Pres. 150 E. 58th St., Ste. 2710 New York, NY 10022 (212) 980-9670 Date Lic.:	02/02-0102 06/22/61	847,944	1,350,000	Diversified	5
Heller Capital Services, Inc. J. Allen Kerr, Pres. 101 Park Ave. New York, NY 10178 (212) 880-7198 Date Lic.:	02/02-0401 09/19/80	2,015,000	0	Diversified	5
Holding Capital Management Corp. Sash A. Spencer, Pres. 685 Fifth Ave. 14th Floor New York, NY 10022 (212) 486-6670 Date Lic.:	02/02-0413 11/19/81	866,697	500,000	Diversified	5
Intergroup Venture Capital Corp. Ben Hauben, Pres. 230 Park Ave. New York, NY 10017 (212) 661-5428 Date Lic.:	02/02-0345 08/07/78	502,500	400,000	Diversified	5
Interstate Capital Co., Inc. David Scharf, Pres. 380 Lexington Ave. New York, NY 10017 (212) 986-7333 Date Lic.:	02/02-0408 10/22/80	1,249,999	3,500,000	Diversified	5
Irving Capital Corp. Andrew McWethy, V.P. 1290 Avenue of the Americas New York, NY 10019 (212) 408-4800 Date Lic.:	02/02-0321 12/06/76	9,000,000	0	Diversified	1

Licensee	License No.	Private Capital	SBA Leverage	Investment Policy	Owner Code*
Key Venture Capital Corp. John M. Lang, Pres. 60 State St. Albany, NY 12207 (518) 447-3180 Date Lic.:	02/02-0418 12/20/83	3,000,000	2,000,000	Diversified	1
Kwiat Capital Corp. Sheldon F. Kwiat, Pres. 576 Fifth Ave. New York, NY 10036 (212) 391-2461 Date Lic.:	02/02-0416 09/25/81	510,000	500,000	Diversified	5
M & T Capital Corp. J.V. Parlato, Pres. One M & T Plaza Buffalo, NY 14240 (716) 842-5881 Date Lic.:	02/02-0268 12/29/67	5,007,486	0	Diversified	1
MH Capital Investors, Inc. Edward L. Kock III, Pres. 140 E. 45th St., Ste. 3100 New York, NY 10017 (212) 808-0105 Date Lic.:	02/02-0501 11/06/86	20,000,000	0	Diversified	1
MRN Capital Co. Robert E. Schulman, Pres. 150 Great Neck Rd. Great Neck, NY 11021 (516) 466-5752 Date Lic.:	02/02-0431 04/23/82	1,011,700	0	Diversified	5
Multi-Purpose Capital Corp. Eli B. Fine, Pres. 31 S. Broadway Yonkers, NY 10701 (914) 963-2733 Date Lic.:	02/02-0232 03/18/63	210,300	165,000	Diversified	5

Licensee	License No.	Private Capital	SBA Leverage	Investment Policy	Owner Code*
NYBDC Capital Corp. Marshall R. Lustig, Pres. 41 State St. Albany, NY 12207 (518) 463-2268 Date Lic.:	02/02-0303 11/02/73	500,000	770,000	Diversified	4
NYSTRS/NV Capital, Ltd. Partnership Raymond A. Lancaster, Pres. One Norstar Plaza Albany, NY 12207 (518) 447-4050 Date Lic.:	02/02-0493 02/07/86	1,035,250	0	Diversified	2
NatWest USA Capital Corp. Orville G. Aarons, Gen. Mgr. 175 Water St. New York, NY 10038 (212) 602-1200 Date Lic.:	02/02-0492 02/06/86	10,000,000	0	Diversified	1
Nelson Capital Corp. Irwin Nelson, Pres. 591 Stewart Ave. Garden City, NY 11530 (516) 222-2555 Date Lic.:	02/02-0297 06/12/73	500,000	1,500,000	Diversified	5
Noro Capital Ltd. Harvey J. Wertheim, Pres. 767 Third Ave. New York, NY 10017 (212) 661-5281 Date Lic.:	02/02-0399 10/15/80	2,000,000	5,000,000	Diversified	5
Norstar Capital Inc. Raymond A. Lancaster, Pres. One Norstar Plaza Albany, NY 12207 (518) 447-4043 Date Lic.:	02/02-0482 04/12/85	3,950,000	0	Diversified	1

Licensee	License No.	Private Capital	SBA Leverage	Investment Policy	Owner Code*
Preferential Capital Corp. Bruce Bayroff, Secretary-Treasurer 16 Court St. Brooklyn, NY 11241 (212) 855-2728 Date Lic.:	02/02-0372 09/14/79	509,380	500,000	Diversified	5
Questech Capital Corp. Earl W. Brian, M.D., Pres. 600 Madison Ave., 21st Floor New York, NY 10022 (212) 758-8522 Date Lic.:	02/02-0415 06/26/81	5,000,000	10,000,000	Diversified	5
R & R Financial Corp. Imre Rosenthal, Pres. 1451 Broadway New York, NY 10036 (212) 790-1441 Date Lic.:	02/02-0135 04/27/62	505,000	300,000	Diversified	3
Rand SBIC, Inc. Donald Ross, Pres. 1300 Rand Bldg. Buffalo, NY 14203 (716) 853-0802 Date Lic.:	02/02-0311 05/05/76	1,605,000	1,800,000	Diversified	6
Realty Growth Capital Corp. Lawrence Beneson, Pres. 331 Madison Ave., Fourth Floor East New York, NY 10017 (212) 661-8380 Date Lic.:	02/02-0097 03/29/63	500,000	1,080,000	100% Real Estate Specialist	5
S & S Venture Associates, Ltd. Donald Smith, Pres. 333 Seventh Ave. New York, NY 10001 (212) 736-4530 Date Lic.:	02/02-0383 04/25/80	510,000	1,500,000	Diversified	5

Licensee	License No.	Private Capital	SBA Leverage	Investment Policy	Owner Code*
Small Business Electronics Investment Corp. Stanley Meisels, Pres. 1220 Peninsula Blvd. Hewlett, NY 11557 (516) 374-0743 Date Lic.:	02/02-0026 09/01/60	600,000	450,000	Diversified	5
Southern Tier Capital Corp. Harold Gold, Secretary-Treasurer 55 S. Main St. Liberty, NY 12754 (914) 292-3030 Date Lic.:	02/02-0095 06/28/61	350,111	800,000	Major Group 70 (Hotels and Rooming Houses)	5
TLC Funding Corp. Philip G. Kass, Pres. 141 S. Central Ave. Hartsdale, NY 10530 (914) 683-1144 Date Lic.:	02/02-0380 02/29/80	980,000	2,940,000	Diversified	5
Tappan Zee Capital Corp. 120 N. Main St. New City, NY 10956 (914) 634-8890 (See listing under New Jersey for full information.)					
Telesciences Capital Corp. Mike A. Petrozzo, Contact 26 Broadway, Ste. 841 New York, NY 10004 (212) 425-0320 Date Lic.:	02/02-0341 09/14/78	1,250,000	0	Diversified	4
Vega Capital Corp. Victor Harz, Pres. 720 White Plains Rd. Scarsdale, NY 10583 (914) 472-8550 Date Lic.:	02/02-0270 08/05/68	2,402,861	6,950,000	Diversified	6

Licensee	License No.	Private Capital	SBA Leverage	Investment Policy	Owner Code*
Venture SBIC, Inc. Arnold Feldman, Pres. 249-12 Jericho Turnpike Floral Park, NY 11001 (516) 352-0068 Date Lic.:	02/02-0334 11/23/77	612,000	1,800,000	Diversified	5
WFG-Harvest Partners, Ltd. Harvey J. Wertheim, G.P. 767 Third Ave. New York, NY 10017 (212) 838-7776 Date Lic.:	02/02-0490 09/30/85	1,000,000	0	Diversified	1-P
Walnut Capital Corp. 20 Exchange Place, 31st Floor New York, NY 10005 (212) 425-3144 (See listing under Illinois for full information.)					
Winfield Capital Corp. Stanley M. Pechman, Pres. 237 Mamaroneck Ave. White Plains, NY 10605 (914) 949-2600 Date Lic.:	02/02-0292 04/19/72	1,000,000	3,000,000	Diversified	5
Wood River Capital Corp. Elizabeth W. Smith, Pres. 645 Madison Ave. New York, NY 10022 (212) 750-9420 Date Lic.:	02/02-0361 05/09/79	11,512,000	26,000,000	Diversified	5
North Carolina Delta Capital, Inc. Alex B. Wilkins, Jr., Pres. 227 N. Tryon St., Ste. 201	04/10-0086	1,250,000	5,000,000	50% Real Estate	3

Licensee	License No.	Private Capital	SBA Leverage	Investment Policy	Owner Code*
Charlotte, NC 28202 (704) 372-1410 Date Lic.:	11/29/61				
Falcon Capital Corp. P.S. Prasad, Pres. 400 W. Fifth St. Greenville, NC 27834 (919) 752-5918 Date Lic.:	04/04-0091 04/14/64	504,237	500,000	Diversified	5
First Union Capital Corp. Ted Brooks, Pres. 924 B St. P.O. Box 310 North Wilkesboro, NC 28674 (919) 651-5194 Date Lic.:	04/04-0075 05/02/62	1,363,000	10,345	Diversified	6
Heritage Capital Corp. Herman B. McManaway, Pres. 2290 Jefferson First Union Plaza Charlotte, NC 28282 (704) 334-2867 Date Lic.:	04/04-0047 10/21/61	2,050,265	2,500,114	50% Real Estate	3
Kitty Hawk Capital, Ltd. Partnership Walter H. Wilkinson, Pres. One Tryon Center, Ste. 2030 112 S. Tryon St. Charlotte, NC 28284 (704) 333-3777 Date Lic.:	04/04-0189 07/23/80	1,905,000	3,000,000	Diversified	5-P
NCNB SBIC Corp. Troy S. McCrory, Jr., Pres. One NCNB Plaza, T-39 Charlotte, NC 28255 (704) 374-5583 Date Lic.:	04/04-0232 07/19/84	2,500,000	0	Diversified	1

Licensee	License No.	Private Capital	SBA Leverage	Investment Policy	Owner Code*
NCNB Venture Co., Ltd. Partnership S. Epes Robinson, G.P. One NCNB Plaza, T-39 Charlotte, NC 28255 (704) 374-5723 Date Lic.:	04/04-0231 07/19/84	10,000,000	0	Diversified	1-P
Ohio A.T. Capital Corp. Robert C. Salipante, V.P. 900 Euclid Ave., T-18 Cleveland, OH 44101 (216) 687-4970 Date Lic.:	05/05-0197 06/04/84	1,000,000	0	Diversified	1
Banc One Capital Corp. James E. Kolls, V.P. 100 E. Broad St. Columbus, OH 43215 (614) 463-5832 Date Lic.:	05/06-0020 01/17/62	440,000	0	Diversified	1
Capital Funds Corp. Carl G. Nelson, Chief Investment Officer 800 Superior Ave. Cleveland, OH 44114 (216) 344-5774 Date Lic.:	05/06-0011 12/09/60	3,700,000	0	Communications	1
Clarion Capital Corp. Morton A. Cohen, Pres. 35555 Curtis Blvd. Eastlake, OH 44094 (216) 953-0555 Date Lic.:	05/07-0023 09/25/68	8,891,858	10,500,000	Diversified	1
First Ohio Capital Corp. Michael J. Aust, Gen. Mgr. 606 Madison Ave. (Mail: P.O. Box 2061; Toledo 43603) Toledo, OH 43604	05/05-0163	2,000,000	1,300,000	Diversified	1

Licensee	License No.	Private Capital	SBA Leverage	Investment Policy	Owner Code*
(419) 259-7146 Date Lic.:	04/14/82				
Gries Investment Corp. Robert D. Gries, Pres. Statler Office Tower, Ste. 720 Cleveland, OH 44115 (216) 861-1146 Date Lic.:	05/06-0031 03/24/64	682,957	1,412,400	Diversified	5
Miami Valley Capital, Inc. W. Walker Lewis, Chairman Talbott Tower, Ste. 315 131 N. Ludlow St. Dayton, OH 45402 (513) 222-7222 Date Lic.:	05/05-0143 01/02/80	1,446,709	1,250,000	Diversified	2
National City Capital Corp. Michael Sherwin, Pres. 623 Euclid Ave. Cleveland, OH 44114 (216) 575-2491 Date Lic.:	05/05-0137 02/08/79	2,500,000	4,000,000	Diversified	1
River Capital Corp. 796 Huntington Bldg. Cleveland, OH 44114 (216) 781-3655 (See listing under Virginia for full information.)					
SeaGate Venture Management, Inc. Donald E. Breese, Senior V.P. 245 Summit St., Ste. 1403 Toledo, OH 43603 (419) 259-8588 Date Lic.:	05/05-0203 07/19/85	1,010,000	0	Diversified	1
Tamco Investors (SBIC) Inc.	05/05-0116	350,000	1,050,000	Grocery Stores	4

Licensee	License No.	Private Capital	SBA Leverage	Investment Policy	Owner Code*
Nathan H. Monus, Pres. 375 Victoria Rd. Youngstown, OH 44515 (216) 792-3811 Date Lic.:	06/21/77				
Tomlinson Capital Corp. H. F. Meyer, Pres. 13700 Broadway Cleveland, OH 44125 (216) 587-2003 Date Lic.:	05/05-0105 09/18/75	550,000	300,000	Grocery Stores	4
Oklahoma Alliance Business Investment Co. Barry Davis, Pres. 17 E. Second St. One Williams Center, Ste. 2000 Tulsa, OK 74172 (918) 584-3581 Date Lic.:	06/10-0012 08/12/59	3,469,367	2,660,000	Diversified	5
First Oklahoma Investment Capital Corp. Tom A. Archibald, V.P. 210 W. Park Ave., Ste. 400 Oklahoma City, OK 73102 (405) 272-4669 Date Lic.:	06/06-0225 11/30/79	1,285,000	1,500,000	Diversified	1
Southwest Venture Capital, Inc. Donald J. Rubottom, Pres. 2700 E. 51st St., Ste. 340 Tulsa, OK 74105 (918) 742-3177 Date Lic.:	06/06-0186 12/27/76	500,000	500,000	Diversified	5
Western Venture	06/06-0248	2,007,500	3,000,000	Diversified	2

Licensee	License No.	Private Capital	SBA Leverage	Investment Policy	Owner Code*
Capital Corp. William B. Baker, Chief Operating Officer 4900 S. Lewis Tulsa, OK 74105 (918) 749-7981 Date Lic.:	08/03/81				
Oregon First Interstate Capital, Inc. 227 S.W. Pine St., Ste. 200 Portland, OR 97204 (503) 223-4334 (See listing under California for full information.)					
Northern Pacific Capital Corp. John J. Tennant, Jr., Pres. 1201 S.W. 12th Ave., Ste. 608 (Mail: P.O. Box 1658; Portland 97207) Portland, OR 97205 (503) 241-1255 Date Lic.:	10/13-0014 01/18/62	911,464	800,000	Diversified	5
Norwest Growth Fund, Inc. 1300 S.W. Fifth St., Ste. 3108 Portland, OR 97201 (503) 223-6622 (See listing under Minnesota for full information.)					
Pennsylvania Capital Corp. of America Martin M. Newman, Pres. 225 S. 15th St., Ste.	03/03-0040	1,302,135	1,315,000	Diversified	6

Licensee	License No.	Private Capital	SBA Leverage	Investment Policy	Owner Code*
920 Philadelphia, PA 19102 (215) 743-1666 Date Lic.:	08/09/84				
Central Capital Corp. Robert Murray, Pres. Philadelphia National Bank Bldg., 7th Floor Broad & Chestnut Sts. Philadelphia, PA 19107 (215) 629-2836 Date Lic.:	03/03-0140 04/20/79	1,000,000	1,000,000	Diversified	1
Enterprise Venture Capital Corp. of Pennsylvania Don Cowie, CEO 227 Franklin St., Ste. 215 Johnstown, PA 15961 (814) 535-7597 Date Lic.:	03/03-0179 09/11/85	1,147,649	0	Diversified	1
Erie SBIC George R. Heaton, Pres. 32 W. Eighth St., Ste. 615 Erie, PA 16501 (814) 453-7964 Date Lic.:	03/03-0177 07/19/85	1,080,000	1,000,000	Diversified	5
First SBIC of California Daniel A. Dye, Contact P.O. Box 512 Washington, PA 15301 (412) 223-0707 (See listing under California for full information.)					
First Valley Capital Corp. Matthew W. Thomas, Pres.	03/03-0160	510,000	0	Diversified	1

Licensee	License No.	Private Capital	SBA Leverage	Investment Policy	Owner Code*
One Center Sq., Ste. 201 Allentown, PA 18101 (215) 776-6760 Date Lic.:	08/19/83				
Meridian Capital Corp. Knute C. Albrecht, Pres. Blue Bell West, Ste. 122 650 Skippack Pike Blue Bell, PA 19422 (215) 278-8907 Date Lic.:	03/03-0127 07/22/77	1,820,000	0	Diversified	1
PNC Capital Corp. Gary J. Zentner, Pres. Pittsburgh National Bldg. Fifth Ave. & Wood St. Pittsburgh, PA 15222 (412) 355-2245 Date Lic.:	03/03-0152 08/12/82	3,194,971	1,000,000	Diversified	1
Rhode Island Domestic Capital Corp. Nathaniel B. Baker, Pres. 815 Reservoir Ave. Cranston, RI 02910 (401) 946-3310 Date Lic.:	01/01-0333 12/11/84	500,000	1,000,000	Diversified	1
Fleet Venture Resources, Inc. Robert M. Van Degna, Pres. 111 Westminster St. Providence, RI 02903 (401) 278-6770 Date Lic.:	01/01-0067 12/13/67	6,509,800	1,500,000	Diversified	1
Moneta Capital Corp. Arnold Kilberg, Pres. 285 Governor St. Providence, RI 02906 (401) 861-4600 Date Lic.:	01/01-0322 05/04/84	500,000	0	Diversified	5

Licensee	License No.	Private Capital	SBA Leverage	Investment Policy	Owner Code*
Old Stone Capital Corp. Arthur C. Barton, Exec. V.P. One Old Stone Sq., 11th Floor Providence, RI 02903 (401) 278-2559 Date Lic.:	01/13-0008 07/20/61	6,991,500	11,370,000	Diversified	3
River Capital Corp. 55 S. Main St. Providence, RI 02903 (401) 861-7470 (See listing under Virginia for full information.)					
Wallace Capital Corp. Lloyd W. Granoff, Pres. 170 Westminister St., Ste. 300 Providence, RI 02903 (401) 273-9191 Date Lic.:	01/01-0338 12/22/86	1,015,000	0	Diversified	4
South Carolina Carolina Venture Capital Corp. Thomas H. Harvey III, Pres. 14 Archer Rd. Hilton Head Island, SC 29928 (803) 842-3101 Date Lic.:	04/04-0201 01/19/81	792,100	700,000	Diversified	5
Charleston Capital Corp. Henry Yaschik, Pres. 111 Church St. P.O. Box 328 Charleston, SC 29402 (803) 723-6464 Date Lic.:	04/04-0042 06/21/61	1,012,409	500,000	Diversified	5
The Floco Investment Co., Inc.	04/04-0032	491,900	0	Food Retailers	5

Licensee	License No.	Private Capital	SBA Leverage	Investment Policy	Owner Code*
William H. Johnson, Sr., Pres. Hwy. 52, North (Mail: P.O. Box 919; Lake City 29560) Scranton, SC 29561 (803) 389-2731 Date Lic.:	07/05/61				
Lowcountry Investment Corp. Joseph T. Newton, Jr., Pres. 4444 Daley St. P.O. Box 10447 Charleston, SC 29411 (803) 554-9880 Date Lic.:	04/04-0021 07/28/60	1,908,950	3,000,000	Grocery Stores	4
Reedy River Ventures John M. Sterling, Pres. 400 Haywood Rd. P.O. Box 17526 Greenville, SC 29606 (803) 297-9198 Date Lic.:	04/04-0198 07/16/81	1,796,300	3,200,000	Diversified	5-P
Tennessee Financial Resources, Inc. Milton Picard, Chairman 2800 Sterick Bldg. Memphis, TN 38103 (901) 527-9411 Date Lic.:	04/05-0064 03/21/62	1,000,320	0	Diversified	5
Leader Capital Corp. James E. Pruitt, Jr., Pres. 158 Madison Ave. P.O. Box 708 Memphis, TN 38103 (901) 578-2405 Date Lic.:	04/04-0237 06/23/86	1,000,000	0	Diversified	3
Suwannee Capital Corp. Peter R. Pettit, Pres.	04/04-0136	2,383,929	500,000	Grocery Stores	5

Licensee	License No.	Private Capital	SBA Leverage	Investment Policy	Owner Code*
3030 Poplar Ave. Memphis, TN 38111 (901) 325-4315 Date Lic.:	07/11/78				
Texas Alliance Business Investment Co. 911 Louisiana One Shell Plaza, Ste. 3990 Houston, TX 77002 (713) 224-8224 (See listing under Oklahoma for full information.)					
Allied Bancshares Capital Corp. D. Kent Anderson, Chairman 1000 Louisiana, Seventh Floor (Mail: P.O. Box 3326; Houston 77253) Houston, TX 77002 (713) 224-6611 Date Lic.:	06/06-0219 11/01/79	19,057,008	19,000,000	Diversified	1
Americap Corp. James L. Hurn, Pres. 7575 San Felipe Houston, TX 77063 (713) 780-8084 Date Lic.:	06/06-0265 03/01/83	1,045,000	3,600,000	Diversified	1
Ameriway Venture Partners I James L. Hurn, G.P. 7575 San Felipe Houston, TX 77063 (713) 780-8084 Date Lic.:	06/06-0290 11/19/85	1,055,000	1,000,000	Diversified	1-P
Banctexas Capital, Inc. Alfred Bowman, Pres. 1601 Elm St., Ste. 800 Dallas, TX 75201 (214) 969-6382 Date Lic.:	06/06-0242 02/27/81	1,003,500	500,000	Diversified	1

Licensee	License No.	Private Capital	SBA Leverage	Investment Policy	Owner Code*
Brittany Capital Co. Robert E. Clements, Pres. 1525 Elm St. 2424 LTV Tower Dallas, TX 75201 (214) 742-5810 Date Lic.:	06/10-0152 08/04/69	750,000	2,425,000	Diversified	5-P
Business Capital Corp. James E. Sowell, Chairman 4809 Cole Ave., Ste. 250 Dallas, TX 75205 (214) 522-3739 Date Lic.:	06/06-0253 09/30/82	510,000	800,000	Diversified	5
Capital Marketing Corp. John Myrick, Pres. 100 Nat Gibbs Dr. P.O. Box 1000 Keller, TX 76248 (817) 656-7380 Date Lic.:	06/10-0150 06/24/68	11,082,311	32,390,000	Grocery Stores	4
Capital Southwest Venture Corp. William R. Thomas, Pres. 12900 Preston Rd., Ste. 700 Dallas, TX 75230 (214) 233-8242 Date Lic.:	06/10-0065 07/13/61	4,715,585	16,000,000	Diversified	6
Central Texas SBI Corp. David G. Horner, Pres. P.O. Box 829 Waco, TX 76703 (817) 753-6461 Date Lic.:	06/10-0076 03/29/62	600,000	75,000	Diversified	1
Charter Venture Group, Inc. Winston C. Davis, Pres.	06/06-0237	1,000,000	1,000,000	Diversified	1

Licensee	License No.	Private Capital	SBA Leverage	Investment Policy	Owner Code*
2600 Citadel Plaza Dr., Ste. 600 Houston, TX 77008 (713) 863-0704 Date Lic.:	10/10/80				
Citicorp Venture Capital, Ltd. 717 N. Harwood St. Dallas, TX 75201 (214) 880-9670 (See listing under New York for full information.)					
Energy Assets, Inc.	06/06-0211	683,109	500,000	Various Firms In Energy Industry	4
Laurence E. Simmons, Exec. V.P. 4900 Republic Bank Center Houston, TX 77002 (713) 236-9999 Date Lic.:	04/12/79				
Energy Capital Corp. Herbert F. Poyner, Pres. 953 Esperson Bldg. Houston, TX 77002 (713) 236-0006 Date Lic.:	06/06-0231 09/09/80	11,285,613	1,500,000	Diversified	5
Enterprise Capital Corp. Fred Zeidman, Pres. 3501 Allen Pkwy. Houston, TX 77019 (713) 526-8070 Date Lic.:	06/10-0154 05/08/70	5,000,000	10,000,000	Diversified	3
FCA Investment Co. William J. Moore, Mgr. 3000 Post Oak, Ste. 1790 Houston, TX 77056 (713) 965-0061 Date Lic.:	06/06-0289 08/19/85	1,017,000	0	Diversified	5

Licensee	License No.	Private Capital	SBA Leverage	Investment Policy	Owner Code*
Ford Capital, Ltd. Gerald J. Ford, Pres. 1525 Elm St. (Mail: P.O. Box 2140; Dallas 75221) Dallas, TX 75201 (214) 954-0688 Date Lic.:	06/06-0292 10/06/86	7,965,000	0	Diversified	1-P
Grocers SBI Corp. Milton E. Levit, Pres. 3131 E. Holcombe Blvd., Ste. 101 Houston, TX 77021 (713) 747-7913 Date Lic.:	06/06-0187 02/14/77	1,000,000	1,000,000	Grocery Stores	4
Interfirst Venture Corp. James O'Donnell, Pres. 901 Main St., 10th Floor P.O. Box 83000 Dallas, TX 75283 (214) 977-3160 Date Lic.:	06/10-0056 06/22/61	12,500,044	9,000,000	Diversified	1
Livingston Capital, Ltd. J. Livingston Kosberg, G.P. 5701 Woodway, Ste. 332 Houston, TX 77057 (713) 977-4040 Date Lic.:	06/06-0220 01/07/80	1,000,000	1,450,000	Diversified	5-P
MVenture Corp. Wayne Gaylord, Sr., V.P. Main at Ervay P.O. Box 662090 Dallas, TX 75266 (214) 741-1469 Date Lic.:	06/06-0188 12/08/76	16,250,000	35,000,000	Diversified	1
Mapleleaf Capital Corp. Edward Fink, Pres.	06/06-0239	3,000,002	2,000,000	Diversified	2

Licensee	License No.	Private Capital	SBA Leverage	Investment Policy	Owner Code*
55 Waugh, Ste. 710 Houston, TX 77007 (713) 880-4494 Date Lic.:	10/06/80				
Mid-State Capital Corp. Smith E. Thomasson, Pres. 510 N. Valley Mills Dr. Waco, TX 76710 (817) 772-9220 Date Lic.:	06/06-0287 03/04/85	1,400,000	0	Diversified	2
Neptune Capital Corp. Richard C. Strauss, Pres. 5956 Sherry La., Ste. 800 Dallas, TX 75225 (214) 739-1414 Date Lic.:	06/06-0293 12/23/86	1,050,000	0	Diversified	5
Omega Capital Corp. Theodric E. Moor, Jr., Pres. 755 S. 11th St., Ste. 250 P.O. Box 2173 Beaumont, TX 77704 (409) 832-0221 Date Lic.:	06/06-0260 08/12/82	530,000	500,000	Diversified	5
Red River Ventures, Inc. Delwin W. Morton, Pres. 777 E. 15th St. Plano, TX 75074 (214) 422-4999 Date Lic.:	06/06-0170 02/21/74	1,251,000	1,500,000	Diversified	3
Republic Venture Group, Inc. Robert H. Wellborn, Pres. P.O. Box 225961 Dallas, TX 75265 (214) 922-5078	06/10-0059	11,000,000	0	Diversified	1

Licensee	License No.	Private Capital	SBA Leverage	Investment Policy	Owner Code*
Date Lic.:	06/26/61				
Retzloff Capital Corp. Steven Retzloff, Pres. 15000 N.W. Freeway, Ste. 310A Houston, TX 77240 (713) 466-4690	06/06-0279	2,500,000	4,000,000	Diversified	5
Date Lic.:	12/08/83				
Rust Capital Ltd. Jeffrey Garvey, Partner 114 W. Seventh St., Ste. 1300 Austin, TX 78701 (512) 479-0055	06/06-0209	7,000,000	12,000,000	Diversified	3-P
Date Lic.:	05/04/79				
SBI Capital Corp. William E. Wright, Pres. 6305 Beverly Hill La. (Mail: P.O. Box 771668; Houston 77215) Houston, TX 77057 (713) 975-1188	06/06-0244	2,250,000	2,700,000	Diversified	5
Date Lic.:	10/22/81				
San Antonio Venture Group, Inc. Domingo Bueno, Pres. 2300 W. Commerce St. San Antonio, TX 78207 (512) 223-3633	06/06-0190	1,051,000	0	Diversified	4
Date Lic.:	03/23/78				
South Texas SBIC Arthur E. Buckert, Treasurer 120 S. Main St. P.O. Box 1698 Victoria, TX 77901 (512) 573-5151	06/10-0019	1,500,000	1,000,000	Diversified	1
Date Lic.:	05/08/61				
Southwestern Venture Capital of Texas, Inc. James A. Bettersworth, Pres.	06/06-0234	1,326,000	1,000,000	Diversified	2

Licensee	License No.	Private Capital	SBA Leverage	Investment Policy	Owner Code*
1336 E. Court St. P.O. Box 1719 Seguin, TX 78155 (512) 379-0380 Date Lic.: or 1250 N.E. Loop 410, Ste. 300 San Antonio, TX 78209 (512) 822-9949	11/24/80				
Sunwestern Capital Corp. Thomas W. Wright, Pres. 3 Forest Plaza 12221 Merit Dr., Ste. 1680 Dallas, TX 75251 (214) 239-5650 Date Lic.:	06/06-0266 03/07/83	2,102,645	5,500,000	Diversified	5
Sunwestern Ventures Co. Thomas W. Wright, Pres. 3 Forest Plaza 12221 Merit Dr., Ste. 1680 Dallas, TX 75251 (214) 239-5650 Date Lic.:	06/06-0286 10/22/84	10,000,000	5,000,000	Diversified	5
Texas Commerce Investment Co. Fred Lummis, V.P. Texas Commerce Bank Bldg., Ste. 3100 712 Main St. Houston, TX 77002 (713) 236-5332 Date Lic.:	06/06-0258 06/09/82	8,700,000	0	Diversified	1
United Mercantile Capital Corp. Joe Justice, Gen. Mgr. 444 Executive Center Blvd., Ste. 222	06/06-0184	629,888	1,200,000	Diversified	5

Licensee	License No.	Private Capital	SBA Leverage	Investment Policy	Owner Code*
(Mail: P.O. Box 66; El Paso 79940) El Paso, TX 79902 (915) 533-6375 Date Lic.:	11/16/76				
Wesbanc Ventures, Ltd. Stuart Schube, G.P. 2401 Fountainview, Ste. 950 Houston, TX 77057 (713) 977-7421 Date Lic.:	06/06-0288 05/28/85	2,550,000	0	Diversified	1-P
Virginia James River Capital Associatcs A. IIugh Ewing, Managing Partner 9 S. 12th St. (Mail: P.O. Box 1776; Richmond 23219) Richmond, VA 23214 (804) 643-7323 Date Lic.:	03/03-0146 05/15/81	1,144,875	2,500,000	Diversified	5-P
Metropolitan Capital Corp. John B. Toomey, Pres. 2550 Huntington Ave. Alexandria, VA 22303 (703) 960-4698 Date Lic.:	03/04-0107 12/02/70	1,826,893	2,590,000	Diversified	4
River Capital Corp. Peter Van Oosterhout, Pres. 1033 N. Fairfax St. Alexandria, VA 22314 (703) 739-2100 Date Lic.:	03/01-0320 06/29/82	5,000,000	20,000,000	Diversified	1
Sovran Funding Corp. David A. King, Jr., Pres. Sovran Center, Sixth Floor One Commercial Plaza	03/03-0176	5,000,000	0	Diversified	1

Licensee	License No.	Private Capital	SBA Leverage	Investment Policy	Owner Code*
P.O. Box 600 Norfolk, VA 23510 (804) 441-4041 Date Lic.:	02/11/85				
Tidewater Industrial Capital Corp. Armand Caplan, Pres. United Virginia Bank Bldg., Ste. 1424 Norfolk, VA 23510 (804) 622-1501 Date Lic.:	03/04-0065 02/13/62	758,200	760,000	Diversified	4
Tidewater SBI Corp. Robert H. Schmidt, Pres. 1214 First Virginia Bank Tower 101 St. Paul's Blvd. Norfolk, VA 23510 (804) 627-2315 Date Lic.:	03/04-0100 02/05/65	1,000,000	500,000	Diversified	4
UV Capital A. Hugh Ewing III, Managing G.P. 9 S. 12th St., 3d Floor Richmond, VA 23219 (804) 643-7358 Date Lic.:	03/03-0175 10/29/84	5,050,505	0	Diversified	5
Washington Capital Resource Corp. T. Evans Wyckoff, Pres. 1001 Logan Bldg. Seattle, WA 98101 (206) 623-6550 Date Lic.:	10/10-0171 05/19/80	1,124,873	1,000,000	Diversified	5
Northwest Business Investment Corp. C. Paul Sandifur, Pres. 929 W. Sprague Ave. Spokane, WA 99204 (509) 838-3111 Date Lic.:	10/13-0005 03/16/61	238,680	0	Diversified	5
Peoples Capital Corp. Robert E. Karns, Pres.	10/10-0174	1,730,000	0	Diversified	1

Licensee	License No.	Private Capital	SBA Leverage	Investment Policy	Owner Code*
1415 Fifth Ave. Seattle, WA 98171 (206) 344-5463 Date Lic.:	03/05/81				
Seafirst Capital Corp. R. Bruce Harrod, Pres. Columbia Seafirst Center 701 Fifth Ave. P.O. Box 34103 Seattle, WA 98124 (206) 442-3520 Date Lic.:	10/10-0166 06/18/80	3,000,000	5,500,000	Diversified	1
Washington Trust Equity Corp. John M. Snead, Pres. Washington Trust Financial Center P.O. Box 2127 Spokane, WA 99210 (509) 455-4106 Date Lic.:	10/10-0170 02/21/80	700,000	0	Diversified	1
Wisconsin Bando-McGlocklin Investment Co., Inc. George Schonath, Investment Advisor 13555 Bishops Court, Ste. 225 Brookfield, WI 53005 (414) 784-9010 Date Lic.:	05/05-0147 09/02/80	3,000,000	8,900,000	Diversified	5
Capital Investments, Inc. Robert L. Banner, V.P. Commerce Bldg., Ste. 400 744 N. Fourth St. Milwaukee, WI 53203 (414) 273-6560 Date Lic.:	05/07-0003 05/25/59	3,159,044	7,580,000	Diversified	6
M & I Ventures Corp. John T. Byrnes, Pres. 770 N. Water St. Milwaukee, WI 53202	05/05-0202	3,030,000	0	Diversified	1

Licensee	License No.	Private Capital	SBA Leverage	Investment Policy	Owner Code*
(414) 765-7910 Date Lic.:	08/19/85				
Marine Venture Capital, Inc. H. Wayne Foreman, Pres. 111 E. Wisconsin Ave. Milwaukee, WI 53202 (414) 765-2274 Date Lic.:	05/05-0195 05/02/84	3,000,000	0	Diversified	1
MorAmerica Capital Corp. 600 E. Mason St. Milwaukee, WI 53202 (414) 276-3839 (See listing under Iowa for full information.)					
Super Market Investors, Inc. John W. Andorfer, Pres. 23000 Roundy Dr. (Mail: P.O. Box 473; Milwaukee 53202) Pewaukee, WI 53072 (414) 547-7999 Date Lic.:	05/05-0136 01/25/79	500,000	750,000	Grocery Stores	4
Twin Ports Capital Co. Paul Leonidas, Pres. 1228 Poplar Ave. Superior, WI 54880 (715) 392-8131 Date Lic.:	05/05-0188 03/20/84	510,000	0	50% Grocery Stores	4
Wisconsin Community Capital, Inc. Francis J. David, Gen. Mgr. 14 W. Mifflin St., Ste. 314 Madison, WI 53703 (608) 256-3441 Date Lic.:	05/05-0204 12/17/85	1,005,000	0	Diversified	5
Wyoming Capital Corp. of	08/08-0048	1,000,000	1,000,000	Diversified	3

Licensee	License No.	Private Capital	SBA Leverage	Investment Policy	Owner Code*
Wyoming, Inc.					
Scott Weaver, Mgr.					
P.O. Box 3599					
145 S. Durbin St.					
Casper, WY 82602					
(307) 234-5351					
Date Lic.:	09/27/79				

SBIC LICENSEES
TOTALS BY STATES

State	No. of SBICs					Total Private Cap	Total Obligations to SBA
	Size 1	Size 2	Size 3	Size 4	Total		
Alabama	0	0	2	1	3	11,666,800	6,500,000
Alaska	0	0	1	0	1	2,500,000	0
Arizona	0	1	1	1	3	18,600,000	500,000
Arkansas	0	2	1	0	3	2,237,859	3,750,000
California	0	17	22	5	44	152,844,645	61,514,000
Colorado	0	1	2	0	3	4,150,000	5,500,000
Connecticut	0	7	1	2	10	24,482,128	46,905,000
Delaware	0	0	0	0	0	0	0
District of Columbia	0	1	3	0	4	8,784,708	10,500,000
Florida	0	3	5	1	9	20,152,378	39,208,804
Georgia	0	1	2	0	3	5,699,200	4,500,000
Hawaii	0	1	0	0	1	1,000,000	500,000
Idaho	0	0	0	0	0	0	0
Illinois	0	2	4	3	9	83,333,581	16,700,000
Indiana	0	1	5	0	6	11,000,040	1,400,000
Iowa	0	0	1	0	1	5,000,000	12,150,440
Kansas	0	0	1	0	1	1,075,240	0
Kentucky	0	1	1	0	2	2,540,000	3,600,000
Louisiana	0	3	4	0	7	10,542,731	9,015,000
Maine	0	1	0	0	1	1,000,000	1,000,000
Maryland	0	1	1	1	3	20,428,217	5,513,720
Massachusetts	1	5	11	6	23	102,493,406	121,075,000
Michigan	0	1	2	1	4	38,487,265	0
Minnesota	0	4	5	2	11	72,722,486	42,570,000
Mississippi	0	1	0	0	1	800,000	509,000
Missouri	0	2	3	0	5	10,167,000	2,900,000
Montana	0	0	0	0	0	0	0
Nebraska	0	1	0	0	1	500,000	0
Nevada	0	1	0	0	1	1,000,000	800,000
New Hampshire	0	1	1	0	2	2,142,500	0
New Jersey	0	3	4	0	7	12,768,767	18,322,000
New Mexico	0	3	0	0	3	2,120,276	4,430,000

State	No. of SBICs					Total Private Cap	Total Obligations to SBA
	Size 1	Size 2	Size 3	Size 4	Total		
New York	2	25	21	14	62	376,324,655	228,395,000
North Carolina	0	1	5	1	7	19,572,502	11,010,459
North Dakota	0	0	0	0	0	0	0
Ohio	0	5	5	1	11	22,571,524	19,812,400
Oklahoma	0	1	3	0	4	7,261,867	7,660,000
Oregon	0	1	0	0	1	911,464	800,000
Pennsylvania	0	2	5	0	7	10,054,755	4,315,000
Puerto Rico	0	0	0	0	0	0	0
Rhode Island	0	2	1	2	5	15,516,300	13,870,000
South Carolina	0	2	3	0	5	6,001,659	7,400,000
South Dakota	0	0	0	0	0	0	0
Tennessee	0	1	2	0	3	4,384,249	500,000
Texas	0	9	17	10	36	155,359,705	171,640,000
Utah	0	0	0	0	0	0	0
Vermont	0	0	0	0	0	0	0
Virginia	0	2	4	1	7	19,780,473	26,350,000
Washington	1	1	3	0	5	6,793,553	6,500,000
West Virginia	0	0	0	0	0	0	0
Wisconsin	0	2	5	0	7	14,204,044	17,230,000
Wyoming	0	1	0	0	1	1,000,000	1,000,000
TOTAL	4	120	157	52	333	1,289,975,977	935,845,823

SBIC LICENSEES
TOTALS BY PRIVATE CAPITAL SIZE CLASS

Total Private Capital Size Class	Total No. of SBICs	Total Private Capital	Total Obligations to SBA
Size 1—$300,000 or less	4	898,980	215,000
Size 2—$300,001 to $1 million	120	85,705,766	94,981,492
Size 3—$1 million to $5 million	157	355,766,157	403,985,611
Size 4—more than $5 million	52	847,605,074	436,663,720
TOTAL	333	1,289,975,977	935,845,823

SBIC LICENSEES
TOTALS BY TYPE OF OWNERSHIP

Total Private Capital Size Class	Total No. of SBICs	Total Private Capital	Total Obligations to SBA
Bank Dominated	96	753,335,773	232,038,712
Bank Associated	13	64,780,806	18,200,000
Financial Organization	21	62,999,527	117,865,554

Total Private Capital Size Class	Total No. of SBICs	Total Private Capital	Total Obligations to SBA
Nonfinancial Organization	29	45,165,810	85,560,000
Individually Owned	158	304,275,888	383,210,492
40' Act Company	16	59,418,173	98,971,065
TOTAL	333	1,289,975,977	935,845,823

SBIC LICENSEES
PRIVATE CAPITAL BY TYPE OF OWNERSHIP

Type of Ownership	Private Capital Size Class							
	Size 1		Size 2		Size 3		Size 4	
	No.	Dollars	No.	Dollars	No.	Dollars	No.	Dollars
Bank Dominated	0	0	19	15,877,759	46	120,290,474	31	617,167,540
Bank Associated	0	0	1	501,118	10	15,879,688	2	48,400,000
Financial Organization	0	0	6	4,817,552	12	34,190,475	3	23,991,500
Nonfinancial Organization	2	450,000	16	10,678,460	9	16,382,843	2	17,654,507
Individually Owned	2	448,980	75	52,463,411	70	143,189,669	11	108,173,828
40' Act Company	0	0	3	1,367,466	10	25,833,008	3	32,217,699

PART II: 301(D) SBIC LICENSEES

Licensee	License No.	Private Capital	SBA Leverage	Investment Policy	Owner Code*
Alabama					
Alabama Capital Corp. David C. Delaney, Pres. 16 Midtown Park, East Mobile, AL 36606 (205) 476-0700	04/04-5203	1,550,000	4,650,000	Diversified	5
Date Lic.:	07/28/81				
Tuskegee Capital Corp. A. G. Bartholomew, Pres. 4453 Richardson Rd. Hampton Hall Bldg. Montgomery, AL 36108 (205) 281-8059	04/04-5215	850,000	0	Diversified	5
Date Lic.:	02/09/83				

*Owner Code: 1, bank dominated (50 percent or more owned by bank or bank holding company); 2, bank associated (10 percent to 49 percent owned by bank or bank holding company); 3, financial organization other than bank or bank holding company (public or nonpublic); 4, nonfinancial organization (public or nonpublic); 5, individually owned (privately held); 6, 40' act company. An owner code followed by "P" signifies partnership.

Licensee	License No.	Private Capital	SBA Leverage	Investment Policy	Owner Code*
Alaska					
Calista Business Investment Corp. Alex Raider, Pres. 516 Denali St. Anchorage, AK 99501 (907) 277-0425	10/10-5181	750,000	750,000	Diversified	5
Date Lic.:	03/31/83				
Arkansas					
Capital Management Services, Inc. David L. Hale, Pres. 1910 N. Grant St., Ste. 200 Little Rock, AR 72207 (501) 664-8613	06/06-5207	1,006,310	2,500,000	Diversified	5
Date Lic.:	03/14/79				
Kar-Mal Venture Capital, Inc. Amelia Karam, Pres. 2821 Kavanaugh Blvd. Little Rock, AR 72205 (501) 661-0010	06/06-5185	500,000	1,000,000	Diversified	4
Date Lic.:	11/23/77				
Power Ventures, Inc. Dorsey D. Glover, Pres. 829 Hwy. 270, North Malvern, AR 72104 (501) 332-3695	06/06-5235	500,000	1,000,000	Diversified	5
Date Lic.:	02/26/81				
Worthen Finance and Investment, Inc. Larry K. Stephens, Pres. 200 W. Capitol Ave. Little Rock, AR 72201 (501) 378-1672	06/03-5168	3,010,000	2,000,000	Diversified	1
Date Lic.:	10/31/83				
California					
ABC Capital Corp. Anne B. Cheng, Pres. 2225 W. Commonwealth Ave., Ste. 216 Alhambra, CA 91801 (818) 570-0653	09/09-5352	1,000,000	3,000,000	Diversified	5
Date Lic.:	01/09/85				

Licensee	License No.	Private Capital	SBA Leverage	Investment Policy	Owner Code*
Allied Business Investors, Inc. Jack Hong, Pres. 428 S. Atlantic Blvd., Ste. 201 Monterey Park, CA 91754 (213) 289-0186 Date Lic.:	09/09-5309 12/29/82	600,000	950,000	Diversified	5
Ally Finance Corp. Percy P. Lin, Pres. 9100 Wilshire Blvd., Ste. 408 Beverly Hills, CA 90212 (213) 550-8100 Date Lic.:	09/09-5299 06/04/82	600,000	950,000	Diversified	5
Asian American Capital Corp. David Der, Pres. 1251 W. Tennyson Rd., Ste. 4 Hayward, CA 94544 (415) 887-6888 Date Lic.:	09/09-5279 02/23/81	635,000	1,000,000	Diversified	5
Associates Venture Capital Corp. Walter P. Strycker, Pres. 425 California St., Ste. 2203 San Francisco, CA 94104 (415) 956-1444 Date Lic.:	09/09-5222 06/26/78	540,000	525,000	Diversified	5
Astar Capital Corp. George Hsu, Pres. 7282 Orangethorpe Ave., Ste. 8 Buena Park, CA 90621 (714) 739-2218 Date Lic.:	09/09-5370 11/06/86	1,020,000	0	Diversified	5
Business Equity and Development Corp. Ricardo Olivarez, Pres. 1411 W. Olympic Blvd., Ste. 200 Los Angeles, CA 90015	09/12-5151	1,873,034	1,000,000	Diversified	5

Licensee	License No.	Private Capital	SBA Leverage	Investment Policy	Owner Code*
(213) 385-0351 Date Lic.:	03/19/70				
Charterway Investment Corp. Harold H. M. Chuang, Pres. 222 S. Hill St., Ste. 800 Los Angeles, CA 90012 (213) 687-8539 Date Lic.:	09/09-5338 04/04/84	1,588,336	1,000,000	Diversified	5
Continental Investors, Inc. Lac Thantrong, Pres. 8781 Seaspray Dr. Huntington Beach, CA 92646 (714) 964-5207 Date Lic.:	09/09-5144 06/18/80	2,000,000	5,000,000	Diversified	5
Dime Investment Corp. Chun Y. Lee, Pres. 3701 Wilshire Blvd., Ste. 608 Los Angeles, CA 90010 (213) 739-1847 Date Lic.:	09/09-5298 07/07/82	500,000	1,500,000	Diversified	5
Equitable Capital Corp. John C. Lee, Pres. 855 Sansome St. San Francisco, CA 94111 (415) 434-4114 Date Lic.:	09/09-5331 03/08/79	502,997	1,505,000	Diversified	5
First American Capital Funding, Inc. Luu Trankiem, Pres. 9872 Chapman Ave., Ste. 216 Garden City, CA 92641 (714) 638-7171 Date Lic.:	09/09-5332 05/02/84	734,000	1,968,000	Diversified	5
Jeanjoo Finance, Inc. Chester Koo, Pres. 700 S. Flower St., Ste. 3305 Los Angeles, CA 90017	09/09-5361	1,000,000	0	Diversified	5

Licensee	License No.	Private Capital	SBA Leverage	Investment Policy	Owner Code*
(213) 627-6600 Date Lic.:	09/20/85				
LaiLai Capital Corp. Hsing-Jong Duan, Pres. 1545 Wilshire Blvd., Ste. 510 Los Angeles, CA 90017 (213) 484-5085 Date Lic.:	09/09-5285 11/24/82	1,000,000	700,000	Diversified	5
Los Angeles Capital Corp. Kuytae Hwang, Pres. 606 N. Larchmont Blvd., Ste. 309 Los Angeles, CA 90004 (213) 460-4646 Date Lic.:	09/09-5323 08/30/83	1,006,500	1,500,000	Diversified	5
Magna Pacific Investments David Wong, Pres. 977 N. Broadway, Ste. 301 Los Angeles, CA 90012 (213) 680-2505 Date Lic.:	09/09-5362 12/03/85	1,000,000	1,080,000	Diversified	5
Myriad Capital, Inc. Chuang-I Lin, Pres. 113 E. Savarona Way Carson, CA 90746 (213) 327-7539 Date Lic.:	09/09-5272 09/16/80	1,334,530	5,338,120	Diversified	5
New Kukje Investment Co. George Su Chey, Pres. 958 S. Vermont Ave., Ste. C Los Angeles, CA 90006 (213) 389-8679 Date Lic.:	09/09-5343 01/10/85	1,000,000	1,000,000	Diversified	5
Opportunity Capital Corp. J. Peter Thompson, Pres. 50 California St., Ste. 2505	09/12-5155	2,510,849	2,290,535	Diversified	2

Licensee	License No.	Private Capital	SBA Leverage	Investment Policy	Owner Code*
San Francisco, CA 94111 (415) 421-5935 Date Lic.:	09/23/71				
Pacific Capital Fund, Inc. Eduardo B. Cu Ujieng, Pres. 675 Mariners' Island Blvd., Ste. 103 San Mateo, CA 94404 (415) 574-2688 Date Lic.:	09/09-5265 07/27/81	1,040,000	2,000,000	Diversified	5
Positive Enterprises, Inc. Kwok Szeto, Pres. 399 Arguello St. San Francisco, CA 94118 (415) 386-6606 Date Lic.:	09/09-5256 06/06/80	505,000	505,000	Diversified	5
RSC Financial Corp. Frederick K. Bae, Pres. 223 E. Thousand Oaks Blvd., Ste. 310 Thousand Oaks, CA 91360 (805) 496-2955 Date Lic.:	09/09-5161 09/28/72	526,508	2,000,000	Diversified	3
United Business Ventures, Inc. Gary L. Roberts, CEO 711 Van Ness Ave., 5th Floor San Francisco, CA 94102 (415) 929-6104 Date Lic.:	09/09-5176 11/01/74	1,010,000	1,000,000	Diversified	4
Wilshire Capital, Inc. Kyu-Han Lee, Pres. 3932 Wilshire Blvd., Ste. 305 Los Angeles, CA 90010 (213) 388-1111 Date Lic.:	09/09-5355 02/15/85	2,073,207	0	Diversified	4
Worthen Finance and Investment, Inc. 3660 Wilshire Blvd., Ste. 1110					

Licensee	License No.	Private Capital	SBA Leverage	Investment Policy	Owner Code*
Los Angeles, CA 90010 (213) 480-1908 (See listing under Arkansas for full information.)					
Colorado					
Mile Hi Small Business Investment Co. Samuel E. Matthews, Pres. 1999 Broadway, Ste. 2100 Denver, CO 80202 (303) 293-2431	08/08-5058	550,000	0	Diversified	5
Date Lic.:	06/18/84				
District of Columbia					
Allied Financial Corp. David J. Gladstone, Pres. 1666 K St., N.W., Ste. 901 Washington, DC 20006 (202) 331-1112	03/03-5163	2,000,000	3,000,000	Diversified	6
Date Lic.:	08/09/83				
Broadcast Capital, Inc. John E. Oxendine, Pres. 1771 N St., N.W., Ste. 421 Washington, DC 20036 (202) 429-5393	03/03-5147	2,000,000	3,000,000	Communications Media	5
Date Lic.:	11/26/80				
Consumers United Capital Corp. Donna Barnes, Pres. 2100 M St., N.W. Washington, DC 20036 (202) 872-5274	03/03-5171	1,008,000	0	Diversified	4
Date Lic.:	04/22/85				
Fulcrum Venture Capital Corp. Larry Edler, Pres. 2021 K St., N.W., Ste. 714 Washington, DC 20006 (202) 833-9580	03/03-5135	2,000,000	2,000,000	Diversified	3
Date Lic.:	07/05/78				

Licensee	License No.	Private Capital	SBA Leverage	Investment Policy	Owner Code*
Minority Broadcast Investment Corp. Walter L. Threadgill, Pres. 1820 Jefferson Pl., N.W. Washington, DC 20036 (202) 293-1166 Date Lic.:	03/03-5142 08/07/79	1,000,100	1,500,100	Communications	5
Syncom Capital Corp. Herbert P. Wilkins, Pres. 1030-15th St., N.W., Ste. 203 Washington, DC 20005 (202) 293-9428 Date Lic.:	03/03-5137 07/10/78	2,250,000	5,125,000	Communications Media	4

Florida

The First American Lending Corp. Roy W. Talmo, Chairman 1926 Tenth Ave., North (Mail: P.O. Box 24660; West Palm Beach 33416) Lake Worth, FL 33460 (305) 533-1511 Date Lic.:	04/04-5162 09/27/79	500,000	500,000	Diversified	1
Horn & Hardart Capital Corp. Morton Farber, Mgr. 701 S.E. Sixth Ave. Del Ray Beach, FL 33444 (305) 265-0751 Date Lic.:	04/04-5228 09/11/85	1,000,000	0	Diversified	5
Ideal Financial Corp. Ectore T. Reynaldo, Gen. Mgr. 780 N.W. 42d Ave., Ste. 303 Miami, FL 33126 (305) 442-4665 Date Lic.:	04/04-5190 03/07/83	500,000	500,000	Diversified	5
Pro-Med Investment Corp. Mrs. Marion Rosemore, Pres. 1380 N.E. Miami	04/04-5240	1,000,000	0	Diversified	6

Licensee	License No.	Private Capital	SBA Leverage	Investment Policy	Owner Code*
Gardens Dr., Ste. 225 North Miami Beach, FL 33179 (305) 949-5915 Date Lic.:	11/28/86				
Safeco Capital, Inc. Rene J. Leonard, Pres. 835 S.W. 37th Ave. Miami, FL 33135 (305) 443-7953 Date Lic.:	04/04-5158 08/30/79	500,000	1,000,000	Diversified	5
Universal Financial Services, Inc. Norman Zipkin, Pres. 3550 Biscayne Blvd., Ste. 702 Miami, FL 33137 (305) 573-1496 Date Lic.:	04/04-5153 09/15/78	500,000	1,000,000	Diversified	5
Venture Group, Inc. Ellis W. Hitzing, Pres. 5433 Buffalo Ave. Jacksonville, FL 32208 (904) 353-7313 Date Lic.:	04/04-5219 04/25/83	500,000	500,000	Diversified	5
Verde Capital Corp. Jose Dearing, Pres. 255 Alhambra Circle, Ste. 720 Coral Gables, FL 33134 (305) 444-8938 Date Lic.:	04/04-5156 11/22/78	1,428,000	5,700,000	Diversified	5
Georgia Renaissance Capital Corp. E. Raleigh Murphy, Pres. 230 Peachtree St., Ste. 1810 Atlanta, GA 30303 (404) 658-7000 Date Lic.:	04/04-5236 12/05/86	1,000,000	0	Diversified	5
Sunbelt Funding Corp. Charles H. Jones, Pres. 3590 Riverside Dr. P.O. Box 7006	04/04-5197	4,001,200	3,500,000	Diversified	5

Licensee	License No.	Private Capital	SBA Leverage	Investment Policy	Owner Code*
Macon, GA 31298 (912) 474-5137 Date Lic.:	12/18/80				
Hawaii					
Pacific Venture Capital, Ltd. Dexter J. Taniguchi, Pres. Waiakamilo Sq., Ste. 302 1405 N. King St. Honolulu, HI 96817 (808) 847-6502 Date Lic.:	09/09-5182 06/25/80	721,000	700,000	Diversified	4
Illinois					
Amoco Venture Capital Co. Gordon E. Stone, Pres. 200 E. Randolph Dr. Chicago, IL 60601 (312) 856-6523 Date Lic.:	05/07-5083 12/22/70	2,976,750	6,603,000	Diversified	4
Chicago Community Ventures, Inc. Phyllis George, Pres. 104 S. Michigan Ave., Ste. 215–218 Chicago, IL 60603 (312) 726-6084 Date Lic.:	05/05-5089 06/14/72	1,005,000	2,005,000	Diversified	4
Combined Opportunities Inc. Wallace Buya, Pres. 1525 E. 53d St. Chicago, IL 60615 (312) 753-9650 Date Lic.:	05/07-5084 01/12/71	500,000	500,000	Diversified	4
The Neighborhood Fund, Inc. James Fletcher, Pres. 1950 E. 71st St. Chicago, IL 60649 (312) 684-8074 Date Lic.:	05/05-5124 04/03/78	500,000	950,000	Diversified	1
Peterson Finance and Investment Co.	05/05-5176	1,035,000	1,020,000	Diversified	2

Licensee	License No.	Private Capital	SBA Leverage	Investment Policy	Owner Code*
Thomas Lhee, Pres. 3300 W. Peterson Ave., Ste. A Chicago, IL 60659 (312) 583-6300 Date Lic.:	02/07/84				
Tower Ventures, Inc. Robert T. Smith, Pres. Sears Tower, BSC 43-50 Chicago, IL 60684 (312) 875-0571 Date Lic.:	05/05-5104 06/30/75	2,000,000	3,000,000	Diversified	4
The Urban Fund of Illinois, Inc. E. Patric Jones, Pres. 1525 E. 53d St. Chicago, IL 60615 (312) 753-9650 Date Lic.:	05/07-5080 05/04/71	650,000	1,129,000	Diversified	1
Kentucky Equal Opportunity Finance, Inc. Franklin Justice, Jr., V.P. 420 Hurstbourne La., Ste. 201 Louisville, KY 40222 (502) 423-1943 Date Lic.:	04/05-5096 09/24/70	1,434,391	1,600,000	Diversified	4
Louisiana SCDF Investment Corp. Martial Mirabeau, Mgr. 1006 Surrey St. P.O. Box 3885 Lafayette, LA 70502 (318) 232-3769 Date Lic.:	06/10-5157 04/26/73	2,700,010	3,119,549	Diversified	4
Maryland Albright Venture Capital, Inc. William A. Albright, Pres. 8005 Rappahannock Ave. Jessup, MD 20794 (301) 799-7935 Date Lic.:	03/03-5141 08/10/79	500,000	2,000,000	Diversified	5

Licensee	License No.	Private Capital	SBA Leverage	Investment Policy	Owner Code*
Security Financial and Investment Corp. Han Y. Cho, Pres. 7720 Wisconsin Ave., Ste. 207 Bethesda, MD 20814 (301) 951-4288 Date Lic.:	03/03-5158 12/29/83	510,000	500,000	Diversified	5
Massachusetts New England MESBIC, Inc. Etang Chen, Pres. 50 Kearney Rd., Ste. 3 Needham, MA 02194 (617) 769-5148 Date Lic.:	01/01-5318 10/26/82	500,000	1,500,000	Diversified	5
Transportation Capital Corp. 230 Newbury St., Ste. 21 Boston, MA 02116 (617) 536-0344 (See listing under New York for full information.)					
Michigan Dearborn Capital Corp. Michael LaManes, Pres. P.O. Box 1729 Dearborn, MI 48121 (313) 337-8577 Date Lic.:	05/05-5135 12/14/78	1,858,190	1,000,000	Diversified	4
Metro-Detroit Investment Co. William J. Fowler, Pres. 30777 Northwestern Hwy., Ste. 300 Farmington Hill, MI 48018 (313) 851-6300 Date Lic.:	05/05-5126 06/01/78	2,000,000	6,000,000	Grocery Stores	4
Motor Enterprises, Inc. James Kobus, Mgr. 3044 W. Grand Blvd. Detroit, MI 48202 (313) 556-4273 Date Lic.:	05/15-5024 04/13/70	1,250,000	2,000,000	Diversified	4

Licensee	License No.	Private Capital	SBA Leverage	Investment Policy	Owner Code*
Mutual Investment Co., Inc. Jack Najor, Pres. 21415 Civic Center Dr. Mark Plaza Bldg., Ste. 217 Southfield, MI 48076 (313) 557-2020 Date Lic.:	05/05-5144 04/21/80	1,452,077	4,400,000	Diversified	5
Minnesota Control Data Community Ventures Fund T. F. Hunt, Jr., Pres. 3601 W. 77th St. France Place, MNB07V Minneapolis, MN 55435 (612) 921-4391 Date Lic.:	05/05-5134 01/29/79	2,502,500	5,000,000	Diversified	4
Mississippi Sun-Delta Capital Access Center, Inc. Howard Boutte, Jr., V.P. 819 Main St. Greenville, MS 38701 (601) 335-5291 Date Lic.:	04/04-5175 09/25/79	1,258,100	0	Diversified	5
Nebraska Community Equity Corp. of Nebraska William C. Moore, Pres. 6421 Ames Ave. Omaha, NE 68104 (402) 455-7722 Date Lic.:	07/07-5078 08/16/77	787,000	1,800,000	Diversified	4
New Jersey Capital Circulation Corp. Judy Kao, Mgr. 208 Main St. Fort Lee, NJ 07024 (201) 947-8637 Date Lic.:	02/02-5484 03/28/85	1,000,000	200,000	Diversified	5
Formosa Capital Corp. Philp Chen, Pres. 605 King George Post Rd. Fords, NJ 08863	02/02-5485	1,000,000	0	Diversified	5

Licensee	License No.	Private Capital	SBA Leverage	Investment Policy	Owner Code*
(201) 738-4710					
Date Lic.:	08/22/85				
Rutgers Minority Investment Co. Oscar Figueroa, Pres. 92 New St. Newark, NJ 07102 (201) 648-5287	02/02-5283	1,499,000	905,000	Diversified	4
Date Lic.:	07/28/70				
Zaitech Capital Corp. Mr. Fu-Tong Hsu, Pres. 2083 Center Ave. Fort Lee, NJ 07024 (201) 944-3018	02/02-5494	1,000,000	0	Diversified	5
Date Lic.:	06/05/86				
New Mexico					
Associated Southwest Investors, Inc. John R. Rice, Gen. Mgr. 2400 Louisiana, N.E. Bldg. #4, Ste. 225 Albuquerque, NM 87110 (505) 881-0066	09/14-5086	707,000	1,700,000	Diversified	4
Date Lic.:	12/09/71				
New York					
American Asian Capital Corp. Howard H. Lin, Pres. 130 Water St., Ste. 6-L New York, NY 10005 (212) 422-6880	02/02-5316	503,000	500,000	Diversified	5
Date Lic.:	11/12/76				
Avdon Capital Corp. A. M. Donner, Pres. 805 Ave. L Brooklyn, NY 11230 (718) 692-0950	02/02-5456	1,000,000	1,500,000	Diversified	5
Date Lic.:	04/21/83				
Bethela Capital Corp. Min Ja Oh, Pres. 269 W. 39th St. New York, NY 10018 (212) 302-3104	02/02-5378	566,700	1,012,000	Diversified	5
Date Lic.:	05/09/80				

Licensee	License No.	Private Capital	SBA Leverage	Investment Policy	Owner Code*
CVC Capital Corp. Jeorg G. Klebe, Pres. 131 E. 62d St. New York, NY 10021 (212) 319-7210 Date Lic.:	02/02-5338 03/22/78	3,255,000	6,000,000	Television Industry	5
Capital Investors & Management Corp. Rose Chao, Mgr. 3 Pell St., Ste. 3 New York, NY 10013 (212) 964-2480 Date Lic.:	02/02-5363 02/06/80	500,000	1,500,000	Diversified	5
Cohen Capital Corp. Edward H. Cohen, Pres. 8 Freer St., Ste. 185 Lynbrook, NY 11563 (516) 887-3434 Date Lic.:	02/02-5335 03/01/78	710,000	2,100,000	Diversified	5
Columbia Capital Corp. Mark Scharfman, Pres. 419 Park Ave., South New York, NY 10016 (212) 696-4688 Date Lic.:	02/02-5462 09/09/83	1,150,478	2,000,000	Diversified	5
East Coast Venture Capital, Inc. Zindel Zelmanovitch, Pres. 313 W. 53d St., 3d Floor New York, NY 10019 (212) 245-6460 Date Lic.:	02/02-5470 07/14/86	1,000,000	400,000	Diversified	5
Elk Associates Funding Corp. Gary C. Granoff, Pres. 600 Third Ave., 38th Floor New York, NY 10016 (212) 972-8550 Date Lic.:	02/02-5377 07/24/80	3,604,661	8,785,000	Transportation	5

Licensee	License No.	Private Capital	SBA Leverage	Investment Policy	Owner Code*
Equico Capital Corp. Duane Hill, Pres. 1290 Avenue of the Americas, Ste. 3400 New York, NY 10019 (212) 397-8660 Date Lic.:	02/02-5286 05/07/71	10,550,000	10,295,000	Diversified	4
Everlast Capital Corp. Frank J. Segreto, Gen. Mgr. 350 Fifth Ave., Ste. 2805 New York, NY 10118 (212) 695-3910 Date Lic.:	02/02-5468 07/30/84	1,800,000	1,000,000	Diversified	5
Exim Capital Corp. Victor K. Chun, Pres. 290 Madison Ave. New York, NY 10017 (212) 683-3375 Date Lic.:	02/02-5351 01/05/79	660,000	1,500,000	Diversified	5
Fair Capital Corp. Robert Yet Sen Chen, Pres. 3 Pell St., 2d Floor New York, NY 10013 (212) 964-2480 Date Lic.:	02/02-5437 09/27/82	508,000	500,000	Diversified	5
Fans Capital Corp. Mr. Fon-May Fan, Pres. 136-40 39th Ave., Unit #E3 Flushing, NY 11354 (718) 746-8119 Date Lic.:	02/02-5483 09/26/86	1,010,000	0	Diversified	5
Freshstart Venture Capital Corp. Zindel Zelmanovich, Pres. 313 W. 53d St., 3d Floor New York, NY 10019 (212) 265-2249 Date Lic.:	02/02-5447 02/24/83	633,525	1,500,000	Diversified	5
Hop Chung Capital Corp. Yon Hon Lee, Pres. 74-A Mott St.	02/02-5368	500,000	1,000,000	Diversified	5

Licensee	License No.	Private Capital	SBA Leverage	Investment Policy	Owner Code*
New York, NY 10013 (212) 267-2727 Date Lic.:	07/18/80				
Ibero American Investors Corp. Emilio Serrano, Pres. 55 Saint Paul St. Rochester, NY 14604 (716) 262-3440 Date Lic.:	02/02-5369 09/28/79	1,311,471	1,897,000	Diversified	5
Intercontinental Capital Funding Corp. James S. Yu, Pres. 60 E. 42d St., Ste. 740 New York, NY 10165 (212) 286-9642 Date Lic.:	02/02-5421 09/30/81	500,000	1,000,000	Diversified	5
Intergroup Funding Corp. Ben Hauben, Pres. 230 Park Ave. New York, NY 10017 (212) 661-5428 Date Lic.:	02/02-5376 11/15/79	510,000	1,000,000	Transportation	5
International Paper Cap. Formation, Inc. Bernard L. Riley, Pres. 77 W. 45th St. New York, NY 10036 (212) 536-6000 Date Lic.:	02/02-5432 11/05/81	1,000,000	1,000,000	Diversified	5
Japanese American Capital Corp. Stephen C. Huang, Pres. 19 Rector St. New York, NY 10006 (212) 964-4077 Date Lic.:	02/02-5367 08/07/79	525,000	1,490,000	Diversified	5
Jardine Capital Corp. Evelyn Sy Dy, Pres. 8 Chathan Sq., Ste. 700 New York, NY 10038 (212) 406-0112 Date Lic.:	02/02-5495 12/22/86	1,000,000	0	Diversified	5

Licensee	License No.	Private Capital	SBA Leverage	Investment Policy	Owner Code*
Medallion Funding Corp. Alvin Murstein, Pres. 205 E. 42d St., Ste. 2020 New York, NY 10017 (212) 682-3300 Date Lic.:	02/02-5393 06/23/80	5,238,250	11,734,000	Transportation	5
Minority Equity Capital Co., Inc. Donald F. Greene, Pres. 275 Madison Ave. New York, NY 10016 (212) 686-9710 Date Lic.:	02/02-5288 05/17/71	2,204,047	3,104,046	Diversified	4
Monsey Capital Corp. Shamuel Myski, Pres. 125 Rte. 59 Monsey, NY 10952 (914) 425-2229 Date Lic.:	02/02-5474 01/17/85	1,000,000	1,000,000	Diversified	5
New Oasis Capital Corp. James Huang, Pres. 114 Liberty St., Ste. 404 New York, NY 10006 (212) 349-2804 Date Lic.:	02/02-5379 02/06/80	500,000	1,500,000	Diversified	5
North American Funding Corp. Franklin F. Y. Wong, V.P. 177 Canal St. New York, NY 10013 (212) 226-0080 Date Lic.:	02/02-5418 03/05/81	500,000	1,500,000	Diversified	5
North Street Capital Corp. Ralph McNeal, Pres. 250 North St., RA-65 White Plains, NY 10625 (914) 335-6306 Date Lic.:	02/02-5285 10/16/70	2,200,000	1,500,000	Diversified	4
Pan Pac Capital Corp. Dr. In Ping Jack Lee, Pres. 121 E. Industry Court	02/02-5386	503,000	1,505,000	Diversified	5

Licensee	License No.	Private Capital	SBA Leverage	Investment Policy	Owner Code*
Deer Park, NY 11729 (516) 586-7653 Date Lic.:	06/11/80				
Pierre Funding Corp. Elias Debbas, Pres. 131 S. Central Ave. Hartsdale, NY 10530 (914) 683-1144 Date Lic.: or 270 Madison Ave. New York, NY 10016 (212) 689-9361	02/02-5396 01/22/81	1,759,600	4,839,800	Transportation	5
Pioneer Capital Corp. James G. Niven, Pres. 113 E. 55th St. New York, NY 10022 (212) 980-9090 Date Lic.:	02/02-5274 09/02/69	701,261	1,400,000	Diversified	5
Rainbow Bridge Capital Corp. Nai-Ching Sun, Pres. 449 Broadway New York, NY 10013 (212) 219-0707 Date Lic.:	02/02-5297 06/12/80	500,000	1,500,000	Diversified	5
Roedel Associates, Ltd. Robert Cohen, Pres. 77-51 141st St. Flushing, NY 11367 (212) 591-2838 Date Lic.:	02/02-5454 04/06/83	500,000	0	Diversified	5
Situation Venture Corp. Sam Hollander, Pres. 502 Flushing Ave. Brooklyn, NY 11205 (212) 855-1835 Date Lic.:	02/02-5323 02/16/77	1,000,200	3,000,000	Diversified	5
Square Deal Venture Capital Corp. Mordechai Z. Feldman, Pres.	02/02-5374	546,000	1,200,000	Diversified	5

Licensee	License No.	Private Capital	SBA Leverage	Investment Policy	Owner Code*
135-56 39th Ave., Ste. 440 Flushing, NY 11354 (212) 939-9802 Date Lic.:	09/28/79				
Taroco Capital Corp. David R. C. Chang, Pres. 19 Rector St., 35th Floor New York, NY 10006 (212) 964-6877 Date Lic.:	02/02-5318 09/10/76	1,010,000	3,030,000	Chinese Americans	5
Transportation Capital Corp. Melvin L. Hirsch, Pres. 60 E. 42d St. New York, NY 10165 (212) 697-4885 Date Lic.:	02/02-5388 06/23/80	4,968,100	6,765,000	Diversified	5
Triad Capital Corp. of New York Lorenzo J. Barrera, Pres. 950 Southern Blvd. Bronx, NY 10459 (212) 589-6541 Date Lic.:	02/02-5455 11/25/83	545,253	500,000	Diversified	2
Trico Venture, Inc. Avruhum Donner, Pres. 805 Ave. L Brooklyn, NY 11230 (718) 692-0950 Date Lic.:	02/02-5496 06/27/86	1,000,000	700,000	Diversified	5
United Capital Investment Corp. Paul Lee, Pres. 60 E. 42d St., Ste. 1515 New York, NY 10165 (212) 682-7210 Date Lic.:	02/02-5480 02/05/85	1,030,000	2,000,000	Diversified	5
Venture Opportunities Corp. A. Fred March, Pres. 110 E. 59th St., 29th Floor New York, NY 10022	02/04-5151	575,000	2,300,000	Diversified	5

Licensee	License No.	Private Capital	SBA Leverage	Investment Policy	Owner Code*
(212) 832-3737 Date Lic.:	12/01/78				
Watchung Capital Corp. S. T. Jeng, Pres. 431 Fifth Ave., 5th Floor New York, NY 10016 (212) 889-3466 Date Lic.:	02/02-5371 02/19/80	500,000	1,000,000	Diversified	5
Worthen Finance and Investment, Inc. 535 Madison Ave., 17th Floor New York, NY 10022 (212) 750-9100 (See listing under Arkansas for full information.)					
Yang Capital Corp. Maysing Yang, Pres. 41-40 Kissena Blvd. Flushing, NY 11355 (516) 482-1578 Date Lic.:	02/02-5429 04/12/83	500,000	1,500,000	Diversified	5
Yusa Capital Corp. Christopher Yeung, Chairman 622 Broadway New York, NY 10012 (212) 420-1350 Date Lic.:	02/02-5467 07/31/84	1,035,000	2,000,000	Diversified	5
Ohio Center City MESBIC, Inc. Michael A. Robinson, Pres. Centre City Office Bldg., Ste. 762 40 S. Main St. Dayton, OH 45402 (513) 461-6164 Date Lic.:	05/05-5153 07/29/81	500,000	500,000	Diversified	5
Rubber City Capital Corp. W. R. Miller, Pres.	05/05-5201	1,000,000	0	Diversified	5

Licensee	License No.	Private Capital	SBA Leverage	Investment Policy	Owner Code*
1144 E. Market St. Akron, OH 44316 (216) 796-9167 Date Lic.:	08/14/85				
Pennsylvania Alliance Enterprise Corp. W. B. Priestley, Pres. 1801 Market St., 3d Floor Philadelphia, PA 19103 (215) 977-3925 Date Lic.:	03/03-5066 10/20/71	3,030,200	2,700,000	Diversified	4
Greater Philadelphia Venture Capital Corp., Inc. Wilson E. DeWald, Pres. 920 Lewis Tower Bldg. 225 S. 15th St. Philadelphia, PA 19102 (215) 732-3415 Date Lic.:	03/03-5112 03/31/72	756,583	1,505,000	Diversified	2
Salween Financial Services, Inc. Dr. Ramarao Naidu, Pres. 228 N. Pottstown Pike Exton, PA 19341 (215) 524-1880 Date Lic.:	03/03-5157 07/01/83	800,000	725,000	Diversified	5
Puerto Rico North America Investment Corp. Santigo Ruz Betacourt, Pres. Banco CTR #1710, M Rivera Ave. Stop 34 (Mail: P.O. Box 1831 Hato Rey Station 00919) Hato Rey, PR 00936 (809) 751-6178 Date Lic.:	02/02-5308 11/07/74	750,000	2,250,000	Diversified	5
Tennessee Chickasaw Capital Corp. Tom Moore, Pres. 67 Madison Ave. Memphis, TN 38147	04/04-5128	500,000	500,000	Diversified	1

Licensee	License No.	Private Capital	SBA Leverage	Investment Policy	Owner Code*
(901) 523-6404					
Date Lic.:	08/30/77				
Tennessee Equity Capital Corp.	04/04-5157	502,000	750,000	Diversified	5
Walter S. Cohen, Pres.					
1102 Stonewall Jackson Court					
Nashville, TN 37220					
(615) 373-4502					
Date Lic.:	01/19/79				
Tennessee Venture Capital Corp.	04/04-5176	500,000	500,000	Diversified	5
Wendell P. Knox, Pres.					
162 Fourth Ave. North, Ste. 125					
P.O. Box 2567					
Nashville, TN 37219					
(615) 244-6935					
Date Lic.:	09/28/79				
Valley Capital Corp.	04/04-5216	1,145,000	0	Diversified	5
Lamar J. Partridge, Pres.					
Krystal Bldg., Eighth Floor					
100 W. Martin Luther King Blvd.					
Chattanooga, TN 37402					
(615) 265-1557					
Date Lic.:	10/08/82				
West Tennessee Venture Capital Corp.	04/04-5218	1,250,000	0	Diversified	5
Robert Fenner, Mgr.					
152 Beale St., Ste. 401					
P.O. Box 300					
Memphis, TN 38101					
(901) 527-6091					
Date Lic.:	12/16/82				
Texas					
Chen's Financial Group, Inc.	06/06-5281	1,000,000	2,000,000	Diversified	5
Samuel S. C. Chen, Pres.					
1616 W. Loop, South, Ste. 200					
Houston, TX 77027					
(713) 850-0879					
Date Lic.:	03/05/84				

Licensee	License No.	Private Capital	SBA Leverage	Investment Policy	Owner Code*
Evergreen Capital Co., Inc. Shen-Lim Lin, Chairman 8502 Tybor Dr., Ste. 201 Houston, TX 77074 (713) 778-9770 Date Lic.:	06/06-5264 07/07/83	1,001,000	2,000,000	Diversified	5
MESBIC Financial Corp. of Dallas Donald R. Lawhorne, Pres. 12655 N. Central Expressway, Ste. 814 Dallas, TX 75243 (214) 991-1597 Date Lic.:	06/10-5153 02/26/70	3,070,332	3,050,000	Diversified	2
MESBIC Financial Corp. of Houston Lynn H. Miller, Pres. 811 Rusk, Ste. 201 Houston, TX 77002 (713) 228-8321 Date Lic.:	06/06-5180 11/12/76	854,900	854,000	Diversified	2
MESBIC of San Antonio, Inc. Domingo Bueno, Pres. 2300 W. Commerce San Antonio, TX 78207 (512) 224-0909 Date Lic.:	06/06-5217 09/19/79	751,000	750,000	Diversified	5
Minority Enterprise Funding, Inc. Frederick C. Chang, Pres. 17300 El Camino Real, Ste. 107-B Houston, TX 77058 (713) 488-4919 Date Lic.:	06/09-5230 03/09/79	1,000,000	2,650,000	Diversified	5
Southern Orient Capital Corp. Min H. Liang, Pres. 2419 Fannin, Ste. 200	06/06-5240	550,000	1,650,000	Diversified	5

Licensee	License No.	Private Capital	SBA Leverage	Investment Policy	Owner Code*
Houston, TX 77002 (713) 225-3369 Date Lic.:	12/29/80				
United Oriental Capital Corp. Don J. Wang, Pres. 908 Town & Country Blvd., Ste. 310 Houston, TX 77024 (713) 461-3909 Date Lic.:	06/06-5254 07/07/82	1,000,000	1,500,000	Diversified	5
Virginia Basic Investment Corp. Frank F. Luwis, Pres. 6723 Whittier Ave. McLean, VA 22101 (703) 356-4300 Date Lic.:	03/03-5156 07/29/83	500,000	0	Diversified	5
East West United Investment Co. Bui Dung, Pres. 815 W. Broad St. Falls Church, VA 22046 (703) 237-7200 Date Lic.:	03/03-5125 01/22/76	500,000	1,500,000	Diversified	5
Washington Finance and Investment Corp. Chang H. Lie, Pres. 100 E. Broad St. Falls Church, VA 22046 (202) 338-2900 Date Lic.:	03/03-5150 06/03/82	1,005,000	2,000,000	Diversified	5
Wisconsin Future Value Ventures, Inc. William P. Beckett, Pres. 622 N. Water St., Ste. 500 Milwaukee, WI 53202 (414) 278-0377 Date Lic.:	05/05-5198 11/09/84	1,020,000	0	Diversified	5

301(D) SBIC LICENSEES
TOTALS BY STATES

State	No. of SBICs					Total Private Capital	Total Obligations to SBA
	Size 1	Size 2	Size 3	Size 4	Total		
Alabama	0	1	1	0	2	2,400,000	4,650,000
Alaska	0	1	0	0	1	750,000	750,000
Arizona	0	0	0	0	0	0	0
Arkansas	0	2	2	0	4	5,016,310	6,500,000
California	0	13	11	0	24	25,619,961	35,811,655
Colorado	0	1	0	0	1	550,000	0
Connecticut	0	0	0	0	0	0	0
Delaware	0	0	0	0	0	0	0
District of Columbia	0	0	6	0	6	10,258,100	14,625,100
Florida	0	7	1	0	8	5,928,000	9,200,000
Georgia	0	1	1	0	2	5,001,200	3,500,000
Hawaii	0	1	0	0	1	721,000	700,000
Idaho	0	0	0	0	0	0	0
Illinois	0	3	4	0	7	8,666,750	15,207,000
Indiana	0	0	0	0	0	0	0
Iowa	0	0	0	0	0	0	0
Kansas	0	0	0	0	0	0	0
Kentucky	0	0	1	0	1	1,434,391	1,600,000
Louisiana	0	0	1	0	1	2,700,010	3,119,549
Maine	0	0	0	0	0	0	0
Maryland	0	2	0	0	2	1,010,000	2,500,000
Massachusetts	0	1	0	0	1	500,000	1,500,000
Michigan	0	0	4	0	4	6,560,267	13,400,000
Minnesota	0	0	1	0	1	2,502,500	5,000,000
Mississippi	0	0	1	0	1	1,258,100	0
Missouri	0	0	0	0	0	0	0
Montana	0	0	0	0	0	0	0
Nebraska	0	1	0	0	1	787,000	1,800,000
Nevada	0	0	0	0	0	0	0
New Hampshire	0	0	0	0	0	0	0
New Jersey	0	3	1	0	4	4,499,000	1,105,000
New Mexico	0	1	0	0	1	707,000	1,700,000
New York	0	28	14	2	44	61,113,546	99,556,846
North Carolina	0	0	0	0	0	0	0
North Dakota	0	0	0	0	0	0	0
Ohio	0	2	0	0	2	1,500,000	500,000
Oklahoma	0	0	0	0	0	0	0
Oregon	0	0	0	0	0	0	0
Pennsylvania	0	2	1	0	3	4,586,783	4,930,000
Puerto Rico	0	1	0	0	1	750,000	2,250,000
Rhode Island	0	0	0	0	0	0	0
South Carolina	0	0	0	0	0	0	0
South Dakota	0	0	0	0	0	0	0
Tennessee	0	3	2	0	5	3,897,000	1,750,000

State	No. of SBICs					Total Private Capital	Total Obligations to SBA
	Size 1	*Size 2*	*Size 3*	*Size 4*	*Total*		
Texas	0	6	2	0	8	9,227,232	14,454,000
Utah	0	0	0	0	0	0	0
Vermont	0	0	0	0	0	0	0
Virginia	0	2	1	0	3	2,005,000	3,500,000
Washington	0	0	0	0	0	0	0
West Virginia	0	0	0	0	0	0	0
Wisconsin	0	0	1	0	1	1,020,000	0
Wyoming	0	0	0	0	0	0	0
TOTAL	0	82	56	2	140	170,969,150	249,609,150

301(D) SBIC LICENSEES

TOTALS BY PRIVATE CAPITAL SIZE CLASS

Total Private Capital Size Class	Total No. of SBICs	Total Private Capital	Total Obligations to SBA
Size 1—$300,000 or less	0	0	0
Size 2—$300,001 to $1 million	82	55,619,727	82,153,000
Size 3—$1 million to $5 million	56	99,561,173	145,427,150
Size 4—more than $5 million	2	15,788,250	22,029,000
TOTAL	140	170,969,150	249,609,150

301(D) SBIC LICENSEES

TOTALS BY TYPE OF OWNERSHIP

Total Private Capital Size Class	Total No. of SBICs	Total Private Capital	Total Obligations to SBA
Bank Dominated	5	5,160,000	5,079,000
Bank Associated	6	8,772,917	9,219,535
Financial Organization	2	2,526,508	4,000,000
Nonfinancial Organization	23	46,766,295	60,656,595
Individually Owned	102	104,743,430	167,654,020
40' Act Company	2	3,000,000	3,000,000
TOTAL	140	170,969,150	249,609,150

301(D) SBIC LICENSEES

PRIVATE CAPITAL BY TYPE OF OWNERSHIP

Type of Ownership	Private Capital Size Class							
	Size 1		Size 2		Size 3		Size 4	
	No.	*Dollars*	*No.*	*Dollars*	*No.*	*Dollars*	*No.*	*Dollars*
Bank Dominated	0	0	4	2,150,000	1	3,010,000	0	0
Bank Associated	0	0	3	2,156,736	3	6,616,181	0	0

Type of Ownership	Private Capital Size Class							
	Size 1		Size 2		Size 3		Size 4	
	No.	*Dollars*	*No.*	*Dollars*	*No.*	*Dollars*	*No.*	*Dollars*
Financial Organization	0	0	1	526,508	1	2,000,000	0	0
Nonfinancial Organization	0	0	5	3,215,000	17	33,001,295	1	10,550,000
Individually Owned	0	0	68	46,571,483	33	52,933,697	1	5,238,250
40' Act Company	0	0	1	1,000,000	1	2,000,000	0	0

Small Press Publishers

Small presses are the avant-garde of small businesses; therefore, knowing what they are doing and why can be a good source of trends and industry information. The small press publishers are on the cutting edge: They are especially helpful in spotting new business ideas and opportunities. TOWERS Club, U.S.A. publishes a monthly newsletter, *The Original Writers Entrepreneurial Research Service.*

> Jerry Buchanan
> *The Original Writers Entrepreneurial Research Service*
> TOWERS Club, U.S.A.
> P.O. Box 2038
> Vancouver, WA 98668
> (206) 574-3084

Quality Books, Inc. specializes in small press distribution to the library market. Tom Drewes offers a wealth of knowledge about the industry.

> Tom C. Drewes, Pres.
> Quality Books, Inc.
> 918 Sherwood Dr.
> Lake Bluff, IL 60044
> (312) 295-2010

The Newsletter Clearinghouse publishes the valuable *Newsletter on Newsletters. Publishing Newsletters,* by Howard Penn Hudson (Charles Scribner & Sons, New York), is the newsletter industry's venerable guide to all aspects of the trade. It is available in many bookstores or from the following source.

> The Newsletter Clearinghouse
> 44 W. Market St.
> P.O. Box 311
> Rhinebeck, NY 12572
> (914) 876-2081

Success in Newsletter Publishing: A Periodical Guide, by Frederick G. Goss, is an alternative guide to getting and keeping subscriptions, setting subscription rates, and selling subscriptions. It is available from the NAA, an association of newsletter publishers.

> Mike Kibler
> Newsletter Association of America
> 1401 Wilson Blvd., Ste. 403
> Arlington, VA 22209
> (703) 527-2333

The Oxbridge Dictionary of Newsletters is a 500+-page directory of American and Canadian newsletters.

Patricia Hagood
Oxbridge Communications
150 Fifth Ave., Ste. 301
New York, NY 10011
(212) 741-0231

The third edition of the *Newsletter Directory,* edited by Brigitte T. Darnay, is a descriptive guide to more than 8,000 subscription, membership, and free newsletters, bulletins, digests, updates, and similar serial publications issued in the United States and is available in print or on-line.

Gale Research Co.
Book Tower
Detroit, MI 48226
(800) 223-GALE

The Committee of Small Magazine Editors and Publishers is an organization of small presses and magazine publishers.

Committee of Small Magazine Editors and Publishers
P.O. Box 703
San Francisco, CA 94101
(415) 922-9490

Folio: The Magazine for Magazine Management is exclusively concerned with all aspects of magazine publishing.

Folio
Folio Magazine Publishing Co.
125 Elm St.
P.O. Box 4006
New Canaan, CT 06840
(203) 972-0761

A first-rate publication, *Small Press* deals with the nuts-and-bolts of publishing, including electronic (desktop) publishing.

Meckler Publishing Corp.
Small Press
11 Ferry Lane, West
Westport, CT 06880
(203) 226-6967

Available from Ad-Lib Publications are *Book Marketing Made Easier, Directory of Short Run Book Printers,* and *Formaides for Successful Book Publishing,* all of which were written by John Kremer.

Ad-Lib Publications
P.O. Box 1102

Fairfield, IA 52556
(515) 472-6617

Acropolis Books, Ltd. offers many excellent management books.
Alphonse Hackl, Pres.
Acropolis Books, Ltd.
2400-17th St., N.W.
Washington, DC 20009
(202) 387-6800

Freelance Writer's Report is a newsletter for freelancers which covers writing and
marketing.
Freelance Writer's Report
Cassell Communications, Inc.
P.O. Box 9844
Fort Lauderdale, FL 33310
(305) 485-0795

Publish! is the how-to magazine of desktop publishing.
Publish!
PCW Communications, Inc.
501 Second St., Ste. 600
San Francisco, CA 94107
(415) 546-7722

Sources of Small Business Information

In this chapter, you'll find fundamental organizations designed to help small businesses as well as difficult-to-classify sources. This chapter is more than a reference: Each source listed may be of value to your business, helping you to solve an immediate problem or to prevent a future problem.

GENERAL SOURCES

Formed in 1979, the Walter E. Heller Institute for the Advancement of Small Business Enterprise has the the following objectives: "to help small business survive; to give the small business person a greater sense of self-esteem; and to make sure that small businesses and entrepreneurs don't disappear."

> Walter E. Heller Institute for the Advancement of Small Business
> 105 W. Adams St.
> Chicago, IL 60603
> (312) 621-7000

The *Small-Business Reporter* is a series of more than 50 pamphlets on small business subjects, which are offered for a small postage and handling charge. A free *Publications Index* is available from the following source.

> *Small Business Reports*
> Bank of America
> 211 Main St., 4th Floor
> P.O. Box 37000
> San Francisco, CA 94105
> (415) 974-0749

The Center for Entrepreneurial Management is a worldwide, nonprofit association of about 3,000 entrepreneurs. CEM publishes *The Entrepreneurial Manager,* a monthly newsletter, and sells more than 100 books and tapes on the subjects of entrepreneurship and small business management.

> Joseph R. Mancuso, Pres.
> Center for Entrepreneurial Management, Inc.
> 180 Varick St., Penthouse
> New York, NY 10014-4606
> (212) 633-0060

American Express has a new Small Business Partnership and offers an increasing number of services to small businesses.

American Express/I.D.S.
900 IDS Tower, Unit 409
Minneapolis, MN 55474
(612) 372-3131

American Express
1650 Los Gamus
San Rafael, CA 94903
(800) 962-AMEX

Founded in 1975, the Entrepreneurship Institute is a nonprofit corporation which helps local communities to pool their resources to help benefit small businesses. Their locally funded Entrepreneurship Forums provide entrepreneurs with information on state and local programs, as well as networking opportunities.

Jan Zupnick
Entrepreneurship Institute
3592 Corporate Dr., Ste. 100
Columbus, OH 43229
(614) 895-1153

Mark Stevens is one of the best writers in the field of small business. His books are both helpful and informative.

Mark Stevens
15 Breckinridge Rd.
Chappaqua, NY 10514
(914) 238-3569

The Small Business Resource Guide is a 90-page soft-cover booklet compiled by American Telephone and Telegraph. Its information is inaccurate but specific; therefore, I list it as a resource but do not recommend it.

Braddock Publications
10001 Connecticut Ave., N.W.
Washington, DC 20036
(202) 296-1317

The American Express Partnership with Small Business

American Express has announced the formation of the Small Business Partnership, a new initiative aimed at gaining a better understanding of the needs of small businesses. American Express President Louis V. Gerstner, Jr., noted that through the partnership, the company will provide small business owners with the information and services to help them to manage their companies more effectively while planning for future growth.

Also announced were the findings of the Small Business Management Survey, which was commissioned by the Small Business Partnership to assess the needs of small businesses. The survey of 500 small business owners across the United States found that although small business owners see growth, not profits, as their key business objective, the majority report that they are too busy with day-to-day operations to plan properly for long-term growth.

A Partnership Advisory Council, made up of ten small business leaders, will act as a "sounding board" to counsel the company on how best to serve small business needs. Members of the Partnership Advisory Council include MIT economist and small business expert David Birch (chairperson) and Mary Kelley McCurry (vice-chairperson), the immediate past president of the National Association of Women Business Owners.

The Small Business Partnership will:

- Develop and publish the *American Express Small Business Growth and Climate Indices,* which offer the first comprehensive assessment of the U.S. small business performance and operating environment
- Conduct annual surveys of small business management
- Publish a quarterly newsletter, *The Small Business Resource,* which will be available at no charge to small business owners
- Organize and sponsor small business seminars on issues critical to small businesses
- Provide access to cost-effective tools to enhance owner and company security, expense control and management, cash and asset management, and employee benefits through American Express companies, IDS Financial Services, Travel-Related Services Company, Inc., and AMEX Life Assurance Company
- Offer a toll-free number to provide small business owners with easy access to information about the partnership: (800) 962-AMEX

Underscoring the needs of small businesses for better information and service, Partnership Chairperson David Birch said, "Today, small, growing companies are the pulse of our economy and are a major source of job creation. During 1984–85, small businesses produced nine times as many net new jobs as large businesses, and they will be responsible for at least 60 percent of the more than 2 million new jobs expected to be created in 1987. Small companies will play an increasingly important role in keeping America globally competitive in the 1990s. To ensure small businesses' continued contribution to this country's economy, it is imperative that their owners have access to the best financial information and financial tools."

SPECIALTY SOURCES

Nightingale is an excellent source of motivational audiotapes.
Nightingale
Conant Corp.
7300 N. Lehigh Ave.
Chicago, IL 60648
(312) 677-3100

Laissez Faire Book is an excellent source of libertarian and free-enterprise books.
Andrea Rich
Laissez Faire Books

532 Broadway
New York, NY 10012
(212) 925-8992

H. Ross Perot thought Joe Batten's books and tapes on Tough-Minded Team Building were the best he had read.
Joe Batten
Batten, Batten, Hudson & Swab
820 Keosauquaway
Des Moines, IA 50309
(515) 244-3176

The Marquis Company is the leading publisher of *Who's Who* directories. Editions cover a wide variety of fields.
Marquis *Who's Who*
200 E. Ohio St.
Chicago, IL 60611
(800) 428-3898

Success Motivation Institute is a good source of motivational and inspirational audiotapes.
Success Motivation Institute
500 Lakewood Dr.
Waco, TX 76710
(817) 776-1230

Some experts will tell you that it's best to read a financial report from the back (skipping the window dressing and getting to the heart of the matter). Wherever you decide to start, reading a financial report can be a complex operation. Merrill Lynch offers a free booklet, *How to Read a Financial Report,* which should be of help.
Merrill Lynch
Sales Promotion
25 Broadway, 25th Floor
New York, NY 10004
(212) 237-7455

OFFBEAT SOURCES

The *Grammar Hotline Directory* lists 26 U.S. and Canadian hotlines that answer questions about spelling, punctuation, grammar, and sentence structure. To get a copy of the directory, send a stamped, self-addressed envelope to the following address.
Grammar Hotline Directory
Writing Center
Tidewater Community College

1700 College Crescent
Virginia Beach, VA 23456

Free Attractions is a listing of close to 4,000 museums, galleries, wineries, historical sights, and gardens that are open to the public free of charge. The cost is $11.95.
VanMeer Publications
P.O. Box 1289
Clearwater, FL 33517

The National Institute on Drug Abuse (NIDA) has established a Drug-Free Workplace Helpline to help employers achieve a drug-free workplace. Helpline staff can provide consultation to employers about establishing urine-testing programs, initiating employee-education programs, and establishing or modifying existing employee-assistance programs to deal with drug-related problems of employees. Upon request, written information pertinent to drug abuse in the workplace, including NIDA's recently released monograph, *Urine Testing for Drugs of Abuse,* will be sent to callers. Referrals to practitioners and consultants for on-site assistance will be made, where appropriate. The helpline operates Monday through Friday, from 9:00 A.M. to 8:00 P.M. EST: (800) 843-4971.

The latest in Price Waterhouse's series of *Guides for Smaller Businesses and Entrepreneurs* is *Reports You Need to Manage Your Business.* It explains how to focus on and monitor the essential information required for running and expanding a business. "Too many times, the entrepreneur is swamped with information," says Donald Rappaport, national director of smaller-business services for Price Waterhouse. "There has to be a system to keep out the 'noise'—the data that don't directly bear on profit and efficiency."

Based on the results of a survey of more than 800 smaller businesses, authors Thomas E. Hoffmeister and Mary Marks conclude that the key reports an entrepreneur needs are:

The Operating Budget
The Cash-Flow Forecast
The Daily/Weekly Flash Report
The Financial Statements
The Open-Order/Job Report
The Sales-Analysis Report
The Product-Cost Report
The Payroll Summary
The Stock-Status Report
The Accounts-Receivable Report
The Accounts-Payable Report
The Key-Employee Profile
The Fixed-Assets Summary

The guide features sample formats for these key reports and describes their uses. The reports are designed so that readers, including nonfinancial managers, can adapt them to use in their own companies. *Reports You Need to Manage Your Business* is available, at a cost of $5, from local Price Waterhouse offices, or from the following source. Also ask for a free subscription to *Business Review,* Price Waterhouse's newsletter for small business owners and entrepreneurs.

Donald Rappaport, National Dir.
Smaller Business Services
Price Waterhouse
1801 K St., N.W.
Washington, DC 20006-1394
(202) 296-0800

Speakers

ASSOCIATIONS

The National Speakers Association, with a membership of about 3,000, sponsors seminars for professional and semiprofessional speakers. It also publishes a newsletter for its members, *Speak Out.*

    P. Douglas Kerr
National Speakers Association
4747 N. Seventh St., Ste. 310
Phoenix, AZ 85014
(602) 265-1001

The American Society of Association Executives publishes a directory of members, which includes an excellent who's who of speakers. The directory fee is $100.

    R. William Taylor
American Society of Association Executives
1575 I St., N.W.
Washington, DC 20005
(202) 626-2723

Five thousand speakers, including many celebrity speakers, are members of the International Platform Association.

    Dan T. Moore
International Platform Association
P.O. Box 250
Winnetka, IL 60092
(312) 446-4321

MISCELLANEOUS SERVICES

Somers White is an excellent speaker who personally knows most professional speakers. He is a source of material on speaking.

    Somers White
Somers White & Associates
4736 N. 44th St.
Phoenix, AZ 85018
(602) 952-9292

Ronald B. Myers is an extremely effective public speaker.
Ronald B. Myers
P.O. Box 20431
Columbus Circle Station
New York, NY 10023
(212) 315-2618

Success Leaders Speakers Service can help make planning for small, growing businesses easier.
Success Leaders Speakers Service
Dr. Dupree Jordan, Jr., Pres.
3960 Peachtree Rd., N.E., Ste. 425
Atlanta, GA 30319
(404) 233-3312

PUBLICATION

Sharing Ideas, a lively newsletter for public speakers, is also a speakers' bureau, an agents' association, and a good deal of help for speakers.
Dottie Walters
Sharing Ideas
International Group of Agents and Bureaus
Royal Publishing
18825 Hicrest Rd.
P.O. Box 1120
Glendora, CA 91740
(818) 335-8069
(818) 335-1855

Tax Information

ASSOCIATIONS

The Association of Tax Consultants is a group who supply information to the providers of tax information.

Association of Tax Consultants
P.O. Box 16184
Portland, OR 97233
(503) 249-1040

The following groups are trade associations of the providers of tax advice.

Institute of Tax Consultants
6628–212th St., S.W.
Lynnwood, WA 98036
(206) 774-3521

National Association of Tax Consultants
454 N. 13th St.
San Jose, CA 95112
(408) 298-1458

PUBLICATIONS

The Research Institute of America is an excellent source of up-to-date tax bulletins and newsletters.

Research Institute of America
RIA Bldg.
589 Fifth Ave.
New York, NY 10017
(212) 755-8900

The Commerce Clearing House is a strong source for reference books and tax interpretations.

Commerce Clearing House
4025 W. Peterson
Chicago, IL 60646
(312) 583-8500

The *Prentice-Hall Tax Guide* offers tax advice in many forms.

Prentice-Hall
Route 9W

Englewood Cliffs, NJ 07632
(201) 592-2000

The IRS offers dozens of free publications on a variety of tax issues. It also offers a toll-free hotline service for questions on federal tax matters; in 1986 about 40 million calls were handled. For more information, contact your local tax office or the following source.

Public Affairs Division
Internal Revenue Services
Department of the Treasury
1111 Constitution Ave., N.W., Rm. 2315
Washington, DC 20224
(202) 566-4024
(800) 424-5454; (202) 633-6487 (hotline)
(800) 424-1040 (another tax hotline)

Established in 1925, the *Kiplinger Tax Letter* is a good source of advice on personal and business taxes. It is published on alternate Mondays of each month.

Kiplinger Tax Letter
1729 H St., N.W.
Washington, DC 20006
(202) 887-6400

How to Handle Tax Audits is a series of booklets provided to subscribers.

How to Handle Tax Audits
Irving Schreiber
Panel Publishers
14 Plaza Rd.
Greenvale Station, NY 11548
(516) 484-0006

Small Business Tax Control, published in a double-size, three-ring binder, contains more than 250 tax briefs written in simple language. Every month the reader receives revised and supplemental briefs, as well as a six-page *Tax Prompter.* All briefs emphasize tax-savings ideas and are written specifically for the small business owner.

Small Business Tax Control
Capital Publications, Inc.
1300 N. 17th St.
Arlington, VA 22209
(703) 528-1100

How the IRS Selects Individual Income Tax Returns for Audit is a 142-page report, released by the Department of the Treasury. It is available from the following sources.

U.S. General Accounting Office
441 G St., N.W., Rm. 4522

Washington, DC 20548
(202) 275-6241

Consumer Information
Superintendent of Documents
U.S. Government Printing Office
Washington, DC 20402
(202) 783-3238

The *Federal Index* indexes federal speeches, rulings, regulations, bills, hearings, and so on from October 1976 to the present. The following source can provide information about on-line cost and availability.

Federal Index
Capitol Services, Inc.
415 Second St., N.E.
Washington, DC 20002
(202) 546-5600

BNA's Weekly Tax Report summarizes official tax actions and tax-policy developments. The cost is $476 per year.

BNA's Weekly Tax Report
Bureau of National Affairs, Inc.
1231–25th St., N.W.
Washington, DC 20037
(202) 258-9401
(800) 372-1033

Warren, Gorham and Lamont, Inc. publishes the quarterly *Tax Law Review.* The cost is $48 per year.

Tax Law Review
Warren, Gorham and Lamont, Inc.
210 South St.
Boston, MA 02111
(617) 423-2020

Clark Boardman Co., Ltd. publishes *R&D Partnerships: Structuring the Transaction; A How-to Guide for Lawyers, Accountants and Tax Shelter Professionals* by Lee R. Petillon and Robert J. Hull. The cost is $85 per year.

Clark Boardman Co., Ltd.
435 Hudson St.
New York, NY 10014
(212) 929-7500
(800) 221-9428

Trade Shows and Conventions

Trade Show Week is a weekly newsletter. An annual directory is also published.
   Trade Show Week
   12233 W. Olympic Blvd., Ste. 236
   Los Angeles, CA 90064
   (213) 826-5696

To locate specific trade shows or conventions, I recommend the *Encyclopedia of Associations* or the *World Guide to Trade Associations,* both available from the following source.
   Gale Research Co.
   Book Tower
   Detroit, MI 48226
   (313) 961-2242
   (800) 223-GALE

Successful Meetings Magazine is a monthly which publishes an annual directory of trade shows.
   Stan Itzkowitz
   Successful Meetings Magazine
   633 Third Ave.
   New York, NY 10017
   (212) 986-4800

An association of associations, the American Society of Association Executives can tell you when any specific group is planning a trade show or convention.
   American Society of Association Executives
   1575 I St., N.W.
   Washington, DC 20005
   (202) 626-2723

Travel

ASSOCIATION

The American Society of Travel Agents offers books and seminars and is an excellent source of information. This industry association has local chapters.

American Society of Travel Agents
4400 McArthur Blvd., N.W.
Washington, DC 20007
(202) 965-7520

MISCELLANEOUS SERVICES

Access American, Inc. is a good source of insurance for the traveler.

Edward Shulman, CEO
Access America, Inc.
600 Third Ave., 4th Floor
New York, NY 10016
(212) 490-4061

The Kapco Group Ltd. is a discount travel agency which offers rebates mainly for airline tickets to customers.

Ken Rubel
The Kapco Group, Ltd.
5901 N. Cicero Ave.
Chicago, IL 60646
(312) 736-5200
(800) 63-KAPCO

A no-frills travel agency, McTravel, Inc. refunds part of its commission to its customers.

Richard Dickieson, CEO
McTravel, Inc.
130 S. Jefferson
Chicago, IL 60606
(312) 876-1116

Faredeal is a discount travel group.

Andrew Kahr
Faredeal
First Deposit Corp.

450 Sansome St., Ste. 900
San Francisco, CA 94111
(415) 981-0279
(800) 992-3350

The American Participants program will pay experts who can contribute to foreign societies' understanding of the United States to travel abroad and participate in seminars or symposia. Subjects covered by the program include economics, international political relations, U.S. societal and political processes, arts and humanities, and science and technology.

American Participants
Office of Program Coordination and Development
U.S. Information Agency
301 Fourth St., S.W., Rm. 550
Washington, DC 20547
(202) 485-2764

PUBLICATIONS

Samples of the travel periodicals listed below can be obtained for little or no cost.

Entree is published monthly. The cost is $30 per year; a sample is free.
Entree
P.O. Box 5148
Santa Barbara, CA 93108
(805) 969-5848

The Hideaway Report is published monthly. The cost is $65 per year; a sample costs $5.
The Hideaway Report
Harper Associations, Inc.
P.O. Box 300
Fairfax Station, VA 22039
(703) 978-7397

International Travel News is published monthly. The cost is $11 per year; a sample is free.
International Travel News
2120-28th St.
Sacramento, CA 95818
(916) 457-3643

Economy Traveler is published bimonthly. The cost is $20 per year; a sample costs $1.
Economy Traveler
P.O. Box 547

Menlo Park, CA 94026-0547
(415) 753-0140

Travel Smart is published monthly at $39 per year (less for new subscribers); a sample costs $1.
    Travel Smart
    Communications House
    Dobbs Ferry, NY 10522
    (914) 693-8300

Travel Smart for Business is aimed at the frequent business traveler. A sample costs $10.
    Travel Smart for Business
    Communications House
    Dobbs Ferry, NY 10522
    (914) 693-8300

ROCK-BOTTOM PRICES ON VACATION TRAVEL

You can save 50 percent or more on vacation-travel costs. All you need is the flexibility to take a vacation on short notice or to take pot luck with time you've already set aside.

Charter flights, land arrangements, and cruises frequently become available at distress prices when tour operators seek to get what they can rather than let the space stay unsold. In addition, many tour operators prefer not to publicize the availability of distress merchandise. Sometimes flights or ships are departing in just a few days; other vacation offerings may be for several weeks away.

Here's the deal: Membership organizations specializing in short-notice packages offer a broad array of alternatives. For a modest fee—typically $35 to $50 a year—you can learn about available deals from frequently updated telephone hotlines or mailings. You get information via a telephone hotline, select a trip, pay the reduced price, and receive a voucher.

You must act quickly. But there's no indication you are traveling at a discount. You get the same privileges as full-fare customers. Club membership often covers your family or other traveling companions.

Some travel discount clubs are:

Stand-Buys, Ltd.
311 W. Superior St.
Chicago, IL 60610
(800) 621-5839

Discount Travel International
Ives Bldg.
Narbeth, PA 19072
(800) 253-6200

Moments Notice
40 E. 49th St.
New York, NY 10017
(212) 486-0503

Worldwide Discount Travel Club
1674 Meridian Ave.
Miami Beach, FL 33139
(305) 534-2082

Venture Capital

ASSOCIATIONS

The National Association of Small Business Investment Companies is an association of about 700 SBICs. It publishes a monthly newsletter and sponsors an excellent annual conference on venture capital. A membership directory is available for a $1 handling charge (request in writing only).

National Association of Small Business Investment Companies
1156 15th St., N.W., Ste, 1101
Washington, DC 20005
(202) 833-8230

The National Venture Capital Association is a loose federation of venture capital sources. Its membership directory is free on request.

National Venture Capital Association
1655 N. Fort Myer Dr., Ste. 700
(703) 528-4370

The Webster Association of Venture Capitalists offers a free directory of 130 members.

Western Association of Venture Capitalists
3000 San Hill Rd., Bldg. 2, Ste. 215
Menlo Park, CA 94025
(415) 854-1322

MISCELLANEOUS SERVICES

Venture Capital Connection claims to be a computer dating service for entrepreneurs. Investors register for one year for a $200 fee. Entrepreneurs register for six months for a $200 fee. Entrepreneurs file a three-page summary of their business plans. Mr. Murphy also publishes a newsletter, The California Technology Stock Letter.

Michael Murphy
Venture Capital Connection
155 Montgomery St., Ste. 1401
San Francisco, CA 94104
(415) 982-0125

For a $55 fee, the Venture Capital Hotline will give you up to ten venture capital sources from its data bank.

Lance J. Strauss
Venture Capital Hotline
560 Carmel Rancho Blvd., Ste. 16
Carmel, CA 93923
(800) 237-2380
(800) 252-2380 (in CA)
(408) 625-0700

The Venture Capital Network is a nonprofit corporation. This unique service matches entrepreneurs needing capital with venture capital sources. Investors register for one year for a $200 fee. Entrepreneurs register for six months for a $100 fee. A faculty member of the University of New Hampshire, Bill Wetzel knows of other similar services across the country. In fact, he is assisting nine other regional centers to become "angel" networks.

Dr. William Wetzel
Venture Capital Network
P.O. Box 882
Durham, NH 03824
(603) 862-3369
(603) 862-3556

David Silver claims to have raised more capital than anyone in the world. His Silver Press is a wonderful source of books and information.

A. David Silver
The Silver Press
524 Camino Del Monte Sol
Santa Fe, NM 87501
(505) 983-3868

A source of information on venture capital clubs around the world, the International Venture Capital Institute, Inc. publishes a directory and a newsletter. There are about 100 clubs in the United States and another dozen or so overseas.

Carroll Greathouse
The International Venture Capital Institute, Inc.
A Division of Baxter Associates
P.O. Box 1333
Stamford, CT 06904
(203) 323-3141

PUBLICATION

Stanley Pratt's *Guide to Venture Capital Sources* is the most valuable venture capital guide available today. His firm, Venture Economics (formerly Capital Publishing), also publishes a valuable venture capital newsletter.

Stanley Pratt
Venture Economics, Inc.
16 Laurel Ave., P.O. Box 348

Wellesley Hills, MA 02181
(617) 431-8100

VENTURE CAPITAL NETWORK

Venture Capital Network assists nonprofit organizations outside New England to replicate its service in their local areas. The following is a list of organizations that currently receive such assistance.

Indiana Seed Capital Network
David Clegg
Institute of New Business Ventures, Inc.
One N. Capital, Ste. 420
Indianapolis, IN 46204
(317) 634-8418

Venture Capital Network of New York, Inc.
Claire Barnett
TAC
State University College of Arts and Science
Plattsburgh, NY 12901
(518) 564-2214

Midwest Venture Capital Network
Virginia Wojtkowski
P.O. Box 4659
St. Louis, MO 63108
(314) 534-7204

Atlanta Economic Development Corp.
Hattie Harlow
230 Peachtree St., N.E., Ste. 1810
Atlanta, GA 30303
(404) 658-7000

The Computerized Ontario Investment Network
James Carnegie
Ontario Chamber of Commerce
2323 Yonge St.
Toronto, Ont.
Canada M4P 2C9
(416) 482-5222

Upper Peninsula Venture Capital Network, Inc.
Richard Anderson
206 Cohodas Administration Center
Northern Michigan University
Marquette, MI 48955
(906) 227-2406

Investment Contact Network
Rollie Tillman
Institute for the Study of Private Enterprise
The University of North Carolina at Chapel Hill
312 Carroll Hall 012A
Chapel Hill, NC 27514
(919) 962-8201

Technology Commercialization Center
Jack L. Bishop, Jr.
Northwestern University
906 University Pl.
Evanston, IL 60201
(312) 491-3750

Mississippi Venture Capital Clearinghouse
Bill Parkin
Mississippi Research and Development Center
3825 Ridgewood Rd.
Jackson, MS 39211
(601) 982-6425

ASSOCIATION OF VENTURE CAPITAL CLUBS

The term *venture capital club* is misleading: Venture capital clubs are actually small but localized groups of entrepreneurs who are seeking venture capital. A fun and inexpensive way of meeting other entrepreneurs, these independent groups have sprung up in each region of the United States and have sponsored networking events.

MEMBER CLUBS

Alabama

Birmingham Venture Club
William Featheringill
P.O. Box 10127
Birmingham, AL 35202
(205) 323-5461

Montgomery Venture Group
Philip L. Sellers
P.O. Box 1013
Montgomery, AL 36192
(205) 834-5100

California

Orange Coast Venture Group
Linder C. Hobbs
P.O. Box 7282
Newport Beach, CA 92658
(714) 261-0130

Channel Islands Venture Association
Mark B. Shappee
500 Esplanade Dr., #810
Oxnard, CA 93030
(805) 988-1207

San Diego Venture Group
Robert D. Weaver
701 B St., Ste. 1900
San Diego, CA 92101
(619) 457-2797

Colorado

Colorado Venture Group
Jon Fitzgerald
7353 S. Alton Way, Penthouse
Englewood, CO 80112
(303) 850-7611

Connecticut

Connecticut Venture Group
Ginger M. More, Pres.
P.O. Box 1333
Stamford, CT 06904
(203) 323-3143

Florida

Gold Coast Venture Capital Club
Oscar Ziemba
110 E. Atlantic Ave., Ste. 208 E
Delray Beach, FL 33444
(305) 272-1040

Acorn
Dan Horvath
302 N. Barcelona St.
Pensacola, FL 32501
(904) 433-5619

Illinois

Chicago Venture Capital Network
Tim Eckerman
32 W. Randolph St., Ste. 1450
Chicago, IL 60601
(312) 236-3623

Kentucky

Central Kentucky Venture Capital Club
Ralph M. Mobley
P.O. Box 508
Elizabethtown, KY 42701
(502) 769-1410

Michigan

New Enterprise Forum
Thomas S. Porter
912 N. Main St.
Ann Arbor, MI 48104
(313) 662-0550
(313) 663-3213 (Porter)

Southeastern Michigan Venture Group
Carl Meyering
Renaissance Center Station
P.O. Box 43181
Detroit, MI 48243
(313) 446-7169
(313) 886-2331 (Meyering)

Missouri

Missouri Venture Forum, Inc.
Larry R. Kirchenbauer

8000 Maryland Ave., Ste. 1540
St. Louis, MO 63105
(314) 862-5475

Nebraska

Nebraska Venture Group
Mary L. Woita
Nebraska Business Development Center
University of Nebraska
1313 Farnam-on-the-Mall
Omaha, NE 68182-0248
(402) 554-8381

New Jersey

Southern New Jersey Venture Capital
  Club
Ralph B. Patterson
1200 Campus Dr., RR #30
Mount Holly, NJ 08060
(609) 261-6000

New Mexico

Venture Capital Club of New Mexico
John Kallman
524 Camino del Monte Sol
Santa Fe, NM 87501
(505) 983-1815
(505) 471-0970 (Kallman)

New York

Long Island Venture Group
George O. Goldner, Chairman
Russell M. Moore, Secretary
Business Research Institute
Hofstra University
Hempstead, NY 11550
(516) 560-5175

Ohio

Columbus Investment Interest Group
Sue Erwin, Dir.
37 N. High St.
Columbus, OH 43215
(614) 221-1321

Puerto Rico

Puerto Rico Venture Capital Club
Antonio Vazquez
P.O. Box 2284

Hato Rey, PR 00919
(809) 787-9040

Tennessee

Western Tennessee Venture Capital Club
Ben Bewley
P.O. Box 382012
Germantown, TN 38138
(901) 726-5907

Texas

East Texas Venture Capital Group
P.O. Box 2763
Beaumont, TX 77704
(409) 898-0227

or

Thomas S. Bell
Bell & Associates
485 Milam
Beaumont, TX 77701
(409) 832-5901

South Texas Venture Capital Club
Alan Mason
c/o John J. Krouser
JMB Enterprises
3407 Buckhaven
San Antonio, TX 78230
(512) 496-7553 (Krouser)

Utah

Mountain West Venture Group
Roy Jesperson
P.O. Box 210
Salt Lake City, UT 84144
(801) 533-0777

Washington

Northwest Venture Group
Jeff Jordan
P.O. Box 3293
Kirkland, WA 98033
(206) 746-1973

Wisconsin

Wisconsin Venture Network
Jim Gormley
1011 N. Mayfair Rd., #303
Milwaukee, WI 53226

(414) 453-1353
(414) 276-0200 (Gormley)

Canada

Venture Capital/Entrepreneurship Club of
   Montreal Inc.
Claude Belanger
3420 St-Hubert, Ste. 12
Montreal, Que. H2L 3Z7
Canada
(514) 526-9490

Toronto Venture Capital Club
Jerry Steiner
825 Eglinton Ave., West, Ste. 207
Toronto, Ont. M5N 1E7

Canada
(416) 789-2654

South Africa

Cape Town Venture Capital Association
Colin Hultzer
c/o Arthur Andersen & Co.
Shell House, 12th Floor
Cape Town, South Africa 8001

Johannesburg Venture Capital Club
G. R. Rosenthal
c/o Arthur Andersen & Co.
Commissioner St.
Carlton Centre, 37th Floor
Johannesburg, South Africa 2000

NETWORKING FOR VENTURE CAPITAL

I've been asked repeatedly, "How do you write the perfect business plan?" In fact, some people have gone so far as to say, "Show me the perfect business plan and I'll copy it for my business." Well, it doesn't work that way. Every business is different, so every business plan requires a different strategy to show each deal off to its best advantage. I could show you what I think is a perfect business plan for a high-tech business, but it wouldn't do you a bit of good if you were trying to raise capital for a service business. The real key to raising capital is showing your business plan to the *right* venture source.

That's why prospecting is the most important part of preparing your plan. One of the biggest mistakes an entrepreneur can make is to write a really terrific plan and then spend his time showing it around to the wrong venture sources. It's demoralizing, and the experience will drain your enthusiasm and wear you out. For most entrepreneurs, this idea is a bit revolutionary. When I mention that an entrepreneur should spend at least three months prospecting, people look at me strangely. "What are we supposed to do," they ask, "spend three months walking up and down Wall Street?"

The answer is no. Wall Street has nothing to do with it. Believe it or not, new entrepreneurs shouldn't be prospecting for venture capitalists: They should prospect for *other entrepreneurs.* This may sound like a strange idea, but it works.

Begin by studying Stanley Pratt's *Guide to Venture Capital Sources* (available in most libraries or from Venture Economics, 16 Laurel Ave., P.O. Box 348, Wellesley Hills, MA 02181; [617] 431-8100). Look for venture sources that invest in your industry. Call or write to several good candidates and ask for a list of their portfolio investments.

Presenting Your Plan

You've spoken with other successful entrepreneurs and now you're ready to present your business plan to the several venture capitalists that you've carefully selected. How can you make it more likely that *they* will select *you?* The chapter on Business Plans discusses the presentation process in great detail. Here are a few highlights:

- Have the plan hand-delivered by someone who knows both the investor and your plan. Ideally, this person has been following developments in your business plan for at least six months. Good choices are bankers, consultants, lawyers, accountants, and other entrepreneurs.
- Don't focus your energies on presenting a pretty cover. According to test results, investors notice the company name first, and then (in order of importance) the geographical location of the company, the length of the plan (they prefer short ones), and the cover quality.
- To maintain the interest of venture capitalists, structure the plan with a succinct summary page to open, followed by the full plan. Setting a teaser summary or only highlights from the plan may aggravate or frustrate the reader.
- Don't be easily discouraged. The two most successful venture-capital deals in the northeastern United States—Digital Equipment Corporation and Data General Corporation—were both turned down a number of times before receiving a "yes."

Let's say that one of the firms you've selected is Adler & Company in New York. You're working on a software product and you've noted that they invest in high technology. After compiling a list of all of their investments, you see that they've invested in a total of seven software companies.

Your next step is to get the names of the entrepreneurs behind those companies and to start calling them. Introduce yourself: "I'm an entrepreneur down here in Tampa, and I notice that your operation is right up in St. Pete. I'm putting together a business plan, and I thought you might be able to look it over and give me a few tips. Do you work on Saturdays? Well, could I drop it by next Saturday morning, so you could have a look at it?"

Call him back a week later: "Hi, I wonder if I could come by again next Saturday and talk about the problems I'm having putting the finishing touches on the plan." And soon the entrepreneur is involved. Entrepreneurs love to get those kinds of phone calls, and they love to help each other.

Everything you may have heard about entrepreneurs being ornery and independent is true. But there's also a camaraderie that exists among entrepreneurs, which can be very valuable to someone just starting out—if that person knows how to take advantage of it.

So now this entrepreneur from St. Pete is involved. His firm is one of Adler & Company's portfolio investments, so he's going to talk to Fred Adler periodically. He tells Adler, "A funny thing happened the other day, Fred. So-and-so, who works over at the Widget Company, came over, and I gave him a hand with his business plan. He's got a pretty neat idea." And maybe a couple of months later he says, "Fred, you remember so-and-so who worked over at the Widget Company? Well, now he's working full time on his own deal." A little later, he tells Adler: "You remember so-and-so? He's got a prototype together, and it's working pretty well. I think it looks like a good deal." So Adler says, "Why don't you give me his phone number?"

All of this got started because you phoned the entrepreneur. If you're sharp enough, you might say, "I see you have a board of directors. What kind of support do they provide?" That's usually all you have to say, and when it comes time to put your board together, he'll be one of your key people.

How many people do you have to approach? In my example, it took only one phone call to get the ball rolling. In reality, you may have to speak with several different entrepreneurs before things start happening. But even if it takes six months, the contacts you make along the way will be invaluable.

I'd like to say that I invented this technique myself, but I didn't. I only discovered it. How? By asking venture capitalists where they get their leads. More than half told me their leads came from existing portfolio companies! It's common sense: After all, a venture source obviously has confidence in the people he invests in and trusts their judgment.

You may ask, "Aren't entrepreneurs concerned about creating competition for themselves—especially if I'm in the same business that they're in?" Maybe, but most of the time they'll be willing to help. Furthermore, if the entrepreneur's business is so similar to yours that he turns you down for that reason, his venture capitalist probably wouldn't do the deal anyway. Before they decide to invest in a company, financial backers will always check their portfolio companies for possible conflicts.

Of course, you may also be concerned about having your idea stolen. But you shouldn't be. The entrepreneurs you'll be talking to are so caught up in their own business that they don't have the time or the staff to steal someone else's ideas.

And more important, much of what makes your idea attractive is you—your energy, your enthusiasm, and a host of other intangible features. For example, Fred Smith of Federal Express came up with his revolutionary idea for an overnight air-freight service in 1965 when he was a student at Yale. He wrote a paper about it for an economics class, but his professor called it impractical and gave the paper a "C." It took six years to actually put the company together: Only Fred Smith could bring all the intangibles together and make it happen.

Remember, venture capitalists get thousands of calls every year, but entrepreneurs get very few, if any. In fact, it's very possible that an entrepreneur will be flattered to get your call. And if you're persistent, you can find an entrepreneur who'll both listen and help.

THE SECRET PHRASE THAT RAISES CAPITAL

Here's the situation: You've been in a financial negotiation for three months. You've got a terrific business plan—even your venture capitalist admits that—but the two of you just can't come to terms. So now you're meeting for the umpteenth time and half of you is thinking, "Maybe I should just get up and walk; I'm just wasting my time." But the other half is thinking, "I've got three months invested in this deal; they've got the money; they like my plan; I'd be a fool not to stick it out." What do you do? Well, there's a seven-word phrase that will help you close the deal. But before I tell you what those seven words are, I should explain how and why they work.

The biggest mistake an entrepreneur can make when he deals with a venture capitalist is to lose sight of what the venture capitalist is really after. It may sound like he wants too much equity or control, but what it really comes down to is dollars, pure and simple. His job is to make a profit on his investments. When the venture capitalist makes what you consider to be an unreasonable offer ("Just give me my terms, and I'll have a check ready for you in the morning"), you don't have to panic. You don't automatically have to give up control in order to obtain financing (which is what it may sound like when he says "my terms").

Playing on His Turf

What do you do if you're not willing to agree to his terms? Do you check around, hoping to arouse enough interest to play one source off against the other? That might be a good ploy in theory. But the reality is that you're playing on his turf, and shopping a deal around tends to alienate venture capitalists more often than it entices them.

What's the secret to closing the deal? Good old-fashioned persistence? I subscribe to the theory that if a batter stands in the batter's box long enough, the pitcher will hit the bat with the ball. However, persistence alone won't raise a nickel. Should you try to get the financier to review everything he thinks looks good about the deal—everything that attracted him to it in the first place? This tactic will bring you back to square one, but it won't get you any closer to closing the deal. As special as you may think your company is, chances are the venture capitalist has seen, and even turned down, deals very similar to yours. Getting your business off the ground might be your dream, but the art of raising capital isn't the art of selling dreams. The art of raising capital is the art of reducing risk.

Dream sellers will always get into trouble during negotiations, because they'll rhapsodize, "You ought to see how beautiful she looks. She's tall and thin and she's got this and that. . . ." But that's not the way raising capital works; in fact, it's just the opposite. What you want to say is, "The risk on this deal is *zero*—the down side is *zero!* Now let's talk about the up side."

Here's an example of what I mean by the up side. Let's say I own 100 acres of land up at Cheboque Point, in Yarmouth, Nova Scotia—a piece of oceanfront property. In fact, this is a good example because it's true. Eighteen months ago, I paid $100,000 for this property; a few months later, I needed some cash, so I decided to sell a piece. I divided it into two equal parcels and put one of the parcels on the market. What do you think the asking price was?

If you guessed $100,000, you guessed right. This example illustrates the most important thing to remember about investors: An investor's foremost concern is getting his money back. Investors not only make investments but also expect to recoup those investments.

Here's another example. Did you ever watch the gamblers in the casinos in Las Vegas or Atlantic City? If you watch for a long time, you'll notice that some of them, at about two or three in the morning, pull all the money out of their pockets, put it down on a table, and count it. They divide it into two piles, put one pile back into their pockets, and continue to play with the other pile. What did they put into their pockets? Cab fare? The money for a phone call home? No. What a smart gambler puts back into his pocket is his initial stake—the money he came in with.

World's Best Money-Raisers

Before I give you a third example, I want to explain how the best money-raisers in the world raise money. Who are the best money-raisers in the world? Politicians? The banker's brother? No. The best money-raisers are venture capitalists. A successful venture capitalist can pick up the phone and raise $100 million in less than one hour. (Most entrepreneurs have trouble getting someone to cosign a $10,000 note.) Why is a venture capitalist so successful when it comes to raising money? The answer lies with the seven-word phrase I mentioned earlier. And after one more example, I'm going to tell you what those seven words are.

I speak at a number of conferences where venture capitalists are assembled, and it's always interesting to watch two of the giants come into a room and meet. Imagine that Bill from Widget Venture runs into Frank from Mega Venture. What do they talk about? Does Bill mention he made $600 million in the last quarter? Does Frank say that his average annual rate of return for the past 17 years has been 41.26 percent? Do they say hello and leave it at that? No. They talk about the success of their *last* fund.

Widget Venture may run four or five different funds of $100 million to $200 million each, but Frank from Mega Venture is really interested only in Widget's last fund. The rest is already history. So Frank may say to Bill, "I understand you put together $120 million for fund 6. How long did it take you to get your principal back to your partners?" And Bill will answer, "Eleven months." Then Bill will ask Frank how long it took Mega's last fund to get its principal back to his partners, and so on. The only thing that venture capitalists ever compare is how fast they returned the original investment to their partners.

When the gambler puts his original capital back into his pocket, he's basically doing the same thing that the venture capitalist does. He returns the original investment and continues playing on his winnings. Of course, the venture capitalists are a *little* more sophisticated. They raise money in ten-year limited partnerships. But it is the same strategy. They try to rush the original investment back to the partners, and then "play with the winnings" for the balance of the ten-year period. The partners have to wait the full ten years to get their winnings, but they get their principal back right away.

The lesson is that no matter who the investor is, his first concern is getting back his initial investment. When a negotiation seems to have reached an impasse, the seven key words you must say to get the signature are, *"You get all your money back first."* No other words will strike as close to the heart of a venture capitalist as these seven: *"You get all your money back first."*

Protect His Initial Investment

Here's a final example. Let's say a young company goes public at $10 a share, but a few months after the initial public offering, the company runs into some problems, and the stock drops to $5 a share. The entrepreneur begins breaking his back to raise the earnings and the stock price. The superhuman effort pays off: The earnings reach and even begin to exceed the original projections. But the company's stock follows a different pattern; after a slow climb back up, the stock price hits 10 and holds there. Why? Because, despite the strong recent performance, the stockholders (investors) remember the initial setback, and when the stock gets back to its original price, they begin to bail out. This "jump-off" point further illustrates the principle I've been describing: The investor is adamant, almost fanatical, about recovering his initial investment. In the stock case, he isn't left with any winnings to play with, but he's recovered his initial investment, and he's ready to start all over again.

The approaches of these four categories of investors (the landowner, the gambler, the venture capitalist, and the stockholder) are very different, but the rationale is the same: Protect the original capital. That's why selling dreams to a venture capitalist will never work. He wants to make sure the risk on his investment is held to a minimum. So, if you've tried everything you know to close a deal and it still seems to hang up on a few points, try that seven-word phrase and see what happens. And always remember that, as great as your dream for your company may be, you're on the venture capitalist's turf. You have to speak his language, not your own. So talk about his dream. Tell him, "You get all your money back first."

ROMANCING THE MONEY PEOPLE

A lot of people think that raising venture capital is a sticky, if not impossible, business. But it can be quite exciting. The first thing to bear in mind is that venture capitalists *like* to finance companies—that's why they're in the business of investing. Your job is to make them like your business enough to put their money into it. And the way to do that is to romance them.

How? Well, you begin at the very beginning—with your business plan. If a plan doesn't distinguish itself, it's not going to be read, let alone financed. And that's where the romance comes in. The romance is the hook (and anyone who knows about romance knows what it's like to get hooked).

Let's look at what will make a venture capitalist fall in love with your plan.

A history of success. More than anything else, a venture capitalist wants some kind of assurance of success. And as the old saying goes, "Nothing succeeds like success." If you or your team have done it once, the investors will be more likely to believe you can do it again.

A well-recognized market. Cures for cancer or herpes come with an automatic market—a restaurant doesn't. Everybody has to eat, you say. However, unless you can show why people will want to eat your food (I'm talking about an in-depth analysis, not just a few great recipes), you're going to be short on romance.

Somebody big is behind it. There's no better way to make a venture capitalist fall in love with your plan than to show him that someone already has. That's not romance, that's sex appeal.

Potential for going public. In this respect, raising capital is a lot like the fashion business: Buyers try to decide what the public is going to want to wear in two years; venture capitalists speculate on whether your stock will appeal to investors in three to seven years.

I don't want your money as much as I want your advice. This sounds like pure flattery, but it's really much more than that, and it's won the heart of many venture capitalists. Tell potential investors that you want them on your board—that their experience and expertise are at least as necessary to your success as their money is. Don't worry: Money always follows advice.

If your company dies tomorrow, is the world going to suffer? Before there was a personal computer, people didn't know they needed one. Now it's a multibillion-dollar market. If you have a plan for a product that will create a permanent market, you've got the romance.

Another factor to keep in mind is that venture capitalists often make emotional decisions. (I'm sure some will say that venture capitalists have no emotions, but the truth is that no decisions about money are unemotional.) Often, the coolest decisions are made emotionally, and then justified by logic.

Now that you know how to get an investor hooked, it's time to learn how to reel him in. After all, what's a romance without a marriage?

It's just like. . . . The first example concerns a venture capitalist I know in Boston. Let's call him Frank. Frank is the dean of venture capital for the New England area. He's been at it for more than 20 years and runs about $150 million in a half-dozen funds. Over the past 20 years, his average annual rate of return has been well over 45 percent. He's invested in Wang Laboratories, Unitrode, and Damon Engineering, to name just a few. But the two deals he missed (both in Massachusetts, surprisingly enough) were Digital Equipment (DEC) and Data General (DG), and they were two of the biggest venture-capital deals in history. When Frank comes home, his wife says, "How are you, sweetheart? Nice to see you. Did any deals come along today that looked like Digital or Data General?" Frank is immediately interested if the front end of your plan looks like DEC or DG. It pays to know not only the deals venture capitalists have made (or lost) money on but also the deals they've missed.

The other guys have deep pockets. The second example is the story of In-Line Technologies, a company in New Bedford, Mass., run by Gene St. Onge and Hank Bok. A few years back, St. Onge and Bok went to see a well-known New York venture capitalist at his Fifth Avenue apartment. During the course of a two-hour breakfast meeting, the venture capitalist spent about an hour and a half talking about a painting that his wife had just bought. Then he discussed business for a half hour.

At the end of the meeting, the venture source agreed to put up half of the $200,000 St. Onge and Bok were trying to raise. But he put two conditions on the deal. First, he *wasn't* going to visit the company and analyze it because that process alone would cost him about $25,000. Second, if they ran out of money, they shouldn't call him for more. "I'm going to make a little investment with you guys," he said, "but I can't afford to spend a lot of time with your people, so don't call me up whenever you have a problem."

The second lesson emerges from this example. Having secured a promise for $100,000 from a well-known venture capitalist, St. Onge and Bok had no problem raising the other $100,000. In fact, their deal was oversubscribed, and they actually had to turn away money. Everyone assumed that the other guy had deep pockets and the deal was safe. When the Rockefellers, or General Electric, or one of the other big venture firms backs a deal, it automatically gains credibility. As a result, venture capitalists will pay more careful attention to your business plan, and lower-level investors (friends and relatives) will also have more confidence in your deal. Frederick Smith of Federal Express claims that an early commitment from venture capitalists was crucial in raising the $90 million it took to launch his company.

If it goes bad. . . . After about six months, In-Line Technologies did run short of money (a common experience for an entrepreneurial venture). St. Onge and Bok remembered that they had been instructed not to come back if they ran short of money, but they also knew that current investors are the best investors. This important piece of information is worth repeating: *Your best investors are your current investors.* So they called their New York connection: "Hello, Mr. Venture Capitalist, this is Gene and Hank. That's right, we're the guys who had breakfast with you six months ago and looked at your wife's new painting. Well, the news is that we need another $200,000 to keep us going."

As you might expect, the venture capitalist wasn't really quite as cavalier as he appeared to be at their first meeting. Long before he sat down to breakfast with St. Onge and Bok, he'd sent their business plan out to one of his portfolio companies on the West Coast, where he served as a director. This company needed the technology that In-Line had developed, and the CEO and an executive vice-president had both expressed interest in the plan. The venture capitalist had his interests well protected from the beginning because one of his portfolio companies was ready, willing, and even anxious to pick up In-Line if it ever went bad.

To make a long story short, the West Coast company flew in and bought In-Line Technologies within 30 days. All of the In-Line investors made a healthy profit on what turned out to be a short-term investment. The third lesson emerges from this example: Your business plan should always offer a contingency plan *if it goes bad.*

Once you've successfully romanced one of the money men, go ahead with the deal (with the marriage). More often than not, an investor isn't going to give you the money you need and then stand back and let you run the company your way. It's very likely he'll sit on your board and make strong suggestions that you won't always agree with. So, make sure your investor, like your spouse, is someone you can live with. Furthermore, make sure the promises you make while courting are promises you can keep. Like marriages, venture-capital deals don't always work out. But if you hold up your end of the bargain, you'll find there is such a thing as a happy ending.

Women Entrepreneurs

Women are emerging as a major force in the entrepreneurial world, and organizations and publications are springing up to help them. Additions to the list of sources below are welcomed; these recommendations will be published in a newsletter.

ASSOCIATIONS

A nonprofit group of women in business, the American Woman's Economic Development Corporation has more than 2,000 members nationwide. Services offered include counseling, networking sessions, conferences, lectures, and training programs.

> Beatrice Fitzpatrick
> American Woman's Economic Development Corp.
> 60 E. 42d St.
> New York, NY 10165
> (212) 692-9100

The Committee of 200 is a 240-member network of high-powered entrepreneurial and corporate women. Services offered include spring and fall conferences, a newsletter, and regional meetings.

> Lydia Lewis
> Committee of 200
> 500 N. Michigan Ave.
> Chicago, IL 60611
> (312) 661-1700

The Interagency Commission on Women's Business Enterprise works to obtain federal contracts for women-owned businesses and to get a larger share of SBA loans to women. Educational programs and counseling for women's start-up companies are also provided.

> Interagency Commission on Women's Business Enterprise
> SBA's Office of Women in Business
> Office of the Chief Counsel for Advocacy
> Small Business Administration
> Washington, DC 20416
> (202) 653-6087

An 800-member organization consisting predominantly of black women, The National Association of Black Women Entrepreneurs is open to women of all races.

Services offered include monthly workshops, networking sessions, and a newsletter.

Marilyn Hubbard
National Association of Black Women Entrepreneurs
P.O. Box 1375
Detroit, MI 48231
(313) 341-7400

The National Association of Female Executives is a nonprofit organization with 250,000 members. Services offered include networking and discounts on car rentals, airlines, and so on. *The Female Executive* is published six times a year.

National Association of Female Executives
1041 Third Ave.
New York, NY 10021
(212) 371-0740

The National Association of Women Business Owners is a dues-based national organization which represents women in all types of businesses. It sponsors "Mega-marketplace," an annual convention which brings women entrepreneurs together with government agencies, private corporations, and banks.

Natalie Holmes
National Association of Women Business Owners
600 S. Federal St.
Chicago, IL 60605
(312) 922-0465
(312) 346-2330

An independent, nonprofit organization, the Women's Business Development Center serves as a clearinghouse for business information. It provides information on creative financing and conducts broad-based economic development research. Training programs, conferences, workshops, and trade shows are sponsored.

The Women's Business Development Center
77 Columbia St.
Albany, NY 12207
(518) 465-5579

The Women's Economic Development Corporation serves 500 active clients; fees are adjusted based on service provided and ability to pay. Services offered include training seminars, individual counseling, and a revolving loan fund for clients.

Kathy Keely
Women's Economic Development Corp.
1885 University Ave., West
St. Paul, MN 55104
(612) 646-3808

PUBLICATIONS

Savvy is an influential monthly women's business magazine. It lists the top 60 American businesses run by women. The cost is $18 per year.

> *Savvy*
> 3 Park Ave.
> New York, NY 10011
> (212) 340-9200
> (800) 423-1780 (subscriptions)

The monthly magazine *Working Mother* helps working mothers balance work and family life. The cost is $12.95 per year.

> *Working Mother*
> 230 Park Ave.
> New York, NY 10169
> (212) 309-9800
> (800) 525-0643 (subscriptions)

Working Woman is a monthly magazine that offers practical advice to career-oriented women. The cost is $12 per year.

> *Working Woman*
> 342 Madison Ave.
> New York, NY 10036
> (212) 559-2080
> (800) 247-5470 (subscriptions)

The books listed below are available in local bookstores.

An Executive's Advice to Her Daughter, by Eliza G. Collins, Harper & Row, $3.95.

Feminine Leadership: Or How to Succeed in Business Without Being One of the Boys, by Marilyn Loden, Times Books, $16.95.

What You Get When You Go for It: Startling Accounts from Professional Women About Their Male Colleagues, by Beth Milwid, Dodd, Mead & Company, $17.95.

Women Who Want to Be Boss: Business Revelations from America's Top Female Executives, by Marilyn Jensen, includes advice from Mary Kay Ash, Cathleen Black, Helen Gurley Brown, Carolyn Jones, Sylvia Porter, and Donna Shalala, Doubleday & Company, $15.95.

A Woman's Guide to Her Own Franchised Business, by Anne Small and Robert S. Levy ($3.50), and *A Woman's Guide to Starting a Small Business,* by Mary Lester ($2.50), are available from the following source.

Pilot Books
103 Cooper St.
Babylon, NY 11702
(516) 422-2225

A book publisher run by women, Dodd, Mead & Company, Inc. offers excellent titles on women and business.
Lynne Lumsden, CEO
Dodd, Mead & Co., Inc.
71 Fifth Ave.
New York, NY 10003
(212) 627-8444

REGIONAL ORGANIZATIONS

The Minnesota Women's Network is a dues-based regional organization. Services offered include educational workshops, meetings, and support groups. It provides 1,000 members with general membership and offers Executive Forum membership for upper-management women.
Minnesota Women's Network
1421 Park Ave.
Minneapolis, MN 55404
(612) 375-9496

Women's Own Network is a dues-based regional organization with 50 members. It provides business referrals or contracts; members share advice, information, and experiences.
Suzanne Zeman
Women's Own Network
P.O. Box 608
Cambridge, MA 02140
(617) 497-7170

A nonprofit regional support organization for women, Women Entrepreneurs has 120 members. Educational (meetings, seminars, newsletter) and networking services are provided.
Women Entrepreneurs
1275 Market St., Ste. 1300
San Francisco, CA 94103-1424
(415) 626-8142

Index